ADVANCES IN

EXPERIMENTAL
SOCIAL PSYCHOLOGY

VOLUME 14

CONTRIBUTORS TO VOLUME 14

Irwin Altman

Barbara B. Brown

Bella M. DePaulo

Russell H. Fazio

Suzanne M. Miller

Charlan Jeanne Nemeth

Martin T. Orne

Robert Rosenthal

Arnold Upmeyer

Anne Vinsel

William M. Waid

Mark P. Zanna

Miron Zuckerman

ADVANCES IN

Experimental

Social Psychology

EDITED BY

Leonard Berkowitz

DEPARTMENT OF PSYCHOLOGY
UNIVERSITY OF WISCONSIN
MADISON, WISCONSIN

VOLUME 14

1981

ACADEMIC PRESS
A Subsidiary of Harcourt Brace Jovanovich, Publishers

New York   London   Toronto   Sydney   San Francisco

ACADEMIC PRESS, INC.
111 Fifth Avenue, New York, New York 10003

HM
251
.A35 / 36,534

United Kingdom Edition published by
ACADEMIC PRESS, INC. (LONDON) LTD.
24/28 Oval Road, London NW1 7DX

LIBRARY OF CONGRESS CATALOG CARD NUMBER: 64-23452

ISBN 0-12-015214-2

PRINTED IN THE UNITED STATES OF AMERICA

81 82 83 84   9 8 7 6 5 4 3 2 1

CONTENTS

v

Direct Experience and Attitude–Behavior Consistency

Russell H. Fazio and Mark P. Zanna

Predictability and Human Stress: Toward a Clarification of Evidence and Theory

Suzanne M. Miller

Perceptual and Judgmental Processes in Social Contexts

Arnold Upmeyer

Jury Trials: Psychology and Law

Charlan Jeanne Nemeth

CONTRIBUTORS

Numbers in parentheses indicate the pages on which the authors' contributions begin.

Irwin Altman, *Department of Psychology, University of Utah, Salt Lake City, Utah 84112* (107)

Barbara B. Brown, *Department of Psychology, University of Utah, Salt Lake City, Utah 84112* (107)

Bella M. DePaulo, *Department of Psychology, University of Virginia, Charlottesville, Virginia 22901* (1)

Russell H. Fazio, *Department of Psychology, Indiana University, Bloomington, Indiana 47401* (161)

Suzanne M. Miller, *Department of Psychology, Temple University, Philadelphia, Pennsylvania 19122* (203)

Charlan Jeanne Nemeth, *Department of Psychology, University of California, Berkeley, California 94720* (309)

Martin T. Orne, *Institute of Pennsylvania Hospital, and University of Pennsylvania, Philadelphia, Pennsylvania 19139* (61)

Robert Rosenthal, *Psychology and Social Relations, Harvard University, Cambridge, Massachusetts 02138* (1)

Arnold Upmeyer, *Institut für Psychologie, Technische Universität Berlin, D-1000 Berlin 10, Federal Republic of Germany* (257)

Anne Vinsel, *Department of Psychology, University of Utah, Salt Lake City, Utah 84112* (107)

William M. Waid,[1] *Institute of Pennsylvania Hospital, and University of Pennsylvania, Philadelphia, Pennsylvania 19139* (61)

Mark P. Zanna, *Department of Psychology, University of Waterloo, Waterloo N2L 3G1, Ontario, Canada* (161)

Miron Zuckerman,[2] *Department of Psychology, University of Rochester, Rochester, New York 14627* (1)

[1]Present address: Unit for Experimental Psychiatry, 111 N. 49th Street, Philadelphia, Pennsylvania 19139.
[2]Present address: 6 David Yellin Street, Tel Aviv 62964, Israel.

ADVANCES IN
EXPERIMENTAL
SOCIAL PSYCHOLOGY

VOLUME 14

VERBAL AND NONVERBAL
COMMUNICATION OF DECEPTION[1]

Miron Zuckerman*

DEPARTMENT OF PSYCHOLOGY
UNIVERSITY OF ROCHESTER
ROCHESTER, NEW YORK

Bella M. DePaulo

DEPARTMENT OF PSYCHOLOGY
UNIVERSITY OF VIRGINIA
CHARLOTTESVILLE, VIRGINIA

Robert Rosenthal

PSYCHOLOGY AND SOCIAL RELATIONS
HARVARD UNIVERSITY
CAMBRIDGE, MASSACHUSETTS

[1]Preparation of this article was supported in part by a grant from the Office of Naval Research (N00014-76-C-0001), the National Science Foundation, the University of Virginia Research Council, and the National Institute of Mental Health. This article is dedicated to all those researchers who, in response to our requests, went back to their old data files, their old computer outputs, and the backs of their old envelopes in order to provide us with the necessary data for the quantitative summaries that are reported.

*Present address: 6 David Yellin Street, Tel Aviv 62964, Israel.

1

I. Introduction

A. DEFINING THE SCOPE OF THE ARTICLE

Lying is a common aspect of interpersonal relationships. It has many forms and comes under many names—white lies, faking, bluffing, acting, cover-ups, put-ons, and others (Bok, 1978). This variety illustrates the numerous functions of lies, their heterogeneous nature, and their pervasiveness. Although at present there is no evidence to indicate just how prevalent deception actually is, if one adopts the position that social interactions are dramaturgical enactments of impression management (see Goffman, 1959), lying emerges as an almost indispensable component of everyday life. Consistent with this perspective, it has also been suggested that lying is at times highly adaptive and even essential for survival (Kraut, 1980; Leakey & Lewin, 1978).

Almost everything that can be said about lying can be said about lie detection. It is a necessary condition for social relationships, if only to hold in check potentially dangerous liars. From an evolutionary point of view, "Just as natural selection inevitably produces would be cheaters, it will inevitably give rise to individuals capable of detecting cheating" (Leakey & Lewin, 1978, p. 192[2]; but see DePaulo, 1980, for a somewhat different point of view suggesting that under some circumstances it may be more beneficial to overlook lies than to detect them). The development of the polygraph as a means of psychophysiological detection of deception is yet another aspect of the attempt to counter lie-telling when the stakes are particularly high.

Lying and lie detection are the two components that, together, make up the exchange we call communication of deception. From the above comments it is clear that one can analyze such communication at different levels (e.g., relatively macro- vs. relatively microanalysis) and from different points of view (e.g., evolutionary, sociological, physiological, etc.). This article presents a primarily psychological point of view and a relatively microanalysis of the verbal and nonverbal exchange between the deceiver and the lie detector. A definition of deception is presented in the next section. It is followed by discussions of the deceiver's perspective (i.e., strategies of deception and behaviors associated with

---

[2]In this regard, it is interesting to note that, according to Premack and Woodruff (1978), chimpanzees may be able to lie as well as to detect lies.

lie-telling), the lie-detector's perspective (i.e., behaviors associated with judgments of deception and strategies of lie detection), and the outcomes of the communication process (i.e., accuracy of lie detection).

B. DEFINING DECEPTION

How is deception defined in the relevant literature? Actually, a few years ago the literature was scant. Writing in 1976 about the issues that concern us here, Krauss, Geller, and Olson noted that "rather little consideration has been given to such questions as these" and, furthermore, that "for the most part [the available research is] neither programmatic nor very informative" (pp. 2–3). Now, however, the situation has changed dramatically. Research on humans as lie detectors has burgeoned and some preliminary reviews have already appeared (e.g., DePaulo, Zuckerman, & Rosenthal, 1980a,b; Kraut, 1980; Knapp & Comadena, 1979; Miller & Burgoon, 1981).

Following Krauss *et al.* (1976, p. 2), most researchers operationalized deception as an act that is *intended* to foster in *another person* a belief or understanding which the deceiver *considers* false. Two characteristics follow from this definition. First, deception has a dual nature. It is comprised of both the communication of some specific information and a metacommunication about the sincerity of the message (see DePaulo, 1980). Specifically, the deceiver transmits a false message (while hiding the true information) and also attempts to convince the perceiver of his or her sincerity. The perceiver, on the other hand, makes a metacommunicational judgment regarding the deceiver's honesty and also decides what to make of the content of the message. Ekman and Friesen (1969a) referred to this duality when they termed the behaviors that give away the deception (without revealing the hidden information) deception cues and the behaviors that betray the concealed information leakage cues. Second, deception is defined as an intentional and conscious act that is directed at another person. These criteria exclude three deception-related phenomena from the present discussion: self-deception, intentionally transparent lies, and mistaken lies. According to Gur and Sackeim (1979) self-deception occurs when the individual holds simultaneously two contradictory beliefs and, because of motivational reasons, is not aware of holding one of them (see also Demos, 1960; Fingarette, 1969). The lack of awareness and the targeting of the self as the object of deception are at variance with our criteria. Intentionally transparent lies occur when the deceiver wishes the deception to be uncovered. Zuckerman, DeFrank, Hall, Larrance, and Rosenthal (1979) hypothesized that this occurs when social rules prevent senders from verbally telling the truth but leave them the option of making their beliefs known nonverbally. Sarcastic remarks and some white lies may fit this description. Zuckerman *et al.* (1979) found that subjects were able to communicate with either facial expressions or tone of voice that they were lying. Clearly, however, this form of lie-telling is not meant to foster a false belief in another person. Finally, instances when senders do not know the truth and mistakenly provide false information also do not fit the present criteria of deception.

II.   The Deceiver's Perspective

A. STRATEGIES OF DECEPTION

In order to foster a false belief in another person, deceivers must manage their own behavior carefully. This exercise in self-presentation must be directed at the two components of the deceptive message; in Ekman and Friesen's terms, the deceiver must show neither leakage nor deception cues.

With regard to leakage, an important consideration is whether the deception conceals only a neutral fact or some felt emotion (cf. Ekman, 1980; Hemsley, 1977; Nieters, 1975). The latter is probably more likely to affect the deceiver's nonverbal and perhaps verbal expressions and, other things being equal, is perhaps more difficult to hide. Ekman (1980) stated that in addition to felt emotion, the deceiver may need to conceal a secondary affect that he or she has about the information that is being withheld. For example, if the deception conceals a fact (e.g., age) or an affect (e.g., hatred) that causes the deceiver to feel ashamed, he or she must conceal the shame as well as the information that has caused it. With regard to deception cues, the question of interest is whether the cues which the deceiver attempts to conceal are veridical cues of deception (i.e., cues actually associated with deception) or cues that the deceiver thinks are related to deception but which, in fact, are not. The correspondence between cues actually associated with deception and cues believed to be associated with deception will be discussed in Section III,A.

How well can deceivers manage their self-presentation? The folk wisdom is that people are able to control the verbal but not the nonverbal components of their behavior. Freud (1905) expressed this belief in a well-known quote: "if his lips are silent, he chatters with his fingertips; betrayal oozes out of him at every pore" (p. 94). Recently, however, Ekman and Friesen (1969a, 1974) suggested that certain nonverbal channels are more controllable than others. According to their model, controllability is a function of three channel characteristics: sending capacity, external feedback, and internal feedback. Sending capacity refers to the number of discriminable messages that can be sent, the speed of transmission, and the visibility or salience of the channel. External feedback refers to the extensiveness of reactions from other people. Internal feedback refers to the sender's awareness of his or her own expressions. On the basis of these criteria, Ekman and Friesen argued that the face is more controllable than the body (i.e., hands, legs, and feet). The face can send a large number of messages at a fast rate; it is visible and attended to by others; and finally, senders are more aware of their facial expressions than of their body movements. Several studies from outside the field of deception provide evidence consistent with the views of the body as a "leaky" channel and the face as a "controlled" channel (DePaulo & Fisher, 1981; DePaulo, Leiphart, & Dull, 1980f).

Since the face is more controllable, it is less likely to give away deception. Stated differently, the channel that is most informative when the communicator is truthful is most misleading when the communicator is deceptive. Exceptions to this general rule are microexpressions (also termed micromomentary expressions; Haggard & Isaacs, 1966), very brief muscular movements in the face that ordinarily can be detected only when a film or videotape is shown in slow motion. Ekman and Friesen (1969a) suggested that these expressions are the remnants of masked or squelched displays and, as such, can provide deception and leakage cues. Haggard and Isaacs (1966) reported that, in clinical interviews, microexpressions were more likely to occur in the context of conflict; that is, they were associated with both denial statements and verbal blocking and tended to be incompatible with the regular facial expressions that preceded or followed them. These findings gave rise to their view that microexpressions reflect unacceptable impulses, a position that is consistent with the Ekman and Friesen formulation.

More recently, investigators have attempted to extend Ekman and Friesen's leakage hierarchy to other channels, particularly to tone of voice (see Rosenthal & DePaulo, 1979a,b). An attempt to apply Ekman and Friesen's leakage criteria to tone of voice may imply that vocal cues are relatively controllable (DePaulo et al., 1980b). A person's speech is highly salient, people react to it, and one cannot help but be aware of his or her own voice. However, it is unclear how much of the salience and the feedback, both external and internal, pertain to the tone of voice as opposed to the verbal component of the speech. In fact, research by Holzman and Rousey (1966) implies that people are less aware of their tone of voice than would be expected. Specifically, in trying to account for people's negative reactions to hearing tape recordings of their own voices, Holzman and Rousey conceptualized the voice as a leaky channel: "among the things subjects heard in their voices [was] something they had not wanted to hear, something expressed which they had not wanted to express but which nevertheless had been conveyed by voice qualities" (p. 85). Since people do not ordinarily react negatively to their naturally occurring voice (as opposed to a tape recording of their voice), it appears that people may not really listen to their voices. Even when they do, their natural voices differ from their tape-recorded voices (because of the altered "bone- to air-conduction ratio," Holzman & Rousey, 1966) and from the voices that others hear. Thus, the self-feedback provided by the vocal channel may be more illusory than real.

More direct evidence regarding the controllability of vocal cues comes from comparisons between the information provided by the verbal content and tone of voice of the same message. Thus, Weitz (1972) showed that the friendliness of whites' behavior toward blacks was positively correlated with friendliness inferred from tone of voice but negatively correlated with friendliness inferred from verbal attitudes. It appeared that tone of voice revealed the whites' true, although unacknowledged, feelings about blacks. Analogously, Bugental and Love (1975) reported that mothers of children with problems in school used a less assertive tone of voice when expressing affective verbal content (positive or negative) than when making neutral statements. In contrast, mothers of normal children displayed the opposite pattern. According to Bugental and Love, a mother's tone of voice may have revealed confidence or insecurity about her ability to control her children. Similarly, Bugental, Henker, and Whalen (1976) reported that, in a free-interaction situation, subjects who felt powerless, that is, believed in external control ("externals"), showed less assertiveness in tone of voice than in verbal content. In contrast, subjects who believed in internal control ("internals") showed the opposite pattern. Finally, Bugental, Caporael, and Shennum (1980) reported that, in interactions with unresponsive children, external adults had less assertive voice intonation and internal adults have more assertive voice intonation when making affective than when making neutral statements. With responsive children, the voice intonations of both external and internal adults were more assertive when expressing affective than when expressing neutral statements.

These studies indicate that the tone of voice leaks information that is not expressed in the verbal content of the speech. A study by Zuckerman, Larrance, Spiegel, and Klorman (1981b) indicated that tone of voice is also less controllable than facial expression. Specifically, they showed that senders were better able to modify (suppress and exaggerate) facial expressions than tone of voice, indicating that the latter cannot be manipulated effectively. Senders were also able to predict their ability to send information via facial expressions but not via tone of voice, indicating greater awareness of face than voice. Finally, sending accuracy under suppression (i.e., the information leaked in spite of instructions to suppress expressions) was more highly correlated with sending accuracy under exaggeration for vocal than for facial expressions. The last finding was interpreted as follows: (a) Since the voice is a leaky channel, whatever it leaks under suppression is a good predictor of what it sends under exaggeration; (b) since the face is relatively controllable, what it leaks under suppression is not a good predictor of what it sends under exaggeration. The picture emerging from the above discussion is of a deceiver who is probably unable to control all channels simultaneously and who probably controls some better than others. The implications of the differences in controllability among channels for strategies of lie detection will be discussed in Section III,B.

B. BEHAVIORAL CORRELATES OF DECEPTION

1. Theoretical Background

Deception is not an affect and, thus, is unlikely to be associated with a specific verbal or nonverbal expression. However, deception does involve various processes or factors that influence behavior (see Kraut, 1980). Four such factors—control, arousal, felt emotion, and cognitive processing—will be discussed here.

a. Attempted Control.   Paradoxically, deceivers' very attempts to control their behavior may serve as cues to deception. The controlled behavior may appear planned, rehearsed, and lacking in spontaneity. In addition, unless deceivers know their craft well, they may try too little or, more probably, too much, thus staging a too slick and excessive presentation (Knapp, Hart, & Dennis, 1974). Finally, since people probably cannot simultaneously control all channels, and since some channels are not completely controllable to begin with, a discrepancy may develop; for example, face and body, face and voice, or macro- and microexpressions may convey different impressions to observers.

b. Arousal.   The idea that deception produces arousal (Hemsley, 1977) derives from research on psychophysiological detection of lying (for reviews, see Lykken, 1974; Orne, Thackray, & Paskewitz, 1972; Podlesny & Raskin, 1977; Waid & Orne, 1981). Despite the recent controversy regarding the application of this research to field settings (Lykken, 1978, 1979; Raskin, 1978; Raskin & Hare, 1978; Raskin & Podlesny, 1979), the above reviews indicate that, in the laboratory, truth and lie-telling are associated with different autonomic responses. There are various interpretations for this phenomenon. Davis (1961) suggested three possibilities: the conditioned response theory, the conflict theory, and the punishment theory. The conditioned response theory assumes that a present lie evokes autonomic responses because the question evoking the lie was conditioned to a dishonest and, therefore, traumatic experience. (A variant of this explanation would be that the present lie, rather than the question evoking it, was conditioned to past lying which sometimes led to unpleasant consequences.) The conflict theory suggests that the enhanced responsivity to lying is a consequence of conflicting tendencies to tell the truth and to lie. The punishment theory attributes the enhanced responsivity to the anticipation of punishment if the lie is discovered. Neither the conditioned response nor the punishment theory is very relevant to the laboratory situation, which ordinarily does not involve crimes or punishments.

Other approaches attribute the autonomic activity associated with deception to the specific information (termed "guilty knowledge") that the deceiver has regarding the crucial question (Lykken, 1959, 1960), to the deceiver's motivation to succeed on the deception task (Gustafson & Orne, 1963, 1965), or to differential habituation curves formed by the single lie stimulus versus the multiple truth stimuli (the one card that requires a lie response versus the four cards that require truth responses in the typical lie detection study; Lieblich, Kugelmass, & Ben-Shakhar, 1970; Ben-Shakhar, Lieblich, & Kugelmass, 1975). According to this last approach, the greater are the number of truth stimuli, the more the habituation and, therefore, the less the reactivity to these stimuli. (A similar point of view would be that the more frequent neutral stimuli draw less attention and hence elicit less reactivity than the "crucial" question; see Waid & Orne, 1981.) In the typical study on nonverbal lie detection, there are equal numbers of deceptive and honest messages, and the idea of differential habituation or attention does not apply. However, studies by Ben-Shakhar (1977) and Hemsley (1977; Experiment 1) indicated that differences in the number of stimuli cannot account for all the differences in autonomic responses to truth and deception.

Whatever produces arousal in the studies on physiological responses can also produce arousal in studies on nonverbal behavior. Following Berlyne (1971), Hemsley (1977) suggested that this arousal would cause an increase in the intensity and frequency of nonverbal behaviors under deception. More specific predictions were formulated with regard to such arousal-related responses as pupil dilation, eyeblinks, fundamental frequency (voice pitch), and speech disturbances.

A number of studies have shown that subjects react with pupil dilation to arousal-producing stimuli such as a signal for the firing of a gun (Nunnally, Knott, Duchnowski, & Parker, 1967; Scott, Wells, Wood, & Morgan, 1967; Simpson, 1969; Simpson & Hale, 1969). Similarly, an increase in eyeblinks was viewed by Meyer (1953) as an index of generalized arousal. High fundamental frequency was related to stress in an analysis of pilots' radio transmissions before versus during flight difficulties (Williams & Stevens, 1969). In the laboratory, Hecker, Stevens, von Bismarck, and Williams (1968) showed that fundamental frequency rose under stress, but only if subjects did not reduce their vocal amplitude. In a different study, Fairbanks (1940) found that posed vocal expressions of fear and anger were associated with higher fundamental frequency than were grief, contempt, and indifference. A review of the relevant literature (Scherer, 1980a) indicated that experimentally induced stress increases fundamental frequency; a related review (Scherer, 1980b) showed that emotions classified as high in arousal are characterized by vocal expressions of high fundamental frequency, whereas emotions low in arousal are characterized by low fundamental frequency. Turning to speech disturbances, Kasl and Mahl (1965) reported that manipulations of the level of anxiety in an interview produced concomitant changes in speech errors and hesitations, which were also related to palmar sweat. These studies suggest that if deception gives rise to arousal, it should be associated with increases in pupil dilation, eyeblink rate, fundamental frequency, and speech disturbances.

It is possible, however, that the general autonomic responsivity to deception reflects specific emotions. If so, cues to deception may be accounted for by the particular affects that are involved rather than by general arousal. This possibility is discussed next.

c. *The Affective Approach.* The affects most commonly associated with deception are guilt and anxiety (e.g., Ekman, 1980; Knapp *et al.*, 1974; Kraut, 1980)—guilt about engaging in deception and anxiety about being caught. Ekman (1980) added to this list "duping delight," that is, the joy associated with meeting the challenge of a successful deception. [Anxiety and duping delight are related to Davis's (1961) punishment notion and Gustafson and Orne's (1963, 1965) motivation to succeed, respectively.] Finally, Mehrabian (1971) suggested that of three dimensions of behavior, evaluation (positivity/negativity), status (dominance/submission), and responsiveness (active/passive), only evaluation is relevant to deception.[3] According to this model, deception is characterized by negative or "nonimmediate" behaviors; of course, nonimmediacy may simply reflect guilt and anxiety. Any of the emotions mentioned above can account for the autonomic reactivity associated with deception, but the nonverbal responses are now viewed as a direct reflection of these affects rather than as the consequence of arousal.

The extent to which deception fosters guilt, anxiety, and/or duping delight varies according to the purpose of the deception, its social context, and characteristics of the deceiver. In this regard, it is unlikely that the usual laboratory experiment arouses guilt since, more often than not, the deception is sanctioned and, in fact, required by the experimenter. Anxiety and duping delight are often minimal, too, although some experimenters did attempt to manipulate subjects' motivation to do well on the deception task. However, if lying has been conditioned to unpleasant experience in the past, deception in the lab may elicit negative affects in spite of its inconsequential context.

The experience of negative affects under deception can influence behavior in several ways. There may be an increase in direct expressions of negative affects, for example, facial and vocal cues might become less pleasant. Another indicator of discomfort and anxiety is the occurrence of adaptors (Ekman & Friesen, 1972)—behaviors that satisfy some self-needs or body needs (e.g., grooming, scratching, etc.). Other behavioral correlates of deception may indicate an attempt to disassociate oneself from the deceptive message so as to minimize the negative experience. This strategy, termed indirectness (Knapp *et al.*, 1974) or withdrawal (Miller & Burgoon, 1981) might result in evasive responses or attempts to change the conversation topic as well as in less eye

_____

[3]However, DePaulo, Wilson, and Lanier (1981f) have found that senders (judged from an audiotape) sound relatively more dominant when lying than when telling the truth.

contact, less direct body orientation, and more distance from the addressee (see Mehrabian, 1971). Finally withdrawal can also cause a decrease in the frequency of illustrators, hand movements that accompany and change (emphasize, augment, etc.) what is being said verbally (Ekman, 1980).

   d. *Cognitive Factors in Deception.*   Creating the details of a lie is a more difficult task than telling the truth. The deceiver must formulate a deceptive message that does not contain logical inconsistencies and does not contradict what the listener might already know. Consistent with this view, DePaulo, Finkelstein, Rosenthal, and Eisenstat (1980e) found that subjects took more time to prepare deceptive statements than truthful ones. To the extent that lying is a complex task, it may give rise to speech characteristics, pupillary responses, and gestures indicative of such complexity.

   Goldman-Eisler (1968) showed that when subjects are required to make verbal statements of greater cognitive complexity, they start the response later and pause more frequently. Hess and Polt (1964) suggested that dilation of the pupil indicates the amount of mental effort exerted during problem solving. Kahneman and his colleagues (Kahneman, 1973; Kahneman & Beatty, 1967; Kahneman & Peavler, 1969; Kahneman, Tursky, Shapiro, & Crider, 1969) also found that size of dilation varies according to the mental effort or processing load required by a task. In fact, their investigations showed that the pupillary response was sensitive enough to indicate within a trial the second-to-second variation in the processing load imposed by the task. Finally, Ekman and Friesen (1972) suggested that a high level of concentration and absorption in a speech would lead to a decrease in the frequency of illustrators.

   Thus, it can be suggested that the higher cognitive complexity of lie-telling may result in more speech pauses or hesitations, longer response latencies, increased pupil dilation, and fewer illustrators. The increase in pupil dilation was previously predicted on the basis of increases in arousal, which is probably correlated with complexity of the task; the decrease in illustrators was previously predicted on the basis of decrease in the speaker's involvement in the deceptive message. On the other hand, the prediction regarding the increase in response latency seems inconsistent with the idea that arousal associated with deception increases the intensity (and decreases the latency?) of the deceiver's responses. Evidence relevant to these predictions as well as other data on behavioral correlates of deception are presented in the following section.

2. *Empirical Findings*

   An often cited quotation from a 900 B.C. papyrus veda describes the behavior of a liar: "He does not answer questions, or they are evasive answers; he speaks nonsense, rubs the great toe along the ground, and shivers; his face is discolored; he rubs the roots of the hair with his fingers" (Trovillo, 1939, p.

849). Some three thousand years later, Horvath (1973) wrote that "a lying subject will usually be evasive and will not answer the examiner's question" (p. 140); Reid and Inbau (1977) mentioned that lying subjects tend to move about and display a high level of nervousness; and Morris (1977) stated that hair grooming is one of the behavioral manifestations of deception. The question is whether these observations are supported by empirical data.

Appendix I presents all the studies known to the authors that have examined verbal and nonverbal behaviors associated with deception except those behaviors or combinations of behavior studied only once, including eye movement (Hemsley, 1977), mouth movement (Hemsley & Doob, 1979), stiffness of posture and evasiveness (Kraut & Poe, 1980), various verbal measures (DePaulo, Rosenthal, Rosenkrantz, & Green, 1981e; Knapp et al., 1974), and immediacy and relaxation (Mehrabian, 1971). Appendix I also omits one study on children's nonverbal behaviors (Feldman, Devin-Sheehan, & Allen, 1978)[4] and another that is based on the subjective impressions of individual polygraph examiners (Horvath, 1973).

Most of the studies presented involved judges who were required to count the frequency or measure the duration of a particular behavior when senders were lying and when they were telling the truth; in a few instances, the measure was based on readings of some mechanical device such as a pupillometer (Heilveil, 1976) or, conversely, the subjective impressions of judges (e.g., pleasantness ratings of facial expressions, Zuckerman et al., 1979). Most investigators reported rates of occurrence for each behavior rather than absolute values, thus controlling for response length. It appears that Gagnon (1975), Hocking and Leathers (1980), and Knapp et al. (1974) did not exercise such control, at least for some of their variables. In the study by Gagnon, deception did not affect response length, $F < 1$; deceptive responses were somewhat shorter in the Knapp et al. study, $F(1,36) = 3.19$, $p < .10$, $d = .60$, $r = .29$; and Hocking and Leathers did not report results for this variable. Our impression is that the effects of the lack of control on the overall pattern of results was minimal.

For each of the behaviors listed in Appendix I, the entries express the difference in the occurrence of that cue between deceptive and truthful messages in standard deviation units (Cohen's d, 1977), defined conceptually as $(M_1 - M_2)/\sigma$ and computed as $2r/\sqrt{1-r^2}$ or, equivalently, as $2\sqrt{F}/\sqrt{df}$ in this article. In this and all other appendices, ds were based on statistics provided by the author(s) in the article or in personal communications; when no statistics were available, the ds were derived from the statement that results were either significant or not significant (in the latter case, results are presented as 0). Positive ds in Appendix I indicate that the behavior under consideration occurred more fre-

---

[4]Here and in other places in this article, discussion of developmental studies is deferred to Section IV,C.

quently under deception. The left side of Table I presents a summary of Appendix I, that is, the number of studies measuring a particular behavior, their mean d, and the combined z associated with this d [zs were computed according to procedures outlined in Rosenthal (1978, 1980) and Rosenthal and Rubin (1978)]. It can be seen that 8 of 19 (42%) behaviors distinguished reliably between truth- and lie-telling, a proportion that exceeds substantially the 5% that would be expected by chance.

The results provide support for the view that deception is arousing. Three of the four arousal-associated behaviors—pupil dilation, speech errors, and pitch—increased significantly under deception; the fourth behavior, blinking, also increased, but the increase was not significant ($z = 1.43$, $p = .15$). The view that

TABLE I
BEHAVIORS ASSOCIATED WITH DECEPTION[a]

	All studies			Low motivation		High motivation		
Behavior	N[b]	Mean d	Combined z	N[b]	Mean d	N[b]	Mean d	z of difference
Visual channel								
Pupil dilation	3	1.49	5.11***	1	1.19	1	1.52**	.57
Gaze	15	− .11	− .66	9	.04	6	− .33	1.76
Blinking	5	.61	1.43	3	1.39***	2	− .56**	4.76***
Smiling	16	− .09	−1.52	7	− .17*	9	− .02	1.65
Head movements	8	− .27	−1.70	3	.14	5	− .52**	2.85**
Gestures	11	− .12	− .16	5	.12	6	− .32	1.11
Shrugs	3	.48	1.96*	2	.17	1	1.10*	.67
Adaptors	12	.40	3.77***	5	.69***	7	.19	2.00*
Foot and leg movements	8	− .06	− .48	3	− .07	5	− .06	.42
Postural shifts	10	− .08	−1.38	4	.16	6	− .24*	2.11*
Auditory channel								
Response latency	13	− .13	− .82	7	− .17	6	− .09	.40
Response length	15	− .12	−1.29	6	.18	9	− .32**	3.04**
Speech rate	9	− .02	− .85	3	.31	6	− .18	1.55
Speech errors	10	.23	2.18*	2	.56*	8	.14	.49
Speech hesitations	8	.62	3.96***	4	.82**	4	.44*	.38
Pitch	4	.68	2.26*	2	.08	2	1.28**	1.98*
Negative statements	3	1.32	5.65***	1	.20	2	1.88***	4.21***
Irrelevant information	4	.73	2.90**	3	.88**	1	.28	1.19
Self-references	2	− .28	−1.15	1	− .12	1	− .44	.67

[a]Positive values indicate that an increase (negative values, that a decrease) in the behavior was associated with deception.

[b]N, Number of studies.

*$p < .05$.

**$p < .01$.

***$p < .001$.

lying is a cognitively complex activity received somewhat weaker support. Two indicators of complex cognitive processing—increase in pupil dilation and increase in speech hesitations—were significantly associated with deception; two others—decrease in illustrators (defined as gestures in Table I) and increase in response latency—were not significantly related to deception. It is possible of course, that the category of gestures includes more than just illustrators and consequently does not allow a good test of the relationship between the latter behavior and deception.

Some of the remaining findings in Table I, as well as single studies of behaviors not included in Table I, provide support for the two remaining views of factors involved in deception—attempted control and felt emotion.

With regard to control, Zuckerman *et al.* (1979) found that deceptive answers gave rise to impressions of less personal involvement; DePaulo, Davis, and Lanier (1980d) and DePaulo, Lanier, and Davis (1981b) reported that deceptive answers were viewed as more rehearsed and less spontaneous; and DePaulo and Rosenthal (1979a) reported that deceptive responses were seen as more discrepant than truthful ones. The lower level of involvement and spontaneity of lies is consistent with their characterization as planned and controlled activities; the impression of discrepancy may indicate that not all channels could be controlled to the same degree.

The lower involvement associated with deception may also signal withdrawal, which is an indicator of negative affect. A decrease in self-references may also indicate withdrawal, but its relationship to deception was not significant (see the bottom line in Table I). Stronger evidence of withdrawal during deception comes from a study on nonimmediate expression in lie- and truth-telling (Wagner & Pease, 1976). Nonimmediate expressions make the relationship between communicators and the objects of their messages less direct. For example, "I like John's company" is a less immediate statement than "I like John" (for a detailed analysis of nonimmediacy, see Wiener and Mehrabian, 1968). Originally, nonimmediacy was identified as a mode of negative expressions— nonimmediate statements were rated as more negative and negative statements were judged as more nonimmediate (Mehrabian, 1966, 1967; Wiener & Mehrabian, 1968). Wagner and Pease (1976) showed, however, that deceptive statements were more nonimmediate than truthful ones, regardless of whether the deceivers attempted to convey positive or negative expressions. Perhaps the expression of nonimmediacy in deception reflects both withdrawal and negative affects. Finally, Table I shows that deception is associated with a nonsignificant decrease in smiling ($z = -1.52$, $p = .13$) and with significant increases in adaptors and verbal negative statements, three behaviors that can serve as indicators of negative affects.

The two remaining correlates of deception presented in Table I—increases in shrugs and amount of irrelevant information—do not fit any specific approach to deception. Shrugs may indicate a lack of confidence in what is being said or not knowing what to say; irrelevant information may be a necessary substitute for information that the deceiver cannot supply. Admittedly, however, it is not terribly difficult to explain the association of almost any behavior with deception. The reason is that deception is many things, involving different processes and taking various forms. One would almost expect that the same behavior would be related differently to different types of lies.

In an exploratory attempt to distinguish among different types of lies, the studies included in Appendix I were classified according to two dimensions, motivation to succeed on the deception task (low or high) and the amount of planning involved in the deception (low, medium, or high). Motivation was considered high if subjects were promised some monetary reward for doing well on the deception task (e.g., Knapp *et al.*, 1974) or if the deception was described as a test of some skill or ability (e.g., Kraut, 1978a). Level of planning was considered high if the deceptive communication was rehearsed with the subjects (e.g., Hemsley, 1977) or if subjects needed only to say no (or yes) in response to all the questions (e.g., Cutrow, Parks, Lucas, & Thomas, 1972). Level of planning was considered medium if, after the question was asked, subjects were allowed to pause and prepare their answer (e.g., DePaulo & Rosenthal, 1979b). Level of planning was considered low if subjects did not know in advance the content of the questions and were not given time to prepare the answers (e.g., Exline, Thibaut, Hickey, & Gumpert, 1970). The classification of studies according to both motivation and planning appears in the two left-hand columns in Appendix I.

The right-hand part of Table I presents the differences in ds between deceptive and truthful communications for low- and high-motivation studies as well as the zs of the difference between the significance levels associated with each d (Rosenthal & Rubin, 1979). It can be seen that of the 19 visual and auditory cues, more were significantly associated with deception in the high-motivation studies than in the low-motivation studies (9 versus 5). Furthermore, there were seven significant differences between the low- and high-motivation levels where only one would be expected by chance. In general, it appears that the highly motivated deceivers tried harder to control their behavior and consequently moved less and displayed more behavioral rigidity. Specifically, compared with the low-motivation condition, deception under high motivation was associated with less blinking, less head movement, fewer adaptors, and fewer postural shifts; on the other hand, it was also associated with higher pitch, a response that is relatively less controllable.

Level of planning produced less dramatic results than did motivation. Compared with deception under low level of planning, the highly planned deception was associated with more postural shifts ($p < .05$), fewer gestures ($p < .05$), more smiling ($p < .10$), and, in particular, shorter response latencies ($p < .001$).

In fact, under low level of planning, lie-telling was associated with longer latencies than truth-telling ($p < .05$) whereas under high level of planning, lie-telling was associated with shorter latencies ($p < .001$). Evidently, the well-prepared deceivers tended to jump the gun whereas the unprepared liars took their time so as to prepare their responses more carefully.

It is appropriate to conclude this section with a brief note on three "exotic" behaviors that may or may not be correlated with deception. The first and perhaps least exotic behavior has to do with several semantic cues to deception. Bolinger (1973) argued that there are specific linguistic forms which characterize deception, for example, deletion of references to persons associated with a cognitive appraisal, as in the phrase "credible deterrent"—"credible to whom?" the listener may ask. Alker (1976) operationalized some of Bolinger's ideas as well as his own in a content analysis of presidential press conferences that are known to have been, at least partially, deceptive (e.g., Kennedy's press conference after the Bay of Pigs invasion). Unexpectedly, the linguistic indices of deception yielded lower scores for the deceptive conferences than for truthful ones. Alker raised the possibility that presidents simply know all too well how to lie, but it is clear that the issue awaits further research.

A second behavior is facial microexpressions, which Ekman and Friesen (1969a) mentioned as a possible cue to deception. In a subsequent report, Ekman and Friesen (1974) wrote that, although naive judges were unable to detect deception from facial expressions, "experienced facial analysts" achieved a high level of accuracy; perhaps these experts obtained their information from facial microexpressions. From the more popular literature, a recent interview with Bennet (1978) indicated that this investigator could detect microexpressions "in the faces of the speakers at the precise moment they laid a lie on their classmates" (p. 34). Interestingly, Bennet mentioned that microexpressions were characterized by rapid eye movement, a cue that was significantly related to deception in a study by Hemsley (1977, Experiment 2). Perhaps there is more to Bennet and to microexpressions than meets the eye. Certainly it is an intriguing topic for future research.

An even more "mysterious" behavior than microexpression is the pattern of stress-related tremors in the voice that are measured by the Psychological Stress Evaluator (PSE). Developers of the PSE, Dektor Counterintelligence and Security of Springfield, Virginia, claim that their instrument detects deception. It is not clear, however, just what is being measured in a PSE voice analysis (Podlesny & Raskin, 1977), and even the existence of voice tremors is considered problematic (Shipp & McGlon, 1973). More important, controlled studies indicated that the PSE instrument did not discriminate between truth and deception above the chance level, although a conventional GSR analysis did (Horvath, 1978, 1979). At present, there appears to be no evidence in support of the validity of the PSE (see also Podlesny & Raskin, 1977; Rice, 1978).

III.   The Lie Detector's Perspective

A.   BEHAVIORAL CORRELATES OF JUDGMENT OF DECEPTION

The finding that truth- and lie-telling are associated with different behaviors gives rise to two more problems: (a) Which behaviors are associated with *judgments* of deception and (b) what is the degree of correspondence between the behaviors actually discriminating deception and those correlated with judgments of deception (cf. DePaulo *et al.*, 1981e; Krauss *et al.*, 1976; Kraut, 1978a; Kraut & Poe, 1980).

Appendix II summarizes the findings of the available studies on the relationship between behavioral cues and perceived deception. Like Appendix I, the present summary includes all behaviors that were examined in two or more studies. Two different paradigms have been used in this research. In the first paradigm, one group of judges rates the truthfulness of deceptive and honest messages and a different group of judges rates the behavioral cues associated with each message. A correlational analysis indicates which behaviors are related to judgments of deception. It should be noted that if both the truthfulness ratings and the behavioral data discriminate actual deception, their intercorrelation will be "inflated." Of the studies reported in Appendix II, Harrison, Hwalek, Raney, and Fritz (1978), DePaulo *et al.* (1981e), and Zuckerman *et al.* (1979) computed the relevant correlations separately for deceptive and honest messages and averaged the results across the type of message. Ekman and Friesen (1972), Kraut and Poe (1980), and Krauss *et al.* (1976) apparently did not control for actual deception, but in these studies either the truthfulness ratings or the behavioral cues were not related to actual deception. Kraut (1978a) and Streeter *et al.* (1977) also did not control for actual deception and the correlations they report may be somewhat "inflated."

The second paradigm (Baskett & Freedle, 1974; Hemsley & Doob, 1979; Friedman, 1979) involves the preparation of two or more messages, identical in all aspects except the behavioral cue of interest (e.g., response latency; Baskett & Freedle, 1974); truthfulness ratings of the various messages are subsequently examined as a function of the variation in the behavioral cue.

The entries in Appendix II were computed in the same way as the entries in Appendix I, except that perceived deception replaced actual deception; positive *d*s indicate that the behavior under consideration was associated with judgments of deception rather than judgments of truth. Table II presents a summary of cues to perceived deception that is analogous to the summary of cues to actual deception in Table I. It can be seen that of 10 behaviors, 8 (80%) were significantly associated with perceived deception, a proportion that is higher than the proportion (42%) of behaviors associated with actual deception. This difference provides strong support for Kraut's (1980) assertion that behavioral cues are more strongly associated with judgments of deception than with actual deception.

TABLE II

BEHAVIORS ASSOCIATED WITH JUDGMENT OF DECEPTION AND BELIEFS ABOUT DECEPTION

Behavior	Judgment of deception			Beliefs about deception, mean d^b
	N of studies	Mean d^a	Combined z	
Visual channel				
Gaze	4	$-.45$	$-3.25**$	-1.25
Smiling	5	$-.32$	$-2.97**$	.31
Adaptors	3	.30	.51	3.16
Postural shifts	2	.50	$3.00**$	1.34
Auditory channel				
Response latency	5	.36	$3.61***$	.68
Response length	4	$-.11$	$-.61$	.46
Speech rate	2	$-.67$	$-2.84**$	1.35
Speech errors	4	.27	$2.00*$	2.06
Speech hesitations	2	.58	$3.17**$	1.28
Pitch	2	.68	$2.82**$	.95

[a] Positive values indicate that an increase (negative values, that a decrease) in the behavior was associated with judgment of deception.

[b] Positive values indicate that an increase (negative values, that a decrease) in the behavior was believed to be associated with deception; after Zuckerman et al., 1981a.

$*p < .05.$
$**p < .01.$
$***p < .001.$

Research on communicator credibility provides supplementary evidence for some of the speech-related variables in Table II. Credibility involves two factors, competence and trustworthiness (cf. McGuire, 1969; Miller & Burgoon, 1981). Competence, also termed authoritativeness, refers to the communicator's ability or expertise; trustworthiness, also termed benevolence, refers to his or her sincerity and honesty. Other credibility dimensions, such as dynamism, are viewed by Miller and Burgoon as antecedent conditions affecting both competence and trustworthiness.

It was shown that increases in the number of speech errors (nonfluencies) and speech hesitations (pauses) resulted in lower credibility ratings, although the effect appears greater for competence and dynamism than for trustworthiness (Lay & Burron, 1968; McCroskey & Mehrley, 1969; Miller & Hewgill, 1964; Sereno & Hawkins, 1967). Increase in pitch produced lower competence and benevolence ratings (Brown, Strong, & Rencher, 1974) as well as impressions of lower potency and persuasiveness and higher nervousness (Apple et al., 1979, Experiments 2 and 3); however, pitch did not affect ratings on the evaluation and activity factors (Apple et al., 1979, Experiment 2), and its effects on ratings of fluency and emphaticness depended on the particular questions that were asked

(Apple *et al.*, 1979, Experiment 3). Faster speech rate produced higher ratings of competence (Smith, Brown, Strong, & Rencher, 1975), more persuasion and higher ratings of knowledge, intelligence, and objectivity (Miller, Maruyama, Beaber, & Valone, 1976), and higher preference ratings, better recall, and more attention (MacLachlan, 1979); in some investigations, however, a curvilinear relationship emerged so that, relative to low and high speech rates, the normal rate produced higher ratings of the speaker's benevolence (Brown, Strong, & Rencher, 1973; Brown *et al.*, 1974; Smith *et al.*, 1975) and general effectiveness (persuasiveness, fluency, etc.; Apple *et al.*, 1979, Experiment 3). Overall, it appears that suspicion of deception is based on the same acoustical variables that give rise to negative impressions of the speaker—speech errors and hesitations, higher pitch, and lower speech rate. Other variables have also been related to speaker effectiveness. For example, Sharp and McClung (1966) and McCroskey and Mehrley (1969) found that poor organization of a message, operationalized by randomizing some of the sentences, produced more negative ratings of the speaker. Although this variable has not previously been examined in the lie detection research, it may be a promising correlate of both actual and perceived deception (see Scherer, 1979, for an extensive review of impressions of speech characteristics).

What is the correspondence between cues to perceived and actual deception? A quantitative answer to this question was first provided in a study by DePaulo *et al.* (1981e). These investigators first computed correlations of each of 20 verbal and paralinguistic cues with both actual deception and perceived deception; they then computed a single correlation between the 20 correlations associated with actual deception and the 20 correlations associated with perceived deception. The latter correlation was substantial, $r(18) = .47$, $p = .04$, indicating that the verbal and paralinguistic cues to actual deception serve, to some extent, as cues to perceived deception (at least for the cues that were examined in the study). The generality of the result was greatly increased when the same type of correlation between actual and perceived cues to deception was computed separately for every combination of sender sex, perceiver sex, and type of affect (positive vs negative). The resulting 8 correlations ranged from .33 to .83 with a median r of .52, $p < .002$. The analogous correlation in the present data between the 10 d estimates of cues to perceived deception (Table II) and the corresponding 10 d estimates of cues to actual deception (Table I) was .64 ($p < .05$). When two studies not controlling for actual deception (Kraut, 1978a; Streeter *et al.*, 1977) were excluded from the computation of ds in Table II, the correlation between cues to perceived and actual deception changed very little ($r = .69$, $p < .05$).

Three other correlates of actual deception that were not included in Table I—impressions of planning or rehearsal, discrepancy among channels, and nonimmediacy of speech—were also examined as correlates of perceived deception. DePaulo *et al.* (1980d) and DePaulo *et al.* (1981b) found that rehearsed responses, whether deceptive or not, were rated as more deceptive than responses that were not rehearsed. Argyle, Alkema, and Gilmour (1970) reported that inconsistency between verbal and nonverbal cues on the positivity dimension (e.g., positive verbal cues paired with negative nonverbal cues) was interpreted as indicating insincerity; no such effect was reported for a similar inconsistency on the dominance dimension (Argyle, Salter, Nicholson, Williams, & Burgess, 1970). Friedman (1979) replicated these results. Finally, Wagner and Pease (1976) reported that subjects rated positive statements less positively and negative statements less negatively when they were nonimmediate than when they were immediate. In a similar study in which subjects directly indicated their perceptions of deceptiveness, DePaulo (1981) found that nonimmediate statements were rated as more deceptive than immediate statements. Thus, there seems to be additional support for the correspondence between behaviors actually discriminating deception and behaviors perceived to be discriminating deception.

It should be noted that what we have called correlates of perceived deception were the behaviors that were correlated with judgments of deception and not behaviors that judges said they used in detecting deception. It is not clear, therefore, whether lie detectors know which cues they actually do use.

In a study by Zuckerman, Koestner, and Driver (1981a), subjects were asked to indicate on a 9-point scale the effects of deception on each of the 19 behaviors listed in Table I ($+4$ = behavior increases under deception, 0 = behavior does not change under deception, -4 = behavior decreases under deception). Approximately half of the subjects indicated these effects for others' behavior, whereas the rest indicated these effects for their own behavior. Estimates of d for the believed association between each behavior and deception in the "others" condition were correlated (.89) with the corresponding d estimates for the "self" condition. Averaged d estimates across the two conditions for only 10 behaviors are presented in the right-hand column of Table II. The correlation between these estimates of behaviors believed to be associated with deception and the d estimates of behaviors related to judgment of deception was .44; however, the correlation between the d estimates of beliefs about deception and the d estimates of behaviors associated with actual deception was only .11. It appears, therefore, that people have some knowledge of at least the cues they use in lie detection. Several other studies lead to the same conclusion.

In two studies by Hemsley (1977, Experiments 2 and 3) the following behaviors were mentioned more often as indicators of deception than of truthfulness: gaze aversion, smiling, nervous hand gestures, postural shifts, longer response latencies, and speech nonfluencies; length of response was also mentioned, but only by very few respondents, and even then it was related to both truth and deception. With the exception of smiling, the list appears consistent with the cues to perceived deception reported in Table II. In a different survey (cited in Hocking & Leathers, 1980), 65% of the respondents mentioned reduced eye contact as indicative of deception, 62% mentioned "shakiness" or "trembling,'' and 54% mentioned fidgeting. Perhaps shaking, trembling, and fidgeting correspond to postural shifts which actually affect decisions about deception (see Table II). Finally, Hemsley and Doob (1978) reported that of 21 subjects who watched a gaze-averting witness in a simulated trial, 17 reported being aware of the witness's gazing behavior, and 10 stated that because of this behavior they rated his testimony as less honest. Interestingly, gaze aversion is also mentioned by subjects as behavior that must be controlled in deception (Hemsley, 1977, Experiment 2; Matarazzo, Wiens, Jackson, & Manaugh, 1970).

Finally, what can be said about awareness of ability to detect lies? Correlations between confidence in accuracy of lie detection and actual accuracy were examined in six studies and range from −.01 to .39, with a median of .06 (Atmiyanandana, 1976; Brandt, Miller, & Hocking, 1980b; Bauchner, 1976, cited in Brandt *et al.*, 1980b; Hocking, 1976, cited in Brandt *et al.*, 1980b; Matarazzo *et al.*, 1970; Nieters, 1975). Thus, it appears that judges know better what they do when attempting to detect deception than how good they are at doing it.

B. STRATEGIES OF LIE DETECTION

Lie detection is a two-factor process: perceiving or attending to the relevant cues and then interpreting them. In actual research, of course, it is not always possible to distinguish between attention and interpretation.

The question of which cues perceivers attend to was originally formulated with regard to the relative influence of the visual and auditory channels on perceivers' judgments. A number of studies indicated that perceivers were more influenced by visual cues, particularly facial expressions (Bugental, Kaswan, & Love, 1970; DePaulo, Rosenthal, Eisenstat, Roger, & Finkelstein, 1978; Mehrabian & Ferris, 1967), but the evidence is by no means uniform (see Krauss, Apple, Morency, Wenzel, & Winton, 1981). Thus, it is important to examine the factors that influence the amount of attention accorded to each channel. One such factor may be the extent to which the message involves deception (see DePaulo *et al.*, 1978). Thus, if the face does not provide deception and/or leakage cues, subjects who suspect deception should attend relatively less to the face and relatively more to tone of voice. There is both direct and indirect support for this hypothesized strategy.

In one study, DePaulo *et al.* (1978) administered to subjects the Nonverbal Discrepancy Test, an instrument comprised of multiple-channel visual (face or body) plus auditory cues (content filtered or random spliced) that are either consistent (visual and auditory components convey the same message), moderately discrepant, or extremely discrepant. Judgments of the discrepant items were more influenced by the visual than the auditory cues. This effect, termed video primacy, was somewhat stronger for the moderately discrepant cues than for the extremely discrepant cues. DePaulo *et al.* suggested that subjects viewed the extremely discrepant messages as more deceptive and consequently assigned more weight to the vocal cues. This interpretation is consistent, of course, with the previously reported relationship between discrepancy and perceived deception. Zuckerman, Blanck, DePaulo, and Rosenthal (1980b) and Blanck, Rosenthal, Snodgrass, DePaulo, and Zuckerman (1981) found that the decrease in video primacy for highly discrepant items was more pronounced for older children, indicating that the distrust toward discrepant items and the resulting decoding strategy may be a learned phenomenon.

In the DePaulo *et al.* (1978) study, deceptiveness was not directly manipulated. This was done, however, in a study by Zuckerman, Spiegel, DePaulo, and Rosenthal (1980c). The discrepancy test was administered with the information that the stimulus person in the test never lied, sometimes lied, or very often lied. It was found that subjects who expected more deception showed less video primacy for discrepancies involving the face but not for discrepancies involving the body; highly suspecting subjects were also more likely to disbelieve the facial expressions (but not the body cues) associated with consistent auditory cues. Thus, suspicion of deception led subjects to discount the readily faked face more than the leakier voice and body.

Another method for determining the relative influence of various channels on the perceiver is to examine correlations between judgments of single channels (e.g., face or voice alone) and those of the multiple channel. These correlations indicate the extent to which each single channel contributes to observers' impressions of the full audiovisual record. Ekman, Friesen, O'Sullivan, and Scherer (1980) examined such correlations for ratings of deceptive messages as well as honest ones. They found, for three samples of perceivers, that, when the senders were lying, judgments of personality and affect that were made from audiovisual cues correlated more highly with judgments of speech (words plus tone) than with judgments made from either face or body cues. However, when senders were telling the truth, there were no differences among the correlations of the three channels with the criterion. Interestingly, the judges in this study were not told that some of the messages involved deception. Perhaps changes in pitch or other voice qualities associated with deception drew attention to the vocal channel when senders were lying (Ekman *et al.,* 1980, p. 27). This interpretation received some support from a study by Zuckerman *et al.* (1980a). Again, single channel (face and filtered speech) ratings of truthfulness and affects were correlated with multiple-channel ratings for deceptive and honest messages. It was found that when senders were honest, ratings of the audiovisual cues were more highly correlated with ratings of the face than with ratings of filtered speech; when senders were lying the pattern was reversed. In this study, however, judges knew that the messages involved deception and, in fact, were quite accurate at detecting it. Perhaps suspicion of deception led subjects to rely on the vocal component of those audiovisual messages involving deceit.

These studies imply that when judges expect a deceptive message they are more influenced by the vocal channel. It is not entirely clear whether this strategy means that subjects attend relatively more to the voice than to the face or that they attend equally to both but then weight the vocal channel more heavily. We also do not know whether these strategies are planned and deliberate or unconscious and unintended.

The question of consciousness notwithstanding, the reliance on vocal cues when deception seems likely implies that the more leaky channels are also treated as such. That is, even if judges cannot verbalize the belief that the voice is leakier than the face, their strategy at detecting deception implies that they behave according to such a belief. Further evidence in support of the correspondence between actual and perceived leakiness is provided by Rosenthal and DePaulo (1979a,b). They hypothesized that as nonverbal cues become more leaky and less controllable, women would lose some of their advantage over men in accuracy of decoding (see Hall, 1978, 1980; Rosenthal, Hall, DiMatteo, Rogers, & Archer, 1979), perhaps because women are socialized not to read those cues that senders are trying to conceal. Their results showed that women's decoding superiority to men was greater for the facial than for the vocal channel. It is interesting to note that lie detectors and women may treat the vocal channel in almost opposite manners for identical reasons. Lie detectors may attend to it in order to detect deception; women may not attend to it so as to avoid detecting concealed information. Like the lie detector, women may not be able to verbalize their strategy but do behave as if they believe that the voice is leakier than the face.

An important question is whether greater reliance on the vocal channel actually improves the accuracy of lie detection. A study by DePaulo, Lassiter, and Stone (1981c) suggests that it does. Their subjects were given access to audiovisual messages but were instructed to pay special attention to the tone of voice, to the words, or to the visual cues; control subjects did not receive any attentional instructions. It was found that perceivers were more accurate at detecting lies in the attend-to-tone and attend-to-words conditions than in the visual and control conditions. These results have two implications. First, tone of voice, perhaps in combination with words, may serve as a particularly good indicator of deception. Second, the lie detector must adopt an attend-to-tone strategy in order to take advantage of the available information. Stated differently, the presence or absence of deception cues is only a necessary condition for the detection of deception. It is the detector's strategy that will determine whether such cues will be put to use.

Lie detectors can also play an active role in the interpretation of the cues they have perceived. In Section III,A, it was shown that the variables correlated with the attribution of deception correspond fairly well to variables correlated with actual deception. It seems, therefore, that the identification of deception depends on whether the relevant cues are leaked by the deceiver and perceived by the lie detector. A quite different approach to the inference of deception is suggested in a study by Kraut (1978a, Experiment 2). This investigator showed that observers suspicious of a self-serving answer became even less trusting when the answer was preceded by a long pause; in contrast, judges trusting a self-damaging answer became even more trusting if it was preceded by the same period of hesitation. Kraut suggested that the pause preceding the self-serving answer was interpreted as the time needed to create the lie whereas the pause preceding a self-damaging answer was interpreted as the time needed to decide on the answer and phrase it in the least damaging way. Thus, the view that perceived deception is related to constant nonverbal and verbal cues is now challenged by the view that a behavioral cue is a nonspecific activator (see Ellsworth & Langer, 1976) that is interpreted according to the context in which it is perceived.

Some nonverbal behaviors (e.g., eye contact) serve as nonspecific activators in the attribution of affect (Ellsworth & Langer, 1976). In all likelihood, more cues fulfill this function in the attribution of deception because deception gives rise to different and sometimes conflicting affects. For example, smiling, a signal generally associated with a positive affect can indicate either a positive affect associated with righteous honesty or the duping delight associated with deception. Thus, a smiling sender may cause a suspicious perceiver to become more suspicious and a trusting perceiver to become more trusting. Of course, the position that there are no specific cues to deception cannot be carried to an extreme; after all, a list of such cues is presented in Table II. Still, the cues in this list may operate differently in contexts other than the psychological experiments in which they have been studied. It is clear that the issue cannot be resolved without more data. In all likelihood, the specificity of the relationship between cues and perceived deception may vary as a function of different cues, different situations, different liars, and different lie detectors.

That inference of deception may be determined by factors other than the objective cues was also documented in a study by Atkinson and Allen (1979). They found that observers who organized behaviors in smaller units or chunks were more likely to perceive the target person's behavior as deliberate (deceptive) than observers who employed a more global analysis. Following Newtson (1973), Atkinson and Allen suggested that observers will shift to a fine level of analysis after they encounter an unexpected behavioral event. They also suggested that an unexpected event can serve as a cue to deception. Even in the absence of an unexpected event, it seems plausible that suspicious observers will pay more attention to the behaviors at hand, divide them into smaller units, and arrive at the conclusion that their suspicion was justified. Of course, whether such a self-fulfilling process occurs depends on whether suspicion actually gives rise to a more fine-grained analysis of behavior.

Overall, the studies presented in this section illustrate the extensive influence of the observer's strategy on the perception and interpretation of behavior. The weights associated with various nonverbal inputs, the meaning attributed to various cues, the accuracy of detection, and the extent to which behavior appears as honest or deceptive may vary, at least in part, as a function of the lie detector's strategy, even when the behavioral stimuli remain constant.

IV. Outcomes of Deceptive Communication: Accuracy of Lie Detection

A. METHODOLOGICAL ISSUES

1. Defining Accuracy

Accuracy of lie detection includes both whether the detectors recognized that deception was occurring (deception accuracy) and whether they identified the concealed information (leakage accuracy). Both types of accuracy depend on the sender's skill at deceiving and the perceiver's skill at detecting—for example, high detection accuracy may indicate that the deceiver did not lie well, that the perceiver was able to see through the deception, or both. Thus, the usual paradigm for studying differences in the ability to deceive is to hold the level of lie detection constant by having, say, one group of judges or randomly distributed judges in the various experimental conditions. Conversely, to examine detecting ability, investigators use one set of deceivers that is rated by all different detectors (for more general discussions of this issue, see Rosenthal, 1981; Rosenthal & DePaulo, 1980).

Some investigators separate accuracy at detecting lies from accuracy at identifying the truth. In reality, these two indices are related because of what Zuckerman *et al.* (1979) have termed the "deceiver's demeanor bias" and the "perceiver's bias." The deceiver's demeanor refers to the sender's tendency to appear honest (or dishonest) consistently, regardless of whether he or she delivers an honest or a deceptive message. Because of this tendency, accuracy at conveying honesty should be negatively correlated with accuracy at conveying deception. The perceiver's bias refers to the detector's tendency to interpret messages as honest (or dishonest) consistently; because of this tendency, ability to detect honesty should be negatively related to the ability to detect deception. Correlational analyses supporting the existence of both biases were reported by Zuckerman *et al.* (1979).

What is the direction of the biases? Findings from 15 available studies (see Appendix III for a presentation of the separate studies) indicate that, overall, truthful messages were detected with more accuracy than deceptive ones (mean d of difference $= .86$, median difference $d = .35$, combined $z = 9.41$, $p < .001$). The fact that detection accuracy was higher under truth than under deception indicates that judges were more likely to call messages truthful than deceptive. Note that this truthfulness bias may be due to the senders' truthful demeanors, to the detectors' tendencies to perceive truthfulness, or to both. More important, accuracy of scores for only lie-telling (or only truth-telling) may reflect the biases as well as the abilities to deceive and/or to detect deception. Such confounding is avoided when the unweighted mean accuracy of truth- and lie-telling combined is considered (see Zuckerman *et al.*, 1979). Which accuracy scores an investigator should use depends on the purpose of the investigation. For example, in order to determine whether perceivers can distinguish deception from truth above chance level, it is necessary to examine the overall level of accuracy. Similarly, comparison of detection accuracy among channels must be based on overall accuracy because different channels may vary in the extent to which they give rise to a particular bias. On the other hand, in order to examine personality correlates of the ability to deceive, the investigator may need to distinguish between accuracy of lie- and truth-telling because the bias may now become the focus of the investigation. This issue will be examined again in Section IV,B,5.

2. *Ecological Validity*

Both the deceiver and the lie detector play very different roles in and outside the laboratory. These issues have been discussed at length by others (DePaulo, 1980; DePaulo, Zuckerman, & Rosenthal, 1980b,c; Knapp & Comadena, 1979; Kraut, 1980; Kraut & Poe, 1980), so we will only summarize their arguments briefly here.

In the laboratory, the deceiver usually does not have much at stake and must follow instructions as to the context and method of deception; in the field, the stakes are generally higher and so is the deceiver's freedom. In the laboratory, the lie detector is required to detect deception; in the field, the issue of deception may be less salient and the detector less on the alert. On the other hand, the lie detector in the field is not limited to a short presentation of the deceptive message (a 20-sec clip is not unrepresentative), can probe the deceiver in order to test various possibilities, and does not have to reach a decision within a specified period of time. Finally, the lie detector in the laboratory can be misled by his or her stereotypes about who is likely to lie, since lying and truth-telling are determined randomly by the experimenter. In the field, some "grain-of-truth" stereotypes may increase, or at least not diminish, detection accuracy.

Note that some of the above factors may facilitate lie detection in the laboratory, whereas others may facilitate lie detection in the field. Most importantly, findings from the laboratory should be generalized to the field only with due caution.

B. CHANNEL EFFECTS IN THE DETECTION OF DECEPTION

1. *Deception Accuracy*

Appendix IV presents the available studies that provide data on deception accuracy. For each study, the difference between obtained and chance accuracy was transformed into standard deviation units (Cohen's *d*, 1977) according to the procedures outlined in Section II,B,2. Positive ds indicate that deception accuracy was above chance level, whereas negative values indicate that accuracy was below chance level. These accuracy data are presented according to channels so that a single study may provide as many ds as the number of channels examined. In fact, the appendix includes 72 d estimates but only 35 separate studies.

A few comments are in order about the division of findings into channels. In general, the facial channel includes studies of facial cues above the neck, whereas the body channel includes studies of body cues from the neck down. The face-and-body channel, however, includes studies that examined only a partial view of the upper body; it was decided that these latter studies fit better the face-and-body category than the face-alone category. The speech channel includes all studies that examined deceivers' unaltered speech, either live or tape-recorded. In contrast, the tone-of-voice channel includes studies of standard-content or content-filtered speech (see Rogers, Scherer, & Rosenthal, 1971; Starkweather, 1956), and the transcript channel includes studies of the transcription of a live or taped message.

With the exception of tone and transcript, the channels presented in Appendix IV can be categorized into eight types created by the presence or absence of three kinds of cues: face, body, and speech. The mean accuracy d for each of these types, as well as for those of tone and transcript, are presented in Table III.

It should be noted that, although all ds in the table are positive and some are substantial, in reality even a big effect may correspond to only a few percentage points above chance accuracy. In fact, the examination of actual percentage accuracy indicates that most of the results fall in the .45–.60 range with a chance level of .5 (see Kraut, 1980; Knapp & Comadena, 1979; Miller & Burgoon, 1981).

TABLE III

ACCURACY OF DETECTING DECEPTION (IN STANDARD DEVIATION UNITS)

| | Visual cues | | | | |
| | Face | | No face | | |
Auditory cues	Body	No body	Body	No body	Means
Speech	1.00(21)[a]	.99(9)	1.49(3)	1.09(12)	1.14
No speech	.35(6)	.05(7)	.43(4)	.00[b]	.21
Means	.68	.52	.96	.54	.68

Transcript only: .70(6)
Tone only: .20(4)

[a] Number of studies upon which d is based is enclosed in parentheses.
[b] Theoretical accuracy.

Which cues produce greater deception accuracy? In accordance with Ekman and Friesen's (1969a) leakage model, the face did not seem to give away deception cues and may even have provided misleading information. Specifically, deception accuracy in the absence of facial cues (mean $d = .75$) was higher than deception accuracy in their presence (.60). Furthermore, of all the channels and channel combinations in Table III, only accuracy of the facial channel (.05) was not significantly greater than chance (combined $z = .66$); accuracy of all the remaining channels was greater than chance at $p < .05$ (one-tailed) or better.

In contrast to the face, the availability of body cues increased deception accuracy from .53 to .82, and the availability of speech cues increased accuracy even more, from .21 to 1.14. Comparison of face, body, and speech as single channels revealed the same order of accuracy; speech was most accurate (1.09), followed by the body (.43), and the face (.05). Additional support for this hierarchy comes from studies that actually compared these channels. Thus, combining the results of three available studies (Hocking et al., 1979; Rotkin, 1979; Wilson, 1975) showed that deception accuracy of the speech-only channel was higher than that of the body (mean d of difference $= .98$, combined $z = 3.30$, $p < .001$); combining the results of four available studies (Ekman & Friesen, 1974; Hocking et al., 1979; Littlepage & Pineault, 1979a; Wilson, 1975) indicated that deception accuracy of the body was higher than that of the face (mean d of difference $= .90$, combined $z = 4.48$, $p < .001$). It is interesting to note that a reexamination of the behavioral cues significantly associated with deception (see Table I) revealed the same speech–body–face order; for the voice, 5 out of 9 (56%) cues were associated with deception, for the body, only 2 out of 5 (40%), and for the face, only 1 out of 5 (20%). It should be noted, however, that these results could be a function of the particular cues that researchers selected to study.

Table III also reveals that tone only and transcript only both provide cues to deception. For both channels, accuracy of deception was above chance, although accuracy of transcript was much higher. Furthermore, the difference between accuracy of tone (.20) and that of speech (1.09) can be conceptualized as the amount of information added by the transcript; analogously, the difference between accuracy of transcript (.70) and of speech (1.09) can be conceptualized as the amount of information added by paralanguage cues. The surprising finding, of course, is the power (i.e., the accuracy) of the word, either written or spoken. The assumption that nonverbal channels are more important in the communication of deception than the verbal cues is simply not true (see DePaulo, Rosenthal, Green, & Rosenkrantz, 1981d). Krauss et al. (1981) reached the same conclusion with regard to affective communication not involving deception.

What are the semantic cues to deception? In Section II,B we noted that deceptive messages are associated with more negative statements, irrelevant information, nonimmediacy, and less involvement. Alker's (1976) exploratory study of deceptive presidential press conferences was also described. To our knowledge, there are no other studies on the semantic structure associated with deception, perhaps because of the paucity of good coding schemes (see Clark & Clark, 1977; Kraut *et al.*, 1980). How words reveal deception is a question that at present has no clear answer.

2. Leakage Accuracy

What is the relationship between deception and leakage accuracy? On some occasions (e.g., bluffing in a poker game), the lie and the hidden message are so intertwined that whatever tips off the perceiver about the deception also betrays the withheld information. On other occasions, however, a perceiver may be aware of a lie but not of the withheld information. On yet other occasions (e.g., those involving self-deception), a perceiver may become aware of the hidden information, although the cues associated with *intentional* lying may be missing. In short, leakage accuracy or the extent to which perceivers can read a concealed message is conceptually distinct from deception accuracy and, hence, is a research topic in its own right.

In what was probably the first investigation of leakage, Ekman and Friesen (1969a) examined facial expressions and body behavior of two patients in clinical interviews. It was found that body behavior yielded information not available from the face and inconsistent with the general impression the patients tried to convey. Although this evidence supported Ekman and Friesen's leakage model, they expressed reservations about the lack of independent criteria for the patient's true and dissimulated affects; generalization was also limited since the sample size was so small.

Turning to experimental work on leakage, a study by DePaulo and Rosenthal (1979b) can illustrate the general paradigm and research strategies that are in use. The basic design is a 2 (truth and deception) × 2 (pro and con messages) factorial. The pro and con messages used by DePaulo and Rosenthal were expressions of liking and disliking for persons the senders knew. Under the truth condition, senders described someone they liked (L) and someone they disliked (D), truthfully. Under deception, they described the person they disliked as if they liked him or her ("dislike as though like," DL) and the person they liked as if they disliked him or her ("like as though dislike," LD).

The basic design is presented in Table IV, which indicates that there are two types of leakage estimates—(1) absolute and (2) relative.

1. Since judges of senders' expressions are told to rate the senders' true affects, they should rate LD descriptions (in which the true affect is liking) as higher in liking than the DL descriptions (in which the true affect is disliking). This difference in liking ratings (LD − DL) is termed "absolute leakage." In the DePaulo and Rosenthal (1979b) study, absolute leakage was negative; that is, judges assigned higher liking ratings to the DL descriptions than to the LD descriptions and, in that sense, were inaccurate detectors.

TABLE IV
EXPERIMENTAL DESIGN FOR RESEARCH ON LEAKAGE ACCURACY

	Mode of expression	
Expressed message	Truth	Lie
General model		
Pro	L ("like")	DL ("dislike as though like")
Con	D ("dislike")	LD ("like as though dislike")
Absolute leakage = LD−DL		
Relative leakage = (L−DL) + (LD−D)		
Numerical example		
Pro	10	7
Con	2	4
Absolute leakage = 4 − 7 = −3		
Relative leakage = (10−7) + (4−2) = 5		

2. Judges should also rate L descriptions (honest expressions of liking) as higher in liking than DL descriptions (faked expressions of liking) and rate D descriptions (honest expressions of disliking) as lower in liking than LD descriptions (faked expressions of disliking). These differences in liking ratings [(L − DL) + (LD − D)] are termed "relative leakage." In the DePaulo and Rosenthal (1979b) study, relative leakage was positive, indicating that judges assigned higher liking values to L than to DL and lower liking ratings to D than to LD. The lower part of Table IV presents hypothetical values for liking ratings that illustrate negative absolute leakage and positive relative leakage.

What are the channel effects on absolute and relative estimates of leakage? An exact answer is impossible because of the small number of relevant studies and the great variety of experimental designs and methods of analysis. Thus, we will only attempt to describe the overall pattern of the results.

Four studies (DePaulo & Rosenthal, 1979b; DePaulo et al., 1981d; Lippa, 1976; Zuckerman, Amidon, Bishop, & Pomerantz, 1980a) utilized the full 2 × 2 leakage design presented in Table IV. (A fifth study by Feldman et al., 1978, examined leakage in children and will be discussed in Section IV,C,6.) Relative leakage was positive in all studies; absolute leakage was positive in the study by Zuckerman et al. (1980a) and negative in the remaining three studies. It appears that in general perceivers are more likely to read the message that deceivers intend to communicate than the message that is concealed; at the same time, perceivers seem less convinced by dissimulated than veridical messages.

The studies by DePaulo et al. (1981d), Lippa (1976), and Zuckerman et al. (1980a) allowed comparison between facial leakage and leakage in other channels. The face showed the least absolute leakage in the studies by Lippa (1976) and Zuckerman et al. (1980a) and the least relative leakage in the studies by DePaulo et al. (1981d) and Zuckerman et al. (1980a).

All other studies on leakage utilized only two cells in the leakage paradigm, that is, subjects were instructed to send a single message, either pro or con, that was truthful for some and deceptive for others. The drawbacks of this partial design are that (a) generalizability is limited since only one message is used, (b) the comparison between the true and false messages yields an estimate of relative leakage but does not allow an estimate of absolute leakage, and (c) behaviors associated with deception cannot be examined because of a confound, that is, any behavioral difference between the true and deceptive messages may reflect either deception or leakage cues (see Krauss *et al.*, 1976).

Of the studies using a partial leakage design, two (Feldman, Jenkins, & Popoola, 1979; Parham, Feldman, Popoola, & Oster, 1980) examined only the facial channel. The college-aged senders in the Feldman *et al.* (1979) study showed negative relative leakage, or what DePaulo and Rosenthal (1979b) called hamming—that is, facial expressions of dissimulated liking were rated more positively than expressions of truthful liking. The truth and deception conditions in the Parham *et al.* (1980) study did not produce a main effect on ratings of senders' facial expressions.

Ekman, Friesen, and Scherer (1976; analysis of data reported by Ekman and Friesen, 1976) and Feldman (1976) compared relative leakage of face and body and obtained contradictory results. Ekman *et al.* (1976) obtained more leakage for body cues, whereas Feldman (1976) obtained more leakage for the face. Ekman *et al.* (1976) also reported no leakage of information in speech and filtered-speech channels.

Finally, Gagnon (1975) utilized yet another variation of the leakage design; he had subjects opposed to strict army obedience make either pro- or antiobedience statements (comparable to the pro–truth and con–deception conditions in Table IV). He also had judges infer from audiovisual cues (speech plus face plus body) or audio cues the speakers' espoused as well as their true attitudes. It was found that for both audiovisual and audio cues the correspondence between espoused and true attitudes was greater in the truth condition, indicating the existence of relative leakage.

The strongest conclusions about leakage detection are that, overall, naive perceivers are not likely to pick up leakage cues unless the dissimulated expressions are compared to veridical cues and that the face provides fewer leakage cues than do other channels.

C. OTHER FACTORS AFFECTING ACCURACY OF LIE DETECTION

1. *Publicness of Interaction*

A number of investigators have proposed that people tend to control behaviors more carefully in public situations. Ekman and Friesen (1969b) suggested the term display rules for the norms that prescribe appropriate expressions in public. In private, display rules may not operate and people may behave differently. Thus, Mahl (1968) reported that patients seated back to back with the interviewer engaged in fewer communicative gestures (illustrators) and in more idiosyncratic "autistic" action (adaptors) than those seated face to face. In the case of deceptive communication, the public situation has a special advantage for the deceiver who can plan his or her strategy according to the perceiver's own reactions to the deception (Krauss *et al.*, 1976). It seems, then, that the deceiver's self-presentation is easier and deception accuracy lower in a public interaction. This issue was examined by Krauss *et al.* (1976), Feldman (1976), and Feldman *et al.* (1979).

Krauss *et al.* (1976) had deceivers interact with interviewers either face to face or via an intercom system. Accuracy of detecting deception was higher in the intercom condition, particularly for the visual channel (facial expresions). Inspection of the mean scores suggested that detection from speech (words plus tone) and audiovisual cues (face plus speech) was not affected by the experimental conditions. Since the intercom subjects knew that their voices were monitored but did not know that their facial expressions were observed, they may have relaxed control over their faces but not over their voices (cf. DePaulo, 1980). However, judges who rated the deceivers' filtered speech rather than their original voices were again more accurate at detecting deception in the intercom condition (Streeter *et al.*, 1977). Apparently, deceivers did not control those vocal aspects that became apparent only when the content was unintelligible.

Feldman (1976) had teacher–subjects praise a student–confederate whom they were previously induced to like or dislike and who either performed well or poorly; the interaction was either public (face-to-face) or private (confederate could not see the teacher). The teachers' expressions were rated more pleasant in the liking condition, particularly if the interaction was private and especially for bodily (relative to facial) expressions. Teachers' expressions were also rated more pleasant when the student performed well, but this effect was more pronounced in the public condition. Thus, one type of leakage was greater in private and the other in public. Finally, Feldman *et al.* (1979) examined facial expressions of subjects who either told the truth or lied about the taste of a sample drink. Leakage of subjects' true opinion was greater in the private than in the public condition.

Overall, it appears that detection accuracy is higher when deceiver and lie detector do not engage in direct, face-to-face contact.

2. A Question of Awareness

It is almost a truism that a deceiver's behavior reflects his or her subjective feelings about the deception rather than the objective fact of whether or not deception has been committed (e.g., Marston, 1920). Thus, the salience of the deception in the deceiver's mind is an important determinant of his or her conduct. Interestingly, the only evidence pertaining to this issue comes from a controversy that came to light and to a possible resolution in the first quarter of this century.

The starting point was the discovery of the association test as a means of studying mental processes and, possibly, the detection of crimes (Jung, 1910). Jung reported that deceivers' associations to crime-related stimuli had longer reaction times, perhaps because of their need to avoid implicating responses. Several investigators replicated this finding, including Yerkes and Berry (1909) and Henke and Eddy (1909). Marston (1920) changed the experimental procedure from an association to an arithmetic task and reported that performing the arithmetic problems counter to instructions took either more or less time than performing them according to instructions. The difference between association and arithmetic tasks notwithstanding, Goldstein (1923) suggested that the two types of reaction times characterized two types of reactions to the deceptive act. Specifically, Goldstein replicated Marston's results but also found that increases in reaction times characterized subjects who reported consciousness of deception, strain, and conflict over disobeying the arithmetic instructions; shorter reaction times characterized a lack of either awareness or unpleasantness related to the deception. In a second experiment, Goldstein attempted to increase awareness of deception and did obtain only increases in reaction times; however, his manipulation of awareness might have changed the nature of the task so that the increase in awareness was possibly confounded with the type of task.

It is possible, then, that level of self-awareness determines, at least in part, the deceiver's behavior and, hence, the accuracy of detection. Interestingly, most studies of lie detection are probably conducted under conditions of high self-awareness, since subjects know they are being videotaped or observed (Carver, 1979; Duval & Wicklund, 1972). However, deceivers who know that they are being videotaped may also try to monitor their behavior (see Section IV,C,1), thus countering the effects of high self-awareness. Of course, self-awareness can be measured as a personality disposition (Fenigstein, Scheier, & Buss, 1975) or manipulated by the presence or absence of a mirror—procedures that are not confounded with the private–public manipulations. Goldstein's (1923) findings can thus be extended to behaviors other than response latency as well as to the question of detection accuracy.

3. Familiarity

Behaviors associated with deception may vary among people either because of individual differences in the mediating processes—degree of controllability, level of arousal, affective responses, and complexity of task (see Section II,B,1)—or because the same process (e.g., the same level of anxiety) gives rise to different responses in different people. Thus, Friedhoff, Alpert, and Kurtzberg (1964) reported that the act of deception led subjects to either decrease or increase the loudness of their responses. The finding that deceivers either increase or decrease their reaction times (Goldstein, 1923; Marston, 1920) also implies a person-specific reaction to deception. Hayano (1980) also suggested that cues to deception in a poker game "are initially seen as a deviation or break in the baseline pattern, such as when a quiet player suddenly acts loudly or a noisy player begins to act meekly" (p. 118).

To the extent that deceptive acts are conceptualized as a deviation from the truthful baseline, familiarity with this baseline ought to increase accuracy of detection. In fact, both Ekman and Friesen (1974) and Brandt et al. (1980b) found that perceivers who saw a sample of the deceiver's truthful behavior were more accurate at detecting deception on subsequent trials than observers who had no prior familiarity with the deceiver's behavior. However, Brandt, Miller, and Hocking (1980a) showed that the relationship between familiarity and detection accuracy may not be completely linear. They manipulated level of familiarity, showing observers the same baseline sample once, twice, three times (the number of times it was shown in the Brandt et al., 1980b, study), six times, or not at all (control condition). It was found the the more times the observers watched the baseline, the higher their lie-detection accuracy, except for the six-times, or high-familiarity, condition, which was comparable in accuracy to the control condition.

Brandt et al. (1980a) suggested that subjects in the high-familiarity condition experienced an information overload, which produced some perceptual distortion in the processing of the baseline material and consequently a decrease in detection accuracy. Alternatively, subjects in this condition may have become either fatigued or bored and consequently did not perform well on the detection task. Brandt et al. (1980a) also reported a study by Bauchner (1978) which showed that friends of a target person were more accurate at detecting his or her deception than were spouses or strangers. Perhaps too high a level of familiarity masks some obvious cues or, alternatively, makes the person aware of too many subtle nuances and produces an overload that interferes with detection.

4. Arousal

A common criticism of the research on nonverbal deception is that deceivers are not very motivated to lie successfully and, consequently, do not behave differently than truthful subjects (e.g., Kraut, 1980). Actually, it is not clear how highly motivated deceivers would behave. They may try harder and therefore lie more effectively; alternatively, the anxiety generated by the arousing situation may interfere with successful deception (see DePaulo, Davis, & Lanier, 1980). Unfortunately only four studies examined the effects of experimentally manipulated motivation, those by Krauss et al. (1976), DePaulo et al. (1980d), DePaulo et al. (1981b), and Rotkin (1979).

Krauss et al. (1976) informed half of their subjects that the deception task was an indication of intellectual and creative abilities (high arousal). Arousal did not affect deception accuracy as measured by judges participating in the original experiment but did affect deception accuracy as measured by judges' ratings of recorded material from this experiment. Specifically, these subsequent ratings showed that aroused subjects did not lie as effectively as those who did not receive the arousing information, particularly if they communicated through the intercom system rather than face to face. The increase in pitch associated with deception was also slightly more pronounced in the high-arousal condition (Streeter *et al.*, 1977). DePaulo *et al.* (1980d) used an arousal manipulation that was similar to Krauss' (1977) and measured the detection accuracy of judges who observed the deceivers' live performances. The main effect for arousal in this study was not significant. In a subsequent study (DePaulo *et al.*, 1981b), judges rated audiovisual, speech-only, transcript-only, or visual-only segments of the interviews. Again, the main effect for arousal was nonsignificant, but the patterning of deception accuracy did vary as a function of the information available to the judges. When rating highly aroused senders, judges were most successful at detecting deception when they had access to tone-of-voice cues (i.e., audiovisual and speech-only conditions); when rating unaroused senders, judges were most accurate when they had access to words (transcript, speech, audiovisual) and least accurate when they had access only to visual cues. Finally, Rotkin (1979) instructed subjects to lie or tell the truth in response to questions that were preselected as either low or high in arousal. Detection accuracy was higher for the nonarousing questions.

At best, the above results are inconclusive. It is thus appropriate to offer the following speculations as topics for future research. First, arousal may have different effects on deception and leakage cues. The highly motivated deceiver may do well at masking information, but his or her highly charged state may give rise to deception cues; conversely, the less motivated person may not mask well, but he or she is not likely to show deception cues. Second, the relationship between motivation and detection accuracy may be curvilinear, with the least detection at some intermediate optimal level (not too low, so that the deceiver will still be motivated to do a good job, and not too high, so that deception cues do not appear). Third, the effects of arousal on detection accuracy may depend on other factors, such as personality variables, channel of communication.

5. *Personality Variables*

Two personality constructs, Machiavellianism and Self-Monitoring, have attracted attention as possible sources of individual differences in deceiving and lie detection skills. The abilities to deceive and, possibly, to detect lies may be seen as necessary skills for the manipulative Machiavellian person (Christie & Geis, 1970). This view received indirect support from the finding that high-Mach subjects maintained more eye contact while cheating than did low-Mach subjects (Exline *et al.*, 1970). However, subsequent work (Knapp *et al.*, 1974; O'Hair, Cody, & McLaughlin, 1981) failed to replicate these findings. A review of six available studies indicates that high-Mach deceivers were somewhat less detectable than low-Mach (mean d of difference $= -.18$, combined $z = -1.63$, $p = .11$); the corresponding review of five studies on ability to detect lies indicates that the advantage of high- over low-Mach deceivers was even less reliable (mean $d = .23$, combined $z = 1.20$) (see Appendix V for the presentation of the separate studies).

Snyder's (1974) Self-Monitoring Scale measures the ability to control expressive behavior as well as sensitivity to the social conduct of others. Self-control can indicate an ability to deceive, whereas sensitivity to others' expressions can indicate an ability to detect deception. However, a summary of nine studies indicates that, although high self-monitors were less detectable than low self-monitors (mean $d = .13$), this difference was not significant (combined $z = -.62$); similarly, a summary of eight studies indicates that the advantage of high over low self-monitors in detecting ability was not reliable (mean $d = .04$, combined $z = 1.13$) (see Appendix V for the presentation of the separate studies).

Two additional investigations (Lippa, 1976; Elliott, 1979) of the relationships between self-monitoring and expressive behavior utilized a different method of data analysis. Lippa (1976) requested introvert and extrovert subjects to role-play either introverts or extroverts. High self-monitors did a better job at presenting both veridical and faked images of themselves. Elliott (1979) had high and low self-monitors present accurate and fabricated opinions regarding the legalization of marijuana. Again, high self-monitors did a better job regardless of the nature of their message. For example, they were seen as friendlier and more believable than were low self-monitors.

Note that both Lippa (1976) and Elliott (1979) found in essence that high self-monitors were less easily read with respect to their deceptive messages (which were more likely to be identified as honest than deceptive) and more easily read with respect to their truthful messages (which were also more likely to be identified as honest than deceptive). Perhaps the usual accuracy score, which combines accuracy of deceptive and truthful messages, is not correlated with constructs such as Machiavellianism because it does not make sense psychologically. After all, the Machiavellian person should try to appear honest when lying *and* telling the truth. The appropriate scoring system should combine his or her detectability when telling the truth (i.e., the extent to which honesty was perceived as honesty) and his or her lack of detectability when lying (i.e., the extent to which deception was perceived as honesty). In fact, Geis and Leventhal (cited in Geis & Moon, 1980) found that high-Machs were more believed than low-Machs when telling the truth, whereas Geis and Moon (1980) found that high-Machs were more believed than lows when lying; either difference indicates that overall the high-Mach person appears more honest than the low. Future investigations of personality correlates of deception should distinguish between accuracy of truth- and lie-telling.

Finally, Kraut (1980) noted that one possible reason for the lack of correlation between personality variables and accuracy of detection is that the latter, at least as measured in the laboratory experiment, is not a reliable skill; that is, people's accuracy at detecting deception in one sender is not highly related to the accuracy at detecting deception in another (DePaulo & Rosenthal, 1979b; Kraut, 1978a,b). At present, it is not clear whether this low reliability is an attribute of the construct of lie detection or an aspect of its operationalization. It should be noted, however, that when a measure assesses a multidimensional construct (and the ability to detect deception may well be a multidimensional construct), even scores with zero or modest negative internal consistency reliability can be significantly correlated with criterion variables.

6. Age and Sex

Feldman et al. (1979) suggested that children are not as effective at deceiving as adults because they have less control over their nonverbal behavior and because they are less able to see their own behavior from the point of view of a lie detector (cf. Flavell, Botkin, Fry, Wright, & Jarvis, 1968). Saarni (1979a) proposed that younger children are less able to understand and/or use display rules and thus are less able to dissimulate emotions they do not feel. In one study (Saarni, 1979a), it was found that 10-year-olds exceeded 8- and 6-year-olds in ability to verbalize about display rules in response to stimulus photographs displaying interpersonal conflict situations; that is, the older children surpassed the younger ones in the number of spontaneously given display rules and in the complexity of reasoning for their use. In addition, the 6-year-olds gave fewer instances of personal display rule usage than their older counterparts (Saarni, 1979b). In a related study, Saarni (1980) found that first-graders were more likely to express negativity (i.e., less likely to use the appropriate display rules) after receiving a disappointing gift than were third- and fifth-graders.

However, direct investigations of children's ability to dissimulate affect do not always show a clear relationship with age. Feldman et al. (1979) did find that first-graders deceived less well with their faces than did seventh-graders and college students. However, Feldman et al. (1978) found no difference between third- and sixth-graders in deception ability. Feldman and White (1980) tested 5- to 12-year-old children and found that older females deceived better with their faces and less well with their bodies than did younger females; males showed the opposite pattern. Finally, Krauss and Morency (1980) found that, relative to first-graders, fifth-graders were better deceivers with regard to masking unpleasant but not pleasant stimuli. Thus, it appears that deception ability in general increases with age, but the exact change may depend on sex of deceiver, channel of communication, and type of lie.

What about the ability to detect lies? DePaulo, Jordan, Irvine, and Laser (1981e) tested five different age levels (sixth-, eighth-, tenth-, and twelfth-graders and college students) on their abilities to detect deception (deception accuracy) and to identify the emotion that senders tried to hide (leakage accuracy). Results showed a linear increase in deception accuracy but also a linear *decrease* in absolute leakage accuracy. Since there was also a linear increase in ability to detect veridical affects, the accuracy of *relative* leakage remained constant. Stated differently, older subjects were better than younger subjects at reading overt expressions. When the expressed affects corresponded to the senders' actual affects (i.e., when the senders were being honest) then the greater ability of older subjects to read overt expressions led them to more accurate perceptions. However, when senders' expressed affects and true affects did not correspond (i.e., when the senders were lying), then older subjects' greater ability to read expressed affects led them (compared to younger subjects) even further astray from senders' true feelings.

Turning to gender effects in the communication of deception, it is again necessary to distinguish between ability to deceive and ability to detect lies. Hall's (1980) recent review established that, relative to males, females are more accurate senders of nonverbal cues that do not involve deception. However, it is unclear whether this effect extends to the detectability of deception. Specifically, the expressive sender may be able to control his or her behavior and thus become less expressive when deception is concerned. Sex differences in ability to detect lies are also hard to predict. As previously noted, Rosenthal and DePaulo (1979a,b) suggested that females are socialized not to read concealed and/or unintended messages. In fact, analysis of the DePaulo and Rosenthal (1979b) data showed that, compared to males, females were significantly more likely to interpret deceptive messages as the deceiver wanted them interpreted rather than as the deceivers really felt. DePaulo *et al.* (1981e) replicated this effect in the study involving subjects ranging in age from sixth-graders to college students. According to this reasoning, the "traditional" advantage of females over males in decoding ordinary nonverbal messages (see Hall, 1978, 1980) may not extend to accuracy at detecting deception.

Appendix VI presents the available studies on gender effects on accuracy of both detectability and detecting. The results indicate that, compared to males, females were slightly more detectable (mean $d = .04$) as well as more accurate detectors (mean $d = .17$), but neither difference was reliable (combined $zs = 1.06$ and 1.05, respectively). The right-hand column of Appendix VI presents the results of studies on the simultaneous effects of sex of deceiver and sex of detector. It appears that detection accuracy was somewhat higher when the deceiver–detector dyads were composed of the same as opposed to the opposite sexes (mean $d = .24$, combined $z = 1.645$, $p = .10$). A separate study not involving deception (Zuckerman, Lipets, Koivumaki, & Rosenthal, 1975) also showed higher communication accuracy, particularly in the auditory channel, for same-sex dyads. It should be noted that in most of the above studies the lie detectors rated the deceivers' recorded messages rather than their live presentations; deceivers interacted with the experimenter, a camera, or some anonymous crowd. Thus, the greater detection accuracy in same-sex dyads indicates a greater ability of detectors to read same-sex deceivers rather than a greater detectability of deceiver when communicating with same-sex detectors.

V. Summary and Conclusions

This review focused on three major issues: (1) strategies of deception and behaviors associated with lie-telling (the deceiver's perspective); (2) behaviors associated with judgments of deception and strategies of lie detection (the lie-detector's perspective); and (3) accuracy of lie detection.

Taking up the first issue, we suggested that the kinds of behaviors associated with deception might be best predicted by four different states or processes hypothesized to be associated with deception: attempted control, arousal, affective states, and cognitive complexity. That is, deceivers (more so than truth-tellers) may try to control their verbal and nonverbal displays, they may be aroused, they may experience specific affects (e.g., guilt), and they also may be engaging in a cognitively more demanding task than people who are telling the truth. Thus, cues that have already been shown (or suggested) to be associated with these four states may be the most likely indicators of deception.

We suggested that deceivers' attempts to control their self-presentations may result in behaviors that appear planned, rehearsed, or lacking in spontaneity; because of capacity limitations (the inability to control all channels simultaneously and equally well) discrepancies may develop between various channels. Research relevant to these hypotheses indicated that liars appear less involved in their communications than truth-tellers and that deceptive responses were seen as less spontaneous, more rehearsed, and more discrepant than truthful responses.

Of four behaviors shown in the literature to be associated with arousal— pupil dilation, speech errors, pitch, and blinking—the first three increased significantly during deception, and blinking showed a nonsignificant trend in the predicted direction. The evidence also suggests that deception is associated with increases in behaviors indicative of negative affect; deceptive messages are characterized by more verbal nonimmediacy, more negative verbal statements, more adaptors, and slightly less smiling than truthful messages.

Increased cognitive processing demands have been shown or hypothesized to be associated with increases in pupil dilation, response latency, and speech hesitations, and decreases in illustrators. Relevant studies indicate that pupil dilation and speech hesitations do in fact increase during deception; the relationship to deception of response latency and illustrators was not demonstrated reliably.

Of the ten behaviors that have been examined in more than one study of perceived deception, eight predicted people's judgments about the occurrence of deception. Detectors are more likely to perceive as deceptive those communications that are characterized by less gazing, less smiling, more postural shifts, longer response latencies, slower speech rate, more speech errors, more hesitations during speech, and higher pitch. Although there are more cues that reliably predict perceptions of deception than actual deception, overall the correspondence between cues to actual deception and the cues that are used in perceiver's judgments is substantial.

It was also shown that the extent to which behavior is interpreted as deceptive or honest may depend as much on the detector as on the behavior itself. Thus, in one study, the same behavior that served as a cue to deception for suspicious observers also served as a cue to honesty for trusting observers. Suspicion may also determine the weights perceivers assign to various channels; more suspicious perceivers may pay more attention to leaky channels such as the body and voice and less attention to a controllable channel such as the face. Finally, it was hypothesized that suspicion of deception may lead perceivers to organize the observed behaviors in smaller units—a process that may lead them to confirm their suspicions.

Accuracy at detecting deception is generally greater than chance, though small when expressed in raw accuracy scores. Accuracy is substantially moderated by the channels that are available to the lie detector. Consistent with the Ekman and Friesen leakage model, facial cues seem to be faking cues; that is, perceivers are actually more accurate at detecting deception when they do not have access to facial cues than when they do. The availability of body cues increases perceivers' accuracy at detecting deception, and speech cues (words plus tone) increase accuracy even more.

Our review strongly suggests that success at deceiving and success at detecting deceit are both mediated largely by adeptness at construing and interpreting verbal nuances. Certainly, the outcomes of many other kinds of social interactions, too, are mediated by this same sort of verbal skill. A more thorough understanding of deceptive communications depends critically on new advances in the social psychology of language, a field which is in its infancy. The "counts" of occurrences of specific linguistic cues (such as ums and ers) provide a useful start, but an unraveling of the intricacies of the verbal medium may demand other approaches as well.

Virtually all of the studies that we have reviewed have been laboratory studies in which senders told lies or the truth in accordance with the demands of the experiment. Thus, it might seem appropriate in concluding this chapter to issue a call for more real-life-like research. The problem is that in order to study deception, it is necessary to have an objective criterion for when people are lying and when they are telling the truth. While it might be interesting, for example, to study the lies of high-ranking political officials, such falsehoods are often not identified as such until much later in time, if at all. And so, if we do not know when politicians are lying and when they are telling the truth, we cannot very well study the lie-truth differences in their behavior, nor can we study the accuracy with which their lies are detected by other people. We can, however, increase the ecological validity of the paradigms that are used in our laboratories. We can, for example, examine the precise ways in which deceptions are adapted to particular targets of deception, and we can also study deceivers' active lie-detection strategies (e.g., setting traps to catch the liar, asking leading questions, probing for inconsistencies; see also Kraut, 1980). These kinds of studies are currently in progress (e.g., Toris & DePaulo, 1981).

APPENDIX 1A
STUDIES OF VISUAL BEHAVIORS ASSOCIATED WITH DECEPTION

Studies	Motivation	Planning	Pupil dilation	Gaze	Blinking[a]	Smiling[b]	Head movements[c]	Gestures[d]	Shrugs[e]	Adaptors[f]	Foot and leg movements[f]	Postural shifts[g]
Berrien and Huntington (1943)	High	Low	1.52									
Burns and Kintz (1976)	Low	Low		.70								
Clark (1975)	Medium	High	1.75									
Cutrow et al. (1972)	High	High			-.98							
Ekman and Friesen (1972)	High	High						-1.10	1.10	0		
Exline et al. (1970)	High	Low		-.54								
Finkelstein (1978)	Low	Medium				-.12	-.04	-.12				
Gagnon (1975)	High	Medium					-.84	-.38		.44		
Heilveil (1976)	Low	Low	1.19	-.16							.13	-.78
Hemsley (1977)	Low	High		.29	1.53	1.06		.47		1.40		.61
Hemsley and Doob (1979) Study 1	Low	High		-.65	1.58							
Hemsley and Doob (1979) Study 2	Low	High		-.50	1.05							
Hocking and Leathers (1980)	High	High		-.80	-.15	.06	-.63	-.44		.44	-.42	
Knapp et al. (1974)	High	Medium		-.69		.16	-.15	-.37		.92	.25	
Krauss et al. (1976)	Low	Low		0		0						
Krauss et al. (1976)	High	Low		0		-.74						

(Continued)

APPENDIX 1A (Continued)

Studies	Motivation	Planning	Pupil dilation	Gaze	Blinking[a]	Smiling[b]	Head movements[c]	Gestures[d]	Shrugs[e]	Adaptors[f]	Foot and leg movements	Postural shifts[g]
Kraut (1978a)	High	Low				.21				-.08		-.07
Kraut (1978b)	High	Low				-.07		.43		.07	.12	-.37
Kraut and Poe (1980)	High	Low			.22	.24		-.08		.07		-.14
Matarazzo et al. (1970)	Low	High		0								
McClintock and Hunt (1975)	Low	Low			.21	-1.05		.42		.84	-.38	.19
Mehrabian (1971) Study 1	High	High				.25				-.06		0
Mehrabian (1971) Study 2	High	Medium				-.22	-.52					-.07
Mehrabian (1971) Study 3	High	Low				-.10	-.46					
O'Hair et al. (1981)	High	High		.28		-.50	.51	0	.24	.36	-.30	.16
O'Hair et al. (1981)	Low	Low		.00		-.16	-.04	-.17	.11	.40	-.17	-.31
Schneider and Kintz (1977)	Low	Medium									.27	
Zuckerman et al. (1979)	Low	Medium				-.45						

NOTE. Positive values indicate that deception was associated with an increase in the frequency/duration of the behavior. Negative values indicate a decrease.

[a] Blinking also includes eye flutters in Hocking and Leathers (1980).
[b] Smiling also includes facial attractiveness in Krauss et al. (1976) and facial pleasantness in Mehrabian (1971) and Zuckerman et al. (1979).
[c] Head movements also include affirmative nods in Knapp et al. (1974) and O'Hair et al. (1981) and head nodding in Mehrabian (1971).
[d] Gestures also include illustrators in Ekman and Friesen (1972), Hocking and Leathers (1980), Kraut (1978b), Kraut and Poe (1980), and O'Hair et al. (1981) and hand and arm movements in Finkelstein (1978) and Gagnon (1975).
[e] Shrugs also include hand shrugs in Ekman and Friesen (1972).
[f] Adaptors also include self-manipulations in Finkelstein (1978), Hemsley (1977), and McClintock and Hunt (1975), hand to face gestures and adaptors in Hocking and Leathers (1980), and grooming in Kraut (1978a,b) and Kraut and Poe (1980).
[g] Postural shifts also include rocking rate and trunk swivel rate in Mehrabian (1971; studies 1 and 2, respectively).

APPENDIX 1B
STUDIES OF AUDITORY BEHAVIORS ASSOCIATED WITH DECEPTION

Studies	Motivation	Planning	Response latency	Response length	Speech rate[a]	Speech errors[b]	Speech hesitations[c]	Pitch	Negative statements[d]	Irrelevant information[e]	Self-references[f]
Cutrow et al. (1972)	High	High	-1.68								
DePaulo et al. (1981e)	Low	Medium									-.12
Ekman et al. (1976)	High	High			-.18	1.12	.41		.20		
Gagnon (1975)	High	Medium		-.26	.02	-.70		1.10			
Harrison et al. (1978)	Low	Low	.81	1.26							
Hemsley (1977)	Low	High					1.18			1.20	
Hemsley and Doob (1979) Study 1	Low	High	-1.54				1.14			.99	
Hemsley and Doob (1979) Study 2	Low	High					.53			.46	
Hocking and Leathers (1980)	High	High	.24		.32	.33	.45				
Knapp et al. (1974)	High	Medium		-.73	-.86	.02	.25		2.17		-.44
Krauss et al. (1976)	Low	Low	0	0	0	0					
Krauss et al. (1976)	High	Low	0	0	-.74	.74					
Kraut (1978a)	High	Low	.33	-.32		.04	.33				
Kraut (1978b)	High	Low	.12	.17		.07					
Kraut and Poe (1980)	High	Low	.43	-.26		.10				.28	

APPENDIX 1B (*Continued*)

Studies	Motivation	Planning	Response latency	Response length	Speech rate[a]	Speech errors[b]	Speech hesitations[c]	Pitch	Negative statements[d]	Irrelevant information[e]	Self-references[f]
Manaugh et al. (1970)	Low	Medium	0	0							
Matarazzo et al. (1970)	Low	High	.82	.52							
Mehrabian (1971) Study 1	High	High		0		.56					
Mehrabian (1971) Study 2	High	Medium		−.81	−.61						
Mehrabian (1971) Study 3	High	Low		−.71	.79		.71				
Motley (1974)	Low	High			1.10			0			
O'Hair et al. (1981)	Low	High	−1.02	−.64							
O'Hair et al. (1981)	Low	Low	−.23	−.06							
Streeter et al. (1977)	Low	Low						.15			
Streeter et al. (1977)	High	Low						1.45			
Todd (1976)	High	High							1.59		

NOTE. Positive values indicate that deception was associated with an increase in the frequency/duration of the behavior. Negative values indicate a decrease.

[a] Speech rate also includes confidence ratio in Knapp et al. (1974).

[b] Speech errors also include nonfluencies in DePaulo et al. (1981e), word repetition in Hocking and Leathers (1980), and (non)fluency in Krauss et al. (1976).

[c] Speech hesitations also include the ums and ers in DePaulo et al. (1981e), pausing in Hocking and Leathers (1980) and Knapp et al. (1974), and percentage talk in interaction in Mehrabian (1971, Study 3).

[d] Negative statements also include (lack of) excess positive in DePaulo et al. (1981e) and disparaging statements in Knapp et al. (1974) and Todd (1976).

[e] Irrelevant information also includes volunteering extra information in Kraut and Poe (1980).

[f] Self-references indicate the number of times the deceiver refers to himself/herself, also including the excess others in DePaulo et al. (1981e).

44

APPENDIX II

STUDIES OF BEHAVIORS ASSOCIATED WITH PERCEIVED DECEPTION

Studies	Gaze	Smiling	Adaptors	Postural shifts	Response latency	Response length	Speech rate	Speech errors	Speech hesitations	Pitch
Apple et al. (1979; Study 1)							-.37			1.08
Baskett and Freedle (1974)					-.31[a]					
DePaulo et al. (1981e)							-.93	.45	.68	
Ekman and Friesen (1972)			1.01							
Friedman (1979)		-1.01								
Harrison et al. (1978)					.43	.23				
Hemsley and Doob (1978) Study 1	-.56									
Hemsley and Doob (1978) Study 2	-.69									
Krauss et al. (1976)	0	0			.51	-.17		.68		
Kraut (1978a)		.41	-.32	.39	.49	.06		.22	.49	
Kraut and Poe (1980)	-.54	-.32	.20	.61	.68	-.58		-.28		
Streeter et al. (1977)										
Zuckerman et al. (1979)		-.68								.27

NOTE. Positive values indicate that an increase (negative values, that a decrease) in the frequency/duration of the behavior was associated with judgment of deception.

[a] This reversal is due to the employment of unusually short latencies which tended to be regarded as indices of deceit; within the usual range of latencies employed in other studies, this study also found that longer latencies were indices of deceit, $z = 2.82$, $d = .63$.

45

APPENDIX III
Differences in Detection Accuracy between Truthful and Deceptive Messages

Studies	d^a
Atmiyanandana (1976)	−.01
Ekman and Friesen (1974)	−.81
Fay and Middleton (1941)	−4.85
Fugita et al. (1980)	.18
Harrison et al. (1978)	2.04
Hildreth (1953)	3.02
Littlepage and Pineault (1979a)	.35
Littlepage and Pineault (1979b)	2.23
Littlepage and Pineault (1981)	5.97
Maier (1966)	.48
Maier and Janzen (1967)	−.23
Maier and Thurber (1968)	.09
Rotkin (1979)	1.60
Zuckerman et al. (1979)	.24
Zuckerman et al. (1980a)	2.53

[a] Positive values indicate that truthful messages were more accurately detected than deceptive ones, negative values, the reverse.

APPENDIX IV
Studies of Deception Accuracy for Various Channels and Channel Combinations

Studies	d^a
1. Face and Body and Speech	
Bauchner et al. (1977); Miller et al. (1981)	.47
DePaulo et al. (1980d)	1.33
DePaulo et al. (1981c)	.39
DePaulo and Rosenthal (1979)	1.64
DePaulo et al. (1981d)	.31
Hemsley (1977) Study 1	1.88
Hemsley (1977) Study 2	1.11
Hemsley (1977) Study 3	.66
Hildreth (1953)	−.79
Hocking et al. (1979)	.69
Kraut (1978a)	.95
Kraut and Poe (1980)	−.45

(Continued)

APPENDIX IV (*Continued*)

Studies	d^a
Kraut *et al.* (1980) live	1.63
Kraut *et al.* (1980) video	.71
Littlepage and Pineault (1979b)	4.47
Maier (1966)	.59
Maier and Janzen (1967)	1.02
Maier and Thurber (1968)	.33
Matarazzo *et al.* (1970)	.36
Rotkin (1979)	2.62
Wilson (1975)	1.02
2. Face and Body	
Atmiyanandana (1976)	.26
Bauchner *et al.* (1977); Miller *et al.* (1981)	−.23
DePaulo *et al.* (1981d)	.04
Hocking *et al.* (1979)	−.18
Rotkin (1979)	.51
Wilson (1975)	1.70
3. Face and Speech	
Fugita *et al.* (1980)	.31
Geis and Moon (1980)	2.15
Harrison *et al.* (1978)	1.48
Hemsley and Doob (1979)	1.26
Hocking *et al.* (1979)	.53
Littlepage and Pineault (1978)	1.39
Littlepage and Pineault (1979a)	.12
Littlepage and Pineault (1981)	.67
Zuckerman *et al.* (1980a)	1.00
4. Face	
Ekman and Friesen (1974)	−.16
Hocking *et al.* (1979)	−.40
Littlepage and Pineault (1978)	−.42
Littlepage and Pineault (1981)	.00
Wilson (1975)	−.18
Zuckerman *et al.* (1979)	1.02
Zuckerman *et al.* (1980a)	.46
5. Body and Speech	
Hocking *et al.* (1979)	.39
Littlepage and Pineault (1979a)	1.32
Rotkin (1979)	2.76
6. Body	
Ekman and Friesen (1974)	.15
Hocking *et al.* (1979)	−.19
Rotkin (1979)	.27
Wilson (1975)	1.48

(*Continued*)

APPENDIX IV (*Continued*)

Studies	d^a
7. Speech	
Bauchner et al. (1977); Miller et al. (1981)	−1.28
DePaulo et al. (1981d)	.57
Fay and Middleton (1941)	2.20
Harrison et al. (1978)	1.59
Hocking et al. (1979)	.67
Littlepage and Pineault (1978)	1.36
Littlepage and Pineault (1981)	.68
Maier and Lavrakas (1976) Study 4	.38
Maier and Thurber (1968)	1.28
Rotkin (1979)	4.27
Wilson (1975)	.45
Zuckerman et al. (1980a)	.88
8. Tone of Voice	
DePaulo et al. (1981d)	−.13
Motley (1974)	−.26
Zuckerman et al. (1979)	.37
Zuckerman et al. (1980a)	.84
9. Transcripts	
Bauchner et al. (1977); Miller et al. (1981)	.23
DePaulo et al. (1981d)	.27
Hocking et al. (1979)	.84
Kraut et al. (1980)	1.15
Maier and Thurber (1968)	1.30
Zuckerman et al. (1980a)	.88

[a] Positive values indicate that accuracy of detection is higher than chance, negative values, lower than chance.

APPENDIX V

STUDIES OF PERSONALITY CORRELATES OF THE COMMUNICATION OF DECEPTION

Detectability of sender		Detection accuracy of detector	
Studies	d^a	Studies	d^a
Machiavellianism			
DePaulo and Rosenthal (1979)	−.58	DePaulo and Rosenthal (1980)	0
Geis and Leventhal (unpublished;		Geis and Moon (1980)	0
cited in Geis & Moon, 1980)	0		
Geis and Moon (1980)	−1.29	Krauss et al. (1976)	0
Krauss et al. (1976)	0	Kraut (1978b)	.14
Kraut (1978b)	.58	Kraut et al. (1980)	1.01
Zuckerman et al. (1980a)	.23		
Self-Monitoring			
DePaulo and Rosenthal (1980)	.61	Brandt et al. (1980b)	1.01
Hemsley (1977) Study 3	−.54	DePaulo and Rosenthal (1979)	−1.12
Krauss et al. (1976)	−.96	Geizer et al. (1977)	.60
Kraut (1978b)	.12	Hemsley (1977) Study 3	−.22
Kraut and Poe (1980)	−.04	Krauss et al. (1976)	.37
Kraut et al. (1980)		Kraut (1978b)	−.18
Replication 1	−.63		
Replication 2	−.18	Kraut et al. (1980)	−.26
Zuckerman et al. (1979)	.24	Zuckerman et al. (1980a)	.16
Zuckerman et al. (1980a)	.22		

[a] Positive values indicate that high scores on Self-Monitoring or Machiavellianism are associated with higher detectability or higher detection accuracy. Negative values, the reverse.

APPENDIX VI

STUDIES OF GENDER EFFECTS IN THE COMMUNICATION OF DECEPTION

Sex of sender		Sex of receiver		Sex composition of dyad	
Studies	d^u	Studies	d^u	Studies	d^u
Christensen (1980)	.23	Atmiyanandana (1976)	.20	Christensen (1980)	−.30
DePaulo and Rosenthal (1979)	.34	Christensen (1980)	.31	DePaulo et al. (1980d)	−.24
DePaulo et al. (1980d)	−.09	DePaulo and Rosenthal (1979)	.26	DePaulo et al. (1981c)	.78
DePaulo et al. (1981c)	−.52	DePaulo et al. (1980d)	−.47	DePaulo et al. (1981d)	.74
Fay and Middleton (1941)	−1.00	DePaulo et al. (1981c)	.08	Fay and Middleton (1941)	−.17
Geis and Moon (1980)	.78	Fay and Middleton (1941)	.66	Hemsley (1977; Study 3)	.66
Hemsley (1977; Study 3)	.54	Hemsley (1977) Study 3	.61		
Zuckerman et al. (1979)	.16	Hildreth (1953)	.56		
Zuckerman et al. (1980a)	−.05	Hocking et al. (1979)	−.14		
		Littlepage and Pineault (1978)	−.05		
		Maier and Lavraskas (1976)	.48		
		Maier and Thurber (1968)	.08		
		Rotkin (1979)	−.06		
		Zuckerman et al. (1979)	−.16		

[a] Positive values indicate that accuracy of detection is higher for female senders, female detectors, or same sex dyads; negative values, that accuracy is lower.

REFERENCES

Alker, H. A. *Mystification and deception in presidential press conferences.* Paper presented at the meeting of the American Psychological Association, Washington, D. C., September, 1976.

Apple, W., Streeter, L. A., & Krauss, R. M. Effects of pitch and speech rate on personal attributions. *Journal of Personality and Social Psychology,* 1979, **37**, 715-727.

Argyle, M., Alkema, F., & Gilmour, R. The communication of friendly and hostile attitudes by verbal and non-verbal signals. *European Journal of Social Psychology,* 1970, **1**, 385-402.

Argyle, M., Salter, V., Nicholson, H., Williams, M., & Burgess, P. The communication of inferior and superior attitudes by verbal and non-verbal signals. *British Journal of Social and Clinical Psychology,* 1970, **9**, 222-231.

Atkinson, M. L., & Allen, V. L. Level of analysis as a determinant of the meaning of nonverbal behavior. *Social Psychology Quarterly,* 1979, **42**, 270-274.

Atmiyanandana, V. *An experimental study of the detection of deception in cross-cultural communication.* Unpublished Ph.D. dissertation, Florida State University, 1976.

Baskett, G. D., & Freedle, R. O. Aspects of language pragmatics and the social perception of lying. *Journal of Psycholinguistic Research,* 1974, **3**, 117-131.

Bauchner, J. E. *Accuracy in detecting deception as a function of level of relationship and communication history.* Unpublished Ph.D. dissertation, Florida State University, 1978. (As cited by Brandt *et al.,* 1980a.)

Bauchner, J. E., Brandt, D. R., & Miller, G. R. The truth/deception attribution: Effects of varying levels of information availability. In B. R. Ruben (Ed.), *Communication yearbook I.* New Brunswick, New Jersey: Transaction Books, 1977.

Ben-Shakhar, G. A further study of the dichotomization theory in detection of information. *Psychophysiology,* 1977, **14**, 408-413.

Ben-Shakhar, G., Lieblich, I., & Kugelmass, S. Detection of information and GSR habituation: An attempt to derive detection efficiency from two habituation curves. *Psychophysiology,* 1975, **12**, 283-288.

Bennet, R. Micromoments. *Human Behavior,* 1978, **7**, 34-35.

Berlyne, D. E. *Aesthetics and psychobiology.* New York: Appleton, 1971.

Berrien, F. K., & Huntington, G. H. An exploratory study of pupillary responses during deception. *Journal of Experimental Psychology,* 1943, **32**, 443-449.

Blanck, P. D., Rosenthal, R., Snodgrass, S. E., DePaulo, B. M., & Zuckerman, M. Longitudinal and cross-sectional age effects in nonverbal decoding skill and style. *Developmental Psychology,* 1981, in press.

Bok, S. *Lying: Moral choice in public and private life.* New York: Vintage Books, 1978.

Bolinger, D. Truth is a linguistic question. *Language,* 1973, **49**, 539-550.

Brandt, D. R., Miller, G. R., & Hocking, J. E. The truth-deception attribution: Effects of familiarity on the ability of observers to detect deception. *Human Communication Research,* 1980, **6**, 99-110. (a)

Brandt, D. R., Miller, G. R., & Hocking, J. E. *Effects of self-monitoring and familiarity on deception detection.* Unpublished, North Texas State University, 1980. (b)

Brown, B. L., Strong, W. J., & Rencher, A. C. Perceptions of personality from speech: Effects of manipulations of acoustical parameters. *Journal of the Acoustical Society of America,* 1973, **54**, 29-35.

Brown, B. L., Strong, W. J., & Rencher, A. C. Fifty-four voices from two: The effects of simultaneous manipulations of rate, mean fundamental frequency, and variance of fundamental frequency on ratings of personality from speech. *Journal of the Acoustical Society of America,* 1974, **55**, 313-318.

Bugental, D. B., Caporael, L., & Shennum, W. A. Experimentally-produced child uncontrollability:

Effects on the potency of adult communication patterns. *Child Development,* 1980, **51,** 520–528.

Bugental, D. B., Henker, B., & Whalen, C. K. Attributional antecedents of verbal and vocal assertiveness. *Journal of Personality and Social Psychology,* 1976, **34,** 405–411.

Bugental, D. E., Kaswan, J. W., & Love, L. R. Perception of contradictory meanings conveyed by verbal and nonverbal channels. *Journal of Personality and Social Psychology,* 1970, **16,** 647–655.

Bugental, D. B., & Love, L. Nonassertive expression of parental approval and disapproval and its relationship to child disturbance. *Child Development,* 1975, **46,** 747–752.

Burns, J. A., & Kintz, B. L. Eye contact while lying during an interview. *Bulletin of the Psychonomic Society,* 1976, **7,** 87–89.

Carver, C. S. A cybernetic model of self-attention processes. *Journal of Personality and Social Psychology,* 1979, **37,** 1251–1281.

Christensen, D. *Decoding of intended versus unintended nonverbal messages as a function of social skill and anxiety.* Unpublished Ph.D. dissertation, University of Connecticut, 1980.

Christie, R., & Geis, F. L. (Eds.). *Studies in Machiavellianism.* New York: Academic Press, 1970.

Clark, H., & Clark, E. *Psychology and language,* New York: Harcourt, 1977.

Clark, W. R. *A comparison of pupillary response, heart rate, and GSR during deception.* Paper presented at the meeting of the Midwestern Psychological Association, Chicago, 1975.

Cohen, J. *Statistical power analysis for the behavioral sciences* (Rev. ed.) New York: Academic Press, 1977.

Cutrow, R. J., Parks, A., Lucas, N., & Thomas, K. The objective use of multiple physiological indices in the detection of deception. *Psychophysiology,* 1972, **9,** 578–588.

Davis, R. C. Physiological responses as a means of evaluating information. In A. D. Biderman & H. Zimmer (Eds.), *The manipulation of human behavior.* New York: Wiley, 1961.

Demos, R. Lying to oneself. *Journal of Philosophy,* 1960, **57,** 588–595.

DePaulo, B. M. *Success at detecting deception: Liability or skill?* Paper presented at the conference on the Clever Hans Phenomenon, New York Academy of Sciences, New York, May, 1980.

DePaulo, B. M. *Verbal nonimmediacy and its relationship to deception.* Unpublished data, University of Virginia, 1981.

DePaulo, B. M., Davis, T., & Lanier, K. *Planning lies: The effects of spontaneity and arousal on success at deception.* Paper presented at the Eastern Psychological Association, Hartford, Connecticut, April, 1980. (d)

DePaulo, B. M., Finkelstein, S., Rosenthal, R., & Eisenstat, R. A. *Thinking about deceit.* Unpublished data, University of Virginia, 1980. (e)

DePaulo, B. M., & Fisher, J. P. Too tuned-out to take: The role of nonverbal sensitivity in help seeking. *Personality and Social Psychology Bulletin,* 1981, in press.

DePaulo, B. M., Jordan, A., Irvine, A., & Laser, P. S. *Age changes in the detection of deception.* Submitted for review, University of Virginia, 1981. (a)

DePaulo, B. M., Lanier, K., & Davis, T. *The effects of planning and arousal on telling and detecting lies.* In preparation, University of Virginia, 1981. (b)

DePaulo, B. M., Lassiter, G. D., & Stone, J. I. *Attentional determinants of success at detecting deception.* Submitted for review, University of Virginia, 1981. (c)

DePaulo, B. M., Leiphart, V., & Dull, W. R. *Help-seeking and social interaction: Person situation, and process considerations.* Paper presented at the international conference on the Development and Maintenance of Prosocial Behavior, Warsaw, Poland, July, 1980. (f)

DePaulo, B. M., & Rosenthal, R. Ambivalence, discrepancy, and deception in nonverbal communication. In R. Rosenthal (Ed.), *Skill in nonverbal communication.* Cambridge, Massachusetts: Oelgeschlager, 1979. (a)

DePaulo, B. M., & Rosenthal, R. Telling lies. *Journal of Personality and Social Psychology,* 1979, **37,** 1713–1722. (b)

DePaulo, B. M., Rosenthal, R., Eisenstat, R. A., Rogers, P. L., & Finkelstein, S. Decoding discrepant nonverbal cues. *Journal of Personality and Social Psychology,* 1978, **36,** 313-323.

DePaulo, B. M., Rosenthal, R., Green, C. R., & Rosenkrantz, J. *Verbal and nonverbal revealingness in deceptive and nondeceptive communications.* Submitted for review, University of Virginia, 1981. (d)

DePaulo, B. M., Rosenthal, R., Rosenkrantz, J., & Green, C. R. *Actual and perceived cues to deception.* Submitted for review, University of Virginia, 1981. (e)

DePaulo, B. M., Wilson, T. D., & Lanier, K. Unpublished data, University of Virginia, 1981. (f)

DePaulo, B. M., Zuckerman, M., & Rosenthal, R. Humans as lie detectors. *Journal of Communication,* 1980, **30,** 129-139. (a)

DePaulo, B. M., Zuckerman, M., & Rosenthal, R. Modality effects in the detection of deception. In L. Wheeler (Ed.), *Review of personality and social psychology.* New York: Sage, 1980. (b)

DePaulo, B. M., Zuckerman, M., & Rosenthal, R. The deceptions of everyday life. *Journal of Communication,* 1980, **30,** 216-218. (c)

Duval, S., & Wicklund, R. A. *A theory of objective self awareness.* New York: Academic Press, 1972.

Ekman, P. *Mistakes when deceiving.* Paper presented at the conference on the Clever Hans Phenomenon, New York Academy of Sciences, New York, May, 1980.

Ekman, P., & Friesen, W. V. Nonverbal leakage and clues to deception. *Psychiatry,* 1969, **32,** 88-106. (a)

Ekman, P., & Friesen, W. V. The repertoire of nonverbal behavior: Categories, origins, usage, and coding. *Semiotica,* 1969, **1,** 49-98. (b)

Ekman, P., & Friesen, W. V. Hand movements. *Journal of Communication,* 1972, **22,** 353-374.

Ekman, P., & Friesen, W. V. Detecting deception from the body or face. *Journal of Personality and Social Psychology,* 1974, **29,** 288-298.

Ekman, P., Friesen, W. V., O'Sullivan, M., & Scherer, K. Relative importance of face, body, and speech in judgments of personality and affect. *Journal of Personality and Social Psychology,* 1980, **38,** 270-277.

Ekman, P., Friesen, W. V., & Scherer, K. R. Body movement and voice pitch in deceptive interaction. *Semiotica,* 1976, **16,** 23-27.

Elliott, G. C. Some effects of deception and level of self-monitoring on planning and reacting to a self-presentation. *Journal of Personality and Social Psychology,* 1979, **37,** 1282-1292.

Ellsworth, P. C., & Langer, E. J. Staring and approach: An interpretation of the stare as a nonspecific activator. *Journal of Personality and Social Psychology,* 1976, **33,** 117-122.

Exline, R. V., Thibaut, J., Hickey, C. B., & Gumpert, P. Visual interaction in relation to Machiavellianism and an unethical act. In R. Christie & F. Geis (Eds.), *Studies in Machiavellianism.* New York: Academic Press, 1970.

Fairbanks, G. Recent experimental investigations of vocal pitch in speech. *Journal of the Acoustical Society of America,* 1940, **11,** 457-466.

Fay, P. J., & Middleton, W. C. The ability to judge truth-telling, or lying, from the voice as transmitted over a public address system. *The Journal of General Psychology,* 1941, **24,** 211-215.

Feldman, R. S. Nonverbal disclosure of teacher deception and interpersonal affect. *Journal of Educational Psychology,* 1976, **68,** 807-816.

Feldman, R. S. Nonverbal disclosure of deception in urban Koreans. *Journal of Cross-Cultural Psychology,* 1979, **10,** 73-83.

Feldman, R. S., Devin-Sheehan, L., & Allen, V. L. Nonverbal cues as indicators of verbal dissembling. *American Educational Research Journal,* 1978, **15,** 217-231.

Feldman, R. S., Jenkins, L., & Popoola, O. Detection of deception in adults and children via facial expressions. *Child Development,* 1979, **50,** 350-355.

Feldman, R. S., & White, J. B. Detecting deception in children. *Journal of Communication*, 1980, **30**, 121-128.

Fenigstein, A., Scheier, M. F., & Buss, A. H. Public and private selfconsciousness: Assessment and theory. *Journal of Consulting and Clinical Psychology*, 1975, **43**, 522-527.

Fingarette, H. *Self-deception*. London: Routledge & Kegan Paul, 1969.

Finkelstein, S. *The relationship between physical attractiveness and nonverbal behaviors*. Unpublished honors thesis, Hampshire College, 1978.

Flavell, J. H., Botkin, P. T., Fry, C. L., Wright, J. C., & Jarvis, P. T. *The development of role-taking and communication skills in children*. New York: Wiley, 1968.

Freud, S. Fragments of an analysis of a case of hysteria (1905). *Collected Papers*. Vol. 3. New York: Basic Books, 1959.

Friedhoff, A. J., Alpert, M., & Kurtzberg, R. L. An electro-acoustic analysis of the effects of stress on voice. *Journal of Neuropsychiatry*, 1964, **5**, 266-272.

Friedman, H. S. The interactive effects of facial expressions of emotion and verbal messages on perceptions of affective meaning. *Journal of Experimental Social Psychology*, 1979, **15**, 453-469.

Fugita, S. S., Hogrebe, M. C., & Wexley, K. N. Perceived expertise in detecting deception, successfulness of deception and nonverbal cues. *Personality and Social Psychology Bulletin*, 1980, **6**, 637-643.

Gagnon, L. R. *The encoding and decoding of cues to deception*. Unpublished Ph.D. dissertation, Arizona State University, 1975.

Geis, F. L., & Moon, T. H. *Machiavellianism and deception*. Unpublished, University of Delaware, 1980.

Goffman, E. *The presentation of self in everyday life*. New York: Doubleday, 1959.

Goldman-Eisler, F. *Psycholinguistics: Experiments in spontaneous speech*. New York: Academic Press, 1968.

Goldstein, E. R. Reaction times and the consciousness of deception. *American Journal of Psychology*, 1923, **34**, 562-581.

Gur, R. C., & Sackeim, H. A. Self-deception: A concept in search of a phenomenon. *Journal of Personality and Social Psychology*, 1979, **37**, 147-169.

Gustafson, L. A., & Orne, M. T. Effects of heightened motivation on the detection of deception. *Journal of Applied Psychology*, 1963, **47**, 408-411.

Gustafson, L. A., & Orne, M. T. Effects of perceived role and role success on the detection of deception. *Journal of Applied Psychology*, 1965, **49**, 412-417.

Haggard, E. A., & Isaacs, K. S. Micromomentary facial expressions as indicators of ego mechanisms in psychotherapy. In L. A. Gottschalk & A. H. Auerbach (Eds.), *Methods of research in psychotherapy*. New York: Appleton, 1966.

Hall, J. A. Gender effects in decoding nonverbal cues. *Psychological Bulletin*, 1978, **85**, 845-857.

Hall, J. A. Gender differences in nonverbal communication skills. In R. Rosenthal (Ed.), *Quantitative assessment of research domains*. San Francisco, California: Jossey-Bass, 1980.

Harrison, A. A., Hwalek, M., Raney, D. F., & Fritz, J. G. Cues to deception in an interview situation. *Social Psychology*, 1978, **41**, 156-161.

Hayano, D. M. Communicative competency among poker players. *Journal of Communication*, 1980, **30**, 113-120.

Hecker, M. H. L., Stevens, K. N., von Bismarck, G., & Williams, C. E. Manifestations of task-induced stress in the acoustic speech signal. *Journal of the Acoustical Society of America*, 1968, **44**, 993-1001.

Heilveil, I. Deception and pupil size. *Journal of Clinical Psychology*, 1976, **32**, 675-676.

Hemsley, G. D. *Experimental studies in the behavioral indicants of deception*. Unpublished Ph.D. dissertation, University of Toronto, 1977.

Hemsley, G. D., & Doob, A. N. The effect of looking behavior on perceptions of a communicator's credibility. *Journal of Applied Social Psychology*, 1978, **8**, 136–144.

Hemsley, G. D., & Doob, A. N. *The detection of deception from nonverbal behaviors.* Paper presented at the meeting of the Canadian Psychological Association, Quebec, 1979.

Henke, F. G., & Eddy, M. W. Mental diagnosis by reaction method. *Psychological Review*, 1909, **16**, 399–409.

Hess, E. H., & Polt, J. M. Pupil size in relation to mental activity during simple problem-solving. *Science*, 1964, **143**, 1190–1192.

Hildreth, R. A. *An experimental study of audiences' ability to distinguish between sincere and insincere speeches.* Unpublished Ph.D. dissertation, University of Southern California, 1953.

Hocking, J. E., Bauchner, J., Kaminski, E. P., & Miller, G. R. Detecting deceptive communication from verbal, visual, and paralinguistic cues. *Human Communication Research*, 1979, **6**, 33–46.

Hocking, J. E., & Leathers, D. G. Nonverbal indicators of deception: A new theoretical perspective. *Communication Monographs*, 1980, **47**, 119–131.

Hocking, J. E., Miller, G. R., & Fontes, N. E. Videotape in the courtroom. *Trial*, 1978, **14**, 52–55.

Holzman, P. S., & Rousey, C. The voice as a percept. *Journal of Personality and Social Psychology*, 1966, **4**, 79–86.

Horvath, F. S. Verbal and nonverbal clues to truth and deception during polygraph examinations. *Journal of Police Science and Administration*, 1973, **1**, 138–152.

Horvath, F. An experimental comparison of the psychological stress evaluator and the galvanic skin response in detection of deception. *Journal of Applied Psychology*, 1978, **63**, 338–344.

Horvath, F. Effect of different motivational instructions on detection of deception with the psychological stress evaluator and the galvanic skin response. *Journal of Applied Psychology*, 1979, **64**, 323–330.

Jung, C. G. The association reaction method. *American Journal of Psychology*, 1910, **21**, 219–240.

Kahneman, D. *Attention and effort.* Englewood Cliffs, New Jersey: Prentice-Hall, 1973.

Kahneman, D., & Beatty, J. Pupillary responses in a pitch-discrimination task. *Perception and Psychophysics*, 1967, **2**, 101–105.

Kahneman, D., & Peavler, W. S. Incentive effects and pupillary changes in association learning. *Journal of Experimental Psychology*, 1969, **79**, 312–318.

Kahneman, D., Tursky, B., Shapiro, D., & Crider, A. Pupillary, heart rate, and skin resistance changes during a mental task. *Journal of Experimental Psychology*, 1969, **79**, 164–179.

Kasl, S. V., & Mahl, G. F. The relationship of disturbances and hesitations in spontaneous speech to anxiety. *Journal of Personality and Social Psychology*, 1965, **1**, 425–433.

Knapp, M. L., & Comadena, M. E. Telling it like it isn't: A review of theory and research on deceptive communications. *Human Communication Research*, 1979, **5**, 270–285.

Knapp, M. L., Hart, R. P., & Dennis, H. S. An exploration of deception as a communication construct. *Human Communication Research*, 1974, **1**, 15–29.

Krauss, R. M., Apple, W., Morency, N., Wenzel, C., & Winton, W. Verbal, vocal and visible factors in judgments of another's affect. *Journal of Personality and Social Psychology*, 1981, **40**, 312–319.

Krauss, R. M., Geller, V., & Olson, C. *Modalities and cues in the detection of deception.* Paper presented at the meeting of the American Psychological Association, Washington, D.C., September, 1976.

Krauss, R. M., & Morency, N. *Nonverbal encoding and decoding affect by first and fifth graders.* Paper presented at the meeting of the American Psychological Association, Montreal, 1980.

Kraut, R. E. Verbal and nonverbal cues in the perception of lying. *Journal of Personality and Social Psychology*, 1978, **36**, 380–391. (a)

Kraut, R. E. *Verbal and nonverbal cues in the perception of lying: A replication.* Unpublished, Cornell University, 1978. (b)

Kraut, R. E. Humans as lie detectors: Some second thoughts. *Journal of Communication,* 1980, **30,** 209–216.

Kraut, R. E., & Poe, D. On the line: The deception judgements of customs inspectors and laymen. *Journal of Personality and Social Psychology,* 1980, **39,** 784–798.

Kraut, R. E., Thompson, A., & Lewis, S. H. *Listener responsiveness, deception, and semantic structure in conversation.* Unpublished, Cornell University, 1980.

Lay, C. H., & Burron, B. F. Perception of the personality of the hesitant speaker. *Perceptual and Motor Skills,* 1968, **26,** 951–956.

Leakey, R. E., & Lewin, R. *People of the lake: Mankind and its beginnings.* New York: Anchor Press, 1978.

Lieblich, I., Kugelmass, S., & Ben-Shakhar, G. Efficiency of GSR detection of information as a function of stimulus set size. *Psychophysiology,* 1970, **6,** 601–608.

Lippa, R. Expressive control and the leakage of dispositional introversion-extraversion during role-played teaching. *Journal of Personality,* 1976, **44,** 541–559.

Littlepage, G. E., & Pineault, T. Verbal, facial, and paralinguistic cues to the detection of truth and lying. *Personality and Social Psychology Bulletin,* 1978, **4,** 461–464.

Littlepage, G. E., & Pineault, M. A. Detection of deceptive factual statements from the body and the face. *Personality and Social Psychology Bulletin,* 1979, **5,** 325–328. (a)

Littlepage, G. E., & Pineault, M. A. *Detection of deception of planned versus spontaneous communications.* Paper presented at the annual convention of the Psychonomic Society, November, 1979. (b)

Littlepage, G. E., & Pineault, M. A. Detection of truthful and deceptive interpersonal communications across information transmission modes. *Journal of Social Psychology,* 1981, **114,** 57–68.

Lykken, D. T. The GSR in the detection of guilt. *Journal of Applied Psychology,* 1959, **43,** 385–388.

Lykken, D. T. The validity of the guilty knowledge technique: The effects of faking. *Journal of Applied Psychology,* 1960, **44,** 258–262.

Lykken, D. T. Psychology and the lie detector industry. *American Psychologist,* 1974, **29,** 725–739.

Lykken, D. T. The psychopath and the lie detector. *Psychophysiology,* 1978, **15,** 137–142.

Lykken, D. T. The detection of deception. *Psychological Bulletin,* 1979, **86,** 47–53.

McClintock, C. C., & Hunt, R. G. Nonverbal indicators of affect and deception in an interview setting. *Journal of Applied Social Psychology,* 1975, **5,** 54–67.

McCroskey, J. C., & Mehrley, R. S. The effects of disorganization and nonfluency on attitude change and source credibility. *Speech Monographs,* 1969, **36,** 13–21.

McGuire, W. J. The nature of attitudes and attitude change. In G. Lindzey, & E. Aronson (Eds.), *The handbook of social psychology,* 2nd ed. Reading, Massachusetts: Addison-Wesley, 1969.

MacLachlan, J. What people really think of fast talkers. *Psychology Today,* 1979, **13,** 113–117.

Mahl, G. F. Gestures and body movements in interviews. In J. M. Shlien, H. F. Hunt, J. D. Matarazzo, & C. Savage (Eds.), *Research in psychotherapy.* Vol. 3. Washington, D.C.: American Psychological Association, 1968.

Maier, N. R. F. Sensitivity to attempts at deception in an interview situation. *Personnel Psychology,* 1966, **19,** 55–65.

Maier, N. R. F., & Janzen, J. C. Reliability of reasons used in making judgments of honesty and dishonesty. *Perceptual and Motor Skills,* 1967, **25,** 141–151.

Maier, N. R. F., & Thurber, J. A. Accuracy of judgments of deception when an interview is watched, heard, and read. *Personnel Psychology,* 1968, **21,** 23–30.

Maier, R. A., & Lavrakas, P. J. Lying behavior and evaluation of lies. *Perceptual and Motor Skills,* 1976, **42,** 575–581.

Manaugh, T. S., Wiens, A. N., & Matarazzo, J. D. Content saliency and interviewee speech behavior. *Journal of Clinical Psychology,* 1970, **26,** 17–24.

Marston, W. M. Reaction time symptoms of deception. *Journal of Experimental Psychology*, 1920, **3**, 72–87.

Matarazzo, J. D., Wiens, A. N., Jackson, R. H., & Manaugh, T. S. Interviewee speech behavior under conditions of endogenously-present and exogenously-induced motivational states. *Journal of Clinical Psychology*, 1970, **26**, 141–148.

Mehrabian, A. Immediacy: An indicator of attitudes in linguistic communication. *Journal of Personality*, 1966, **34**, 26–34.

Mehrabian, A. Attitudes inferred from non-immediacy of verbal communications. *Journal of Verbal Learning and Verbal Behavior*, 1967, **6**, 294–295.

Mehrabian, A. Nonverbal betrayal of feeling. *Journal of Experimental Research in Personality*, 1971, **5**, 64–73.

Mehrabian, A., & Ferris, S. R. Inference of attitudes from nonverbal communication in two channels. *Journal of Consulting Psychology*, 1967, **31**, 248–252.

Meyer, D. R. On the interaction of simultaneous responses. *Psychological Bulletin*, 1953, **50**, 204–220.

Miller, G. R., Bauchner, J. E., Hocking, J. E., Fontes, N. E., Kaminski, E. P., & Brandt, D. R. ". . . And nothing but the truth": How well can observers detect deceptive testimony? In B. D. Sales (Ed.), *Perspectives in law and psychology. Vol. II: The trial process.* New York: Plenum, 1981.

Miller, G. R., & Burgoon, J. K. Factors affecting assessments of witness credibility. In R. Bray & N. Kerr (Eds.), *The psychology of the courtroom.* New York: Academic Press, 1981.

Miller, G. R., & Hewgill, M. A. The effect of variations in nonfluency on audience ratings of source credibility. *Quarterly Journal of Speech*, 1964, **50**, 36–44.

Miller, M., Maruyama, G., Beaber, R. J., & Valone, K. Speed of speech and persuasion. *Journal of Personality and Social Psychology*, 1976, **34**, 615–624.

Morris, D. Nonverbal leakage: How can you tell if someone's lying. *New York*, 1977, Oct. 17, 43–46.

Motley, M. T. Acoustic correlates of lies. *Western Speech*, 1974, **38**, 81–87.

Newtson, D. Attribution and the unit of perception of ongoing behavior. *Journal of Personality and Social Psychology*, 1973, **28**, 28–38.

Nieters, J. L. *The differential role of facial and body cues in the recognition of disguised emotional responses.* Unpublished Ph.D. dissertation, Saint Louis University, 1975.

Nunnally, J. C., Knott, P. D., Duchnowski, A., & Parker, R. Pupillary response as a general measure of activation. *Perception and Psychophysics*, 1967, **2**, 149–155.

O'Hair, H. D., Cody, M. J., & McLaughlin, M. L. Prepared lies, spontaneous lies, Machiavellianism and nonverbal communication. *Human Communication Research*, 1981, in press.

Orne, M. T., Thackray, R. I., & Paskewitz, D. A. On the detection of deception: A model for the study of the physiological effects of psychological stimuli. In N. S. Greenfield & R. A. Sternbach (Eds.), *Handbook of psychophysiology.* New York: Holt, 1972.

Parham, I. A., Feldman, R. S., Popoola, O., & Oster, G. D. Intergenerational differences in nonverbal disclosure of deception. Unpublished, Virginia Commonwealth University, 1980.

Podlesny, J. A., & Raskin, D. C. Physiological measures and the detection of deception. *Psychological Bulletin*, 1977, **84**, 782–791.

Premack, D., & Woodruff, G. Does the chimpanzee have a theory of mind? *The Behavioral and Brain Sciences*, 1978, **4**, 515–526.

Raskin, D. C. Scientific assessment of the accuracy of detection of deception: A reply to Lykken. *Psychophysiology*, 1978, **15**, 143–147.

Raskin, D. C., & Hare, R. D. Psychopathy and detection of deception in a prison population. *Psychophysiology*, 1978, **15**, 126–136.

Raskin, D. C., & Podlesny, J. A. Truth and deception: A reply to Lykken. *Psychological Bulletin*, 1979, **86**, 54-59.

Reid, J. E., & Inbau, F. E. *Truth and deception*. Baltimore, Maryland: Williams & Wilkins, 1977.

Rice, B. The new truth machines. *Psychology Today*, 1978, June.

Rogers, P. L., Scherer, K. R., & Rosenthal, R. Content filtering human speech: A simple electronic system. *Behavior Research Methods and Instrumentation*, 1971, **3**, 16-18.

Rosenthal, R. Combining results of independent studies. *Psychological Bulletin*, 1978, **85**, 185-193.

Rosenthal, R. Summarizing significance levels. In R. Rosenthal (Ed.), *Quantitative assessment of research domains*. San Francisco, California: Jossey-Bass, 1980.

Rosenthal, R. Conducting judgement studies. In K. R. Scherer & P. Ekman (Eds.), *Handbook of methods in nonverbal behavior research*. London and New York: Cambridge University Press, 1981, in press.

Rosenthal, R., & DePaulo, B. M. Sex differences in eavesdropping on nonverbal cues. *Journal of Personality and Social Psychology*, 1979, **37**, 273-285. (a)

Rosenthal, R., & DePaulo, B. M. Sex differences in accomodation in nonverbal communication. In R. Rosenthal (Ed.), *Skill in nonverbal communication: Individual differences*. Cambridge, Massachusetts: Oelgeschlager, 1979. (b)

Rosenthal, R., & DePaulo, B. M. Encoders or decoders as units of analysis in research in nonverbal communication. *Journal of Nonverbal Behavior*, 1980, **5**, 92-103.

Rosenthal, R., Hall, J. A., DiMatteo, M. R., Rogers, P. L., & Archer, D. *Sensitivity to nonverbal communication: The PONS test*. Baltimore, Maryland: Johns Hopkins University Press, 1979.

Rosenthal, R., & Rubin, D. B. Interpersonal expectancy effects: The first 345 studies. *The Behavioral and Brain Sciences*, 1978, **3**, 377-386.

Rosenthal, R., & Rubin, D. B. Comparing significance levels of independent studies. *Psychological Bulletin*, 1979, **86**, 1165-1168.

Rotkin, H. G. *Information used in detecting deception*. Unpublished Ph.D. dissertation, New York University, 1979.

Saarni, C. Children's understanding of display rules for expressive behavior. *Developmental Psychology*, 1979, **15**, 424-429. (a)

Saarni, C. *When NOT to show what you feel: Children's understanding of relations between emotional experience and expressive behavior*. Paper presented at the meeting of the Society for Research in Child Development, San Francisco, March, 1979. (b)

Saarni, C. *Observing children's use of display rules: Age and sex differences*. Paper presented at the meeting of the American Psychological Association, Montreal, 1980.

Scherer, K. R. Personality markers in speech. In K. R. Scherer & H. Giles (Eds.), *Social markers in speech*. London and New York: Cambridge University Press, 1979.

Scherer, K. R. Vocal indicators of stress. In J. Darby (Ed.), *The evaluation of speech in psychiatry and medicine*. New York: Grune & Stratton, 1980. (a)

Scherer, K. R. Speech and emotional states. In J. Darby (Ed.), *The evaluation of speech in psychiatry and medicine*. New York: Grune & Stratton, 1980. (b)

Schneider, S. M., & Kintz, B. L. The effect of lying upon foot and leg movement. *Bulletin of the Psychonomic Society*, 1977, **10**, 451-453.

Scott, T. R., Wells, W. H., Wood, D. Z., & Morgan, D. I. Pupillary response and sexual interest reexamined. *Journal of Clinical Psychology*, 1967, **23**, 433-438.

Sereno, K. K., & Hawkins, G. J. The effects of variations in speakers' nonfluency upon audience ratings of attitude toward the speech topic and speakers' credibility. *Speech Monographs*, 1967, **34**, 58-64.

Sharp, H. Jr., & McClung, T. Effects of organization on the speaker's ethos. *Speech Monographs*, 1966, **38**, 182-183.

Shipp, T., & McGlone, R. *Physiologic correlates of acoustic correlates of psychologic stress.* Paper presented at the meeting of the Acoustical Society of America, Los Angeles, November, 1973.

Simpson, H. M. Effects of a task relevant response on pupil size. *Psychophysiology,* 1969, **6,** 115–121.

Simpson, H. M., & Hale, S. M. Pupillary changes during a decision making task. *Perceptual and Motor Skills,* 1969, **29,** 495–498.

Smith, B. L., Brown, B. L., Strong, W. J., & Rencher, A. C. Effects of speech rate on personality perception. *Language and Speech,* 1975, **18,** 145–152.

Snyder, M. Self-monitoring of expressive behavior. *Journal of Personality and Social Psychology,* 1974, **30,** 526–537.

Starkweather, J. Content-free speech as a source of information about the speaker. *Journal of Abnormal and Social Psychology,* 1956, **52,** 394–402.

Streeter, L. A., Krauss, R. M., Geller, V., Olson, C., & Apple, W. Pitch changes during attempted deception. *Journal of Personality and Social Psychology,* 1977, **35,** 345–350.

Todd, W. R. *Linguistic indices of deception as manifested by women: A content analytic study.* Unpublished Ph.D. dissertation, Florida State University, 1976.

Toris, C., & DePaulo, B. M. *The role of suspiciousness in detecting deception and reading leaked cues.* In preparation, University of Virginia, 1981.

Trovillo, P. V. A history of lie detection. *Journal of Criminal Law and Criminology,* 1939, **29,** 848–881.

Wagner, H., & Pease, K. The verbal communication of inconsistency between attitudes held and attitudes expressed. *Journal of Personality,* 1976, **44,** 1–16.

Waid, W. M., & Orne, M. T. Cognitive, social and personality processes in the physiological detection of deception. In L. Berkowitz (Ed.), *Advances in experimental social psychology,* Vol. 14. New York: Academic Press, 1981.

Weitz, S. Attitude, voice, and behavior: A repressed affect model of interracial interaction. *Journal of Personality and Social Psychology,* 1972, **24,** 14–21.

Wiener, M., & Mehrabian, A. *Language within language.* New York: Appleton, 1968.

Williams, C. E., & Stevens, K. N. On determining the emotional state of pilots during flight: An exploratory study. *Aerospace Medicine,* 1969, **40,** 1369–1372.

Wilson, S. J. *Channel differences in the detection of deception.* Unpublished Ph.D. dissertation, Florida State University, 1975.

Yerkes, R. M., & Berry, C. S. The association reaction method of mental diagnosis. *American Journal of Psychology,* 1909, **20,** 22–37.

Zuckerman, M., Amidon, M. D., Bishop, S. E., & Pomerantz, S. D. *Face and tone of voice in the communication of deception.* Unpublished, University of Rochester, 1980. (a)

Zuckerman, M., Blanck, P. D., DePaulo, B. M., & Rosenthal, R. Developmental changes in decoding discrepant and nondiscrepant nonverbal cues. *Developmental Psychology,* 1980, **16,** 220–228. (b)

Zuckerman, M., DeFrank, R. S., Hall, J. A., Larrance, D. T., & Rosenthal, R. Facial and vocal cues of deception and honesty. *Journal of Experimental Social Psychology,* 1979, **15,** 378–396.

Zuckerman, M., Koestner, R., & Driver, R. *Beliefs about cues associated with deception. Journal of Nonverbal Behavior,* 1981, in press. (a)

Zuckerman, M., Larrance, D. T., Spiegel, N. H., & Klorman, R. Controlling nonverbal cues: Facial expressions and tone of voice. *Journal of Experimental Social Psychology,* 1981, in press. (b)

Zuckerman, M., Lipets, M. S., Koivumaki, J. H., & Rosenthal, R. Encoding and decoding nonverbal cues of emotion. *Journal of Personality and Social Psychology,* 1975, **32,** 1068–1076.

Zuckerman, M., Spiegel, N. H., DePaulo, B. M., & Rosenthal, R. *Nonverbal strategies for decoding deception.* Unpublished, University of Rochester, 1980. (c)

COGNITIVE, SOCIAL, AND PERSONALITY PROCESSES IN THE PHYSIOLOGICAL DETECTION OF DECEPTION

William M. Waid* and Martin T. Orne

INSTITUTE OF PENNSYLVANIA HOSPITAL AND
UNIVERSITY OF PENNSYLVANIA
PHILADELPHIA, PENNSYLVANIA

I. Origins and Nature of Lie Detection

A. INTRODUCTION

Interpersonal deception has emerged as a fundamental area of inquiry in social psychology, with some investigators devoting particular attention to its involuntary vocal, gestural, and other nonverbal correlates (e.g., Ekman &

---

*Present address: Unit for Experimental Psychiatry, 111 N. 49th Street, Philadelphia, Pennsylvania 19139.

ADVANCES IN EXPERIMENTAL SOCIAL
PSYCHOLOGY, VOL. 14

Friesen, 1974; DePaulo & Rosenthal, 1979) and others focusing on its physiological correlates (e.g., Barland & Raskin, 1973; Orne, Thackray, & Paskewitz, 1972). The observation that behavior involving conflict and emotion is typically accompanied by marked physiological changes has been the basis of one of the oldest and most widely used psychotechnologies—the physiological detection of deception. Jung (1906) originally envisioned the basic principle as an aid in diagnosis and psychotherapy. In the context of a word-association task, items which evoked larger than usual galvanic skin responses were scrutinized as possible conflict areas of the patient. Though such an approach in therapy has only recently enjoyed a rekindled interest (Abrams, 1973), the deployment of analogous techniques in criminal investigations was swift and widespread (Marston, 1917). Today, their use extends to routine screening of employees for possible malfeasance (Lykken, 1974, 1981).

The controversy in scientific journals (Lykken, 1974, 1978, 1979; Podlesny & Raskin, 1977) as well as in congressional hearings (U.S. Senate, 1978) has had the salutary effect of sharpening the debate concerning the precise scientific status of the polygraph test as a means of assessing the veracity of testimony. While it is important for public policy purposes to obtain valid estimates of the accuracy of current polygraph test techniques, it would be unfortunate if the current controversy were to obscure the need for an understanding of the precise processes by means of which physiological responses may accurately reflect veracity, deception, or other psychological states. Current polygraph testing procedures, which are the justifiable target of some suspicion, do not necessarily represent the ultimate state of the art.

The physiological detection of deception involves the comparison of physiological responses to relevant questions (which evoke a lie from a deceptive person) with responses to control questions. The precise nature of these questions, particularly the control questions, may vary depending on the examiner and the purpose and type of test, as may the collection and use of the physiological data. Some reviews have focused in great detail on what might be considered the psychometric issues involved, that is, the nature of the questions asked, the structure of the tests, and the validity and reliability of different approaches (Lykken, 1974, 1981), whereas others have focused on what are essentially physiological issues—the most accurate physiological response or combination of responses (Podlesny & Raskin, 1977).

The purpose of the research described in the present article, however, is to examine the underlying cognitive, social, and personality processes involved in the physiological response accompanying deception. Deception is only one of the many social behaviors in which physiological arousal plays a role (e.g., Shapiro & Crider, 1969), and there is no specific pattern of physiological response to deception (Orne et al., 1972). Understanding how underlying processes contribute to the physiological response associated with deception would help clarify the reciprocal effects of social psychological and physiological processes in general. In applied settings, the control of such processes, whether experimental or statistical, might permit enhancing the accuracy of polygraph test results. Before describing this research, we shall review the nature of field polygraph testing and the scientific controversy surrounding it.

B. NATURE OF FIELD POLYGRAPH TESTING

An individual who takes a polygraph test usually does so at the request of the police, his attorney, or even an employer. People may, of course, also suggest that they take a polygraph test to clear themselves of suspicion. Typically, though, the person is suspected of a crime, and failure to be judged truthful on the polygraph test can have serious consequences such as dismissal by his employer and/or continuation of a police investigation that could lead to indictment, trial, and ultimately, perhaps, prison.

When the examiner meets the suspect, he reminds him of his right not to take the test and has him sign a consent form testifying that he takes the test "voluntarily." In a properly conducted polygraph test (Reid & Inbau, 1977), the examiner attempts to structure the entire process as an opportunity for the suspect to demonstrate his truthfulness, and, thus, his innocence. The examiner attempts to achieve rapport with the subject, portraying himself as helping the subject prove his truthfulness, with the polygraph being the final arbiter. He explains that the "lie detector" is a scientific instrument which will record his physiological reactions and indicate when and if he is lying. He tends to state flatly that this can be done with certainty, implying that deception would be pointless because the record would reveal it.

The interrogator carefully discusses with the suspect the questions he will ask. There are, of course, different procedures used by different examiners, but the most widely used procedures, the *control question,* the *zone of comparison,* and their various adaptations, all employ a similar pretest strategy. Approximately 12 questions are formulated, including a number of irrelevant items such as "Are you in the United States?" Also included will be certain control questions such as "Besides what you told me about, have you ever stolen anything?" These are subject to extensive discussion in the formulation stage. Finally, three or four relevant questions pertaining to the specific purpose of the interrogation will be included.

Some history is helpful in understanding the rationale for this questioning procedure. Originally (Marston, 1917), the polygraph test involved only relevant and irrelevant questions, the subject being judged deceptive if he responded more to the former than the latter. (Irrelevant questions are still included as buffers so that the subject's typically large response to the first question or two is not to one of the relevant or control questions.) To control for the problem that even an innocent person might respond more to crime-related questions than to irrelevant ones, Reid (1947) instituted the use of carefully crafted *emotional control* questions. The innocent person is believed to respond more to the emotional control question (e.g., "Besides what you told me about, have you ever stolen anything?") than to the relevant question because he is sure of his truthfulness of the latter but not to the former. The guilty individual, in contrast, though perhaps quite responsive to the emotional control question, will be even more responsive to the relevant question to which he is definitely lying. The debate over the validity of such a procedure will be discussed in detail later.

Only after the questions that are to be asked have been carefully worked out with the subject does the actual examination begin. The typical commercial polygraph records respiration, a cardiovascular measure, and the electrodermal response (EDR). Partly because the inflated blood pressure cuff soon becomes uncomfortable, the actual test is limited to about 10 or 12 questions taking only about 3–4 min. During the actual test, the suspect is usually seated so that he cannot see the record on the machine or the interrogator. The interrogator waits long enough (15–20 sec) between each question to allow the three measures to return to fairly stable baselines. Typical recordings from such a test are illustrated in Fig. 1.

The electrodermal response has been found consistently to be the most accurate of the physiological measures in laboratory studies (Orne *et al.*, 1972) and consequently has been the primary dependent variable in most studies of the detection of deception. The findings discussed here will be from the electrodermal channel for the most part, with cardiovascular and respiratory data presented only when they make some point not obvious with the electrodermal data.

In field testing, the scoring of the physiological parameters is frequently not specified in quantitative terms.[1] Instead, deception is diagnosed by globally comparing the subject's physiological responses on relevant items with his responses on items that are presumed to be even more arousing or anxiety provoking to an individual who is not lying.

Between such tests, the examiner will typically administer a *stimulation* test. He instructs the subject to choose a card from a deck of six to eight cards, look at it, and conceal it on his person without the examiner seeing it. A polygraph test is then conducted in which the subject is asked, "Is the number _____ on the card in your possession?" through five or six numbers. The ostensible purpose of the test is to assess the individual's typical response to deception, but

---

[1]Podlesny and Raskin (1977) have described a quasi-systematic scoring procedure that is coming to be used more widely. In this scoring procedure, the examiner rates each relevant and control question pair from −3 (relevant much larger than control) to +3 (control much larger than relevant). The proponents of such rating procedures have not documented that they are as accurate as a purely objective measurement of response amplitudes.

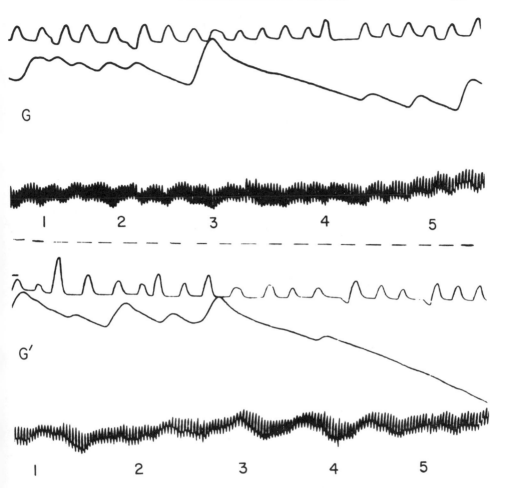

Fig. 1. Peak of tension test records in an actual theft case in which the galvanic skin reflex (GSR) tracing proved to be of considerable value. In fact, this subject's regular test records were devoid of any indications of deception either with respect to relevant or the control questions. No diagnosis could have been attempted had the examiner not conducted the above peak of tension tests in which he utilized the GSR. The subject was a maid in the home of a physician in which a *blue* envelope containing a considerable sum of money disappeared. On the above test, the subject, who professed not to have seen the envelope and not to know the color, was asked the following questions: (1) Was the missing envelope brown?; (2) Was the missing envelope red?; (3) Was the missing envelope blue?; (4) Was the missing envelope yellow?; (5) Was the missing envelope gray? Observe the very pronounced peak of tension in the GSR tracing at *3* on both tests. *G'* was a repeat of *G*. Confronted with an actual display of these records, the subject admitted taking the money and returned it in the same blue envelope. (The upper tracing in each panel is respiration, the middle is GSR or electrodermal response, and the bottom tracing is relative blood pressure.) From Reid and Inbau (1977), with permission.

the actual purpose is to demonstrate to the subject that the polygraph can, indeed, distinguish between truthful and deceptive answers. Such a demonstration is viewed as enhancing the belief in the accuracy of the test and, consequently, enhancing the physiological responses of the deceptive subject while also reducing the fear of false detections among truthful subjects.

In order to ensure that he can make this demonstration, the field polygrapher may arrange matters so that he knows the content of the card even if the polygraph record does not reveal it. This is actually unnecessary in most cases, since the EDR channel of the polygraph, at least, does detect the subject's deception at highly reliable rates, as we will demonstrate later.

Although the stimulation test is seen by the field examiner as a demonstration, it is also, in concept, the perfect lie detection test or, more precisely, *guilty knowledge* detection test, since it features questions in which the critical items and the control items are perfectly matched, except for deception to the critical one. If the subject did not know which item was the critical one, he would respond about equally to all of the items.

If some particular item of crime-related information is available that would be known only to the guilty person, the guilty knowledge technique may be used to determine whether the suspect is deceptive or truthful about the subject of the investigation. In this procedure, a series of questions is asked in an order previously established with the suspect; the crucial item is typically placed third or fourth. In addition to a larger response to the critical item, the operator may look for a gradual increase in the amount of tension elicited by each item as the crucial one is approached and a sudden relaxation once it has passed, leading to the term *peak of tension* test in the field. If, for example, $400 were taken in a theft and this amount is not generally known, the suspect might be asked, "Was the amount taken $200, $300, $400, $500, $600?" The suspect who knows the correct amount should show his maximal response to $400. He may also demonstrate a gradual increase in tension that peaks at $400, with a sudden relaxation as the crucial item is passed.

The crucial feature of the guilty knowledge test is that the innocent person does not know which item is the relevant one and, thus, cannot systematically respond to it more than to the control items. In the typical field *lie* or *guilty person* test, however, it is obvious which questions are relevant.

Although field polygraphers have assumed that the conditions for such a test, the existence of information known only by the guilty person, can be met only rarely, Reid and Inbau (1977) provide many examples of ingenious uses of the test. Thus, the guilty knowledge technique may be increasingly used. Laboratory investigations, which, until recently, generally have used a variation of this procedure are therefore of practical as well as theoretical significance.

Lykken has urged the use in the field of multiple-item guilty knowledge tests, which can be constructed when more than one critical item of information is available. Its validity has been well documented in laboratory studies, in contrast to the control question test, which, though widely used in the field, has only recently been examined under controlled conditions. Furthermore, as we shall discuss, there is significant overlap of guilty person and guilty knowledge tests. Thus, most factors which are found to affect the guilty knowledge test tend to affect the guilty person test in the same way. How accurate are such testing procedures? That question is the crux of the current controversy.

C. ACCURACY OF PHYSIOLOGICAL INDICATORS AND ALTERNATIVE TEST PROCEDURES IN CURRENT FIELD POLYGRAPH TESTS

1. Guilty Person Polygraph Tests

Since field examiners routinely use the control question (i.e., guilty person) test and its variations, it is these tests that have been the subject of field validity studies. Perhaps unintentionally, some investigators (Podlesny & Raskin, 1977) have conveyed the impression that the physiological detection of deception using the control question technique has now been established as a psychophysiological technology which is highly accurate in life situations:

> The control question technique (Reid & Inbau, 1966) and the zone comparison technique, which is a modified control-question procedure (Backster, 1962) are presently employed by many field examiners. . . . There are some laboratory data available concerning the relative power of the control question test in identifying guilty and innocent subjects. In the Barland and Raskin (1975) experiment there were 8% false positives and 4% false negatives. In the Raskin study there were 4% false positives and no false negatives. Finally, a mock crime experiment recently completed in our laboratory compared accuracy rates of control question and guilty knowledge tests (described below). The result was 2% false positives and 8% false negatives for the control question test and 10% false negatives for the guilty knowledge test. Thus, although the control question technique does produce some false positives and false negatives, it is possible to reduce them to a smaller proportion of the cases. (Pp. 786, 787)

These highly accurate results are presumably based entirely on the physiological data since Podlesny and Raskin take pains to assert that a field polygrapher must "base his decisions on the physiological recordings" (p. 788).

There are several reasons that these laboratory results should not be mistaken for estimates of the true accuracy of the physiological data typically gathered in the field polygraph tests. The most compelling is a major, widely circulated study by Horvath (1974, 1977), which reports the best available data evaluating field polygraph testing. Horvath had 10 professional polygraphers interpret over 100 polygraph records from cases sampled scientifically from state police files.

In contrast to the highly accurate detection in laboratory studies presumably simulating field conditions as closely as possible (Barland & Raskin, 1975;

Raskin, 1976, Note 1), Horvath's field polygraphers, interpreting (blind) the physiological records of subjects verified to be deceptive or truthful, correctly detected 77% of the deceptive subjects, but erroneously classified 49% of the innocent subjects as "deceptive." The study overwhelmingly contradicts the premise that laboratory data accurately estimate the actual accuracy of physiological field data and forms the basis for Lykken's sharp critiques of field polygraph test practices (Lykken, 1974, 1978, 1979, 1981).

It would be equally unfortunate, however, if the Horvath (1977) study were assumed to estimate the actual accuracy of field polygraph test decisions. Despite Podlesny and Raskin's assertion that decisions should be made only on the basis of the physiological record, other factors may enter into the decision, as noted by Horvath (1977). Unless the records are scored blind and the decision made by someone other than the examiner of the subject, it cannot be maintained that the decision is based only on the physiological record. In fact, field polygraphers (Horvath, 1973), like other people (Kraut, 1978), appear capable of significant (though, of course, far from perfect) discrimination between deceptive and truthful statements on the basis of involuntary vocal and other nonverbal cues. As Lykken (1978) has noted, this may partially explain the discrepancy between the laboratory data Podlesny and Raskin cite and the results of Horvath (1977) using blind interpretation of physiological records by examiners who never saw the subjects. In Barland and Raskin (1975), the examiner of the subject made the decision on the basis of his own "numerical" scoring (Podlesny & Raskin, 1977) of the record following the examination, as is normally done in the field. The control question tests were preceded by an interview and were interspersed with discussions of the subject's answers to the questions. Thus, there was ample opportunity for the examiner to observe involuntary signs of deception and incorporate these, whether consciously or otherwise, into his final decision. Field polygraphers have the same opportunities. Thus, actual field decisions may be considerably more accurate than is suggested by the Horvath study, but not solely on the basis of the average polygrapher's interpretation of the physiological record. Further, since Horvath explicitly examined the accuracy of polygraphers' interpretations, purely objective measurement of the physiological responses might have yielded more accurate discrimination between truth and deception.

2. Guilty Knowledge Polygraph Tests

More accurate results appear to be obtained with the guilty knowledge test in field settings. Reid and Inbau (1977) describe many ingenious, successful uses of the single-item guilty knowledge technique. Although such field reports are not validity data, they do contradict the assumption widely held in the field (Podlesny & Raskin, 1977) that the guilty knowledge technique is rarely usable. Frequency of use of the guilty knowledge procedure may depend more on the ingenuity and expertise of the examiner than on properties inherent in the field context.

Although no systematic field study of this technique comparable to Horvath's (1977) study of the guilty person technique has been carried out, we have conducted an approximation of such a study. The card test administered for demonstration purposes by most field polygraphers constitutes a single-item guilty knowledge test. Although the outcome of this test does not bear directly on the overall polygraph test, given the possible consequences of the entire test, the field subject can be presumed to feel some concern even about the card test.

We examined the card test charts of 36 suspects tested by a professional polygraph firm. The card test detected 14 of 18 verified innocents ($p < .01$) and 13 of 18 ($p < .01$) verified deceptives. Although these cases were not sampled from the firm's files according to scientific sampling, they were also not selected on the basis of the card test results, which field examiners do not score, so they provide some indication of the validity of the guilty knowledge technique in the field setting.[2]

Similar results were obtained by Kugelmass and Lieblich (1966), who administered a card test to Israeli policemen during selection testing which was supposedly related to their service and future with the force. Under these field-type conditions (the use of the polygraph test in personnel screening) subjects' deception in the card test was detected at highly significant rates. Similar results are obtained in laboratory experiments (e.g., Gustafson & Orne, 1963, 1965a,b).

D. CONCLUSIONS

In summary, the best field evidence to date on the guilty person polygraph procedure (Horvath, 1977) indicates that when only the polygrapher's interpretation of the record is used in making a decision, and there are equal numbers of guilty and innocent subjects, about 75% of deceptive subjects will be correctly identified, but truthful subjects will be correctly identified at only chance levels of accuracy. It may be, however, that actual polygraph test decisions are more accurate since they are based on all the information the examiner has about the case, as well as on involuntary verbal and nonverbal cues given by the subject. Both field and laboratory studies have focused on polygraph tests concerning specific events. It seems likely that the polygraph is less accurate in tests con-

---

[2]According to field polygraphers, guilty subjects may attempt to produce greatly enhanced responses to the critical number in the hope that their response to relevant questions in the control question test will appear less pronounced by comparison, possibly leading the examiner to decide they are truthful. The equal levels of detection in guilty and innocent groups suggest that this tendency was not strong in the present sample.

cerning unspecified events, as is frequently the case in preemployment screening (Lykken, 1981).

The sparse field evidence regarding the guilty knowledge procedure, in contrast, is in accord with the many laboratory demonstrations of the efficacy of this technique. Unfortunately, while the guilty person test appears to result in a high frequency of false positives, the guilty knowledge procedure cannot always be employed.

To the extent that the polygraph test is touted as a *psychophysiological test,* as opposed to an important adjunct to police investigation, the field validity results are disconcerting. Thus, it seems unlikely that adherence to present field procedures will lead to acceptance of the polygraph test as an objective psychophysiological measure. Rather, research is needed which seeks to understand the conditions under which deception and truth can be accurately discriminated solely on the basis of the physiological record.

As Davis noted in 1961, there had been little investigation of the *psychological* processes at work in lie detection until the time of his inquiries. Most research had not gone beyond illustrating that deception could be detected, at least in the laboratory, with one or another physiological measure (Podlesny & Raskin, 1977, have reviewed this literature as well as more recent data of this sort). The more interesting problem, however, is, as Davis phrased it, "Just what general properties of a situation provoke the physiologic reactions that make lie detection possible" (p. 160). We would expand that question: What are the cognitive, behavioral, social, and personality processes that facilitate or interfere with the physiological verification of testimony? The present series of studies addresses this question.

II.   Processes Underlying the Physiological Response to Deception and Its Detection

A.   INTRODUCTION

In field polygraph testing, the actual guilt or innocence of subjects does not become established for a long period of time—if at all. Even more problematic for scientific purposes, the ultimate disposition of the case cannot be considered to be independent of the polygraph test outcome. Suspects who appear truthful may not be investigated with the thoroughness of those who appear deceptive, leading to a possible confounding of legal guilt or innocence with polygraph test results (Orne *et al.,* 1972). A further problem is that cases which are solved constitute a minority of all cases. Consequently, investigators have turned to the experimental laboratory as a context for examining the processes involved in the detection of deception. As in applied social research in general, (e.g., Saks &

Hastie, 1978), results obtained with the experimental method permit stronger causal statements about the variables of interest, but at the expense of some possible generalizability to nonlaboratory settings. For example, the experimental subject cannot be expected to suffer the same degree of apprehension as the field subject. While this must be kept in mind, it would be an obstacle to experimental research only if the detection of deception failed to work under such conditions. Among other observations on the psychological processes that result in augmented physiological responses to deception, Davis (1961) noted that lying even about rather trivial matters, and even in accordance with instructions from an experimenter, yielded high rates of detection. Davis interpreted this to mean that the detection of deception did not depend on the behavior the person attempts to conceal being criminal or antisocial in nature but rather that it was a quite general phenomenon that would work in many different situations, such as counterintelligence, as well as criminal investigations. The material about which experimental subjects attempt deception varies. In some studies subjects commit a mock crime. In others, subjects memorize certain information and attempt to convince the examiner that they have not done so. In still others, a procedure similar to the field stimulation test is used, whereas, in others, the subject may lie about his personal identity and history. Since many studies, including Davis's (1961), document the effectiveness of the psychophysiological detection of deception in such laboratory situations, they appear to provide an appropriate setting for systematically controlled investigations of the factors which may affect the accuracy of field lie detection.

B.   COGNITIVE AND BEHAVIORAL COMPONENTS

Initial studies were designed to identify behavioral and mental components of the interaction between examiner and subject which are responsible for the augmented autonomic response to deception. One basic question has been whether it is the *act of deception* itself that evokes augmented physiological response.

1.   Deceptive Acts versus Deceptive Intentions

In a study addressing this question, Gustafson and Orne (1965a), utilizing a procedure based on the stimulation test employed by field polygraphers, instructed one group of subjects to respond no verbally to each critical and each control question, as is typically the case in field examinations. A second group was also instructed to attempt to appear innocent but was directed by the examiner to remain silent while the physiological responses to the questions were recorded. In both conditions, deception was detected significantly above chance levels, but the verbalization condition yielded significantly more detection than the silent condition. Davis (1961) also reported that detection was achieved even without a verbal response from the subject but that a verbalized deception augmented detection. Kugelmass *et al.* (1967) obtained significant detection even with subjects instructed to answer yes to every question. Even though they were technically telling the truth about the critical number and "lying" about the others, the intent to deceive (conceal the critical number) was sufficient to lead to detection. Reid and Inbau (1977) describe the use of a yes test in the field.

From the perspective of understanding the processes at work in the physiological response to deception, these findings reveal several interesting facts. The verbal *act of deception* itself contributes only part of the stimulation eliciting the physiological response. The *intention to deceive* apparently contributes more to this response, as seen by the fact that even subjects who remain silent when attempting not to be detected physiologically are highly detectable.

A recent study by Dawson (1980) indicates that it is the expectation of giving the answer rather than the verbal answer per se which evokes differential physiological response. Subjects were tested both with the usual guilty person technique requiring an immediate answer and with a delayed (8 sec) answer required, permitting analysis of responses to question and answer separately. Significant discrimination between deceptive and nondeceptive subjects was achieved with the immediate answer test and with the responses to the questions, but not to the answers, in the delayed answer test. Significant differences in discriminative power between the immediate answer test and the responses to questions only on the delayed answer test would require much larger samples than was used in this study. Nonetheless, it is quite suggestive that only 7 of 12 nondeceptive subjects were correctly identified using the typical immediate answer test, while 10 of 12 were correctly identified using the response to questions on the delayed answer test. Amplitude data provided further insights. The EDRs to the usual question-answer stimulus in the immediate answer test had the largest amplitude. The EDRs to the questions in the delayed answer test were about 60-80% of the amplitude of those in the immediate answer test, with responses to the answers only being considerably smaller.

2. Intent to Deceive versus Stimulus Content

It might also be hypothesized that it is the content of the relevant questions, to which the subject has been sensitized by some sort of experience, that evokes the enhanced physiological response, rather than the intent to deceive. In a study (Gustafson & Orne, 1963) addressing this question, one group was treated identically to the silent group in the preceding study, and a second group was treated the same except that no mention was made of deception. The subjects in this second group listened to a series of stimuli that included one with which they had had some prior experience, identical to that of the group explicitly, though silently, attempting deception. Significant detection of critical items was obtained with the group motivated to deceive but not with the unmotivated group.

These results indicate that, at least with relatively nonsalient items of information, as in the stimulation test administered by field polygraphers, little detection
can be obtained physiologically unless the test is explicitly labeled as "lie detection" and the subject is explicitly attempting to deceive. In such cases, it appears
to be the effort to deceive, rather than the question per se, which results in the
augmented autonomic response yielding detection.

3. Nature of Questions

Nonetheless, lie detector tests usually do involve subject matter that may be
inherently arousing and, further, may contain the threat of unpleasant consequences. Another study (Thackray & Orne, 1968a) illustrates that the nature of
the stimulus material does affect detectability. The subjects were told that their
task would be to appear innocent, that is, to appear not to be one of the individuals about whom they would be interrogated, and that they were not to admit
recognizing any of the memorized words. Each subject was introduced to the
examiner, who was, in fact, blind as to the identity of the subjects, as subject
number 26. Using this situation, it was possible to compare the rate of detection
to first name, last name, and date of birth with the rate to three random words that
the subject had overlearned. The mean detection rate for the personal material
was significantly better than for the overlearned words. Other investigators have
reported similar findings (Davis, 1961).

These findings support a conditioned response model (Davis, 1961) which
posits that the critical question has acquired arousal properties that contribute to
detection independently of the effort to deceive or fear of consequences. One's
name is a stimulus to which a person is thoroughly conditioned to respond.
Analogously, in the field situation, a verbal inquiry about a crime a person has
committed would evoke arousal associated with semantic or other symbolic
representations of the crime-related events. The more serious the crime, the more
physiological arousal would be evoked by the question.

The implications of these initial findings for the field use of the physiological detection of deception are worth noting here. There appear to be several
behavioral and cognitive components of the interaction between examiner and
subject that independently produce enhanced physiological response: the act of
deception, the effort to deceive, and any inherently arousing content of the
questions. Since each of these processes independently increases the physiological response and can be examined separately, the polygraph examiner has a
number of different ways of eliciting physiological response. Applied research
should examine whether innocent and guilty subjects respond differentially to
these different components and whether examining the physiological response to
these components separately enhances the accuracy of the test, as suggested by
Dawson's (1980) findings.

The findings on the effects of personal as opposed to impersonal content of questions in laboratory studies suggest that, in field tests, questions about more serious offenses might evoke more arousal than questions about less serious issues. While inherently more arousing stimuli might lead to a greater detection of guilty subjects, they might also be more likely to lead to false detection of innocent suspects when the guilty person procedure is employed. This point is illustrated by additional findings by Horvath (1977). His field polygraph sample included two kinds of cases: crimes against a person (e.g., rape, assault, homicide) and property crimes. Significantly more innocent subjects suspected of a crime against a person were mistakenly classified as deceptive than were those suspected of a property crime. Thus, being asked whether one had killed or raped another person is apparently more arousing than being asked whether one stole something.

4. Awareness

In the normal polygraph test, the subject is well aware that his physiological responses are being monitored to detect whether or not he is telling the truth. In fact, the polygraph is used almost as a stage prop in that its visible presence seems to enhance the subject's concern and consequently his efforts to deceive. As we have indicated, moreover, the effort to deceive appears to be a major factor in making detection possible. Thus, it might be hypothesized that even if we could obtain the physiological responses of an individual without his awareness, we would not very effectively detect deception.

There are, however, separate components of the attempt to deceive. In the polygraph context, the attempt to deceive includes attempts to modify normal physiological responses to social interaction, either by trying not to respond or by trying to produce responses to certain questions. Even without the presence of the polygraph, however, the subject of an interrogation still attempts deception, that is, attempts to speak and act in such a way as to be believed, even though deceiving. Thus, it may be that the attempt to deceive, in the everyday sense, is sufficient to evoke physiological arousal leading to detection even when the subject is unaware that his physiological responses are being monitored. We have investigated these questions using three different approaches.

A preliminary investigation of this problem was carried out in the course of a study by Thackray and Orne (Orne et al., 1972). Prior to a peak-of-tension or guilty knowledge series in a group experiment, the stimuli were presented to the subjects, ostensibly so they would know the stimulus order in the subsequent test. This is a routine part of field peak-of-tension tests. During this presentation, the subjects were led to believe that the equipment, located in an adjacent room, was turned off. Immediately after the presentation, the subjects were interrogated about these same words and were requested to answer no to each item. The difference in detection rates between the preinterrogation presentation and the actual interrogation, though they were higher in the actual interrogation situation, only approached significance ($p < .10$). Any interpretation of this finding must be tempered by the realization that the procedure confounded a number of variables, and no systematic effort was made to establish whether or not the subjects believed the experimenter when they were told that they were not being recorded.

In the context of another study, an attempt was made to test the latter issue more directly. Thackray and Orne (1968a) arranged the situation so that, as the subject was entering the interrogation room, a technician was turning off the polygraph. A number of electrodes were then attached to the subject, and it was explained to him that it would be necessary for some of the sensors, particularly the oximeter, to stabilize over a period of time before the test could take place. Prior to turning on the polygraph and actually taking the test, the subject and the interrogator discussed the questions in a way similar to that of a real-life detection situation, ostensibly in order to avoid confusion and surprise. During this time, the subject's EDR responses were telemetered to another polygraph four rooms away. Once the discussion was completed, the actual examination took place. A subsequent attempt was made to determine whether the subjects believed that a recording was made during the pretrial test period. Only one subject reported such a belief. Nevertheless, significant detection was obtained in both conditions, with no significant difference between conditions.

We have replicated this basic finding using a third method of varying awareness in a guilty person procedure with both deceptive and nondeceptive subjects (Waid, Orne, & Wilson, 1979a). In this study, subjects were attached to a field polygraph in the same room and given a brief demonstration of its operation. The machine was then turned off and an interview and review of the test questions was conducted. Two electrodes unobtrusively terminated not in the field polygraph but in a polygraph in an adjacent room where recordings were made throughout. In both the unaware and aware conditions, deceptive subjects tended to give significantly larger EDRs to the relevant question, whereas innocent subjects did not. The results were more dramatic in the aware condition, however, as indicated by a comparison of individual subjects. During the unaware condition, 10 of 15 deceptive subjects gave a larger EDR to the relevant than to the control question, whereas only 4 of 15 innocent subjects did so [$\chi^2(1) = 3.35$, $p < .10$]. During the aware condition, however, 13 of 15 deceptive subjects gave a larger EDR to the relevant than to the control question, whereas 5 of 15 nondeceptive subjects did so [$\chi^2(1) = 6.81$, $p < .01$].

In each of these studies, order of conditions was a confounding variable, there being no easy way to make plausible a reversal in the order of presentation. In each study, however, novelty and habituation worked against the hypothesis that awareness enhances detectability. Although it is not possible on the basis of these studies to answer the question of how subjects would behave if they were not in a polygraph situation, the findings do suggest that it is not merely the conscious belief that one is being monitored, but, rather, the arousing nature of the question, as well as the attempt to deceive, in its totality, that may be sufficient to evoke differential responsivity, and the specific attempt to deceive the polygraph may further enhance differential responsivity.

5. *Knowledge of Results*

Although the awareness that one's physiological responses are under scrutiny does not enhance detectability dramatically, greater enhancement might be obtained by conveying to the subject information about the effectiveness of the attempted deception. Feedback, or knowledge of results, has pervasive effects in a broad range of psychological processes. The stimulation test is precisely a case of feedback of results to the subject, though in some cases it may be false feedback. False feedback of physiological responses has also been shown to affect psychological processes (e.g., Valins, 1966; Hirschman, 1975).

Although the stimulation test "works," does demonstrating this to the subject affect his subsequent performance? To test this question, Gustafson and Orne (1965b) conducted a study similar to those described but gave subjects feedback concerning the outcome of one test before conducting a second. Subjects were told, as usual, "This is a study in lie detection. Only very stable and emotionally mature individuals are able to fool the lie detector. We want you to try your best to fool the machine. Good luck!" Subjects were shown cards with numbers and were asked to select one, apparently without the experimenter's knowledge. A tape recording was then played on which all the possible numbers were repeated in the form of questions. The subject was instructed to reply no to each number, so that one of his responses would necessarily be a lie.

After the first trial, regardless of the subject's actual physiological responses, the experimenter entered the room and told half the subjects what their card had been—thus indicating that they had been detected. To the other half, the experimenter named the wrong card, thereby leading them to believe they had gone undetected. A second trial was then given to each subject in order to determine the effect of feedback on subsequent detection. These results are presented in Table I.

Subjects who hoped to go undetected because "only mature and stable individuals are able to fool the lie detector" but who were told they had been detected, continued to show augmented responses the next time they were required to lie, making their detection much easier. Exactly the opposite result occurred when the experimenter communicated to the subject that he had effectively deceived the machine. These subjects became less detectable.

Clearly, feedback of results affects physiological response to the detection of deception, but the nature of the feedback is critical to continued success of the detection procedure. If the subject is motivated to escape detection, as is the field subject, and has reason to believe that he has successfully avoided detection once, he becomes less aroused when he deceives subsequently. If he has reason

TABLE I

Number of Successful and Unsuccessful
Detections on Two Trials from Subjects
Attempting to Deceive[a]

	Told detected on Trial 1	Told not detected on Trial 1
Trial 1		
Detected	13	11
Not detected	3	5
Trial 2		
Detected	15	3
Not detected	1	13

[a] Adapted from Gustafson and Orne (1965b).

to believe he has been detected, that is, has responded emotionally or physiologically when deceiving, he will be more responsive physiologically on subsequent deceptions than he would otherwise have been. Such a phenomenon is consistent with studies explicitly concerned with the effects of false physiological feedback and subsequent attitudes and physiological responses. If a subject is led to believe that he has responded emotionally (i.e., physiologically) to a particular stimulus, that stimulus becomes of greater significance to him than other similar stimuli. Such salient stimuli have been shown in other contexts to produce greater arousal than otherwise similar stimuli. Hirschman (1975) has shown that attending to a signal believed to reflect one's own physiological activity is more arousing than attending to the same physical signal not so labeled. This is consistent with the fact that attending to other aspects of the self, for example, one's own voice, is more arousing than attending to otherwise identical stimuli (Holzman, Rousey, & Snyder, 1966). The latter finding suggests a simple modification of the polygraph test that could possibly enhance its effect. Questions would be presented visually with the requirement that the subject himself read the question aloud, pause, and then answer it. Such a procedure would provide the subject with auditory feedback of his own emotional state as well as making it more difficult to engage in evasive mental countermeasures (which will be discussed in a following section).

6. Attention

The subject's cognitive processing of the stimulus information during the test is another potentially important determinant of the physiological response to deception. Recent research on the psychophysiology of attention and memory suggests that such processing might influence the detection of deception. Corteen (1969), for example, reported that incidentally recalled words had produced significantly larger electrodermal responses during presentation than had those that were forgotten. Similar results have been reported by Maltzman, Kantor, and Langdon (1966), by Sampson (1969), and by McLean (1969). Presumably, the more intensely attention is focused on a stimulus, the greater the electrodermal response and the more likely its later recall.

These studies of the role of arousal in human memory suggest the hypothesis that, in the detection of deception, subjects who avoid fully processing the semantic information of each question, instead responding mechanically to each stimulus, would show reduced electrodermal responses and consequently would be detected infrequently. This *truncated* processing could be indexed by the subject's later recall of the test questions: subjects who were detected infrequently being expected to recall fewer of the questions. The purpose of the present study was to test this hypothesis. A reduction in subjects' detectability due to truncated processing would be particularly likely to occur in guilty knowledge tests, since in these tests the subject gives the same answer to each item.

We investigated this hypothesis in three separate experiments (Waid, Orne, Cook, & Orne, 1978). During the polygraph test, the subject was asked if any of a long list of words were code words he had learned. A code word was considered detected if it evoked a larger electrodermal response (EDR) than the largest EDR to any of that word's matched control words. Afterward, without forewarning, a second experimenter asked the subject to remember all the words he had been asked about on the polygraph test. In each experiment the number of code words on which a subject was detected (via the EDR) was positively associated with the number of control words he remembered (code words were always remembered since these had been overlearned). The results suggest that the less thoroughly a subject processes the test words, as indexed by later memory, the less likely he is to be detected.

It is important to observe that the present results were obtained in the guilty knowledge paradigm. Their relevance to the control question procedure more commonly used in field settings remains to be determined. Due to the increased field use of the guilty knowledge test (Reid & Inbau, 1977), however, the present results may be relevant to the field context. They suggest that the effectiveness of the field peak of tension test might be improved by procedures which would enhance the subject's attention, such as requiring the subject to repeat the questions aloud in addition to answering them.

In a subsequent study (Waid, Orne, & Orne, 1981b) we examined whether analogous effects of attention might be observed in the field-type guilty person test. Memory for three different kinds of questions can be scored in the guilty person test: critical, control, and irrelevant. As a consequence, the analysis is more complex, but possibly more informative, than is the case with the guilty knowledge test wherein—at least in our paradigm—only control items can serve as the memory pool. Our previous findings with the guilty knowledge test suggested that in the guilty person test, items that are later recalled should evoke larger skin conductance responses than those that are not, and, across subjects, those who recall many questions (particularly critical ones) should be detected more frequently than those who recall relatively few. Since recall of control questions should also be associated with larger skin conductance responses, high recall of critical questions together with low recall of control questions should be associated with a greater number of critical questions detected physiologically.

The skin conductance amplitude data support this hypothesis and are consistent with our previous findings. The mean amplitude of the skin conductance response to critical and control questions which were later recalled was significantly larger on both first and second guilty person tests than that of critical and control questions which were not recalled (Table II). Thus, whatever attentional or information-processing mechanisms are associated with later recall are also related to larger electrodermal responses.

We next sought to determine whether this phenomenon would account for some of the differences among subjects in physiological detectability. That is, are subjects who recall many questions, particularly critical ones, detected more frequently than subjects who recall few?

The correlation of the number of critical questions recalled with the number of critical questions detected was calculated for each of the three physiological measures separately. Also calculated was the correlation of the detection measures with a differential recall measure (number of relevant questions recalled minus number of control questions recalled divided by number of relevant questions recalled plus number of control questions recalled) which expresses each subject's tendency to recall more relevant than control questions, or vice versa, as a proportion of the total recall of both types of questions.

These results (see Table III) are also consistent with our previous findings to

TABLE II

AMPLITUDE OF THE EDR TO RELEVANT AND CONTROL
QUESTIONS (GUILTY PERSON TESTS) AS A FUNCTION OF
LATER RECALL FOR 40 GUILTY AND 34 INNOCENT
SUBJECTS COMBINED

	Recalled	Not recalled
Test 1		
Relevant	2.96	2.35
Control	2.95	2.41
Test 2		
Relevant	1.66	.98
Control	1.41	1.35

[a]From Waid et al. (1981b).

TABLE III

CORRELATION OF TOTAL NUMBER OF DETECTIONS WITH NUMBER OF QUESTIONS RECALLED (GUILTY PERSON TEST)[a]

Group	Measure	Irrelevant	(Relevant − control)/ (Relevant + control)
Guilty	SCR[b]	.48*	.40*
(N = 39)	Blood pressure	.08	.10
	Respiration	.14	.24
Innocent	SCR	.27	.16
(N = 34)	Blood pressure	.07	.13
	Respiration	.14	.15

[a] From Waid et al. (1981b).
[b] SCR, Skin conductance response in micromhos per centimeter squared.
*$p < .01$

a remarkable degree. The more irrelevant questions a guilty subject later recalls, the more often he is detected via the skin conductance response. The irrelevant questions in the guilty person test are akin to the control questions in the guilty knowledge test in that they are innocuous and of no real import to the subject. Apparently, memory for such stimuli, whether the control items of the guilty knowledge test or the irrelevant questions of the guilty person test, serves as a marker of the intensity of attention or information processing that the subject devotes to the stimuli of the test and the consequent likelihood of responding physiologically and being detected.

The significant positive correlation between number of questions detected using skin conductance and the ratio measure of differential recall indicates that the greater a guilty subject's disposition to recall critical rather than control items, the more frequently he is detected electrodermally. The correlation was not significant, however, among innocent subjects.

The results are consistent with the following model: The more actively a subject attends to a given stimulus, whether critical or control, the larger the skin conductance response it evokes and the more likely it is to be recalled later. Guilty subjects who attend more actively to the critical than to the control stimuli, as indicated by proportionally greater recall of the former than of the latter, respond physiologically more to the critical than to the control stimuli leading to more detections of critical questions. Finally, recall of the irrelevant questions, which are not a part of the detection score, appears to serve as an independent index of the subject's general attentiveness, a factor which also correlates with the number of critical questions detected. This factor would appear to be the same as that tapped by the recall of control questions in the guilty knowledge test, which we have previously reported (Waid et al., 1978).

These results also suggest that procedures should be taken to preclude, or at least reduce, the effectiveness of mental countermeasures subjects might use to lessen their physiological response to relevant questions. Theoretically at least, a number of unobtrusive mental activities, such as counting backward by sevens, might interfere with processing of the test questions sufficiently to dampen responsivity. Since the subject typically is acquainted with the order of the questions in the guilty person test, the deceptive suspect might well utilize such a procedure when the relevant question is approaching, but concentrate completely on the content of the control question when it occurs. To counteract such efforts, subjects might be informed at the outset that they will have to be able to recall the questions asked after the test, or they might be instructed to repeat, or "echo," the question aloud a few seconds after answering. Although these are rather straightforward control procedures, they are not used systematically, if at all, in the field testing procedure.

7. Habituation

Orne *et al.* (1972) reviewed the relationship of detection to habituation, the tendency for the amplitude of physiological responses to decline across a series of similar stimuli. The effects of habituation depend on the unit of analysis. Taking each of a series of tests of a subject as the unit, the accuracy of detection declines across repetitions (Orne *et al.,* 1972). However, taking each question within a test as the unit of analysis, habituation leads to quite different results.

From this perspective, considerable research has been devoted to *dichotomization* and subsequent differential habituation as explanatory mechanisms in the detection of deception. In a number of careful parametric studies (Lieblich, Kugelmass, & Ben-Shakhar, 1970; Ben-Shakhar, Lieblich, & Kugelmass, 1970; Ben-Shakhar, 1977), investigators at the Hebrew University have shown that the smaller the ratio of relevant items to control items, the greater the enhancement of information detection. Such findings have been interpreted (Ben-Shakhar, 1977) to mean that subjects dichotomize the questions into two categories (e.g., relevant and control) and that habituation ensues separately for the two. The greater the number of control items, the smaller the mean response becomes and, thus, the more the response to the relevant item stands out. Although this is a theory of appealing simplicity, it seems to be more a restatement of the operations of the experiment than an account of mechanisms. Moreover, these studies have used a paradigm in which subjects are not instructed to deceive nor to attempt to "beat the polygraph." The guilty person procedure, in which the ratio of relevant to control questions is only 1:1, but in which subjects explicitly attempt deception, yields higher rates of detection (e.g., Waid, Orne, & Wilson, 1979b) than that obtained by Ben-Shakar (1977) even with a ratio of 1:8. Nonetheless, this line of inquiry seems to indicate that with appropriate manipulation of the number of control items, substantial detection of information can be obtained even when subjects have no particular deceptive intent.

C. COPING WITH THE POLYGRAPH TEST: COUNTERMEASURES

In addition to merely attempting to deceive, or employing unobtrusive mental countermeasures such as those we have alluded to, the guilty individual faced with a polygraph test may make explicit preparations to cope with the stress of the polygraph test and escape detection. Attempting to suppress physiological reactions inevitably fails, as shown by the majority of laboratory studies in which subjects are instructed to do precisely that. The opposite strategy, consciously producing augmented responses to control items by thinking emotional thoughts, taking deep breaths, clenching the teeth or sphincter, etc., does not appear successful either. Many of these physical activities produce anomolous tracings in respiration or cardiovascular channels and are readily identified. Even when such identification of artifacts is not attempted by the examiner, such a strategy does not avoid detection, at least with the guilty knowledge test (Lykken, 1960).

Dawson (1980) has reported that even individuals with long training in producing emotions at will, "method" actors, were unable to reduce their detectability. Crude physical self-stimulation, such as pressing on a tack secreted in the shoe, is sometimes attempted and detected (Reid & Inbau, 1977). Such countermeasures can be easily controlled for, though it is by no means certain that the typical field examiner does so.

Some of the tools available for handling day-to-day stress and anxiety might be effective in reducing physiological response to the polygraph test generally and to relevant questions specifically.

1. Tranquilizers

A number of studies, for example, suggest that tranquilizing drugs are an effective countermeasure. Such drugs might offer a fast-acting, readily available avenue to reducing physiological reactivity to the interpersonal stress of the polygraph test.

In the absence of adequate research on the effects of such agents on polygraph test results, professional polygraphers have asserted that drugs are rarely used as countermeasures and that, if used, such drugs would produce overt effects which would be readily discernible to the examiner, who would simply postpone the test. Despite such claims, polygraphers have had no objective way of knowing whether or how often drugs have been used to confound their tests since no plasma or urine analyses for such drugs have ever been made in the context of polygraph tests. In fact, tranquilizers are the most widely prescribed and abused of all drugs, and illicit traffic in such drugs is commonplace. It would be prudent to assume that many determined guilty parties could obtain a tranquilizer prior to testing, possibly even when in jail, since illicit traffic in drugs thrives in preliminary detention centers such as jails. Furthermore, there is no evidence that clinical doses of minor tranquilizers cause impairments of overt behavior or performance which would permit the kind of identification claimed by polygraphers. On the contrary, "The anti-anxiety agents share a similar central depressant action: the ability to produce mild sedation in doses that are generally unlikely to cause soporific effects or to adversely affect the quality of consciousness and the quality of psychomotor performance" (American Medical Association, 1973).

We tested the effects of a tranquilizer—meprobamate—on polygraph test results and also whether the operator could determine which subjects had ingested a tranquilizer on the basis of their behavior and appearance during interaction with him (Waid, Orne, Cook, & Orne, 1981a).

A guilty knowledge polygraph test was administered to 44 male volunteer subjects. Subjects assigned to the guilty condition were divided into three groups . The first group ($N = 11$) was told that they were being given a tranquilizer which would help them avoid detection, and 400-mg meprobamate, the typical minimum clinical dose, was administered orally; the second group ($N = 11$) was also told they were being given a tranquilizer which would help them avoid detection, but a placebo was administered; the third group of subjects ($N = 11$), the no-countermeasure group, was given nothing. After 30 min, a second experimenter, who was blind as to the subjects' innocence or guilt and drug condition, conducted the polygraph test.

The results are presented in Table IV. The electrodermal response yielded significant identification of guilty and innocent subjects, whereas the respiratory and cardiovascular measures did not. This is consistent with other studies in which detection was scored blindly and separately for each channel. Using the electrodermal response, both the no-countermeasure and placebo groups were significantly discriminated from the innocent group ($\chi^2 = 12.03$, $p < .001$ and $\chi^2 = 9.62$, $p < .001$, respectively). The detection of meprobamate subjects, in contrast, was not significant. Most meprobamate subjects were mistakenly classified as truthful with no significant discrimination between meprobamate and innocent groups. The meprobamate group did differ significantly from both the no-countermeasure and placebo groups ($p < .04$ and $p < .01$, respectively) by Fisher's exact probability test.

Finally, the examiner's judgment of whether a subject had received a tranquilizer did not approach significant accuracy. This is not to say that no effects of meprobamate on overt behavior can be observed. Clinicians' ratings of patients discriminate between placebo and tranquilized conditions, but this occurs under conditions where each patient has been observed over a considerable period of time under numerous situations and with repeated drug administrations. The polygraph examiner, in contrast, has little or no previous experience with his

TABLE IV

NUMBER OF SUBJECTS CLASSIFIED AS DECEPTION INDICATED (DI) OR NO DECEPTION INDICATED
(NDI) FOR EACH PHYSIOLOGICAL MEASURE AND OPERATOR'S JUDGMENT OF SUBJECTS AS
TRANQUILIZED (T) OR NOT TRANQUILIZED (NT)[a]

	EDR		Cardio		Breath amplitude		Drug judgment	
	DI	NDI	DI	NDI	DI	NDI	T	NT
Innocent	0	11	1	10	1	10	2	9
Guilty, no counter-measure	9	2	0	11	4	7	5	6
Guilty, placebo	8	3	2	9	3	8	3	8
Guilty, mepro-bamate	3	8	0	11	5	6	0	11

[a]From Waid *et al.* (1981a).

subject to provide some baseline for judging whether the subject has taken a single dose of a tranquilizer (Waid *et al.*, 1981a).

These results challenge the widely held view among polygraph examiners that tranquilizers might depress responsivity uniformly but would not reduce the differential response leading to detection, as well as the view that tranquilized subjects can be recognized. On the contrary, such drugs may pose a serious threat to the detection of deception by means of the polygraph.

2. Self-Hypnosis

Sarbin and Slagle (1979) have reviewed the psychophysiological effects of hypnosis. No effects specific to hypnosis have been observed, but it provides a convenient way of inducing deep relaxation as indicated by sharp declines in skin conductance levels (Morse, Martin, Furst, & Dubin, 1977). A study was designed to test whether such a procedure might reduce the likelihood of detection. A polygraph test was given to 87 male college students under conditions similar to those already described (Waid & Orne, 1980). Of these subjects, 34 were nondeceptive, and 53 were attempting deception. A group of highly hypnotizable individuals ($N = 13$) was included in this latter group and trained, over the course of several sessions, to achieve deep relaxation through self-hypnosis. They were then asked to use this training to help them remain relaxed and escape detection on a polygraph test.

Deceptive subjects were significantly discriminated from nondeceptive subjects, as in earlier studies. Among deceptive subjects, however, those using hypnosis were detected as easily as those with no countermeasure. This lack of effect on the physiological response to deception occurred despite a significant effect of hypnosis on subjective state. The State Anxiety Scale of the State/Trait Anxiety Scale (Spielberger, Gorsuch, & Lushene, 1970) was administered at several points during the session. The three groups did not differ overall in their state anxiety scores, but the effect of trials was highly significant (reflecting an increase in anxiety up to and just after the polygraph test, followed by a subsequent decline), and the interaction between group and trial was also significant. Comparisons of individual means indicated that the self-hypnosis subjects were significantly less anxious than the no-countermeasure guilty subjects on arrival and at all three trials following the polygraph test but did not differ significantly from the no-countermeasure subjects on the two trials immediately preceding the test, though the differences were similar to other trials.

This pattern of results suggests that the practice of self-hypnosis provided some reduction in the state anxiety evoked by the general context of the polygraph test but that it was insufficient to reduce the physiological response to specific stimuli.

Corcoran, Lewis, and Garver (1978) have also examined the effects of hypnotic suppression of arousal on detection. In addition, they examined the effects of biofeedback training in suppressing EDR. Both hypnosis and biofeedback groups showed significant declines in detectability from pre- to posttraining tests, whereas a control group showed no significant decline. While these results are of some practical significance, it is not clear whether the effects are specific to training or are a placebo effect. The control group had no contact with the laboratory in the four weeks between pre- and posttraining tests, whereas the other two groups returned several times for training. Rovner, Raskin, and Kircher (1979) have reported that subjects who received extensive information about the nature of lie detection and were given two practice tests were later detected significantly less than the subjects receiving neither. The effects in Corcoran *et al.* may be due to similar nonspecific, but practically important, factors of experience with the polygraph setting. It is particularly unlikely that these results were due to hypnosis per se since the subjects were not selected for hypnotizability. Effects obtained in an unselected sample, with no control group for comparison, cannot be attributed to hypnosis per se.

D. PERSONALITY AND INDIVIDUAL DIFFERENCES

Another class of variables that is also likely to influence differential responsivity—attributes of the subject such as personality—was, for many years, less thoroughly investigated than the cognitive and behavioral components. (Barland & Raskin, 1973; Orne *et al.*, 1972).

1. Level of Socialization

One personality construct of particular interest, both on the basis of face validity and because of relevant prior work, is socialization. Poorly socialized individuals are characterized by tendencies toward impulsivity, lack of restraint, superficial interpersonal relationships, and a history of interpersonal conflict despite normal intelligence, good superficial social skills, and an absence of neuroticism and social anxiety (Gough, 1960). The behavior pattern of poorly socialized individuals suggests that deception is not unusual for them, and that they might be less aroused while attempting deception and, consequently, less easily detected.

From an empirical perspective, the potential importance of individual differences in socialization is underlined by the finding of Waid (1976) that college students scoring low on the socialization scale (Gough, 1964) of the California Psychological Inventory (CPI) gave smaller electrodermal responses (EDRs) to noxious bursts of noise than did subjects scoring high on socialization. The high and low groups did not differ, however, in the amplitude of the EDR to innocuous 68-dB tones, indicating that the low-socialization subjects were characterized by a reduced SCR specifically to noxious stimuli rather than by a generalized reduction of electrodermal responsivity. Similar findings have been reported for the related construct of psychopathy. Hare (1978) has reviewed the many studies wherein prison inmates diagnosed as psychopathic are found to give smaller EDRs than either nonpsychopathic prisoners or nonprisoner control subjects both in anticipation and in response to noxious stimuli.

The reduced differential electrodermal responsivity of low-socialization subjects strongly suggests the relevance of socialization to the detection of deception since the latter depends precisely on a differentially large response to relevant as opposed to control questions.

To investigate this hypothesis, we asked 15 college students to attempt to deceive a professional polygraph examiner, while 15 others who had nothing to hide also submitted to the examination (Waid et al., 1979b). The examiner was blind as to the deceptive or truthful condition of the subjects. On the basis of the EDR, significant discrimination was made between deceptive and truthful subjects with both guilty person and guilty knowledge polygraph tests. On both types of test, however, subjects who were not detected were significantly less socialized than those who were detected. The reduced susceptibility to detection was mediated by a reduced EDR to deception among low-socialization subjects. Among innocent subjects, the highly socialized were more responsive electrodermally throughout the test, leading some of them to be misclassified as deceptive on at least one test.

It appears that the relatively poorly socialized individual is less likely to be detected by his differential EDR while deceiving than is his highly socialized counterpart. A highly socialized, innocent subject, on the other hand, may, due to his greater overall electrodermal responsivity in the situation, be more likely to be misjudged as deceptive than his less socialized counterpart. Although the effect of socialization might not be the same with cardiovascular or respiratory measures, it should be noted that the skin conductance response has been found to be the most accurate indicator of deception both in the laboratory (Barland & Raskin, 1975; Cutrow, Parks, Lucas, & Thomas, 1972; Thackray & Orne, 1968b) and in one field study which focused on this issue (Barland, 1975). Whether the relationship between socialization and detection would manifest itself in most field settings, however, can be determined only by further research.

The context of a lie detector test is a highly structured one in which the subject's attention is specifically focused on the fact that his "involuntary" responses are being scrutinized. Consequently, it is legitimate to ask whether the reported differences in skin conductance between high- and low-socialization subjects would be found to accompany deception when the subject is unaware that his responses are under scrutiny.

It may be that when the poorly socialized individual is aware that his physiological responses are being scrutinized he exerts more control over his responsivity. Thus, in the unaware condition, he might be just as responsive as the more highly socialized person. On the other hand, it may be that the highly socialized subject is inordinately aroused by the awareness that his responses are being scrutinized. In the unaware condition, he might be just as hyporesponsive as the undersocialized subject.

Alternatively, awareness may not have such differential effects. That is, highly socialized subjects may be markedly aroused and low-socialization subjects little aroused by deception regardless of their awareness of physiological monitoring. (As described above, several studies have found almost equal detection of deception, using the EDR, under aware and unaware conditions.) To examine this question, we (Waid et al., 1979a) had 15 subjects attempt to deceive a polygraph examiner both before (unaware) and during (aware) a polygraph test. Fifteen other subjects made truthful denials to the examiner's questions. Postexperimental inquiry revealed no indications that subjects in the unaware condition knew that any physiological recording took place. Under both aware and unaware conditions, high-socialization subjects gave larger EDRs when deceiving than did low-socialization subjects. They also gave larger EDRs than low-socialization subjects when disclosing significant personal information but did not differ electrodermally when answering routine information questions during a pretest interview (unaware).

In summary, highly socialized subjects gave significantly larger SCRs than their poorly socialized counterparts to deception, self-disclosure, and a variety of intrusive interview questions. Since subjects were apparently unaware that physiological monitoring was taking place, it appears that neither the reduced response of poorly socialized subjects nor the correspondingly augmented response of highly socialized subjects are the result of awareness of being monitored.

2. Autonomic Lability and the Detection of Deception

The autonomic processes monitored during the polygraph test are themselves subject to individual differences and might exert a more direct influence on the outcome of the testing than traits indexed by questionnaire.

The extremely high intraindividual, day-to-day variability in autonomic responses reported by some investigators (Wieland & Mefford, 1970) previously may have made it seem unnecessary to examine the effects of individual differences in autonomic functioning. One particular aspect of autonomic functioning, however, has emerged as a relatively stable characteristic of the person: electrodermal lability (Crider & Lunn, 1971; Lacey & Lacey, 1958). This characteristic of the individual is defined by the frequency with which EDRs occur, either spontaneously or to a series of simple stimuli such as tones (Crider & Lunn, 1971). Although situational factors such as threat (Katkin, 1965, 1966) or task performance (O'Gorman & Horneman, 1979) may increase the frequency of response, individuals tend to maintain their rank on the lability dimension across situations (O'Gorman & Horneman, 1979).

Since the EDR is the most accurate measure in the detection of deception, it seemed important to investigate the role of electrodermal lability as a potential moderator of detection. Intuitively, it would seem that a person who generally tends to give few EDRs spontaneously would be less likely to respond appropriately during the test, even though deceptive, and thus would be less vulnerable to detection than his more labile counterpart. We tested this hypothesis (Waid & Orne, 1980) in studies similar to those previously described. In the first of two studies, volunteer subjects took a guilty knowledge test. The number of nonspecific EDRs occurring between questions was significantly positively correlated with the number of critical items detected.

A second study was conducted to test the reproducibility of the findings and to test their generalizability to the type of polygraph test more frequently used in field settings, the guilty person, or lie detection test. In addition, the rate of nonspecific electrodermal responding was assessed in a manner permitting the correlation of detections with lability independent of the lie detection test itself. The results of the guilty knowledge tests in the second study replicated those of the first quite closely. Guilty subjects again had significantly more detections than innocent subjects but did not differ significantly from them in number of nonspecific EDRs during rest periods.

Similar results were obtained with the guilty person tests. Again, the more labile the subject, whether innocent or guilty, the more questions on which he was detected as deceptive, though the effect was attenuated in comparison with the guilty knowledge tests. Again, using the number of nonspecific EDRs between questions yielded similar results. Finally, it is important to note that the "stabile" subjects were not simply nonresponders electrodermally. No subject failed to give several EDRs at some point in the experiment.

Although the use of cardiovascular and respiratory along with electrodermal measures might be hypothesized to reduce this tendency, the accuracy of these measures has been consistently reported to be substantially less than that of the EDR (Barland, 1975; Barland & Raskin, 1975; Cutrow *et al.*, 1972; Thackray & Orne, 1968b). Further, the effect on these measures of the subject's lability, whether electrodermal, cardiovascular, or respiratory, is unknown but might be similar to the effect of electrodermal lability on electrodermal detection of deception.

A study was designed to determine whether electrodermal lability assessed independently of the polygraph examination relates to likelihood of detection (Waid, Wilson, & Orne, 1981d). Number of nonspecific electrodermal responses during a Day 1 rest period were scored and subjects split into labiles (ten or more nonspecific responses in the 3-min period) and stabiles (two or fewer responses). The number of questions detected on three guilty person tests on each measure are presented in Table V for the 12 labile guilty, 12 stabile guilty, 11 labile innocent, and 11 stabile innocent subjects. Consistent with the findings for the entire sample of 40 guilty and 34 innocent subjects, the effect of guilt on number of detections was highly significant across all three channels [$F(1,40) = 21.50$, $p < .001$]. The effect of lability was also highly significant [$F(1,40) = 13.90$, $p < .001$], and there was no interaction with guilt. That is, labile subjects tended to have more questions detected, that is, respond more to critical than to control

TABLE V
NUMBER OF RELEVANT QUESTIONS EVOKING LARGER
RESPONSES THAN ADJACENT CONTROL QUESTION FOR
THREE PHYSIOLOGICAL MEASURES AS A FUNCTION OF
GUILT AND ELECTRODERMAL LABILITY[a]

Group	Measure	Labile	Stabile
Guilty	SCR	8.00	6.08
	Blood		
	pressure	6.92	6.33
	Respiration	8.25	5.75
Innocent	SCR	3.30	3.20
	Blood		
	pressure	6.80	3.70
	Respiration	6.80	4.60

[a]From Waid *et al.* (1981d).

questions, than their stabile counterparts, whether guilty or innocent. Although the differences between labiles and stabiles were greater for skin conductance and respiration in comparison with blood pressure among guilties and for respiration and blood pressure in comparison with skin conductance among innocents, there were no significant interactions between lability and channel nor among lability, guilt, and channel.

We performed similar analyses for the same groups in the guilty knowledge test. Although guilty subjects were detected more than innocent subjects $[F(1,40) = 9.79, p < .01]$, the differences were not as dramatic as in the preceding guilty person tests. There was no effect of lability $[F(1,40) = 1.04$, not significant], but the interaction between guilt–innocence and measure was significant $[F(2,80) = 6.93, p < .01]$. This significant interaction reflects the fact that there was better discrimination between guilty and innocent subjects with skin conductance than respiratory or blood pressure measures.

A comparison of the two types of test indicates that labile subjects show a decline in the number of detections from guilty person to the later guilty knowledge tests, whereas stabile subjects remain at approximately the same low rate of detection throughout.

Few other individual-difference variables have been examined in the context of the physiological verification of testimony. Most studies have used sample sizes that would be considered too small to permit the emergence of any effect of individual differences even if such measures had been obtained. McCarron (1973) found subjects scoring high on a depression scale to be less responsive physiologically during a guilty knowledge polygraph test. No measures of detectability per se were reported. Ingersoll (1977) and Giesen and Rollison (1980) have reported results consistent with the present ones using different measures of antisocial tendencies. Raskin and Hare (1978), however, found no effects of either clinical diagnoses of sociopathy nor of the Socialization Scale in a prison sample. Lykken (1978) has discussed a number of problems with that study which may explain why no effects were obtained.

E. SOCIAL PSYCHOLOGICAL FACTORS

By its very nature, lying is a social phenomenon. Shapiro and Crider (1969) and Schwartz and Shapiro (1973) have reviewed other social processes that affect physiological responses, some of which might modulate, facilitate, or interfere with the physiological response accompanying deception. Ironically, the explicitly social variables influencing the physiological changes accompanying deception have been the subject of little explicit research. The behavioral and cognitive components of the interaction between examiner and subject discussed earlier have their basis in social relationships, but those relationships have not been systematically explored.

Given the social interactive nature of the polygraph situation, several social variables may modulate the subject's physiological responses. The relative social status of examiner and subject, for example, might well affect responses, particularly in the case of innocent subjects. A falsely accused bank teller might react somewhat differently to questioning by a middle-aged professional examiner than would a falsely accused senator, physician, or attorney. Other social variables that might be likely to affect physiological responses during the polygraph test are ethnic, sex, and age mismatches between examiner and subject. Another sort of social variable, however, led to some interesting results as we investigated an intriguing applied problem.

1. Detection of Deception in Small Groups

Traditionally, of course, polygraph tests are administered to individual subjects, though in many situations there are several suspects, all of whom may take polygraph tests individually. Orne and Thackray (1967), however, suggested the possible advantages of a group polygraph test under certain circumstances. The physiological detection of information, rather than or in addition to guilt, may be an important objective in some contexts (e.g., Kupperman & Trent, 1979). An efficient way to enhance information detection might be available if a number of individuals are withholding the same critical information. One might then average physiological responses across subjects in a manner analogous to the intrasubject average evoked response which is used to enhance otherwise indiscriminable EEG responses to stimulation (Shagass, 1972). The probability of detection achieved in this way might be greater than would be attainable by scoring detections for subjects individually and then attempting to identify the shared information.

Orne and Thackray (1967) used an electronic technique to average the electrodermal response (EDR) across subjects examined in groups. Groups of six or seven deceptive subjects were perfectly discriminated from groups of six or seven nondeceptive subjects on the basis of the group EDR, whereas there was substantial overlap of individual deceptive and individual truthful subjects when the individual subjects' responses were used as the unit of analysis. These results suggest that a group polygraph test might have practical value in field situations in which it is known that a group of individuals share information they are unwilling to divulge. However, Orne and Thackray (1967) did not document an actual increment in information detection as a function of grouping the physiological responses of several deceptive individuals nor as a function of the number of deceptive individuals, confining their study to the discrimination between deceptive and nondeceptive groups in comparison with the discrimination between deceptive and nondeceptive individuals. A subsequent study examined whether the group average evoked physiological response increases information detection beyond that obtained by analyzing the information detection scores of the same individuals. A second purpose was to examine whether the amount of information detected is a positive function of the number of deceptive individuals whose physiological responses make up the group response.

Although we hypothesized that the physiological detection of information would be sharper with a group physiological response rather than with individual responses, other lines of research in social psychophysiology suggested that the physiological detection of individual deceptive subjects would be reduced in a group context. Other social stimuli which increase autonomic arousal similarly to deception are modulated by the broader social context in which they occur. For example, subjects who were frustrated by working on what were actually, unbeknownst to them, insoluble problems showed an increase in arousal, as indexed by skin conductance (Kissel, 1965). The increase in skin conductance during this period was less, however, among subjects who were tested with another subject present and significantly less when the other subject was an acquaintance. Kissel's results suggest that in a detection of deception test the presence of others who are in the same predicament might reduce the arousal evoked in the individual by the test questions.

Research on social facilitation (Zajonc, 1965), in contrast, might suggest that the presence of similar others, that is, coactors, would result in enhanced physiological responses. Geen (1977) has discussed the complex effects of the presence of others on physiological responses. Suffice it to say that the presence of other people enhances physiological activity when the context itself is not very arousing physiologically or when the other people may be perceived as competing with or evaluating the subject. In the context of the group polygraph test we described, this is not the case, although it might be possible to structure the procedure to involve competition.

To summarize, it was first hypothesized that raw physiological data grouped from several deceptive subjects would lead to a greater amount of information detection than would the averaged detections of the separate individuals in the groups. Second, it was hypothesized that the amount of information detected would increase as a function of the number of deceptive individuals combined but that, paradoxically, the greater the number of deceptive individuals tested together, the less the individual's physiological response to deception due to the stress-reducing properties of the presence of others in the same predicament. The study was carried out similarly to those already described. There were 74 subjects who attempted to conceal information from a polygraph operator in a guilty knowledge polygraph test and 74 other subjects who had nothing to hide and attempted to prove their truthfulness to the operator, who was blind to each subject's condition. Each polygraph session consisted of a small ($N = 1$–2), medium ($N = 3$), or large ($N = 4$–7) deceptive group and a small, medium, or large truthful group. Further, computer synthesis was used to partition GSRs into groups ranging from 1 to 25 subjects in size.

To assess the effect of combining the electrodermal responses of members of groups of guilty or innocent subjects, the mean rate of detection per group, using the mean number of detections of the individuals in the group, was compared with the mean number of detections per group using the group EDR to each question.

Guilty groups had more detections than innocent groups [$F(1,42) = 52.6$, $p < .0001$], and more detections were obtained with the grouped EDR than with the average of individual detections in both guilty and innocent groups [$F(1,42) = 53.4$, $p < .0001$]. Among innocent groups, however, the mean number of detections remained below chance levels with either scoring method whereas, among guilty groups, number of detections remained significantly above chance levels with either method.

Within the range of actual group sizes in the present study, there was no significant effect of group size on number of detections per group using the grouped EDR. As described below, however, this was partially due to the depressing effect of large groups on individual group members' detections. When the range of group sizes was expanded and the effects of actual group size on individual detections reduced, by combining subjects from different groups via computer synthesis, significant effects emerged. The amount of information detected was a positive function of group size when all members of the synthesized groups were deceptive. Pearson's r between number of guilty persons in the synthesized group and number of items detected was $r(16) = .69$, $p < .01$, for the 18 synthesized groups with no innocent subjects included.

As expected, no orderly relationship obtained between the number of subjects in the group and frequency of detection when groups containing only innocent subjects were synthesized, and there were no significant differences between group sizes. This result confirms that pooling individuals, even if they are not deceptive, does not adventitiously lead to false detections.

Table VI presents the mean number of detections of individual subjects in small, medium, and large groups in guilty or innocent conditions. The mean number of detections among guilty and innocent groups was significantly related to group size—the smaller the group, the greater the number of detections [$F(2, 144) = 4.41$, $p < .025$]. Comparisons of individual means indicated that this effect was due more to the difference between small and large guilty groups ($p < .05$) than to that between small and large innocent groups ($p < .10$).

Since small guilty group subjects were detected more frequently than the medium and large guilty group subjects, they might be expected to give larger EDRs to the relevant words, relative to the control words, than the remaining groups. Among innocent subjects, however, such should not be the case, since they had no knowledge of which words were relevant. Consistent with this view, among guilty subjects, those in small groups showed a significantly larger EDR difference score than those in the medium and large groups [$t(72) = 1.73$, p

TABLE VI

MEAN NUMBER OF DETECTIONS OF INDIVIDUAL
SUBJECTS AS A FUNCTION OF CONDITION AND GROUP
SIZE

	Group size		
Condition	Small	Medium	Large
Guilty	8.36	6.26	6.19
($N = 74$)			
Innocent	3.18	2.33	1.95
($N = 74$)			

$< .05$], whereas there were no such differences among innocent subjects. The somewhat greater frequency of false detections among small innocent group subjects than among large innocent group subjects could be mediated by a tendency to continue responding, that is, by a failure to habituate, among the presumably more aroused small innocent group subjects. Consistent with this view, innocent subjects in small groups gave more EDRs to stimuli than did those in the other groups [$t(72) = 2.40$, $p < .01$]. Among guilty subjects there was no effect of group size on number of EDRs to stimuli.

Frequency of nonspecific EDRs was positively correlated with number of detections among both guilty [$r(72) = .27$, $p < .01$] and innocent [$r(72) = .50$, $p < .00005$] subjects, consistent with previous findings (Waid & Orne, 1980). This relationship did not mediate the effects of group size, however, since there was no difference among groups in nonspecific EDRs [$F(2, 142) = .05$] nor between guilty and innocent conditions [$F(1, 142) = .01$]. The latter finding is also consistent with previous findings (Waid & Orne, 1980) that subjects who are attempting to convince a polygraph examiner that they are, indeed, telling the truth are just as aroused, as indexed by nonspecific EDRs, as are subjects who are attempting deception. Tonic skin resistance level was not significantly related to number of detections among either guilty or innocent subjects.

On the postexperimental self-report measures, no subject alluded to groups, the number of people lying, or collaboration in response to any of the three questions concerning the purpose of the experiment and strategies for avoiding detection. Although collaboration or other group supports would not be frequently expected answers, it is nonetheless striking that out of 74 subjects, most of whom were run with at least one collaborator, no subject mentioned group support or presence as a possible aid in avoiding detection or as a possible purpose of the experiment. Few subjects reported friends among the members of their groups, and the presence of these few acquaintances was unrelated to group size. Thus, the effects of group size on individual responses could not have been mediated by the fortuitous presence of more friends in the large groups.

In summary, the identification of guilty knowledge was facilitated by combining several individuals' physiological responses into composite, group physiological responses to the polygraph test questions and then identifying items associated with deception. Computer synthesis of "groups" of up to 20 guilty subjects indicated that the amount of information detected is a positive function of group size. Paradoxically, however, the present results also indicate that the individual subjects' physiological responses in the lie detection test are reduced by the presence of similar others.

In a broader sense, these results confirm that social factors other than the subject's deception itself may modulate the physiological responses given in this setting. Although polygraph tests are not ordinarily given in groups, it might be hypothesized, as an extension of the present results, that in the case of a group act of violence or robbery, for example, individual suspects, even if tested alone, might, due to diffusion of responsibility for the crime, whether conscious or otherwise, be less detectable than the typical lie detection suspect accused of an individual act of illegal behavior. Conversely, an innocent person who is the only known suspect in a case might be more aroused in the polygraph test than an innocent subject who knows he is only one among several being tested. Other, less subtle social factors might also affect the polygraph test. The possibility that the race or ethnicity of polygraph examiner and subject might interact, for example, has never been systematically examined.

2. Ethnic Differences and Physiological Response to Stress

Studies in Israel (Kugelmass & Lieblich, 1968), the United States (Sternback & Tursky, 1965), and Japan (Lazarus, 1966) suggest that there are ethnic differences in physiological responses to stress. Such differences might well affect the detection of deception.

Research on the psychophysiological response to cross-racial stimuli suggests that a subject might be more responsive physiologically when examiner and subject differ ethnically (e.g., Rankin & Campbell, 1955; Kugelmass & Lieblich, 1968). Such increased responsivity might increase the likelihood of detection if the subject is deceptive but might also increase the likelihood of a false positive if the subject is truthful (Waid & Orne, 1980). Analogous cross-racial effects have been demonstrated in other psycholegal areas such as eyewitness testimony or person identification (Brigham & Barkowitz, 1978; Malpass & Kravitz, 1969).

These studies prompted us to examine the effects of ethnic differences in our investigations. As a retrospective index of ethnic origin, we used subjects' surnames, classifying them on the basis of their appearance in a standard onomastic reference work (Smith, 1973). Although this index does not take into account the mother's ethnic heritage or the subject's ethnic identity, if any, it has the virtue of objectivity. The ethnic classifications we were able to compare, among subjects all of whom were drawn from native-born American college students, were English, German, Irish, Italian, Jewish, and Scottish. To test for differences in the physiological response to social stress, we compared the skin conductance responses of these groups to a mildly intrusive biographical interview similar to that described earlier (Waid *et al.*, 1979a). We also tested whether any such ethnic differences would emerge specifically to deception in a polygraph test.

The polygraph examiner in two recent studies was a former police captain of Irish heritage. The sessions were carried out as in Waid *et al.* (1981). The mean EDR to selected groups of biographical interview questions was computed as in Waid *et al.* (1979a). The salient fact in these data was that the Irish group gave significantly smaller EDRs than did the remaining ethnic groups. With separation into seven different ethnic groups, insufficient numbers of guilty and innocent subjects were available in each to make a reasonable examination of the effects of ethnicity on the control questions test results. Since subjects in both studies had also been given a stimulation test in which all subjects attempted deception, these data were examined. The number of detections could range from zero to two on this test. The results lent further support to the interethnicity effect. The overall effect of group was significant, and the Irish subjects had the lowest number of detections of any of the groups.

Consistent with other social psychophysiological studies (e.g., Rankin & Campbell, 1955; Porier & Lott, 1967), these data suggest that—at least in the context of a dyadic interaction—people are somewhat less aroused physiologically by an individual of their own ethnic background than by a person of a different ethnic background. Such results might derive from interethnic prejudices but, particularly with the exclusively Western European origins of the ethnic group studies here, would seem more likely due to subtle differences in interactional style, for example, nonverbal characteristics of ethnic groups, different accents, etc. Aside from any ethnic stereotypes or prejudices to which subjects might respond, people of the same ethnic background would experience little if any novelty in social interaction with a conethnic. People of different ethnic backgrounds, in contrast, at least during a fairly formalized dyadic situation such as the polygraph test, might react, probably unconsciously, to subtle differences in proximity, gestural, visual, vocal, and paralinguistic (e.g., accent) behavior.

3. Family Configuration

Another social factor which several studies (e.g., Gerard & Rabbie, 1961; Stotland, Sherman, & Shaver, 1971) prompted us to examine is family configuration. Similarly to ethnicity, birth order and family size are relatively objectively assessed socioecological variables which appear to predispose the individual to characteristic behavior patterns.

Research on the effects of family configuration on later social behavior has revealed two important, broad categories of effect. Firstborns show greater tendencies toward dependency and conformity in experimental studies than do later borns (Warren, 1966), and archival studies indicate that individuals from large families may be more vulnerable to delinquency (e.g., Galle, Gove, & McPherson, 1972; Rahav, 1980). These effects of family configuration on conformity and social conduct are particularly relevant to understanding the detection of deception. If placed in a situation in which they must lie, people who are normally highly conforming (e.g., first borns) might be more aroused physiologically by lying than others (i.e., later borns). Family size might be expected to exert similar effects.

The procedures used to examine this question (Waid, Orne, & Orne, in preparation) were similar to previously described studies. Birth order and family size were of course highly correlated [$r(13) = .78$, $p < .001$], and selecting on the basis of either family size or birth order revealed significant effects. Among 15 guilty subjects, the 7 firstborn subjects gave a larger EDR to relevant than control questions on 4.6 pairs, whereas the 8 later borns did so on only 2.9 pairs [$t(14) = 1.95$, $p < .05$]. Similarly, the 6 subjects from families with 2 or fewer children were detected on a mean of 4.7 relevant/control question pairs whereas those from larger families were detected on only 3.0 pairs [$t(14) = 1.95$, $p < .05$]. (There was 1 only child in the sample, and he was detected on 6 relevant questions.) Family configuration variables had no effect on the response of innocent ($n = 15$) subjects. Neither family configuration variable was significantly related to age, Socialization Scale score, electrodermal lability, or other measures previously found to affect the EDR to deception. Although family size relates to delinquency in large archival samples, it may do so via mechanisms other than the personality processes reflected in the Socialization Scale.

Future research may seek to isolate the independent effects of birth order and family size, as well as seek to understand how they lead to such effects on the physiological response to deception. Regardless, the present results indicate that individual differences stemming from some complex of family configuration variables may affect the physiological detection of deception.

In summary, several social psychological factors, including ethnicity of subject and examiner, family configuration, and the presence of several others attempting deception affected physiological response during the detection of deception. A recent study (Timm, 1979) provides further indication that social psychological factors such as those we have examined may play a role in the physiological response to deception. In a large sample ($n = 270$), Timm (1979) found that subjects who were regular churchgoers were detected significantly more frequently than those who were not. In addition, subjects who indicated that their friends would be impressed to learn that they had "defeated the poly-graph" were detected significantly less frequently than those who did not so indicate. These findings suggest that the physiological reaction accompanying deception may be enhanced or depressed by regular association with a group that is unsupportive or supportive, respectively, of conduct such as deception.

III. Summary and Conclusions

The objective of the research reviewed here differs from that of most re-search on the physiological detection of deception. Most studies have sought to demonstrate the unique advantages of one type of questioning or another (e.g., Lykken, 1959, 1960, 1974; Barland & Raskin, 1975) or to demonstrate the superiority of one or another physiological measure or combination of measures (Podlesny & Raskin, 1977). The purpose of this article, in contrast, has been to examine the underlying cognitive, social, and personality processes that affect the physiological response to deception regardless of psychometric approach or the precise physiological measure used. Understanding how such processes con-tribute to the physiological response accompanying deception may help clarify the more general problem of the nature of the relationship between physiological and social psychological processes as well as suggest methods for the enhance-ment of polygraph test accuracy in applied settings.

To summarize, initial studies examined the behavioral and cognitive com-ponents of the interaction between examiner and subject that result in accurate testing. It was found that several processes independently enhance the physiolog-ical response to otherwise innocuous stimuli. The attempt to deceive, apart from any verbal act of deception or inherently arousing content of the questions, is sufficient to produce considerable physiological response to relevant as opposed to control questions. These other two factors, however, the verbal act of decep-tion and any inherently arousing content of the questions, also independently produced increased physiological response. It was further observed that the at-tempt to deceive (in its everyday sense, as opposed to the attempt to escape physiological detection) was also sufficient to produce enhanced physiological response to relevant questions. Further, while detection was possible even when subjects were unaware of being recorded, results across three separate studies indicated that the awareness of physiological recording appears to additionally augment the physiological response to relevant questions.

Knowledge of the results of an initial test affected the physiological re-sponse to a subsequent test. If a subject who was motivated to escape detection was led to believe he had been detected on the initial test, he continued to be responsive and to be detected on a subsequent test. If, on the other hand, he believed that he had not been detected (regardless of the actual outcome) on the initial test, he subsequently became significantly less responsive and tended to escape detection.

Attention to the test items, as indexed by subsequent recall, was shown to play an important role in the subject's physiological response. Subjects who were less attentive to relevant questions than to control questions, at least as assessed by later memory, tended to escape detection in comparison with subjects who were more attentive to relevant than to control questions. These results suggest the possible utility of unobtrusive cognitive countermeasures in escaping detection.

The effects of several other processes that might block the physiological response to deception were examined directly. A minor tranquilizer was found to reduce the likelihood of detection on a guilty knowledge test. Self-hypnosis, in contrast, appeared to have no effect on physiological response and detection even though it did reduce subjective anxiety somewhat. Since experience with the polygraph setting has been shown to reduce detectability (Rovner *et al.*, 1979), a study which ostensibly discovered effects of both hypnosis and biofeedback was interpreted as being accounted for by nonspecific, but nonetheless practically important, factors of experience with the polygraph setting.

Two individual difference variables have been found to be of fundamental importance in the detection of deception. The higher the subject's level of socialization (i.e., the lower his antisocial tendencies), the more likely he was to give larger EDRs to relevant than to control questions, whether actually deceptive or not. Similar results have been reported by other investigators using different, but conceptually related, scales (Giesen & Rollison, 1980; Ingersoll, 1977). A study by Raskin and Hare (1978) suggests that higher levels of consequences for detection may lessen the effect of this personality dimension.

The greater a subject's resting autonomic lability, as indexed by frequency of nonspecific EDRs, the more detectable he is during the polygraph test on all three commonly used physiological measures—electrodermal, cardiovascular, and respiratory. Thus, the highly "labile" innocent subject may be at some jeopardy of appearing deceptive on the polygraph test, particularly the lie control test.

Several broad social psychological factors were found to affect physiological responding. Subjects were less responsive electrodermally during the polygraph test, whether attempting deception or making truthful denials, if they were accompanied by several other people doing the same thing, if they were of the same ethnic background as the polygraph examiner, and if they were later- as opposed to firstborn. In light of such results, the possible effects of other social psychological variables should be of some concern. Mismatches between subject and examiner in race, age, sex, and social class or status might affect the examiner's demeanor and the subject's physiological response.

It is worth noting the implications of some of these findings for social psychophysiology in general. The effects of socialization and electrodermal lability, for example, underline the importance of individual differences in modulating the physiological response to social stimuli. It is unlikely that the effects of these factors are confined to the context of deception. Poorly socialized individuals may well be less responsive physiologically in a number of critical social settings (see, e.g., House & Milligan, 1976), and this reduced responsivity may contribute to their insensitivity to social responsibilities. Electrodermally labile young adults may be more reactive physiologically to social stress in general. Whether this tendency leads to vulnerability to subsequent stress-related disorders is being investigated.

A methodological, but quite real, criticism of social psychophysiological research is that little is known about the effect that the process of measurement may have on the psychophysiological systems under observation. Thus, it is encouraging for social psychophysiological research that even when a subject is unaware that his responses are under scrutiny, social behavior such as deception evokes physiological arousal similar to that when the recording procedures are highly salient. It seems likely, therefore, that other types of social processes of interest to social psychophysiologists are not unduly affected by the measurement process.

From an applied perspective, it appears that tranquilizers may represent an effective countermeasure to the detection of deception. From a more general perspective, however, this finding provides badly needed support (McNair, 1973) at the physiological level that a minor tranquilizer is effective in reducing the reaction to interpersonal stress without generally impairing social interaction. Such effects are probably not confined to the stress of deception.

Finally, both cognitive and social psychologists have shown increased awareness of the importance of memory in social processes (Isen, Shalker, Clark, & Karp, 1978; Loftus, 1980). The findings of Waid et al. (1981b) indicate that physiological arousal may play a role in memory for social information. In sum, although we have focused on deception as the social behavior of interest, many of the cognitive, social, and personality effects we have described may well apply to the physiological response to other sorts of social interactions.

In conclusion, these findings indicate that the implicit conceptualization of the detection of deception as merely a kind of psychometric instrument, or as merely a psychophysiological technique, must be considerably revised. A more accurate and complete conceptualization must take into account the social nature of deception and its detection. The most significant factors affecting the physiological response accompanying deception appear to be social psychological, involving underlying cognitive, social, and personality processes.

Such findings indicate that the detection of deception is a complex matter rather than a "simple procedure," as it is often conceptualized (e.g., Barland & Raskin, 1973). Nonetheless, they do not support categorical indictments of the detection of deception (e.g., Lykken, 1974, 1981). Social psychological factors also affect subject behavior, self-report, and observer decisions in other areas of psychological assessment.

Schizophrenic patients respond differently to Minnesota Multiphasic Personality Inventory (MMPI) items (Braginsky, Grosse, & Ring, 1966; Ryan & Neale, 1973) and to a psychiatric interview (Braginsky & Braginsky, 1967) depending on the ostensible purpose of the assessment. Rosenhan (1973, 1975) has examined the contextual nature of psychiatric diagnosis of schizophrenia, observing that normal people faking only one symptom, the presence of hallucination, uniformly gained admission to mental hospitals and earned the diagnosis of paranoid schizophrenic. Despite such effects of social psychological context on psychological assessment, techniques such as the MMPI and psychiatric diagnostic categories are of course widely employed. The effort to update and improve such assessment techniques, making them less susceptible to such sources of error is, however, an essential and continual process.

Similar to these demonstrations that traditional psychological and psychiatric assessment techniques must be considered in the social context where they occur, our findings illustrate that the detection of deception is profoundly affected by a variety of social psychological influences. Analogous to traditional psychological techniques, the problems addressed by the detection of deception are endemic and its techniques somewhat effective, though imperfect. Thus, the use of the physiological detection of deception is likely to continue. It is to be hoped, however, that findings such as those reported here will lead to more realistic understanding of the complex processes by which physiological responses may serve to identify deception in different types of individuals and under varying conditions.

ACKNOWLEDGMENTS

The research reported here was supported in part by a grant from the Institute for Experimental Psychiatry.

We thank David F. Dinges, Frederick J. Evans, Alan S. Lert, Kevin M. McConkey, Emily Carota Orne, and William H. Putnam for their comments during the preparation of the manuscript.

REFERENCES

Abrams, S. The polygraph in a psychiatric setting. *American Journal of Psychiatry,* 1973, **130,** 94–97.

American Medical Association Department of Drugs, *American Medical Association Drug Evaluations,* p. 317. Acton, Massachusetts, Publishing Sciences Group, 1973.

Asch, S. E. Effects of group pressure on the modification and distortion of judgments. In H. Geutzkow (Ed.), *Groups, leadership, and men.* Pittsburgh, Pennsylvania: Carnegie, 1951.

Backster, C. Methods of strengthening our polygraph technique. *Police,* 1962, **6** (5), 61–68.

Barland, G. H. *Detection of deception in criminal suspects: A field validation study.* Doctoral dissertation, University of Utah, 1975.

Barland, G. H., & Raskin, D. C. Detection of deception. In W. F. Prokasy & D. C. Raskin (Eds.), *Electrodermal activity in psychological research.* New York: Academic Press, 1973.

Barland, G. H., & Raskin, D. C. An evaluation of field techniques in detection of deception. *Psychophysiology,* 1975, **12,** 321–330.

Ben-Shakhar, G. A further study of the dichotomization theory in detection of information. *Psychophysiology,* 1977, **14,** 408–413.

Ben-Shakhar, G., Lieblich, I., & Kugelmass, S. Guilty knowledge technique: Application of signal detection measures. *Journal of Applied Psychology,* 1970, **54,** 409–413.

Braginsky, B., & Braginsky, D. Schizophrenic patients in the psychiatric interview: An experimental study of their effectiveness at manipulation. *Journal of Consulting Psychology,* 1967, **31,** 453–457.

Braginsky, B., Grosse, M., & Ring, K. Controlling outcomes through impression management: An experimental study of the manipulative tactics of mental patients. *Journal of Consulting Psychology,* 1966, **30,** 295–300.

Brigham, J. C., & Barkowitz, P. Do "they all look alike?" The effect of race, sex, experience, and attitudes on the ability to recognize faces. *Journal of Applied Psychology,* 1978, **8,** 306–318.

Corcoran, J. F. T., Lewis, M. D., & Garver, R. B. Biofeedback-conditioned galvanic skin response and hypnotic suppression of arousal: A pilot study of their relation to deception. *Journal of Forensic Science,* 1978, **23,** 155–162.

Corteen, R. S. Skin conductance changes and word recall. *British Journal of Psychology,* 1969, **60,** 81–84.

Crider, A., & Lunn, R. Electrodermal lability as a personality dimension. *Journal of Experimental Research in Personality,* 1971, **5,** 145–150.

Cutrow, R. J., Parks, A., Lucas, N., & Thomas, K. The objective use of multiple physiological indices in the detection of deception. *Psychophysiology,* 1972, **9,** 578–588.

Davis, R. C. Physiological responses as a means of evaluating information. In A. D. Biderman & H. Zimmer (Eds.), *The manipulation of human behavior.* New York: Wiley, 1961.

Dawson, M. E. Physiological detection of deception: Measurement of responses to questions and answers during countermeasure maneuvers. *Psychophysiology,* 1980, **17,** 8–17.

DePaulo, B. M., & Rosenthal, R. Telling lies. *Journal of Personality and Social Psychology,* 1979, **37,** 1713–1722.

Ekman, P., & Friesen, W. V. Detecting deception from the body or face. *Journal of Personality and Social Psychology,* 1974, **29,** 288–298.

Galle, O. R., Gove, W. R., & McPherson, J. M. Population density and pathology: What are the relations for man? *Science,* 1972, **176,** 23–30.

Geen, R. G. The effects of anticipation of positive and negative outcomes on audience anxiety. *Journal of Consulting and Clinical Psychology,* 1977, **45,** 715–716.

Gerard, H. B., & Rabbie, J. M. Fear and social comparison. *Journal of Abnormal and Social Psychology,* 1961, **62,** 586–592.

Giesen, M., & Rollison, M. A. Guilty knowledge versus innocent associations: Effects of trait anxiety and stimulus context on skin conductance. *Journal of Research in Personality,* 1980, **14,** 1–11.

Gough, H. G. Theory and measurement of socialization. *Journal of Consulting Psychology,* 1960, **24,** 23–30.

Gough, H. G. *Manual for the California psychological inventory.* Palo Alto, California: Consulting Psychologists Press, 1964.

Gustafson, L. A., & Orne, M. T. Effects of heightened motivation on the detection of deception. *Journal of Applied Psychology,* 1963, **47,** 408–411.

Gustafson, L. A., & Orne, M. T. The effects of verbal responses on the laboratory detection of deception. *Psychophysiology,* 1965, **2,** 10-13. (a)

Gustafson, L. A., & Orne, M. T. The effects of perceived role and role success on the detection of deception. *Journal of Applied Psychology,* 1965, **49,** 412-417. (b)

Hare, R. D. Electrodermal and cardiovascular correlates of psychopathy. In R. D. Hare & D. Schalling (Eds.), *Psychopathic behavior: Approaches to research.* New York: Wiley, 1978.

Hirschman, R. D. Cross modal effects of anticipatory bogus heart rate feedback in a negative emotional context. *Journal of Personality and Social Psychology,* 1975, **31,** 13-19.

Holzman, P. S., Rousey, C., & Snyder, C. On listening to one's own voice: Effects on psychophysiological responses and free associations. *Journal of Personality and Social Psychology,* 1966, **4,** 432-441.

Horvath, F. S. Verbal and nonverbal clues to truth and deception during polygraph examinations. *Journal of Police Science and Administration,* 1973, **1,** (2), 138-152.

Horvath, F. S. *The accuracy and reliability of police polygraphic ("lie detector") examiners' judgements of truth and deception: The effect of selected variables.* Doctoral dissertation, Michigan State University, 1974. Ann Arbor, Michigan: University Microfilms, 1975. No. 14, 753.

Horvath, F. S. The effect of selected variables on interpretation of polygraph records. *Journal of Applied Psychology,* 1977, **62,** 127-136.

House, T. H., & Milligan, W. L. Autonomic responses to modeled distress in prison psychopaths. *Journal of Personality and Social Psychology,* 1976, **34,** 556-560.

Ingersoll, B. D. *Detection of deception in primary psychopaths.* Doctoral dissertation, The Pennsylvania State University, 1977. Ann Arbor, Michigan: University Microfilms, 1978. No. 78-8375.

Isen, A. M., Shalker, T. E., Clark, M., & Karp, L. Affect, accessibility of material in memory, and behavior: A cognitive loop? *Journal of Personality and Social Psychology,* 1978, **36,** 1-12.

Jung, C. G. Die psychologische Diagnose des Tatbestandes. *Juristisch-Psychiatrische Grezfragen,* 1906, **4,** 1-61.

Katkin, E. S. Relationship between manifest anxiety and two indices of autonomic response to stress. *Journal of Personality and Social Psychology,* 1965, **2,** 324-333.

Katkin, E. S. The relationship between a measure of transitory anxiety and spontaneous autonomic activity. *Journal of Abnormal Psychology,* 1966, **71,** 142-146.

Kissel, S. Stress-reducing properties of social stimuli. *Journal of Personality and Social Psychology,* 1965, **2,** 378-384.

Kraut, R. E. Verbal and nonverbal cues in the perception of lying. *Journal of Personality and Social Psychology,* 1978, **36,** 380-391.

Kugelmass, S., & Lieblich, I. The effects of realistic stress and procedural interference in experimental lie detection. *Journal of Applied Psychology,* 1966, **50,** 211-216.

Kugelmass, S., & Lieblich, I. The relation between ethnic origin and GSR reactivity in psychophysiological detection. *Journal of Applied Psychology,* 1968, **52,** 158-162.

Kugelmass, S., Lieblich, I., & Bergman, Z. The role of "lying" in psychophysiological detection. *Psychophysiology,* 1967, **3,** 312-315.

Kupperman, R., & Trent, D. *Terrorism, threat, reality, response.* Stanford, California: Hoover Institution Press, 1979.

Lacey, J. I., & Lacey, B. C. The relationship of resting autonomic activity to motor impulsivity. *Research Publications of the Association for Nervous and Mental Diseases,* 1958, **36,** 144-209.

Lazarus, R. S. *Psychological stress and the coping process.* New York: McGraw-Hill, 1966.

Lieblich, I., Kugelmass, S., & Ben Shakhar, G. Efficiency of GSR detection of information as a function of stimulus set size. *Psychophysiology,* 1970, **6,** 601-608.

Loftus, E. F. *Eyewitness testimony.* Cambridge, Massachusetts: Harvard University Press, 1979.

Lykken, D. T. The GSR in the detection of guilt. *Journal of Applied Psychology*, 1959, **43**, 385-388.

Lykken, D. T. The validity of the guilty knowledge technique: The effects of faking. *Journal of Applied Psychology*, 1960, **44**, 258-262.

Lykken, D. T. Psychology and the lie detector industry. *American Psychologist*, 1974, **29**, 725-739.

Lykken, D. T. The psychopath and the lie detector. *Psychophysiology*, 1978, **15**, 137-142.

Lykken, D. T. The detection of deception. *Psychological Bulletin*, 1979, **86**, 47-53.

Lykken, D. T. *A tremor in the blood: Uses and abuse of the lie detector*. New York: McGraw-Hill, 1981.

McCarron, L. T. Psychophysiological discriminants of reactive depression. *Psychophysiology*, 1973, **10**, 223-230.

McLean, P. D. Induced arousal and time of recall as determinants of paired associate recall. *British Journal of Psychology*, 1969, **60**, 57-62.

McNair, D. M. Antianxiety drugs and human performance. *Archives of General Psychiatry*, 1973, **29**, 611-617.

Malpass, R. S., & Kravitz, J. Recognition for faces of own and other race. *Journal of Personality and Social Psychology*, 1969, **13**, 330-334.

Maltzman, I., Kantor, W., & Langdon, B. Immediate and delayed retention, arousal, and the orienting and defensive reflexes. *Psychonomic Science*, 1966, **6**, 445-446.

Marston, W. M. Systolic blood pressure symptoms of deception. *Journal of Experimental Psychology*, 1917, **2**, 117-163.

Morse, D. R., Martin, J. S., Furst, M. L., & Dubin, L. L. A physiological and subjective evaluation of mediation, hypnosis, and relaxation. *Psychosomatic Medicine*, 1977, **39**, 304-324.

O'Gorman, J. G., & Horneman, C. Consistency of individual differences in non-specific electrodermal activity. *Biological Psychology*, 1979, **9**, 13 22.

Orne, M. T., & Thackray, R. I. Group GSR technique in the detection of deception. *Perceptual and Motor Skills*, 1967, **25**, 809-816.

Orne, M. T., Thackray, R. I., & Paskewitz, D. A. On the detection of deception: A model for the study of the physiological effects of psychological stimuli. In N. S. Greenfield & R. A. Sternbach (Eds.), *Handbook of psychophysiology*. New York: Holt, 1972.

Podlesny, J. A., & Raskin, D. C. Physiological measures and the detection of deception. *Psychological Bulletin*, 1977, **84**, 782-799.

Porier, G. W., & Lott, A. J. Galvanic skin responses and prejudice. *Journal of Personality and Social Psychology*, 1967, **5**, 253-259.

Rahav, G. Birth order and delinquency. *British Journal of Criminology*, 1980, **20**, 385-395.

Rankin, R. E., & Campbell, D. T. Galvanic skin response to Negro and white experimenters. *Journal of Abnormal and Social Psychology*, 1955, **51** (1), 30-33.

Raskin, D. C. *Reliability of chart interpretation and sources of errors in polygraph examinations* (U.S. Department of Justice Report No. 76-3, Contract 75-NI-99-0001). Salt Lake City, Utah: University of Utah, 1976.

Raskin, D. C., & Hare, R. D. Psychopathy and detection in a prison population. *Psychophysiology*, 1978, **15**, 126-136. (a)

Raskin, D. C., & Podlesny, J. A. Truth and deception: A reply to Lykken. *Psychological Bulletin*, 1979, **86**, 54-59.

Reid, J. E. A revised questioning technique in lie detection tests. *Journal of Criminal Law, Criminology and Police Science*, 1947, **37**, 542-547.

Reid, J. E., & Inbau, F. E. *Truth and deception: The polygraph ("lie detector") technique*. Baltimore, Maryland: Williams & Wilkins, 1977.

Rosenhan, D. L. On being sane in insane places. *Science*, 1973, **179**, 250-258.

Rosenhan, D. L. The contextual nature of psychiatric diagnosis. *Journal of Abnormal Psychology,* 1975, **84,** 462–474.

Rovner, L. I., Raskin, D. C., & Kircher, J. C. Effects of information and practice on detection of deception. *Psychophysiology,* 1979, **16,** 197. (Abstract)

Ryan, D. V., & Neale, J. M. Test-taking sets and the performance of schizophrenics on laboratory tests. *Journal of Abnormal Psychology,* 1973, **82,** 207–211.

Saks, M. J., & Hastie, R. *Social psychology in court.* Princeton, New Jersey: Van Nostrand Reinhold, 1978.

Sampson, J. R. Further study of encoding and arousal factors in free recall of verbal and visual material. *Psychonomic Science,* 1969, **16,** 221–222.

Sarbin, T. R., & Slagle, R. W. Hypnosis and psychophysiological outcomes. In E. Fromm & R. E. Shor (Eds.), *Hypnosis: Developments in research and new perspectives.* New York: Aldine, 1979.

Schwartz, G. E., & Shapiro, D. Social psychophysiology. In W. F. Prokasy & D. C. Raskin (Eds.), *Electrodermal activity in psychological research.* New York: Academic Press, 1973.

Shagass, C. *Evoked brain potentials in psychiatry.* New York: Plenum, 1972.

Shapiro, D., & Crider, A. Psychophysiological approaches in social psychology. In G. Lindzey & E. Aronson (Eds.), *The handbook of social psychology* (Vol. III, 2nd ed.). Reading, Massachusetts: Addison-Wesley, 1969.

Smith, E. C. *New dictionary of American family names.* New York: Harper, 1973.

Spielberger, C. D., Gorsuch, R. L., & Lushene, R. E. *STAI manual for the state-trait anxiety inventory ("self-evaluation questionnaire").* Palo Alto, California: Consulting Psychologists Press, 1970.

Sternback, R. A., & Tursky, B. Ethnic differences among housewives in psychophysical and skin potential responses to electric shock. *Psychophysiology,* 1965, **1,** 241–246.

Stotland, E., Sherman, S. E., & Shaver, K. G. *Empathy and birth order: Some experimental explorations.* Lincoln, Nebraska: University of Nebraska Press, 1971.

Thackray, R. I., & Orne, M. T. Effects of the type of stimulus employed and the level of subject awareness on the detection of deception. *Journal of Applied Psychology,* 1968, **52,** 234–239. (a)

Thackray, R. I., & Orne, M. T. A comparison of physiological indices in detection of deception. *Psychophysiology,* 1968, **4,** 329–339. (b)

Timm, H. W. *The effects of placebos and feedback on the detection of deception.* Unpublished doctoral dissertation, Michigan State University, 1979.

United States Senate, *Polygraph control and civil liberties protection act.* Hearings before the subcommittee on the Constitution of the committee on the judiciary, 1978.

Valins, S. Cognitive effects of false heart-rate feedback. *Journal of Personality and Social Psychology,* 1966, **4,** 400–408.

Waid, W. M. Skin conductance response to both signaled and unsignalled noxious stimulation predicts level of socialization. *Journal of Personality and Social Psychology,* 1976, **34,** 923–929.

Waid, W. M., & Orne, M. T. Individual differences in electrodermal lability and the detection of information and deception. *Journal of Applied Psychology,* 1980, **65,** 1–8.

Waid, W. M., Orne, E. C., Cook, M. R., & Orne, M. T. Effects of attention, as indexed by subsequent memory, on electrodermal detection of information. *Journal of Applied Psychology,* 1978, **63,** 728–733.

Waid, W. M., Orne, E. C., Cook, M. R., & Orne, M. T. Meprobamate reduces accuracy of physiological detection of deception. *Science,* 1981, **212,** 71–73. (a)

Waid, W. M., Orne, E. C., & Orne, M. T. Selective memory for social information, alertness, and physiological arousal in the detection of deception. *Journal of Applied Psychology*, 1981, in press. (b)

Waid, W. M., Orne, E. C., & Orne, M. T. *Family configuration and social stress in the physiological detection of deception*. 1981, in preparation. (c)

Waid, W. M., Orne, M. T., & Wilson, S. K. Socialization, awareness, and the electrodermal response to deception and self-disclosure. *Journal of Abnormal Psychology*, 1979, **88,** 663–666. (a)

Waid, W. M., Orne, M. T., & Wilson, S. K. Effects of level of socialization on electrodermal detection of deception. *Psychophysiology*, 1979, **16,** 15–22. (b)

Waid, W. M., Wilson, S. K., & Orne, M. T. Cross-modal physiological effects of electrodermal lability in the detection of deception. *Journal of Personality and Social Psychology*, 1981, in press. (d)

Warren, J. R. Birth order and social behavior. *Psychological Bulletin*, 1966, **65,** 38–49.

Wieland, B. A., & Mefford, R. B. Systematic changes in levels of physiological activity during a four-month period. *Psychophysiology*, 1970, **6,** 669–689.

Zajonc, R. B. Social facilitation. *Science*, 1965, **149,** 269–274.

DIALECTIC CONCEPTIONS IN SOCIAL PSYCHOLOGY: AN APPLICATION TO SOCIAL PENETRATION AND PRIVACY REGULATION[1]

Irwin Altman, Anne Vinsel, and Barbara B. Brown

DEPARTMENT OF PSYCHOLOGY
UNIVERSITY OF UTAH
SALT LAKE CITY, UTAH

[1]A version of this article was presented by the senior author as the presidential address to the Society for Personality and Social Psychology, American Psychological Association, New York City, September 1979.

We express our appreciation to the following colleagues for their constructive comments on earlier versions of the chapter: Martin Chemers, Clyde Hendrick, Harold Kelley, Eric Knowles, Richard Lerner, George Levinger, Stephen Margulis, Joseph McGrath, John Meacham, William Prokasy, Joseph Rychlak, Charles Shimp, M. Brewster Smith, Dalmas Taylor, Carol Werner, and Lawrence Wrightsman.

ADVANCES IN EXPERIMENTAL SOCIAL
PSYCHOLOGY, VOL. 14

I. Introduction

The study of interpersonal relationships is a topic of continuing interest in social psychology. Research and theory in this field has focused on the earliest stages of relationship development and addressed such topics as impression formation, initial attraction, and equity and attribution processes of strangers and acquaintances. In addition, theoretical and empirical attention has been broadened to cover analyses of developmental processes and related aspects of long-term, intimate and close relationships (see Burgess & Huston, 1979; Huston & Levinger, 1978; Levinger & Raush, 1977, for representative writings in this vein of research and theory).

This article is in the spirit of the latter approaches to the study of interpersonal relationships. We will examine the long-term development of social bonds, including their growth and deterioration, interaction processes that occur over the history of social relationships, and their holistic, systems-like qualities. The goal of the article is to integrate and extend two lines of theorizing and research conducted over the past decade and a half that have been concerned with aspects of the development, management, and deterioration of interpersonal relationships. One approach, social penetration theory, deals with the development of social relationships from strangership and casual acquaintanceship to the formation of more intimate social bonds (Altman & Taylor, 1973). A second line of investigation treats privacy as a boundary regulation process, with people differentially accessible to others at various times and circumstances (Altman, 1975).

The primary vehicle we will use to extend these two approaches is dialectic analysis. There have been many approaches to dialectics throughout intellectual history, and our version centers around three ideas that are common to many of them: (1) Social processes are characterized by polarities and oppositions, such as openness–closedness and stability–change; (2) oppositions form a unified system; and (3) oppositional processes are dynamic, with openness and closedness changing over time.

Our analysis also makes several assumptions that are different from the balance or homeostasis concepts underlying much of modern social psychology. Instead of assuming a fundamental human motive for stability, balance, or consistency, we assume that people exhibit both stability and change in their social relationships, not primarily one or the other, and that these oppositions cycle over time, one dominating at one time and the other dominating at another.

The first section of the article compares social penetration and privacy regulation frameworks in terms of their similarities and differences and their strengths and weaknesses. The second section examines the concept of dialectics from a historical and philosophical perspective and describes our particular dialectic approach. We then analyze social relationships in terms of the dialectic concepts of openness–closedness and stability–change and complete the article with proposals for research based on an integration of social penetration and privacy frameworks.

II. Social Penetration Theory and Privacy Regulation Theory

A. SOCIAL PENETRATION THEORY

Altman and Taylor (1973) proposed a process-oriented theory of the development, management, and deterioration of social relationships that emphasized the multilevel behavioral quality of social interactions. According to this framework, social relationships involve the interplay of many levels of behavior that function as a unified "system." These encompass verbal, paraverbal, nonverbal, and environmentally oriented behaviors. Verbal behaviors include mutual self-disclosure, paraverbal behaviors have to do with such things as voice tone and intensity, interruptions and pauses, nonverbal behaviors are exemplified by such things as eye contact, head nodding, smiling, gestures, and body positions, and environmental behaviors include personal spacing, territorial behavior, and other uses of the physical environment.

Although these behaviors have traditionally been studied separately, social penetration theory has adopted a *social unit* perspective whereby one attempts to understand patterns, profiles, and combinations of behaviors (Altman 1976a, 1977b; Altman & Taylor, 1973). This approach emphasizes molar units of analysis such as individuals, teams, couples, families, and other whole social entities, rather than behaviors considered one at a time. Another feature of this orientation is the implied change, fluidity, and variegated quality of behavior patterns; that is, a social unit orientation assumes that the expression of intimacy can involve many combinations of behavior that differ among individuals or that differ even for the same person on various occasions.

Another feature of social penetration theory is its emphasis on developmental processes in social relationships. For example, one hypothesis states that people explore and reveal superficial, nonintimate aspects of themselves during the early stages of a relationship and that only gradually do they probe and disclose more personal, intimate aspects of their lives to another person. Thus, we hypothesize a *depth* dimension in the growth of social bonds. This aspect of the theory assumes a directional and cumulative quality of the social penetration process. It is directional in stating that relationship growth proceeds toward greater mutual openness. It is cumulative in presupposing that exchange at more superficial levels of personality occurs before interaction takes place at more intimate levels. As discussed later, our present dialectic perspective hypothesizes that relationships can exhibit cyclical, reversible, and nonlinear processes, not necessarily only unidirectional and cumulative processes.

Social penetration theory also hypothesizes that developing relationships exhibit movement along a *breadth* dimension involving increased amounts of exchange. Combining depth and breadth dimensions yields a variety of types of relationships: (1) narrow breadth and superficial depth relationships, where people have only limited contacts; (2) broad and shallow relationships, where people have frequent but superficial contacts; (3) narrow and deep relationships, involving intimate contacts in a limited area of exchange; and (4) broad and deep relationships, where people interact in a variety of areas and do so at both intimate and superficial levels.

The combination of breadth and depth dimensions suggests a characteristic developmental pattern. At the earliest stages of a relationship people should exchange superficial and limited information. With a rewarding exchange, movement should progress along breadth and depth dimensions, with deeper and more extensive interpersonal exchanges as interactants move from strangership to acquaintance, to friendship and beyond.

A number of studies have examined these features of social penetration theory in a variety of settings and over varying lengths of relationships (Colson, 1968; Frankfurt, 1965; Morton, 1978; Taylor, 1968; Altman & Haythorn, 1965; Keiser & Altman, 1976; Altman & Taylor, 1973; Taylor & Altman, 1975; Taylor, Altman, & Sorrentino, 1969). These studies have consistently demonstrated that the growth of relationships follows the hypothesized course of development from peripheral, superficial aspects of personality to more intimate ones. The disclosure of superficial information usually takes place rapidly during the early stages of a relationship, whereas exposure of intimate aspects of the self occurs only gradually and at later stages of a relationship. A number of these studies also showed that disclosure is greater in superficial areas of exchange at all stages of a relationship; such disclosures occur among casual acquaintances and for those in close relationships as well. Thus, social relationships are a continuing blend of superficial and intimate interaction, a point made by Simmel (1908/1950) at the turn of the century.

There are several other aspects of social penetration theory that have bearing on this article:

1. The rate and level of development of social relationships is hypothesized to be affected by the interpersonal rewards and costs that arise as a result of social interaction. In general, the greater the rewards relative to costs and the larger the absolute amount of rewards, the faster a relationship will progress, and the more intimate it will become (Frankfurt, 1965; Altman & Taylor, 1973; Taylor & Altman, 1975; Taylor et al., 1969).

2. Personality and situational factors play an important role in the development of relationships. People who have predispositions to be open and accessible

progress more rapidly in interpersonal exchange, other factors being equivalent (Frankfurt, 1965; Taylor, 1968). Situational factors, such as extent of anticipated commitment to a relationship, also affect the degree of openness between individuals (Taylor & Altman, 1975; Taylor *et al.,* 1969).

3. The deterioration of social relationships is hypothesized to follow a systematic course that is the opposite of developmental processes. When interpersonal costs outweigh rewards, it is hypothesized that people disengage from one another in a systematic fashion, slowing down interaction in intimate areas first and gradually moving toward more superficial areas of exchange.

Assessment of Social Penetration Theory

There are certain assumptions of social penetration theory that are satisfactory and others that are less so. Indeed, it is now evident that Altman's work on privacy regulation, described in the next section, was partially motivated by the need to escape from certain restrictive assumptions that had been made in social penetration theory.

On the positive side, we still consider it important to study social processes over the course of development of relationships and to examine molar patterns of social behavior. It is interesting that Huston and Levinger (1978), in a comprehensive review of the field, observed that, in spite of years of research, little theoretical or empirical attention has been given to the course of development of relationships. By implication, their review also suggests that research has been fragmented with regard to different aspects of relationship development. For example, research on impression formation is not integrated with research on relationship development, and attraction research is conducted without reference to interaction process. So, we continue to be satisfied with assumptions made by social penetration theory about the importance of studying the development of social relationships from a multibehavioral perspective.

On the other hand, we are less satisfied with other assumptions in our initial theorizing. In particular, we question the idea that the development of successful relationships always follows a unidirectional and cumulative path, with ever-increasing openness of people to one another. Except for a possible slowing down of progress, or a reversal in the case of deteriorating relationships, the theory assumes an ever-opening course of development. Although the humanistic thinking of the late 1960s and early 1970s emphasized "genuineness," "honesty," and unrestricted "openness" as prime requisites to the well-being of relationships, aspects of our data and speculations have suggested that the development of relationships is probably quite complex. For example, the fact that exchanges in nonintimate areas are always more extensive than interactions in intimate areas, regardless of the stage of relationship, raises the possibility of a cycling back and forth between superficial and intimate topics in interactions throughout the history of a social relationship. Furthermore, as Altman and Taylor (1973) discussed, there are psychological dangers in an unlimited openness of people to one another, including mutual intrusion, increased vulnerability and exposure, and the potential loss of individuality and dignity. We will hypothesize later that, while some relationships may generally proceed toward greater openness, they also probably have cycles or phases of closedness between participants. People not only make themselves accessible to one another; they also shut themselves off to one degree or another, break off contact, engage in more distant styles of interaction, and exhibit an ebb and flow of exchange. Thus, even in the healthiest relationship, people cycle in and out of close contact with one another. Furthermore, why should one assume that relationships always proceed only toward greater openness? It may be perfectly possible for people to remain in a long-term relationship and yet gradually decrease their overall openness to a level below that which may have occurred in earlier stages of their bond. The unidirectional nature of social penetration theory and the procedures used to study the process do not allow for the possibilities that growing relationships might exhibit cycles of varying degrees of openness and closedness or that some relationships might not always progress toward increased openness of participants to one another.

Given these doubts, we now realize that Altman had been ambivalent about pursuing a program of studies within the philosophical assumptions of social penetration theory rather than exploring an alternative set of ideas concerning the development of social relationships. Without explicitly making a decision between social penetration theory and these other notions, he chose the latter path and examined several concepts in environmental psychology, especially privacy. These new analyses eventually led to the assumption that the development and management of interpersonal relationships involved people being both open and closed to one another, with such behaviors varying in strength at different times.

B.   PRIVACY REGULATION THEORY

Altman's analysis of several environmental concepts, including privacy, was stimulated in part by an interest in environment behavior relationships during the early 1970s (Altman, 1973b, 1975; Proshansky & Altman, 1979). He first examined existing research on personal space and subsequently analyzed territoriality and crowding. These later analyses did not solve the problems previously raised with respect to social penetration theory, and Altman turned to the concept of privacy (Altman, 1975, 1976b, 1977a), developing a general framework that incorporated the concepts of personal space, territory, crowding, and privacy. By using a conception of privacy regulation as an opening and closing process, he thought that the problems with social penetration would be resolved, but this proved to be only partially true. This research history, beginning with analyses of personal space, territoriality, and crowding, and then turning to privacy, is described next.

1. Personal Space

The concept of personal space captured the attention of social psychologists in the late 1960s as a result of the ideas of Edward T. Hall (1966). Hall described how intimate, personal, social, and public distances between people involved various channels of communication (e.g., hearing, vision, touch, and smell) and how different spatial zones were used in various situations, relationships, and cultures. Perhaps because of apparent ease of measurement and adaptability to laboratory study, as well as intrinsic interest in the topic, studies of personal space grew from a handful in the 1960s to about 250 by the mid-1970s, (see Altman, 1975; Hayduk, 1978; Altman & Vinsel, 1977, for reviews of recent research).

The philosophical ethos underlying this research is well illustrated in studies of personal space invasion. Hall (1966) and others suggested that personal space involves an invisible boundary around a person, intrusion into which can produce stress, withdrawal, or defense. A review of available research by Altman and Vinsel (1977) reported a consistent finding that people react negatively to overly close approaches by others, exhibiting flight or defensive behaviors such as stares, verbal comments, shifts in body positions, and the use of objects to create barriers. From our perspective, it is interesting that this research focuses on how people *close* themselves off from others and how they avoid being overly exposed and vulnerable. This observation contrasts sharply with the ethos of social penetration research, where the underlying concern was with how people *open* themselves to others. Thus, it is not surprising that social penetration research and personal space research remained separate, since each focused on different aspects of social interaction. Indeed, we ourselves did not relate these two areas until recently, as illustrated in the analysis presented later.

2. Territoriality

A similar emphasis on closedness appears in research on human territoriality. Territoriality refers to the occupancy, marking, and control of areas and objects in the physical environment and sometimes includes defense in response to intrusion (Altman, 1975). One line of research indicates that territories are often marked in some way and that markers protect places from invasion (see Altman, 1975; Stokols, 1978; Altman & Chemers, 1980, for reviews of this research). A related theme is that territorial behavior enhances the functioning of social systems by minimizing conflict and smoothing out social interaction. For example, Altman and Haythorn (1967), Altman, Taylor, and Wheeler (1971), and Sundstrom and Altman (1974) found that groups who established territories functioned better than those who did not structure their space. Similar results were obtained by Ley and Cybrwisky (1974) and Newman (1972) in relation to gang conflict and crime in urban settings. Historical and anthropological analyses also repeatedly demonstrate how territorial demarcation stabilizes the operation of social systems (Altman & Chemers, 1980).

Research on territorial behavior, like that on personal space, contrasts with social penetration theory. Research and theorizing about territoriality emphasizes the closing off of people to one another and how the separation of people into their own territories enhances social systems. With few exceptions, research has not examined how territories are used to make people more accessible to others or to facilitate the growth of social relationships.

3. Crowding

A similar philosophical ethos pervades research and theory on crowding (Altman, 1975; Stokols, 1978; Baum & Epstein, 1978). This topic, of long-standing interest to sociologists, attracted psychologists in the late 1960s and has since been the subject of numerous laboratory and field studies. Investigations of both long- and short-term crowding have dealt with coping responses, negative psychological and physiological effects, and the impact of crowding on social behavior and task performance.

Studies of crowding often indicate that the inability to shut out others is threatening and debilitating. Not only has this research noted that excessive contact is negative, but it has examined how people struggle to regain an acceptable level of inaccessibility from others. Thus, a whole field of investigation has evolved that focuses on the benefits obtained by people closing themselves off from others and emphasizes the dangers of being overly open to others. Personal space, territory, and crowding research deal with somewhat different types of social relationships than do social penetration studies; there are different philosophical substrates underlying these areas, one emphasizing openness and the other emphasizing closedness of people to one another.

4. Privacy

Up to this point, Altman had attempted to integrate research and theory in each of the separate areas of personal space, territorial behavior, and crowding. Intuitively, however, Altman was also troubled by the gap between these environmental concepts and social penetration theory. Bearing these issues in mind, he turned to the concept of *privacy* as a possible vehicle for weaving together these various strands of interest.

The topic of privacy has been of considerable interest to a wide variety of disciplines. Philosophers have addressed ethical issues of privacy; sociologists, political scientists, and lawyers have focused on invasion of privacy; architects have attempted to design homes and other places to ensure privacy. For most of these disciplines, it has been assumed that it is important, psychologically, for people to be able to avoid contact with others. Thus, traditional thinking about privacy fits with the assumptions underlying research on personal space, territoriality, and crowding and contrasts with those implicit in social penetration theory.

These different approaches seem totally contradictory when carried to their limits and when each ignores the other. For social penetration theorizing, the idea of unlimited and never-ending openness makes little intuitive sense. Although extensive self-disclosure was valued by some radical encounter group movements of the 1960s, Altman and Taylor (1973) hypothesized that extreme openness might actually increase the probability of conflict, violate self-integrity, and detract from the mutuality that was being sought in human relationships. On the other hand, the philosophical underpinnings of research and theory on privacy, territoriality, personal space, and crowding emphasized the virtues of interpersonal closedness, inaccessibility, and separation. Obviously, if carried to an extreme, closedness can become isolation, loneliness, and alienation. So, to speak about inaccessibility as a monolithic virtue seems as incomplete as to speak about total openness as a desirable goal.

Because Altman assumed, intuitively, that social relationships involve both accessibility and inaccessibility of people to one another, he adapted a dialectic perspective that would incorporate such seemingly contradictory processes within a common framework.

Altman's (1975) dialectic analysis of privacy regulation primarily addressed the oppositional qualities of accessibility and inaccessibility:

> [S]ocial interaction is the continuing interplay or dialectic between forces driving people to come together and to move apart. There are times when people want to be alone and out of contact with others and there are times when others are sought out, to be heard and to hear, to talk and to listen.
> Thus, privacy is not solely a "keep out" or "let in" process; it involves a synthesis of being in contact with others and being out of contact with others. The desire for social interaction or noninteraction changes over time and with different circumstances. The idea of privacy as a dialectic process, therefore, means that there is a balancing of opposing forces—to be open and accessible to others and to be shut off or closed to others—and that the net strength of these competing forces changes over time. (Altman, 1975, p. 23)

Privacy and social penetration theories were similar in their common emphasis on multibehavioral, molar analyses of the mechanisms used to regulate interaction. People were hypothesized to use different patterns of verbal and nonverbal mechanisms to make themselves more or less accessible to others, with differences occurring within and across individuals as a result of personal style, situational demands, and other factors.

Privacy regulation theory also hypothesized that people seek a particular level of contact with others at any given moment, although the specific degree of desired openness or closedness can vary over time and with circumstances. To achieve a desired level of privacy, people were hypothesized to set in motion various combinations of behavioral mechanisms and to adjust and readjust their use in accordance with a desired state of accessibility.

5. Assessment of Privacy Regulation Theory

Privacy regulation theory was to have accomplished several objectives, some implicit and some explicit. One unstated goal of the approach was to counter the overemphasis of social penetration theory on openness as a predominant quality of the development of social relationships. Second, and more explicit, it was designed to avoid the overemphasis on interpersonal closedness which characterized environmental research on personal space, territory, and crowding. By adopting a dialectic orientation, Altman sought a theoretical framework explicitly assuming that social relationships involved both openness and closedness among participants. In some respects, privacy regulation theory achieved these goals and was a philosophical and conceptual advance over social penetration theory.

On the other hand, the dialectic orientation of privacy regulation theory was elementary, incomplete, and distorted in some respects. For example, the concept of opposition was never clearly explicated in terms of the relationship between opposites, the implications of varying degrees of opposition, the extent to which oppositional processes were permanently dominant or subordinate with respect to one another, the unity of opposites, and so on.

A crucial issue only partially addressed by privacy regulation theory concerned the relationship between oppositional processes. As we reexamine earlier writings and references to those writings by others, it becomes clear that Altman implied a universal ideal or an optimum balance of openness and closedness toward which relationships strived. Thus, a homeostatic assumption lurked within the initial privacy framework to the effect that relationships progressed toward some idealized balance or stability of openness and closedness. This became a troubling matter because we did not intuitively believe that relationships operated in this way; nor, as we will discuss later, does dialectic philosophy necessarily assume such a perspective.

Another problem with privacy regulation theory was its failure to deal with the development of social relationships in as thorough a fashion as social penetration theory. Although the privacy regulation theory referred to privacy as a dynamic and changing process, it did so in a vague way. Unlike social penetration theory, it did not describe the conditions of change or the nature and direction of shifting relationships between openness and closedness.

To summarize, the goal of this article is to integrate social penetration and privacy regulation theories into a unified framework that deals with the development and management of social relationships. We have indicated how these two approaches are similar or complementary and how they are different. For example, they are identical in their emphasis on understanding social units through an examination of multilevel patterns of behavior. However, privacy regulation theory avoids social penetration theory's overemphasis on openness of participants to one another through its use of a dialectic perspective that treats both openness and closedness as aspects of social relationships. But the dialectic approach of privacy regulation theory needs clarification. In addition, privacy regulation fails to deal adequately with the development of relationships, whereas social penetration theory is much more explicit on this issue.

The immediately following section describes our approach to dialectic philosophy and sets the stage for the later discussion. The final two sections of this article present an integration and extension of the privacy regulation and social penetration theories.

III. The Concept of Dialectics

Dialectic concepts have a long history in human affairs and thought. They appear in the philosophy and religion of the ancient Chinese and Greeks, in Judeo-Christian theology, in the political and social philosophies of the last several hundred years, and in the mythology and cosmology of many cultures. (For a detailed philosophical analysis see Adler, 1927, 1952; for applications in psychology see Buss, 1979; Riegel, 1979; and Rychlak, 1976.)

In spite of their widespread use, however, there have been rather divergent views about the utility of dialectic ideas. Berengar of Tours, a medieval philosopher, stated, "Dialectic is the art of arts and it is a sign of an eminent mind that it turns all things to dialectic. Anyone who does not do so abandons his principal glory, for it is by his reason that man resembles God" (Stiefel, 1977, p. 349). On the other hand, Sidney Hook (1953), a modern philosopher, stated that "the term dialectic is so infected with ambiguity, that it is not likely to function as a serviceable designation for any concept or intellectual procedure in any inquiry which aims at the achievement of reliable knowledge about ourselves and the world we live in" (p. 713). Although the term *dialectic* has been employed in different ways over the course of history, one can distinguish between dialectics as (1) a style of reasoning or method used to establish the truth or validity of ideas and (2) a world view or substantive conception of the nature of phenomena (Adler, 1927; Hook, 1953; Rychlak, 1976). In addition, dialectical ideas appear in a variety of political philosophies (e.g., Marxism and Maoism) and also in many religious ideologies (see Koenker, 1971, for an analysis of dialectics in Christian theologies of the past several hundred years).

Because of its long history and varied usage, the concept of dialectics must be employed with caution and with as much specificity as possible. Indeed, one should seek some form of operational definition in any particular application of the term. Our approach will be to focus on dialectics as a philosophical and metatheoretical orientation to the nature of phenomena, with less emphasis on its methodological aspects. Specifically, our analysis will address three features of dialectics in relation to social behavior: (1) the idea of opposition or polarity; (2) the unity of opposites; and (3) the dynamic relationship between opposites.

The notion of the world composed of physical and psychological opposites is central to any dialectic perspective (Rychlak, 1976). Previous dialectic philosophies have employed a variety of oppositions, such as fire and water, an upperworld and an underworld, love and hate. Here, we will describe social relationships as involving the oppositions of openness–closedness and stability–change.

A related property of dialectics is that the oppositions assist in the definition of one another and contribute to a unified psychological system. Thus, the idea of harmony in social relationships helps define and is partly defined by the idea of conflict, and the idea of interpersonal closedness contributes to our understanding of openness and vice versa. We will describe openness–closedness and stability–change as intrinsic aspects of social bonds and as parts of a coherent system, not as parallel or separate processes.

Our approach also emphasizes the dynamic qualities of oppositional relationships. The relationship between opposites is not static; opposites exhibit changing relative strengths vis-à-vis one another and often form new levels of interaction or syntheses. Given this synopsis of our operational definition of dialectics, we can turn to a more detailed discussion of the ideas of opposition, unity of opposites, and change.

A. THE IDEA OF OPPOSITION

In spite of the fact that the concept of dialectics has been used in diverse ways, Rychlak (1976) has stated, ''If there is a core meaning in the dialectic [as a world view], it would seem to be the idea of bipolarity, opposition, or contradiction'' (p. 14).

According to Koenker (1971) and Rychlak (1976), the Greek philosopher Anaximander (600 B.C.) was one of the earliest Western scholars to argue that the universe operated according to oppositions of cold and hot, fire and water. In the realm of human affairs, Heraclitus (see Adler, 1952) referred to several oppositional forces that were essential to social processes, such as harmony and conflict. Even earlier, in ancient Chinese and other Eastern philosophies, the idea of opposition was deemed to be inherent in human events and in the functioning of the physical world. Such an approach is vividly represented in the conception of nature as involving yin and yang forces (Wilhelm & Baynes, 1950). Yin forces are ''female'' forces, with properties of passivity, dependence, weakness, nurturance, receptivity, and yielding. Yang forces are dominant, active, creative, aggressive, and represent "male" qualities (Kuo, 1976).

The idea of opposition appears throughout history in a variety of philosophical, religious, anthropological, and psychological analyses of human functioning. For example, religious and cosmological beliefs of many cultures contain opposites such as God and the Devil, an upperworld of Heaven and an underworld of Hell, and related manifestations of good and evil (Altman & Chemers, 1980). In some cases, the notion of opposition is even represented in the design of communities (Fraser, 1968). For example, among the South Nais people of Indonesia, religious values concerning the polarities of sky and earth, sun and moon, and male and female are explicit in community design. Villages are usually located on hilltops, perhaps for defense but also because the village symbolizes the positive upperworld. Within a village the chief's house is located at the highest end of the street and is decorated with birds, flying figures, and symbols of the sun, reflecting his divine status and the upperworld. The lower end of the village contains the homes of commoners, decorated with figures representative of the underworld such as snakes, crocodiles, and lizards. Anthropologists have described how oppositional processes play a similar role in the symbols and mythology of many other cultures (Douglas, 1970; Levi-Strauss, 1963; Murphy, 1971; Turner, 1969).

The idea of opposition not only appears in Western philosophy and political theory, from Aristotle and Plato to Hegel, Kant, Marx, and others, but it is also evident in theorizing about human social and psychological processes. For example, the id and superego of the Freudian personality system reflect dialectic opposition, with the id encompassing primitive urges of self-gratification and the superego representing the forces of society. Similarly, Jung postulated the presence of animus or male qualities and anima or female qualities within every personality, with corresponding oppositional features of activity versus passivity, aggressiveness versus altruism, etc. And Kelly's (1955) role construct theory hypothesizes that people construe their world in terms of unique configurations of oppositional qualities.

Although opposition is a focal aspect of dialectics, it is important to realize that all opposites are not alike. Adler (1927, 1952) identified several types of opposition. At one extreme are contradictions, exemplified by such opposites as human–not human and tall–not tall. In these cases one of the polarities has specific and definable properties (x), whereas its counterpart is defined by the absence of such properties (not x) and therefore includes *everything* that is different from the defined pole (e.g., not human can include animate and inanimate objects; not tall can include average and short people). We are not interested in such opposites; instead, our focus will be on oppositions where both poles are positive entities. For example, in social psychology positively defined opposites might include harmony and conflict, altruism and aggression, and competition and cooperation. In each of these cases one can study opposites either as independent phenomena or as parts of a larger system. Although both approaches are legitimate (and social psychological research has tended to study either pole of various oppositions independently, not in relationship to one another), our goal will be to emphasize the joint functioning of openness-closedness and of stability–change in relation to one another. Given our earlier critique of the emphasis of social penetration theory on openness and the focus of environmental research on closedness, we now seek a conception of relationships that encompasses openness and closedness within a unified framework. In addition, we will propose that social relationships are characterized by both stability and change, with neither more important than the other and with each intrinsic to the functioning of any relationship.

B.   THE UNITY OF OPPOSITES

The unity of opposites is another recurring feature of dialectic philosophy that is incorporated in our operational definition of the term. Specifically, the concept of the unity of opposites encompasses (1) the complementarity and integration of opposites and (2) the relative strength and balance of opposites.

1.   Complementarity and Integration of Opposites

Dialectics polarities not only exhibit opposition, thereby partially excluding one another, but they also complement and provide a definitional base for each other (Adler, 1927, 1952). For example, the idea of interpersonal harmony implies and helps define interpersonal conflict, and vice versa; the concept of openness in human interaction implies the counterpart of closedness, and vice versa. Thus, if people were only open to one another, and if openness was an ever-present, homogeneous process, then it would be difficult to describe; its definition derives in part from its opposite—closedness.

A related idea is that opposites are components of a higher order system. Adler (1927) stated:

> It is required only that the whole be found which includes the given parts in opposition, and implies them. Until this supraordinate class be established, the entities in opposition have the status of wholes in opposition. They imply one another, and partially exclude one another. In this relation of opposition and partial exclusion, they becomes parts which presupposed a whole of higher order. (p. 165)

Within this perspective, openness and closedness can be treated as oppositional qualities that contribute to a higher order boundary regulation system in which they are separate but related components.

2. Strength and Balance of Opposites

The unity of opposites theme also addresses the strength of polarities in relationship to one another. One principle is that polarities always partially intersect and that one or the other pole never becomes so strong that it completely contradicts its opposite. Adler (1927) summarized this point as follows:

> entities in opposition . . . exclude one another partially, rather than absolutely. Were they to exclude one another absolutely, they could not definitively imply one another as parts of some supraordinate class, and could not be in opposition . . . or the negative of the class defined. Furthermore, the absolute exclusiveness of two classes would mean that they had absolutely no identity conditions in common . . . that they could not be members of some common class. (p. 165)

This idea is salient in many dialectic perspectives. For example, the yin-yang concept of Chinese philosophy assumes that some amount of either pole of an opposition is always present, no matter how powerful the other. If one pole completely dominated the other then the larger system of which they were parts and to whose coherence they contributed would not exist.

This aspect of the unity of opposites is important to our conception of openness and closedness as components of a coherent interpersonal system. If, for example, closedness prevailed completely (i.e., if the members of a couple were completely and totally isolated from one another), there would be, in effect, no relationship. Similarly, if participants were totally accessible to one another at all times, it is likely that they would eventually lose their individual identities and the relationship would become nonviable.

A related issue concerns the extent to which dialectic systems more toward some ideal balance between opposites. This is a crucial matter because it bears on assumptions of balance, consistency, and homeostasis. Historically, dialectic philosophy has not always postulated an ideal state toward which systems strive. That is, dialectic systems do not necessarily move toward an equal "balance" of polarities with respect to one another. Thus, equilibrium, in the form of equal and opposite forces (Lewin, 1936), is not, according to dialectic philosophy, necessarily a natural or desirable state of affairs. Nor do systems necessarily strive ideally toward any other relationship between opposites. The relationship between opposites can assume any of a series of relative strengths (excluding 100:0 or 0:100), and none is inherently better than any other.

This idea will be examined in more detail later because it contrasts with the pervasive assumption of much psychological theorizing, namely, that systems move toward homeostasis, balance, or consistency, all of which imply an equalization of psychological processes around a stable point or interval. Also, as we will discuss later, we do not assume any ideal relationship between openness and closedness or stability and change. Instead, we will assume that social relationships can involve a variety of relative strengths of these polarities. What is adaptive can vary from time to time, depending on internal individual factors and external circumstances. Adaptiveness is associated, we believe, with the momentary congruence and fit of oppositional processes to given situations, not with some ultimate or ideal relationship between opposites.

In summary, our operational definition of the unity of opposites theme is that opposites function in a complementary way as part of a unified system, that opposition does not involve complete exclusion of one or the other pole, and that there is a range of relationships between opposites, with no particular one, including equality or balance, being inherently more adaptive than any other one.

C. THE CONCEPT OF CHANGE

Most dialectic approaches include the idea of a changing relationship between opposites. We also assume that relationships between openness-closedness and stability–change in social bonds are dynamic, with opposite poles having differential strength at different times and with the integration of opposites often associated with a new relationship stage. This orientation does not view change as a momentary disturbance or malfunctioning of a social system. Instead, we consider both change and stability to be intrinsic to social relationships and necessary for their adaptation to external and internal factors. Change is necessary if a relationship is to adapt successfully to varying conditions; stability is necessary to lend predictability and order to social functioning. At this point, more specific aspects of change in dialectic systems need to be explored, such as the extent to which change is cumulative, the directionality of change, and sources of change.

1. Change as Cumulative or Pendular

Given that dialectical polarities exhibit changing relationships, the question arises as to whether such processes are cumulative, incorporating prior histories of oppositional tension, or pendular, with each pole successively gaining, losing, and regaining strength.

Our interpretation of dialectic theorizing is that change generally has been treated as a cumulative process, and this approach fits best with our own conception of openness and closedness in social relationships. That is, we will assume that a given opposition has represented within it a history or accumulation of events, much as Lewin (1936, 1964) incorporates both ahistorical and historical processes in a contemporaneous life space. An important notion underlying this and related dialectic approaches is that change resulting from the resolution of opposites can be either qualitative or quantitative. A resolution involving quantitative changes involves adding similar elements to one or the other side of an opposition, with no substantive shift in the relationship between opposites. However, qualitative change involves a wholly new configuration of opposites or a new structural integration of components. For example, qualitative changes may occur when chemical and biological processes cumulate beyond some threshold point to create dramatic alterations of ecological systems.

The concept of cumulative change of either a quantitative or qualitative nature is compatible with most process-oriented theories in psychology and with our own views about the development of social relationships. For example, stage theories of child development usually presume a cumulative process, with quantitative behavioral increments within phases and qualitative shifts as a child moves to a new level of functioning. Similarly, Lewin's (1936, 1964) conception of the life space includes the idea of cumulative change, although he did not distinguish between quantitative and qualitative change. The Freudian description of regression to an earlier stage of development also seems to involve cumulative and qualitative changes in functioning. Our view of social penetration and privacy regulation assumes that the dialectic opposition of openness and closedness is cumulative, with prior histories of interaction incorporated in new relationships between opposites. These changes in openness and closedness are both quantitative and qualitative. Quantitative changes include cumulative additions to already established modes of interaction; qualitative changes involve new modes of interaction, new areas of interaction, or new bases to a relationship.

2. Change as "Growth Oriented" or Not

Another question concerns the extent to which dialectic systems move in a particular direction toward growth, higher levels of integration, or even some ideal state or final synthesis, or whether they simply change without any particular "upward" direction of movement.

The ancient Chinese philosophy of Tao Te Ching (Wilhelm & Baynes, 1950; Kuo, 1976) implies the possibility of an ultimate resolution of oppositions that, if achieved, yields supreme contentment and harmony and unity of the self in relation to others and to the universe. The idea of a "middle path" or Nirvana in Buddhist thinking contains a similar theme (Kuo, 1976): "Buddhists essentially end dialectical development in the state of Original Nature (or Mind), which means that all contradictions are resolved and tensions cease due to the oneness a Buddhist monk achieves with nature" (p. 76).

Similar conceptions appear in many Western philosophies and religions. Judeo-Christian beliefs posit a messianic period of ultimate perfection, which can be achieved by appropriate behaviors and by resolution of oppositions and contradictions. Hegel also theorized about progression toward an ultimate synthesis, as oppositions are successively resolved, and toward eventual achievement of the grand "Idea." Marx applied the Hegelian framework to the materialistic and social world and conceived of social classes in opposition, resulting eventually in a final synthesis in the form of a "classless society." Similar conceptions appeared in the writings of Plato and Socrates, who saw the resolution of dialectic oppositions as leading to a higher level of mental functioning.

An alternative assumption system is that dialectic oppositions do not proceed toward a particular idealized resolution. For example, according to Aristotle (Adler, 1927), dialectic processes do not necessarily culminate in a higher order synthesis; it may simply be that one pole of an opposition prevails momentarily as a resolution. Adler (1927) also reasoned that any synthesis of opposites may never be complete since total resolution yields the paradox of no opposition, thereby destroying a dialectic system. Furthermore, he stated, if one assumes an infinite universe there is always the possibility of some form of opposition to a given thesis, thereby lessening the likelihood of an ultimate synthesis. Or, if one assumes that human psychological functioning involves an "open system" (Brent, 1978b), with unlimited transactions with the social environment, then the idea of an ultimate synthesis is improbable.

A broad range of psychological theorizing assumes that behavior is directed toward some long-range goal. For example, Freudian theory implies that healthy psychological functioning involves an ideal synthesis wherein the ego keeps in balance the competing demands of the id and superego. For Erikson (1962), personality growth involves successive resolution of various crises which are linked with life stages. Thus, in these theories personal development is cumulative and directional and involves the resolution of a variety of oppositional processes as the person moves toward an idealized state. Similar ideas appear in the theorizing of Piaget (Flavell, 1963), who described the cognitive development of children as involving a continual interplay of assimilation (incorporating new information into existing mental schema) and accommodation (changing mental schema in response to new information). Assimilation and accommodation proceed through increasingly sophisticated stages of cognitive development to the point that a child achieves a mature orientation to the environment.

One exception to the notion of an ultimate synthesis of opposites appears in the personal construct theory of George Kelly (1955). He hypothesized that people construe the world in unique ways as they work through an endless array of bipolarities that are peculiar to their experiences. For Kelly, the process of resolving conflicts is cumulative, but unending and not necessarily directional, and it occurs in different ways for different people. In a sense, flexibility of personality is the ideal and reflects the ability of a person to adapt to ever new situational demands. Thus, if there is some ultimate ideal for Kelly, it is individual capability for change and flexibility rather than achievement of some final state.

Our approach, like that of Kelly, does not assume that social relationships have some inherent propensity to move toward more or less openness–closedness, stability–change, or some other ideal state. Rather, as we will discuss later, we assume that, depending on circumstances, relationships can be open or closed and stable or changing. If there is an ideal in our thinking, it is the capability of persons and relationships to exhibit flexible behavioral patterns that are congruent with situational, personal, and interpersonal demands at a given time.

3. Sources of Opposition

Given the idea that psychological and social processes are composed of myriad oppositions, speculation has arisen over the centuries about the origins of such phenomena. Do opposition and change arise from external sources, such as supernatural events or social and environmental phenomena? Or do they stem from events and processes that are intrinsic to characteristics of people and their interactions with one another?

Many philosophical and theological analyses have posited the existence of supernatural or cosmic sources of dialectic processes. Anaximander (ca. 560 B.C.), an early Greek dialectician, hypothesized that opposition and change derive from a universal, eternal, and divine force, *apeiron*, which is "the Boundless or Limitless over against the things that are" (Koenker, 1971). Similarly, traditional Judeo-Christian thinking posits the source of all reality, including opposition and change, to be derived from God. Such primal undifferentiated forces also appear in several versions of ancient Chinese dialectical thinking. Lao Tzu, often regarded as China's greatest dialectical philosopher, conceptualized oppositional processes as coming from the Tao, which is "elusive, evasive, nebulous, silent, invisible, unchanging, unceasing, everrevolving and standing as One" (Kuo, 1976, p. 73).

For some dialectically oriented philosophers, however, the origins of opposition and change were assumed to be internal in the "nature" of things and people. For example, Aristotle stated that opposition simply originates in the disagreements that are inherent in human interaction. Similarly, Plato argued that opposition arises as a result of tension in states of being and processes of becoming (Adler, 1952). For Kant, opposition derived from irreducible contradictions that the human mind cannot escape, and Marx believed that opposition is a result of materialistic and economic conflicts between different segments of society.

Analogous thinking appears in some psychological theorizing where the locus of dialectic opposition is within the person. For example, Freud postulated the existence of libido, a fundamental source of psychic energy, and a primitive id, which together served as the wellspring of human motivation. In somewhat the same way, Rogers (1961) and Maslow (1963) implied the existence of a "primal growth force" in people that affects motivations and actions. Kelly's (1955) personal construct theory also depicts personality as consisting of a variety of oppositional templates for integrating experience that are somewhat unique to every person. There is no indication in Kelly's thinking of an external source of such oppositions; they simply occur as a function of experience.

There has been, therefore, a broad spectrum of thinking regarding the origins of dialectic opposition and change. Our own view leans toward acceptance of both internal and external sources of opposition. We assume that individuals are unique entities and sometimes desire to withdraw or not interact with others. Yet, they also sometimes wish to be in contact with others. The result is that they are motivated to be both open and closed. Similarly, we assume that people have differential desires at various times for stability and change in their social relationships. However, we also recognize that external factors affect the relative strength of openness–closedness and stability–change. Such influences take the form of social pressures exerted by others, societal norms and demands, and various environmental factors. We wish to avoid, here, a discussion of the exact origins of dialectic opposition in external events, unique individual histories, biological and evolutionary roots, or combinations thereof. Although such an analysis may be necessary in the long run, it is not crucial to the immediate goals of this article, nor are we in a position to present a defensible analysis of the matter.

We have suggested that aspects of dialectic thinking appear in several psychological theories. However, the application of dialectic ideas has not always been systematic, nor have there been many attempts to offer a total theoretical perspective based on dialectic concepts. Perhaps an exception to this fragmented approach appears in the writings of a small group of developmental psychologists who have been influenced by the late Klaus Riegel (1976, 1979).

Although we cannot do justice to the ideas of this group, it may be instructive to present selective aspects of their theorizing in relation to our previous discussion. First, the idea of opposition is central, although different theorists emphasize different oppositions. As an exemplar, Riegel (1976, 1979) hypothesized the operation of several oppositions over the life cycle. These involve the interplay of inner-biological, individual-psychological, cultural-sociological, and outer-physical (environmental) dimensions. Each of these domains may interact with the others, in a dialectical fashion, to yield various life crises which need to be resolved or synthesized. For example, the inner-biological and cultural-sociological domains may exhibit opposition and require a resolution when a person is of sufficient physiological maturity to marry but is not deemed to be ready in terms of cultural-sociological characteristics. Or combinations of these domains may sometimes be in synchrony, yielding a congruence or synthesis of opposites. So, Riegel hypothesized the occurrence of successive asynchronies, synchronies, asynchronies, etc., throughout the life cycle. Implicit in this analysis are several of the ideas described earlier, namely, the functioning of opposites as aspects of a unity, the resolution of opposition without total destruction of one or the other pole, and the like.

Another central dialectical idea in the writings of Riegel and his associates is the emphasis on change. For this group of theorists, change, not stability, is the essence of human development. And change is not an interlude between idealized states of stability or balance. Instead, these writers argue, developmental phenomena inherently involve change as a person attempts to address various asynchronies and oppositions at different life stages. In fact, these theorists seem to place greater emphasis on change than on stability: "The individual, the society, and even outer nature are never at rest, and in their restlessness, they are rarely in perfect harmony" (Riegel, 1976, p. 319).

There is an increasing body of literature on the application of dialectic concepts to developmental psychology which can be sampled in the journal *Human Development* and in volumes by Datan and Reese (1977), Reigel and Rosenwald (1975), and Lerner (1976, 1979).

Because the concept of dialectics has had so many applications over the centuries, a goal of the preceding analysis was to outline our approach to the term for subsequent use in an extension of privacy regulation and social penetration theories. An implication of our analysis is that one may satisfy certain defining qualities of the concept of dialectics and not satisfy others. Thus, given the varied usage of the term, no one can be a "perfect" dialectician.

IV. Assumptions about Social Relationships

A. GENERAL PHILOSOPHICAL ASSUMPTIONS

This section sets forth the general assumptions underlying our integration of social penetration and privacy regulation theories. These assumptions are proposed as axiomatic articles of faith with regard to the fundamental nature of human social behavior. The final section of the chapter outlines a number of research questions based on these assumptions.

We assume that human social interaction can be viewed as functioning in accordance with two dialectical processes: openness–closedness and stability–change. We further assume that the oppositional components of these dialectics operate as a unified and dynamic system, that each pole of the two oppositions is equally important to social functioning, and that the interplay of openness–closedness and stability–change is not directed at achieving some ideal or ultimate state.

1. The Openness-Closedness Dialectic

A central assumption underlying privacy regulation theory is that an important facet of human social behavior involves being both open and closed to contact with others. Openness reflects a willingness to join with others, to be affiliative and gregarious, or to be willing to expose the self to another person. Closedness involves shutting oneself off or withdrawing from others. When people are relatively open, they tend to be self-revealing and in contact with one another. When they are closed to contact, they withdraw, become more distant, or are more constrained in their interaction.

The openness–closedness dialectic operates along a number of substantive dimensions. An individual may, for example, be receptive to a specific person while remaining relatively closed to others. Similarly, people may be differentially open or closed in a variety of content areas. Individuals may also differ in receptivity to contact at intimate and superficial levels. For example, they may be willing to discuss superficial topics with a particular other person and not to deal with intimate issues; the opposite may occur with someone else or at another time.

The desire for more or less contact may be expressed by means of a variety of behaviors, ranging from verbal behaviors (e.g., self-disclosure, hostility, and affection), to nonverbal, environmental, and cultural behaviors (e.g., seeking eye contact, shutting one's office door, adhering to cultural customs regarding receptivity or avoidance of others). Therefore, the concepts of openness–closedness can be operationally defined by a variety of behavioral indicators. The discussion to follow, however, focuses primarily on a conceptual level of analysis rather than on specific behavioral indicators of openness and closedness.

We also assume that the interplay of openness–closedness can be conceived of as a *boundary regulation* process whereby individuals (and perhaps groups and larger social systems) maintain viability by regulation of exchanges with the physical and social environment. Under some conditions, the person–environment boundary is relatively open and permeable, and, in other cases, self-environment boundaries may be impermeable to one degree or another. Although either openness or closedness may temporarily dominate, we assume that all viable relationships contain certain elements of both openness and closedness at all times. Indeed, an individual's ability to regulate boundaries with the external world may be a necessary condition for viability and adaptation to a range of situations. We also assume that analogous boundary processes occur in many areas of behavior. Therefore, our focus on interpersonal aspects of self–other accessibility may be only one instance of a generic human process (Altman, 1979). Consider next a few examples of boundary processes in a variety of behavioral domains.

2. General Boundary Systems

Boundary regulation involves relationships between an individual and the physical and social environment. For example, some theories hypothesize that an early stage of child development involves a few perceived boundaries between the child and the world; the environment is psychologically part of the child and the child is part of the environment. Eventually, the child distinguishes between the self and non-self and gains skill at being differentially open or closed to the world. This process is illustrated by the analysis of child development of Mahler,

Pine, and Bergman (1975). At first, according to this view, the child does not differentiate clearly between the mother and itself. With maturation and social development, boundaries slowly evolve, as the child exhibits cycles of openness and closedness in relation to the mother, seeking contact with her in some situations and deliberately breaking away in other circumstances. Mahler *et al.* conceive of extreme degrees of either openness or closedness as maladaptive. Thus, autism may represent an extreme case of closedness where an impenetrable boundary exists between the child and its social world. At the other extreme is an overly dependent relationship such that the child treats the mother as part of itself, reflecting the absence of a separation or boundary between them. For Mahler *et al.*, therefore, healthy child development involves a changing interplay of separation from and contact with the mother and others.

The early sociological perspectives of Cooley (1902/1964) and Mead (1934) imply a similar process. For these theorists, an important stage of social development occurs when a person is able to view the self from the perspective of others, that is, Cooley's "looking glass self" concept and Mead's distinction between "I" and "Me" aspects of the self. In both cases, social growth occurs when the person learns to distinguish between the self and others, suggesting the development of boundary regulation processes.

The importance of successful regulation of openness or closedness in relation to the world is also evident in research on learned helplessness (Seligman, 1975). Here, an organism is placed in a situation where it cannot control environmental stimulation. Aversive events appear in an unpredictable and uncontrollable fashion and are not contingent on the organism's responses. Thus, normal boundary regulation is rendered ineffective. In some experiments, animals almost give up, fail to regulate their self–environment boundaries, and perform poorly on subsequent learning tasks. Such research illustrates the crucial role of boundary management and the negative implications of failure to regulate transactions with the environment.

Another example is the recent theorizing of Blatt and Wild (1976), who view schizophrenia as involving the poor functioning of cognitive, perceptual, and interpersonal boundary processes. In contrast, healthy functioning involves the ability to maintain behavioral and cognitive distinctions between the self and others and to avoid either extreme fusion with or extreme separation from the physical and social world.

3. *Interpersonal Boundary Systems*

A considerable portion of social psychology, including our own work on social penetration and privacy regulation, can be interpreted as dealing with interpersonal boundary processes and, more specifically, with the openness and closedness of people to one another.

A particularly relevant example of interpersonal boundary processes appears in the theorizing of Argyle and Dean (1965). Their view is that social interaction involves the interplay of approach and avoidance forces propelling people toward or away from one another depending on a variety of social and situational factors. For any given relationship, people seek a particular level of intimacy in terms of the momentary strength of approach and avoidance tendencies. At another level of analysis, Bettleheim (1969) and Simmel (1908/1950) emphasize the importance of both social contact and solitude to the formation of intimate relationships.

In another area, research on loneliness (Perlman & Peplau, 1981) and shyness (Zimbardo, 1977) indicate how insufficient accessibility to others can be aversive. Similarly, as we indicated earlier, studies of self-disclosure, personal space, territorial behavior, and crowding all reflect different facets of self-other boundary regulation processes. Thus, the ability or inability to be open or closed to others in accord with one's momentary desires reflects basic social boundary processes.

Although it may be stretching the idea somewhat, certain features of the research on psychological reactance (Brehm, 1966) can also be viewed as attempts to understand how people react to certain types of violation of their self-other boundaries. This research demonstrates that perceptions of restrictions on one's freedom often lead to *reactance,* which includes a psychological state of stress, a drive to restore one's options, and behaviors aimed at reestablishing perceived freedom. Putting this in our terms, reactance may include establishment of desired openness–closedness with respect to others or to facets of the environment.

Thus, the idea of openness–closedness appears to be an important feature of social interaction, psychological development, and adaptive functioning. Although we do not imply that a single theory can encompass all these phenomena, we do believe that the general concept of boundary regulation and its key facets of openness and closedness are ideas potentially worthy of general application.

4. The Stability–Change Dialectic

Most theories in psychology maintain that human behavior is directed toward achieving balance, equilibrium, or consistency. Furthermore, it is generally assumed that this process occurs at physiological, perceptual, cognitive, and behavioral levels of functioning. It is also often postulated that imbalance is aversive and stressful and that people attempt to reduce or eliminate inconsistencies and imbalances. In contrast, we assume that people are oriented toward both stability and change in their social relationships. They not only display and sometimes seek consistency, balance, and equilibrium in their social relationships, but they also exhibit and sometimes search for change, inconsistency, imbalance, and disequilibrium. We further assume that stability and change are equally fundamental to human behavior. Neither is subservient to the other, and together they form a dynamic system such that qualities of either stability or change can be stronger or weaker at one time or another.

We also believe that both stability and change occur with respect to a number of dimensions of social interaction. Of particular interest to the present analysis are the ways in which openness and closedness exhibit patterns or cycles of stability and change at different times over the course of a relationship. As we see it, the dialectic concept of stability–change is an operating parameter which can be applied to a number of substantive dimensions of social interaction, one of which is openness and closedness.

Stability and change may vary on a number of dimensions:

1. *Frequency,* or number of cycles of openness and closedness per unit of time. Thus, if the number of cycles of openness and closedness is high per unit of time, then a pattern of interaction has occurred that involves rapid and frequent shifts by participants in their openness and closedness to one another. It indicates, therefore, an emphasis on changes in openness and closedness. On the other hand, a small number of cycles per unit of time depicts a relatively stable and unchanging pattern of openness and closedness.

2. *Amplitude,* or relative amount of openness or closedness in a given cycle. Thus, high amplitude reflects a large amount of openness (or closedness) during a given period, and low amplitude indicates the opposite.

The combination of amplitude and frequency dimensions yields a variety of stability–change patterns. For example, a high amplitude or high amount of openness (and/or closedness) coupled with a high frequency of openness–closedness cycles depicts a rapidly changing pattern of interaction that involves dramatic shifts in the amount of interaction, that is, rapid shifts from intense open exchange to closed or limited exchange, followed by another intense exchange, all within a very short period. In this example, change is the dominant quality of interaction. Another pattern reflects considerable stability of interaction, for example, when the amplitude of openness (and/or closedness) is high but is coupled with relatively few cycles or shifts in interaction per unit of time.

3. *Regularity,* or repetitiveness in patterns of openness–closedness cycles. This property derives from the frequency and amplitude dimensions. It refers to the degree to which stability–change features of interaction appear in a consistent, regular fashion over a period of time, or the degree to which interaction shows changing patterns of frequency and amplitude of openness–closedness cycles. Thus, one can conceive of cases in which people exhibit consistent and repetitive cycles and amplitudes of openness and closedness during a given period of time. Or one can imagine varying patterns of openness and closedness in a period of time, such as where people first engage in stable cycles of openness (or closedness) of a constant amplitude but then exhibit rapidly changing fre-

quencies in cycles of openness and closedness with varying amplitudes of interaction.

   4. *Relative duration.* Portions of individual cycles may vary widely in the relative duration or time associated with openness and closedness. For example, on some occasions the openness of a given cycle may last longer than the closedness portion, yielding a longer period of accessibility relative to inaccessibility. Or, the opposite may occur, with individual cycles characterized by extensive periods of closedness, and only brief and intermittent durations of openness.

   In summary, the stability–change dimension can operate on a number of substantive aspects of social exchange, such as openness and closedness. Our analysis holds that both stability and change are intrinsic aspects of social relationships, with neither more central than the other. Because this perspective departs from traditional assumptions, it may be helpful to examine aspects of the history of equilibrium, balance, and consistency ideas in psychology.

B. HOMEOSTASIS AND THE MAINTENANCE OF STABILITY

1. Homeostasis and Biological Sciences

   The maintenance of stability has been postulated throughout history as a feature of physical and biological systems. Biological conceptions of equilibrium were proposed by Hippocrates (460–377 B.C.) and appeared over and over again, culminating in the modern dictum of Claude Bernard, the French physiologist of the nineteenth century, who stated, ''It is the fixity of the 'milieu interieur' which is the condition of free and independent life,'' and ''all the vital mechanisms, however varied they may be, have only one object, that of preserving constant conditions of life in the internal environment'' (cited in Cannon, 1932, p. 38).

   It was Walter Cannon's (1932) analysis of biological systems that eventually laid the foundation for assumptions of stability seeking as a fundamental psychological process. Cannon, a physician and physiologist, described how the human body maintains constancy of functioning in a variety of physiological domains—blood and vascular systems, thirst and hunger, salt and mineral regulation, body temperature, acid–base balance, and autonomic and voluntary systems. Physiological systems are finely attuned to even slight deviations in their functioning and are capable of restoring balance by release of stored materials (e.g., glycogen, insulin) or by adaptations of physiological processes (e.g., heat loss or preservation, oxygen consumption). Cannon coined the term *homeostasis* to reflect the idea that the human body has a variety of interlocked and compensating physiological systems and that it is far more complex than simple physical equilibrium systems.

   Cannon's theory involved absolute constancy levels such as a body temperature of 98.6°F. Although some variations around fixed points are possible, physiological systems are designed to maintain a relatively narrow band of ideal functioning. In this sense, Cannon's model involves striving for a particular steady state, and its response to deviation is to reachieve a fixed ideal (Brent, 1978a).

2. Homeostasis and General Psychology

Cannon's model was readily adopted by psychology, especially in the fields of sensation, perception, learning, and physiological psychology. It was parsimonious, and it also provided a potential bridge between physiological and psychological substrates of behavior. However, the concept of homeostasis took many forms in psychological theorizing, and most applications were more flexible than Cannon's absolute fixed point analysis of biological systems.

Although not intended as such, Helson's (1964) adaptation level theory contains certain homeostatic concepts. The adaptation level is a zone of neutrality or a zero point around which new stimulation is judged to be greater or lesser. Unlike physiological homeostasis, however, adaptation level theory does not assume a fixed equilibrium point toward which behavior is directed. Instead, the adaptation level is a floating neutrality point that shifts, depending on prior experience. In addition, there may be wide individual differences in adaptation levels, depending on unique experiences. Brent (1978a) described this type of homeostatic system as allowing two types of response to the disruption of constancy—a return to the original balance point (as in physiological systems) or the development of a new neutral point around which stimulation is judged.

This type of homeostatic system has been broadly applied in psychology.[2] For example, Stagner hypothesized that homeostasis is the bedrock of personality functioning (Stagner, 1951, 1954, 1961, 1977), although he described homeostasis as a dynamic process that was not geared to a fixed balance point, furthermore, Stagner hypothesized that such homeostatic systems are hierarchical, since people may seek out imbalances at one level of functioning in order to obtain homeostasas at another level. In addition, he conjectured that exploratory behavior and stimulus seeking are designed to facilitate homeostasis in the long run by enabling more accurate anticipatory responses.

The concept of homeostasis is also widespread in developmental psychology. According to Brent (1978a), some developmental theories involve several possible responses to imbalance: (1) The system can strive toward an original balance point, similar to physiological systems; (2) the system can move to a new level of constancy, as suggested by Helson and Stagner; (3) the system can move to a wholly new level of structural integration, as posited by various stage

---

[2]For a more detailed analysis of applications of homeostasis concepts in general psychology, see Brent (1978), Stagner (1977), and Cofer and Appley (1964). For a description of the historical uses of equilibrium models in sociology, see Russett (1966).

theories of human development. For example, a theme common to several stage
theories is that development involves qualitative reorganization of social, cognitive, and perceptual response systems in order to achieve more sophisticated
adaptations to the physical and social world. Examples include Piaget's (Flavell,
1963) theory of the development of cognition, which involves qualitative
changes from concrete sensory to formal operational levels, and Erikson's (1962)
hypothesis of eight stages of psychosocial development.

3. Homeostasis and Social Psychology

The assumption of homeostasis also serves as the basis for modern social
psychology. It is especially evident in the writings of Kurt Lewin and Fritz
Heider, the philosophical and theoretical architects of the field, who emphasized
homeostasis as a central human quality.

Heider and Lewin, influenced by the Gestalt tradition, sought to understand
how people established consistency and stability in their perceptual, attitudinal,
and social worlds. According to Heider (1958), a social system consists of (1)
elements that have some relationship to one another (e.g., members of a family,
interacting persons, a person and his or her actions) and (2) sentiments, or
positive and negative feelings about entities in the system. These unit relations
and sentiments function according to balance-directed qualities:

> The relationship between sentiments and unit formation tends toward a balanced state. (p.
> 177)

> by a balanced state . . . is meant a harmonious state, one in which the entities comprising the
> situation and the feelings about them fit together without stress . . . . Harmony exists when
> entities with equal values are united (pp. 180, 210)

> [Unbalanced situations] leave us with a feeling of disturbance that becomes relieved only
> when change within the situation takes place in such a way that a state of balance is
> achieved. (p. 180)

Lewin also assumed that people sought balance, although he used the terms
equilibrium and *quasi-stationary equilibrium*. Similar to Heider's, Lewin's
(1936), analysis of psychological equilibrium involved "a constellation of forces
such that the forces at a point are opposite in direction and equal in strength" (p.
218).

Lewin applied balance concepts to several aspects of behavior, including
child development, personality, social relationships, and social organization. For
example, with respect to small group processes, Lewin (1964) stated:

> Self-regulating processes are well-known in the individual . . . . Similarly, self-regulating
> processes . . . seem to be characteristic of those conglomerations which are "natural
> groups." For instance, if a worker is temporarily absent other workers of his team might

pinch hit for him. In other words, the constellation of forces which keeps the group life on a certain quasi-stationary level may maintain this level in spite of disturbances. (p. 166)

His belief about the applicability of equilibrium concepts to a broad range of fields is clear (Lewin, 1964):

Our consideration of quasi-stationary equilibrium has been based on analytic concepts, which within the realm of social sciences, have emerged first in psychology. The concepts of a psychological force, of tension, of conflicts as equilibria of forces, of force fields and of inducing fields, have slowly widened their range of application from the realm of individual psychology into the realm of processes and events which had been the domain of sociology and cultural anthropology. From what I have been able to learn recently about the treatment of equilibria by mathematical economics, I am convinced that this treatment, although having a different origin and being based perhaps on a different philosophy, is also fully compatible with our considerations. (p. 235)

Lewin's concept of life space also implies equilibrium processes. The life space consists of the person (contemporaneous and historical aspects of personality) and the psychological environment (momentary features of the immediate environment which have psychological importance to the individual). Valences, or positive and negative features of regions of the psychological environment, are linked to the present needs of the person, with resultant psychological forces propelling the person toward certain regions of the environment. As such, the life space at any moment in time is directed toward achieving a state of equilibrium involving the person and the psychological environment.

Heider and Lewin have had a major impact on social psychological theorizing. For example, Newcomb's (1953) theory of communicative acts consists of an individual coorienting simultaneously toward another person and toward an issue, object, or third person, with the system directed at achieving or reestablishing balance: "We shall also make the assumption . . . that certain forces impinging upon the system are relatively strong and persistent, and that thus there are 'strains' toward preferred states of equilibrium" (p. 395). Perhaps the most influential extension of Lewin's and Heider's thinking was cognitive dissonance theory (Festinger, 1956), the essence of which was as follows: "The basic background of the theory consists of the notion that the human organism tries to establish internal harmony, consistency, or congruity among his opinions, attitudes, knowledge, and values. That is, there is a drive toward consonance among cognitions" (p. 260). Furthermore, Festinger stated that dissonant relations between cognitions operate as drive states: "the existence of non-fitting relations among cognitions, is a motivating factor in its own right" (p. 3) and "The presence of dissonance gives rise to pressures to reduce or eliminate the dissonance" (p. 18).

It is important to note that social psychological theories do not posit absolute balance points toward which behavior is directed, as is the case for some physical and biological systems. Instead, the cumulative role of experience results in shifting balance points, along the lines hypothesized by adaptation level theory. Also, homeostatic ideas in social psychology usually do not involve successive developmental stages of balance, as do certain personality and developmental models.

4. Signs of Discontent with Homeostasis

In spite of the pervasiveness of the assumption of homeostasis in psychological theorizing, doubts have been raised about its universality. Some researchers have observed that animals and humans seek out imbalance or inconsistency, explore strange environments, and seek novel stimulation, thereby seeming to act in a way that is contrary to homeostatic notions. To account for such behavior, some have proposed an exploratory or curiosity motive; others have argued that the search for novel experiences is only designed to better serve the more fundamental motive for consistency. Still others have suggested that the social sciences erroneously adopted closed system models of human functioning which are more appropriate to the analysis of limited physical systems. These critics contend that open systems models, with emphases on change and self-ordering capacities, may be more appropriate models for living systems which interact with their environments (Bertalanffy, 1968; Brent, 1978b; Russett, 1966).

A question about the monolithic assumption of homeostasis even appears in Cannon (1932), although his comments on this issue are rarely cited. In a final chapter, Cannon speculated that homeostasis might operate in social systems, although probably at a less sophisticated level of functioning compared with that of biological systems. Most important, however, Cannon hypothesized that homeostatic mechanisms liberated people from the mundane aspects of life so that they could pursue more exciting and novel adventures:

> Bodily homeostasis, as we have learned, results in liberating those functions of the nervous system that adapt the organism to new situations from the necessity of paying routine attention to the management of the details of bare existence. Without homeostatic devices we should be in constant danger of disaster, unless we are always on the alert to correct voluntarily what normally is corrected automatically. With homeostatic devices, . . . we as individuals are free from such slavery—free to enter into agreeable relations with our fellows, free to enjoy beautiful things, to explore and understand the wonders of the world about us, to develop new ideas and interests, and to work and play, untrammeled by anxieties concerning our bodily affairs. The main service of social homeostasis would be to support bodily homeostasis. It would therefore help to release the highest activities of the nervous system for adventure and achievement. With essential needs assured, the priceless unessentials could be freely sought. (p. 323)

> There might be apprehension that social stabilization would tend towards dull monotony, that the excitements of uncertainty would be lacking. That would be true, however, only for the fundamental requirements of existence. There would still be the social disturbances of

new inventions, the social interest in renowned exploits, in the discords of human nature, in reports of fresh ideas, in the intrigues of love and hate, and in whatever events there may be that make life varied and colorful . . . . Just as social stabilization would foster the stability, both physical and mental, of the members of the social organism, so likewise it would foster their higher freedom, giving them serenity and leisure, which are the primary conditions for wholesome recreation, for the discovery of a satisfactory and invigorating social milieu, and for the discipline and enjoyment of individual aptitudes. (p. 324)

In this little known statement Cannon acknowledged that human behavior may be directed toward more than achieving stability alone. In fact, one may interpret his comments to mean that homeostatic processes are in the service of human striving for the unusual and the novel and that is is variety that is the bedrock of human behavior, not the search for stability and balance.

A more explicit view along these lines was expressed by Helson (1964), whose adaptation level theory is often interpreted as a paragon of homeostatic ideas. To the contrary, Helson referred to the interplay of stability and change as crucial to human functioning:

Although recognizing such concepts as homeostasis, striving toward equilibrium, desire for rest, and other more or less steady states, we must not forget that individuals and groups strive for variety, change and novelty as well as for rest, quiet, and the familiar. To infer from our theory that all behavior is directed toward the attainment of equilibrium or fixed end-states is wrong. The desire for pleasure, action, objects, possessions, change of situation, fame, recognition, and all the other things for which men strive is not satisfied by reaching a state of equilibrium (which would be paralleled psychologically by feelings of neutrality or indifference) but rather by attaining greater variety and intensity of satisfactions which come from activities and objects associated with higher levels of adjustment. (p. 49)

impulsion to action (and enjoyment) comes not from situations giving rise to neutral states of the organism but rather from the disparity between stimulation and prevailing adaptation level. (p. 49)

The point of view enunciated here asserts that equilibrium states represent the reference points or zeros from which behavior is measured, predicted, and understood, without implying that the *goal* of behavior is a state of equilibrium. (p. 49)

To emphasize his view, Helson cited Cohen (1958):

Whatever the value of the principle of equilibrium in physiology where it arose, whether it is called constancy, stability, homeostasis or negative feedback, its explanatory value in the domain of the mind is limited . . . . It serves to express the important elements of stability and resistance to change, but it does nothing to convey the part played by instability and the impulse to change in human life. These are just as fundamental, and without them social change would be inconceivable. (p. 52)

Although one finds relatively little discussion of the stability–change issue in social psychology, there are several theorists who, although strong homeostasis proponents, hint at the importance of change and variety in social behavior. For example, Fritz Heider (1958), made a brief reference to the human tendency to seek variety:

> On the other hand, there may also be the tendency to leave the comfortable equilibrium, to seek the new and adventurous. The tension produced by unbalanced situations often has a pleasing effect on our thinking and esthetic feelings. Balanced situations can have a boring obviousness and a finality of superficial self-evidence. Unbalanced situations stimulate us to further thinking; they have the character of interesting puzzles, problems which make us suspect a depth of interesting background. Sometimes they evoke, like other patterns with unsolved ambiguities, powerful esthetic forces of a tragic or comic nature. (p. 180)

Fiske and Maddi (1961) hypothesized that organisms seek varying stimulation, sometimes more and sometimes less than the range of stimulation to which they have been exposed. In a sense, constant, stable stimulation may result in monotony and perhaps even an inability to function in a range of environments:

> Organisms manifest a need to maintain their normal level of activation. This motive is non-specific in the sense that any of a wide range of behaviors may be utilized to furnish stimulation with appropriate impact. When those specific motives are present, the organism commonly attempts to sustain activation by seeking or producing stimulation with variation; it may attend to complex stimulation, it may explore, or it may play. (p. 46)

Maddi (1968) stated the issue even more explicitly and in a way that is close to our own view. For Maddi, both consistency and variety are essential and equal facets of human functioning:

> It is variety that produces the experience of surprise, and a new consistency that produces the subsequent experience of insight and deeper meaning. The total experience is a little like being stretched to a new height. It is the experience of growth. And the experience of growth—clearly satisfying—requires this particular combination of variety and consistency.
>   In conclusion I would suggest that single-minded emphasis on either the consistency or the variety positions . . . is shortsighted. Both consistency and variety are pursued and enjoyed, and it is incumbent upon us to recognize this in some harmonious and creative fashion in our theorizing. (p. 274)

In summary, we have illustrated how the assumption of homeostasis, in one form or another, pervades psychological theorizing. Yet, we have also pointed to a variety of writings that implicitly or explicitly question this assumption and suggest how human behavior is frequently directed at seeking change and instability. Although exploratory and novelty-seeking behaviors have begun to be researched in some fields, present-day research and theory in social psychology is based primarily on the monolithic assumption of homeostasis or stability as the major underpinning of human social behavior. Our view, described next, contrasts with this orientation. Instead, we will assume that human social behavior is directed toward achieving both stability and change in social relationships, according to several characteristics of dialectic systems.

C. SPECIFIC ASSUMPTIONS ABOUT OPENNESS-CLOSEDNESS AND STABILITY-CHANGE

We now state our assumptions about dialectic features of openness-closedness and stability-change in relation to social interaction. These assumptions derive from the earlier analysis of dialectic philosophy and the immediately preceding discussion. Based on these assumptions, we then propose a series of researchable questions and hypotheses that integrate and extend privacy regulation and social penetration theories.

1. *Human social relationships are characterized by (a) openness or contact and closedness or separateness between participants and (b) stability or consistency and change or variety.* We assume that people in a social relationship are open and closed toward one another, with these oppositional processes varying in strength at different times and in different circumstances. More specifically, we assume that social relationships exhibit both stability and change in reference to openness-closedness. That is, openness and closedness do not exist in a static relationship to one another. Although people may exhibit relatively stable openness (or closedness) for a period of time, it is likely that openness eventually gives way to closedness and that closedness is eventually followed by openness. Such cyclical variations in accessibility of people to one another are affected by factors internal and external to social relationships.

These cycles of openness-closedness may exhibit different patterns of stability and change over short and long periods of time. Thus, there may be short-term cycles of changing accessibility-inaccessibility within longer term stable cycles of either openness or closedness. For example, a relationship between two people may be characterized by a high level of accessibility over a period of time, perhaps months. Yet, within that generally stable interval of openness, the participants may exhibit change—coming together and withdrawing over shorter periods of time, sometimes being relatively less open and sometimes being more open. Thus it is possible that there are short-term cyclical fluctuations of accessibility and inaccessibility that are embedded in stable long-term cycles.

A given pattern of openness-closedness can be characterized with respect to stability-change along several dimensions, as discussed earlier. For example, cycles of openness-closedness can differ in (1) the *frequency* with which participants shift from openness to closedness (i.e., the number of cycles per unit of time), (2) the *amplitude,* or absolute amount of openness-closedness, (3) the *regularity,* or redundancy with which given cyclical patterns recur, and (4) the *relative duration,* or proportion of time openness and closedness appear in a given cycle. Finally, stability–change patterns may differ in various content areas and modalities; for example, a member of a couple may increase rapidly in openness to the other's self-disclosure while maintaining a relatively closed stance toward nonverbal intimacy.

Stability and change apply to several aspects of openness–closedness in social relationships. These include self-disclosure, nonverbal behavior, general avoidance and receptivity, and many of the topics discussed throughout this article in relation to social penetration and privacy theory. In addition, participants in a social relationship may seek stability in being able to predict the behavior of their partners, anticipating their dealings with one another and achieving consistency of outcomes in their mutual contacts. For example, social penetration theory hypothesized that relationship development involved the formation of mutually consistent and stable cognitive models by participants about one another. Similarly, attribution theory describes how people attempt to develop stable and orderly explanations for events, including their own behavior and that of others.

On the other hand, people also seek variety, change, and novelty in their social relationships. Even in well-established relationships people challenge and stimulate one another and exhibit a degree of unpredictability in their interactions. The absence of varied experience may be stagnating, satiating, or inhibiting to the growth of a relationship. If another person is totally predictable, if interactions are totally consistent, if a social bond is in a totally steady state, then the relationship may be incapable of growth or expansion. In such cases, people may deliberately act to alter the relationship by challenging one another, generating conflict, or seeking out new experiences in the relationship. Or, obviously, they may turn to new relationships to achieve change. On the other hand, a relationship that is constantly changing and in which there is ever present unpredictability and novelty may not be viable over the long run.

In summary, we will assume that openness–closedness and stability–change are always present in social relationships, with one or the other pole of these dialectics dominating at different times. In addition, openness–closedness and stability–change cycles may occur over long and short periods of time. Finally, we assume that both poles of these oppositions are important to social relationships, with neither being more primary.

2. *Social relationships do not strive toward an ultimate or ideal balance of openness and closedness or of stability and change.* As discussed earlier, psychological theorizing often assumes that human functioning is directed toward some ideal state of affairs such as balance or homeostasis. On the other hand, we assume that adaptive social functioning involves a momentary congruence of psychological processes with the demands of a situation. Thus, an adaptive pattern of openness–closedness and stability–change can take many forms, none of which is necessarily better or worse than any other. In certain situations,

viable relationships may have a relatively greater preponderance of openness over closedness; in other situations viability may be associated with more closedness than openness; still other cases may show an equal balance of these opposites.

We also assume that different patterns of stability and change of openness and closedness can be adaptive over the history of a social relationship. Some successful relationships may proceed gradually toward a relatively greater degree of openness than closedness. Other relationships may begin with relative openness, but over the long term people may gradually withdraw and become more closed to one another, or vice versa. Or participants may value a relationship which shifts rapidly and abruptly from intense interaction to reserve. Still other viable relationships may remain in a stable accessibility or inaccessibility state for a long period of time.

As a related issue, most dialectic philosophies assume that oppositions never totally obliterate one another. The existence of a dialectic system requires the presence of some quality of each polar opposite. Thus, the total domination of a dialectic system by one or the other opposition would yield a static state, with no possibility for change, growth, movement, or adaptation to new circumstances. For these reasons we will assume that, regardless of the openness of a relationship, there will still exist elements of inaccessibility between participants. Thus, participants in a relationship are not likely to ever know one another completely or to have unlimited access to each other's lives. Such a situation would result in the complete mutual absorption of participants, a loss of their separate individualities, and extreme vulnerability and dependence, which could result in the eventual destruction of the relationship. Similarly, a relationship is not likely to survive if there is complete inaccessibility of partners to one another. Obviously, if they never communicate, never reveal themselves, or are never in contact with one another, the relationship would not be likely to continue.

In the same way, both stability and change are assumed to be ever present qualities of social relationships. A social bond with complete stability is not likely to grow or adapt to new circumstances. External and internal events that impinge on a relationship, momentarily or on a long-term basis, usually require adaptation and response modifiability. A totally unchanging relationship is, therefore, not likely to survive outside of a totally encapsulated situation, and such situations rarely occur. In some cases, parties to a relationship may wish for "the world to stop," so they can achieve the glories of a particular moment on a permanent basis. Needless to say, this rarely happens, as external and internal events eventually press the relationship toward change.

The extreme opposite, continuous change and instability, is equally maladaptive. Relationships that are unstable and ever-changing, where nothing is predictable from moment to moment and where there is an unending search for novelty, are also not likely to survive. Some minimal clarity about role relationships, mutual agreement about the rules of a relationship, and other aspects of stability are essential to the viability of a social unit.

In summary, our dialectic perspective assumes that viable social bonds possess elements of both stability and change and of both openness and closedness, with either side of these oppositions possibly stronger than the other at a given moment but with neither pole ever totally dominating. It is only with elements of each oppositional pole present, even to a minimal extent, that a relationship can grow, adapt, and respond to variations in internal and external circumstances.

This section has outlined some fundamental philosophical assumptions that serve as the substrate for our attempts to integrate and extend social penetration and privacy regulation theories. As essentially untestable statements of faith, their value resides in the theoretical ideas they spawn, the questions they provoke, and the research they stimulate. In the next section, we propose a series of theoretically relevant research questions and hypotheses that derive from our assumptions that human social relationships involve a dialectic interplay of openness–closedness and stability–change.

V.   Directions for Research

The long-range goal of our dialectic extension of social penetration and privacy regulation theories is to generate empirically testable hypotheses about the development and management of interpersonal relationships. This section poses a number of research possibilities that derive from our analysis. The topics to be discussed concern openness–closedness and stability–change processes in reference to (1) relationship development, (2) crises in social relationships, (3) intimacy of exchange, (4) personal characteristics of interaction style, and (5) the interpersonal unit—matching and timing of interaction.

The focus of the discussion will be on the amplitude and frequency characteristics of openness–closedness cycles in relation to the preceding topics. We will not address systematically the dimensions of regularity or relative duration of openness–closedness cycles, discussed earlier, because of the complexity associated with these dimensions of stability–change. Where possible, we will offer hypotheses about stability and change in relation to openness and closedness, although such predictions are primarily heuristic, since little guiding data are available in the research literature.

A.   OPENNESS-CLOSEDNESS AND STABILITY-CHANGE IN DEVELOPING
     RELATIONSHIPS

Figure 1 summarizes the basic social penetration and privacy regulation concepts. Figure 1a depicts the development of social relationships in intimate and nonintimate areas of exchange as a function of interpersonal rewards and

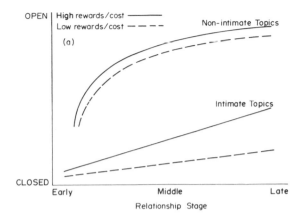

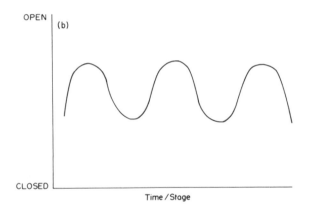

Fig. 1.   Summary of social penetration (a) and privacy regulation (b) frameworks.

costs. These curves are based on theory and empirical research, as discussed in earlier sections. They illustrate the orderly development of social relationships from acquaintanceship to close friendship along a dimension of increasing openness of participants to one another and in relation to reward–cost factors. Figure 1B outlines the basic hypothesis of privacy regulation theory, namely, that people in a relationship exhibit variations in openness and closedness from one time to another.

The curves of Fig. 2 represent two possible configurations of openness–closedness cycles suggested by the present dialectic analysis. These curves suggest that, along with generally increasing openness over the growth of a social bond, people exhibit embedded cycles of openness and closedness. That is, we speculate that a period of openness eventually gives way to a degree of closedness—as people seek a change in their mode of dealing with one another, as they try to absorb the results of their interaction, as they experience psycholog-

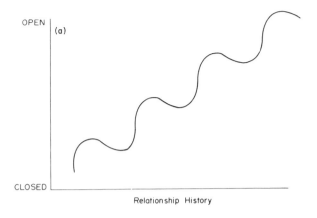

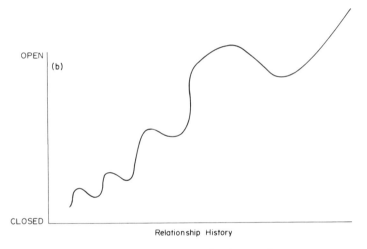

Fig. 2.   Possible openness–closedness cycles.

ical satiation, or because of other factors. This results, over time, in oscillations of openness–closedness, with only two such patterns depicted in Fig. 2.[3]

Figure 2a is a simple case that is essentially an additive combination of the ideas expressed in social penetration and privacy regulation theories. Here, the possibility is raised that people in a growing relationship will exhibit cycles of openness and closedness that are consistent in their amplitude and frequency

[3]Lerner (1979) has also theorized that oscillations occur over the course of a relationship with respect to dimensions of affection, trust, or sharing. According to Lerner, patterns of oscillation within and across these dimensions become less global and more differentiated as relationships develop.

characteristics throughout the history of the relationship. Figure 2b, on the other hand, represents an extension of both theories and is, to us, one example of a more likely pattern of interaction. It suggests that early in a relationship people move quickly in and out of cycles of openness–closedness that have relatively shallow amplitudes, that is, they engage in short, frequent, low-stability bursts of openness–closedness, perhaps as they scan one another in a variety of areas and then back off to assess their interaction. Later in a relationship, as suggested in Fig. 2b, the openness–closedness cycles are slower in frequency, greater in amplitude, and exhibit more stability, as people interact extensively and for lengthier periods and subsequently withdraw slowly but to a considerable extent.

Figures 2a and 2b are oversimplified in several respects. They posit generally upward directions of the overall curve, whereas, as suggested earlier, relationships may also move toward closedness. For example, in some marriages spouses may eventually exhibit more and more closedness from one another but still maintain the relationship. Other relationships may stabilize, with openness and closedness cycles continuing to occur around a given level of interaction. Another possibility is that there may be short-term cycles of openness and closedness within long-term cycles, which in turn may be embedded within still longer-term cycles. That is, a relationship may have a generally closed phase for a period of months, where the parties are relatively withdrawn and distant from one another. Yet, within such a cycle there may be weeks or days where they are relatively open. Participants may also exhibit variations of openness and closedness within a day or within a series of encounters during a day. Little is known about such short- and long-term units of analysis, but the dialectic perspective suggests that such processes may occur.

Figure 2 also portrays quantitative shifts in openness–closedness. More dramatic, qualitative changes in modes of interaction, new patterns of opening or closing mechanisms, and expansion or contraction of areas of exchange have not been depicted.

In summary, our dialectic framework hypothesizes that relationships involve cycles of openness–closedness, whereas our earlier theorizing essentially averaged such cycles and focused on the process of increased openness as a normative sequence of events. To our knowledge, there is no empirical research or other systematic theoretical perspective that addresses the possibilities raised here or that provides guidance on the nature of stability–change dynamics of openness and closedness.

B. RELATIONSHIP CRISES

Social penetration theory hypothesizes that relationship growth and deterioration proceed in a systematic fashion, as shown in Fig. 3a. Generally speaking, the rate and degree of deterioration are hypothesized to be a function of the

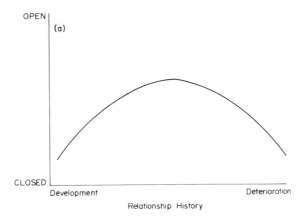

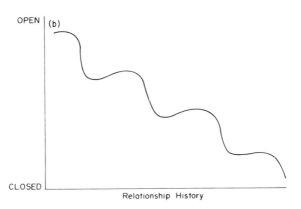

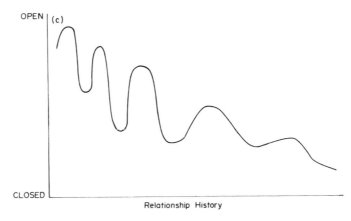

Fig. 3.   Relationship crises.

relative imbalance of costs to rewards, the locus of the costs (e.g., conflict in intimate areas is hypothesized to accelerate the rate and amount of the withdrawal), the relative stability and strength of the relationship, and other factors. The deterioration of relationships is also predicted to proceed from intimate to nonintimate exchange, that is, people are expected to withdraw initially from interaction in more intimate areas and to work their way back to less intimate areas, to the point where the relationship could continue. No successful research has been conducted on the deterioration process, because it is difficult to simulate in the laboratory and because it is not easy to gain access to the history of relationships in naturalistic settings. Our dialectic framework approaches the deterioration of relationships from a somewhat extended perspective. As illustrated in Fig. 3b, a simple combination of social penetration and privacy regulation theories suggests that people in conflict shut themselves off and open themselves up to their partners in a relatively constant cyclical fashion as they attempt to resolve disagreements, express their hostilities, and clarify their positions. In this simplest case, amplitude and frequency of cycles are similar at all times. A more likely possibility is shown in Fig. 3c. This figure depicts a case where people in conflict first come together and pull apart in a series of rapid-fire and intense exchanges and withdrawals. Thus, they might argue intensely about a topic, then seal themselves off from one another, and repeat this process over and over. If the relationship continues to deteriorate, the amplitude and frequency of openness–closedness cycles might slow down as interaction becomes less volatile and less frequent, perhaps to the point that participants primarily exchange civilities and have little contact with one another. We do not suggest that this latter pattern appears in all deteriorating relationships; it may be that a number of patterns occur in various cases of relationship deterioration. The essential point is that our dialectic perspective allows for the integration and extension of the possibilities originally proposed by the social penetration and privacy regulation frameworks. The task remains, of course, to accumulate empirical information on interaction patterns in deteriorating relationships.

C. INTERACTION AT DIFFERENT LEVELS OF INTIMACY

One central idea of social penetration theory, well supported by empirical data, is that interaction in nonintimate areas is more extensive and increases more rapidly than interaction in intimate areas (Fig. 1a). Although our dialectic perspective incorporates this idea, it also provides a more complex conception of relationship development. As shown in Fig. 4, we now expect that interaction in nonintimate and intimate areas involves openness–closedness cycles possessing various patterns of stability and change. Especially interesting is the possibility that amplitude and frequency characteristics of these cycles vary as a function of intimacy.

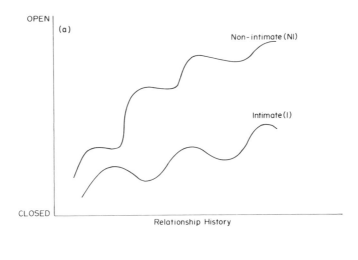

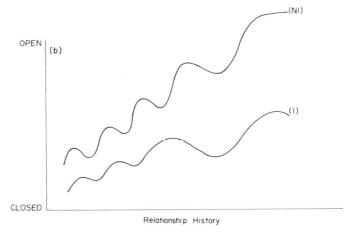

Fig. 4.   Openness–closedness cycles at different levels of intimacy.

Figure 4a presents the simplest possibility, where openness–closedness cycles in nonintimate and intimate areas are identical. It portrays a situation where people interact and withdraw in a regular fashion, with no differences in the stability–change features of cycles in intimate and nonintimate areas. The curves of Fig. 4b, which we consider to be illustrative of more probable patterns, hypothesize changes in frequency and amplitude of openness–closedness at different points in the history of a relationship. In both intimate and nonintimate areas, the curves suggest that openness–closedness cycles are relatively shallow during the early stages of a relationship. Here we expect people to make themselves mutually accessible and inaccessible to a limited extent, neither committing nor withdrawing in an extreme fashion and cycling rapidly in and out of contact with one another. Later, as the relationship progresses, the cycles of openness–closedness should increase in amplitude, with the participants engaging in more extensive explorations and withdrawals and exhibiting slower stability–change shifts.

This pattern is also expected to vary as a function of topic intimacy. More rapid transitions from openness to closedness may occur in nonintimate areas, where people move less cautiously from accessibility to inaccessibility. However, in intimate areas, especially later in relationships as increasingly sensitive interactions occur, there are likely to be slowly changing cycles of contact and withdrawal along with increased amounts of both opening and closing of people to one another. According to social penetration theory and data, such intimate areas of exchange are approached cautiously because of the potential costs, the vulnerability of people to one another, and so on. So, while openness and closedness in intimate areas may increase in amplitude at later points in a relationship, these processes are expected to occur in gradually shifting cycles.

Although we consider the curves of Fig. 4b to be reasonable extensions of social penetration and privacy regulation theories, it is likely that empirical research will reveal a variety of patterns of openness–closedness for different relationship histories. Furthermore, as indicated earlier, our presentation in this section does not incorporate variations in the regularity of cycles per unit of time, whereas it is quite likely that complex shifts in this characteristic of cycles do occur over time.

D. PERSONAL FACTORS IN RELATIONSHIP DEVELOPMENT

Although social penetration theory hypothesizes that individual differences play a role in the growth of relationships, relatively little research has successfully demonstrated how such factors work. This may be true because the search for stable traits associated with self-disclosure was not a useful strategy. An alternative approach, based on the perspective of this article, is that personal qualities are reflected in characteristic patterns of openness–closedness over time. Figure 5a and b illustrates a few such possibilities. Figure 5a depicts profiles of two people who both exhibit relatively shallow amplitudes of openness and closedness cycles. However, the two curves differ in frequency of cycles. The upper curve (person 1) portrays a stable, slowly changing pattern of openness and closedness, and the lower curve (person 2) represents a more rapidly shifting interactive style.

The profiles in Fig. 5a and b are rather different with respect to amplitude qualities. In Fig. 5b, the cycles of openness and closedness involve wide sweeps of accessibility and inaccessibility, which means that the style of interaction involves extensive coming together and pulling apart. Thus, intense, high-

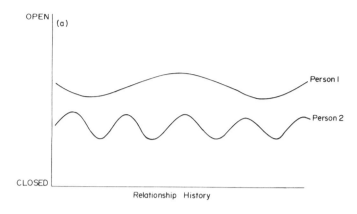

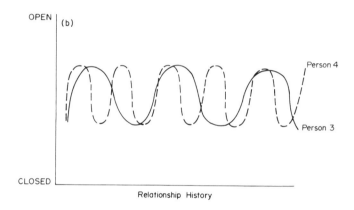

Fig. 5.   Individual differences in cycles.

amplitude interaction is followed by extensive withdrawal, and vice versa. Again, however, the two curves in Fig. 5b reflect differences in frequency of cycles per unit of time, with one curve (person 3) illustrating a relatively stable and slowly changing pattern of interaction and the other curve (person 4) representing a rapidly shifting exchange style.

The combination of amplitude and frequency of cycles yields different personal styles of accessibility, with two extremes depicted by persons 1 and 4 in Fig. 5a and b. The curve for person 1 shows a style of interaction that involves a relatively narrow band of differences in self–other accessibility (amplitude). In addition, changes in openness–closedness are gradual and occur slowly (frequency of cycles). A much different image is conveyed by person 4 in Fig. 5b. Here the pace of interaction shifts quickly from openness to closedness and the intensity of the interaction is high, with wide variations occurring between extensive interaction and extreme withdrawal.

What is presented here is only illustrative, and there are many factors that probably interact with personal styles, for example, topical intimacy, relationship history, and the interaction style of the other participant. The exact contribution of such factors, as in other cases, must await research in the spirit of the approach proposed in this article.

E. THE INTERPERSONAL UNIT: MATCHING AND TIMING OF INTERACTION

Social penetration and privacy regulation theories followed the long-standing tradition in social psychology of focusing on individuals as the unit of study rather than on relationships. Similarly, the discussion up to this point has dealt with openness–closedness and stability–change primarily from the perspective of the individual, not the dyad. We have not addressed such questions as: How does intimate disclosure by one person affect intimate disclosure by another individual? What is the impact of differences in personal predispositions in openness–closedness on the relationship as a whole? What happens to relationship development over time if the participants exhibit different styles of openness and closedness? While there has been some research on reciprocity of interpersonal exchange (Altman, 1973; Huston and Levinger, 1978), little theoretical or empirical attention has been directed at the *interactive* quality of social relationships, where the unit of study is the relationship or the joint behavior of participants.

There are several reasons for this neglect of dyadic units, such as the difficulty of studying interactive processes over time, the inability to unravel complex networks of behavior that occur in interpersonal exchanges, and the absence of conceptual frameworks for dealing with the social relationship as a unit. Although social penetration and privacy regulation theories emphasize temporal processes in social relationships, they do not deal directly with holistic interpersonal units; instead, they focus on the behavior of individuals.

The dialectic perspective outlined here may provide a partial basis for understanding relationships as units by permitting comparison of the cycles of openness–closedness of participants in a social bond. Are cycles of openness–closedness and stability–change congruent or noncongruent, that is, are the participants in synchrony with one another or are they out of phase? Do cycles match in terms of content or level of intimacy, or do they mismatch? Are the members of a pair in phase at all stages of a relationship, or are they in phase at certain times and out of phase at other times?

Figure 6 illustrates hypothetical cases of temporal synchrony and nonsynchrony of interpersonal exchange. The curves in Fig. 6a reflect temporal synchrony or *timing*, where the participants are congruent in their accessibility to

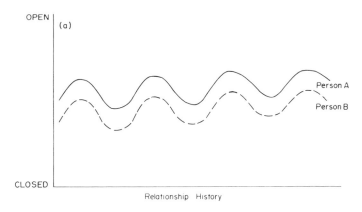

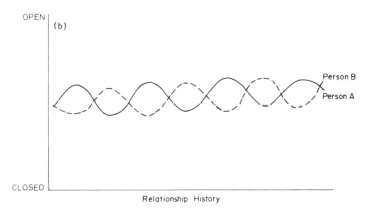

Fig. 6.   Timing and matching of cycles. (a) Timing, (b) mistiming, (c) matching, and (d) mismatching.

one another. When one person is open and available, so is the other person, and when one member is closed, the other is similarly inaccessible. On the other hand, the curves in Fig. 6b portray a relationship where the participants are out of synchrony, or are *mistiming* with respect to openness and closedness. When one person is interested in interaction, the other person is in a closed phased and is not receptive to contact. One might expect that a pattern of mistiming, if continued over an extended period, would not enhance the viability of a relationship. This is not to say that congruent timing is always ideal or that nonsynchrony of timing is undesirable. There are instances, for example, in which one person seeks the advice of another, and it is not appropriate for both parties to be simultaneously open about themselves; or mistiming may help open up new areas of interaction. The general point is that the analysis of timing and mistiming of

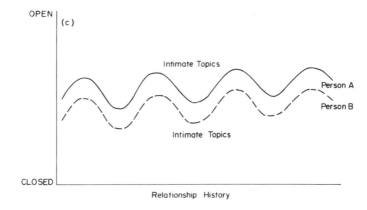

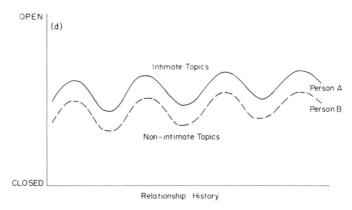

Fig. 6 (*Continued*).

openness–closedness may provide a preliminary basis for understanding individuals in relationships as the unit of analysis.

Figure 6c and d illustrates another concept that may contribute to a relationship-oriented approach. This concept, *matching,* refers to the *substantive synchrony* of openness–closedness cycles. The sets of curves in Fig. 6c and d depict synchrony with respect to timing, that is, a temporal meshing of cycles. However, they are different in their degree of substantive matching. The set in Fig. 6c illustrates both timing and matching. Here the participants are synchronous in openness or closedness and in level of intimacy or subject matter of interaction. The pair of curves in Fig. 6d reflects a different situation. Although there is synchrony with respect to the timing of cycles, the participants are mismatched with respect to topical intimacy. One person is open with regard to an emotionally laden intimate topic, whereas the other person is open with respect to a superficial issue (or vice versa). It is as if one person were discussing a crucial issue of personal values or a mutual sex problem and the other person responding with a discussion of the latest football scores or comments on the weather. Thus, although there is synchrony on the timing of openness and closedness, the people mismatch in the content of their exchange.

The concepts of *timing* and *matching* readily lead to a variety of research-able questions. For example, how viable are relationships with long histories of matching or mismatching and timing or mistiming? Do members of viable rela-tionships exhibit better timing and matching than those in unstable relationships? Does continual good timing and matching result in boredom or a stagnating relationship? To what extent do different relationships progress over time toward greater or lesser synchrony?

An especially important issue concerns matching and timing at different stages of a relationship. It might be expected that some matching and timing is necessary at all stages of relationships. Thus, if participants cannot achieve a sufficient degree of matching and timing early in their relationship, then the bond may not even begin. It is also possible that some mistiming and mismatching may be necessary in the early stages of a relationship to provide stimulation and some unpredictability. Similarly, advanced relationships may not be able to progress or maintain themselves unless sufficient matching and timing are achieved. And relationships may freeze at a given stage of development, or eventually deteriorate, because the participants are unable or unwilling to be-come synchronous in some new, perhaps more intimate, domain. Thus, although they could be "good friends," they may not be able to achieve the status of "lovers." On the other hand, mismatching and mistiming may serve a positive function in well-developed relationships by allowing the exploration of new areas of interaction, facilitating new modes of communication, and providing the possibility for an expansion of the relationship.[4]

Of course, there are many factors beyond matching and timing that contrib-ute to the progress of relationships, several of which have been discussed in this article. The point is, however, that the concepts of matching and timing, derived from our dialectic perspective, may offer a unique possibility for understanding relationship growth, functioning, and viability. And, more important, the con-cepts of matching and timing may facilitate the analysis of the social relationship as a unit of study.

---

[4]Lerner (1979) considered different types of symmetry or synchrony between members of a dyad. He described symmetry in terms of the synchrony or asynchrony between (a) developmental levels of the members of a dyad and (b) the rate of development of dyad members with respect to some characteristic. He hypothesized that different types of relationships (such as graduate student–mentor) may show characteristic progressions in the symmetry of the levels and rates of development of the participants.

VI. A Final Note

The goal of this article was to integrate and extend social penetration theory and privacy regulation theory. We first illustrated how these approaches were similar and dissimilar in their conceptions of interpersonal relationships. For example, they both emphasized temporal processes and the multimodal nature of social relationships. They differed in that privacy theory adopted a partial dialectic perspective on social interaction, in contrast with the more unidirectional approach taken in social penetration theory. Given these and other similarities and differences, we proposed a dialectic assumption system designed to weld these theories into a unified framework and to propose some new directions for theory and research on social relationships.

Our dialectic approach, with its emphasis on openness–closedness and stability–change, contrasts with the current philosophical underpinnings of social psychology, and it may well be that herein lies either a major contribution or a major flaw of this article. Particularly, our approach contrasts with the prevalent assumption in social psychology that human behavior is directed primarily at achieving homeostasis, stability, or consistency. Instead, we made the assumption that social psychological processes can be viewed in terms of various dialectical oppositions and that stability and change are equally fundamental in social relationships. We then proposed a series of questions, expectations, and hypotheses based on a dialectic extension of social penetration and privacy regulation concepts.

The question naturally arises as to the theoretical and empirical value of the approach proposed here. Obviously, it is too early to address this question fully, since we have only posed directions of research that derive from our analysis and have not yet conducted direct empirical tests of the approach. If there is any way to make evaluative judgments at the present time, it is through the theoretical richness, the suggestions of new directions of research, and the generative quality of our ideas and assumptions (Gergen, 1978).

Another issue concerns the place of our approach within the current state of social psychology. Since the mid-1960s, social psychologists have been engaged in introspection and self-analysis about their activities, often termed "the crisis" in social psychology. Although the crisis appears to have become relatively quiescent, our view is that a number of crucial issues continue to be unresolved, especially those associated with central assumptions about the nature of human social behavior.

The crisis in social psychology, born and stimulated in part by the social turbulence of the 1960s, originally focused on the issues of social relevance and research methodology. Critics within and outside the field railed against the seemingly esoteric and abstract body of social psychological research, and chastised the field for failing to help solve the social problems of the times—civil rights and discrimination, environmental degradation, the difficulties of the Vietnam War, etc. A second criticism focused on research methodology and the field's strict reliance on laboratory experimental methods which, it was argued, resulted in irrelevant, narrow, and artificial research. Furthermore, critics stated, laboratory research, with its emphasis on manipulation of independent variables and its tracking of singular outcomes, violated the complex systems-like character of social psychological phenomena, with their multidirectional chains of causation. In many respects, this first stage of the crisis focused on *what* types of research should be conducted (i.e., applied versus basic research) and *how* research should be done (i.e., laboratory versus other methods).

By the middle of the 1970s these issues were more or less resolved. Research had begun to address a variety of social problems, including environmental topics, community action issues, health-related problems, and gerontology, to name a few. In addition, the methodological perspective of social psychology had broadened beyond the traditional laboratory setting to include field experiments, naturalistic observations, and survey, archival, and case studies. So, those aspects of the crisis concerned with *what* to study and *how* to do it have now been largely resolved.

Beginning in the early 1970s, a second type of concern about social psychology has emerged, to a great extent stimulated by Gergen (1973). Gergen's claims concerning the transient, nonuniversalistic, and historical boundedness of social psychological knowledge raised the possibility that our strict adherence to a positivistic philosophy of science may not be appropriate. The impact of social and historical circumstances on phenomena have also been addressed by others in social psychology (Buss, 1979), developmental psychology (Riegel, 1979), and elsewhere (Rychlak, 1977). Whether or not one agrees with such alternative conceptions, the points raised by these authors deal with philosophy of science matters—the basic nature of the field as a science or otherwise, the extent to which its data are universalistic or relativistic, and the appropriateness of different forms of inquiry.

These philosophical questions have not been resolved and will continue to be discussed during the 1980s. However, there are even more fundamental issues that need to be addressed. We refer to the underlying philosophical assumptions that are held to be true about human social behavior. The field's basic articles of faith and its unstated assumptions about the nature of social behavior need to be reassessed, for it is these assumptions that play a central role in shaping the directions of the field. This article has raised questions and proposed alternatives to certain substantive assumptions that have been central to social psychology, and, indeed, to psychology, as a field. Thus, we offered an alternative assumption framework to that of homeostasis, consistency, or balance as prime motive forces, in the form of a dialectic perspective involving openness/closedness and stability–change. Whether or not this assumption system is immediately capable of empirical study, whether or not it requires different research methods, and whether or not it bears in a unique way on the nature of social psychology as a science or otherwise remains to be addressed. Our view is that the future of social psychology depends on a careful analysis of the central assumptions that we make about human social behavior. If such an analysis is not done, then it is certain that research and theorizing in the coming decades will follow the models of the past decades. So it is that research on socially relevant topics such as crowding, health, and related issues are conducted within a homeostatic conception of human social behavior. Thus, while the content of research has varied over the years, the basic structure of our "new" theories continues to be linked to past assumptions about the basis of social behavior. On the other hand, an explicit analysis of our fundamental assumptions will at least allow for the possibility of charting new directions of research and theory and for either the reaffirmation of our previously held beliefs or the adoption of a different assumption system.

Another important point is that no set of assumptions is inherently better or worse than any other set. Alternative assumptions are simply different, leading one along different paths of research and theory. And, ultimately, it is the conceptual richness, new directions of research, and eventual derivative empirical tests that determine the worth of any assumptions about human social behavior.

In the final analysis, we believe that it is better to follow a path based on explicit assumptions rather than one based on implicit or unstated beliefs. In the latter case, change can only come about by fumbling and trial and error. By stating precisely one's beliefs and assumptions, one has more opportunity to either change or continue on a given course. It is this task, namely, the statement, examination, and evaluation of our assumptions and articles of faith about human social behavior, that is crucial to the future of social psychology. Whether or not this self-examination leads to a change in assumptions is irrelevant. What is important is the process of redefining or reaffirming our beliefs about human social behavior.

REFERENCES

Adler, M. J. *Dialectic*. New York: Harcourt, 1927.
Adler, M. J. (Ed.). *The great ideas: A syntopicon of great books of the western world*. Chicago, Illinois: Encyclopaedia Britannica, 1952. Vol. I, pp. 345–352; Vol. II, pp. 282–288, 323–329.
Altman, I. Reciprocity of interpersonal exchange. *Journal for the Theory of Social Behavior*, 1973, **3**, 249–261. (a)
Altman, I. Some perspectives on the study of man-environment phenomena. *Representative Research in Social Psychology*, 1973, **4**, 109–126. (b)
Altman, I. *The environment and social behavior: Privacy, personal space, territory and crowding*. Monterey, California: Brooks/Cole, 1975.

Altman, I. Environmental psychology and social psychology. *Personality and Social Psychology Bulletin,* 1976, **2,** 96-113. (a)

Altman, I. Privacy: A conceptual analysis. *Environment and Behavior,* 1976, **8,** 7-29. (b)

Altman, I. Privacy regulation: Culturally universal or culturally specific? *Journal of Social Issues,* 1977, **33,** 66-84. (a)

Altman, I. Research on environment and behavior: A personal statement of strategy. In D. Stokols (Ed.) *Perspectives on environment and behavior.* New York: Plenum, 1977. Pp. 303-323. (b)

Altman, I. Privacy as an interpersonal boundary process. In M. Von Cranach, K. Foppa, W. Lepenies, & D. Ploog (Eds.), *Human ethology: Claims and limits of a new discipline.* London and New York: Cambridge University Press, 1979. Pp. 95-132.

Altman, I., & Chemers, M. M. *Culture and environment.* Monterey, California: Brooks/Cole, 1980.

Altman, I., & Haythorn, W. W. Interpersonal exchange in isolation. *Sociometry,* 1965, **23,** 411-426.

Altman, I., & Haythorn, W. W. The ecology of isolated groups. *Behavioral Science,* 1967, **12,** 169-182.

Altman, I., & Taylor, D. A. *Social penetration: The development of interpersonal relationships.* New York: Holt, 1973.

Altman, I., & Vinsel, A. M. Personal space: An analysis of E. T. Hall's proxemics framework. In I. Altman & J. F. Wohlwill (Eds.), *Human behavior and environment: Advances in theory and research* (Vol. 2). New York: Plenum, 1977. Pp. 181-259.

Altman, I., Taylor, D. A., & Wheeler, L. Ecological aspects of group behavior in social isolation. *Journal of Applied Social Psychology,* 1971, **1,** 76-100.

Argyle, M., & Dean, J. Eye contact, distance, and affiliation. *Sociometry,* 1965, **28,** 289-304.

Baum, A , & Epstein, Y. M. (Eds.). *Human response to crowding.* Hillsdale, New Jersey: Erlbaum, 1978.

Bertalannfy, L. *General system theory.* New York: Braziller, 1968.

Bettleheim, B. *The children of the dream.* New York: Macmillan, 1969.

Blatt, S. J., & Wild, C. M. *Schizophrenia: A developmental analysis.* New York: Academic Press, 1976.

Brehm, J. W. *A theory of psychological reactance.* New York: Academic Press, 1966.

Brent, S. B. Motivation, steady state, and structural development: A general model of psychological homeostasis. *Motivation and Emotion,* 1978, **2,** 299-332. (a)

Brent, S. B. Prigogine's model for self-organization in nonequilibrium systems: Its relevance for developmental psychology. *Human Development,* 1978, **21,** 374-387. (b)

Burgess, R. L., & Huston, T. L. *Social exchange in developing relationships.* New York: Academic Press, 1979.

Buss, A. R. *A dialectical psychology.* New York: Irvington, 1979.

Cannon, W. B. *The wisdom of the body.* London: Kegan, 1932.

Cofer, C. N., & Appley, M. H. *Motivation: Theory and research.* New York: Wiley, 1964.

Cohen, J. *Humanistic psychology.* London: Allen & Unwin, 1958.

Colson, W. N. *Self-disclosure as a function of social approval.* Unpublished M.A. thesis, Howard University, Washington, D.C., 1968.

Cooley, G. H. *Human nature and the social order.* New York: Schocken, 1964. (Originally published in 1902.)

Datan, N., & Reese, H. W. *Life span developmental psychology.* New York: Academic Press, 1977.

Douglas, M. *Purity and danger.* Baltimore, Maryland: Penguin, 1970.

Erikson, E. H. *Childhood and society.* New York: Norton, 1962.

Festinger, L. *A theory of cognitive dissonance.* New York: Row Peterson, 1956.

Fiske, D. W., & Maddi, S. R. (Eds.). *Functions of varied experience.* Homewood, Illinois: Dorsey, 1961.

Flavell, J. H. *The developmental psychology of Jean Piaget.* Princeton, New Jersey: Van Nostrand-Reinhold, 1963.

Frankfurt, L. P. *The role of some individual and interpersonal factors in the acquaintance process.* Unpublished doctoral dissertation, The American University, Washington, D.C., 1965.

Fraser, D. *Village planning in the primitive world.* New York: Braziller, 1968.

Gergen, K. Social psychology as history. *Journal of Personality and Social Psychology,* 1973, **26,** 309–320.

Gergen, K. Toward generative theory. *Journal of Personality and Social Psychology,* 1978, **36,** 1344–1360.

Hall, E. T. *The hidden dimension.* Garden City, New York: Doubleday, 1966.

Hayduk, L. A. Personal space: An evaluative and orienting review. *Psychological Bulletin,* 1978, **85,** 117–134.

Heider, F. *The psychology of interpersonal relations.* New York: Wiley, 1958.

Helson, H. *Adaptation level theory.* New York: Harper, 1964.

Hook, S. Dialectic in society and history. In H. Feigl & M. Brodbeck (Eds.), *Readings in the philosophy of science.* New York: Appleton, 1953, 701–713.

Huston, T. L., & Levinger, G. Interpersonal attraction and relationships. *Annual Review of Psychology,* 1978, **29,** 115–156.

Keiser, G. J., & Altman, I. Relationship of nonverbal behavior to the social penetration process. *Human Communication Research,* 1976, **2,** 147–161.

Kelly, G. A. *The psychology of personal constructs.* New York: Morton, 1955.

Koenker, E. G. *Great dialecticians in modern Christian thought.* Minneapolis, Minnesota: Augsburg, 1971.

Kuo, You-Yuh. Chinese dialectical thought and character. In J. F. Rychlak (Ed.), *Dialectic: Humanistic rationale for behavior and development.* Basel: Karger, 1976. Pp. 72–86.

Lerner, R. M. *Concepts and theories of human development.* Reading, Massachusetts: Addison-Wesley, 1976.

Lerner, R. M. A dynamic interactional concept of individual and social relationship development. In R. L. Burgess & T. L. Huston (Eds.), *Social exchange in developing relationships.* New York: Academic Press, 1979. Pp. 271–305.

Levi-Strauss, C. *Structural anthropology.* New York: Basic Books, 1963.

Levinger, G., & Raush, H. L. *Close relationships: Perspectives on the meaning of intimacy.* Amherst, Massachusetts: University of Massachusetts Press, 1977.

Lewin, K. *Principles of topological psychology.* New York: McGraw Hill, 1936.

Lewin, K. *Field theory in social science.* New York: Harper, 1964.

Ley, D., & Cybriwsky, R. Urban graffiti as territorial markers. *Annals of the Association of American Geographers,* 1974, **64,** 491–505.

Maddi, S. R. The pursuit of consistency and variety. In R. P. Abelson, E. Aronson, W. J. McGuire, T. M. Newcomb, M. J. Rosenberg, & P. H. Tannenbaum (Eds.), *Theories of cognitive consistency: A handbook.* Chicago, Illinois: Rand McNally, 1968. Pp. 267–274.

Mahler, M., Pine, F., & Bergman, A. *The psychological birth of the human infant: Symbiosis and individuation.* New York: Basic Books, 1975.

Maslow, A. H. The need to know and the fear of knowing. *The Journal of General Psychology,* 1963, **68,** 111–125.

Mead, G. H. *Mind, self and society.* Chicago, Illinois: University of Chicago Press, 1934.

Morton, T. Intimacy and reciprocity of exchange: A comparison of spouses and strangers. *Journal of Personality and Social Psychology,* 1978, **36,** 72–81.

Murphy, R. *The dialectics of social life.* New York: Basic Books, 1971.

Newcomb, T. M. An approach to the study of communicative acts. *Psychological Review,* 1953, **60,** 393–404.

Newman, O. *Defensible space.* New York: Macmillan, 1972.

Perlman, D., & Peplau, L. A. Toward a social psychology of loneliness. In R. Gilmour & S. Duck (Eds.), *Personal relationships in disorder.* New York: Academic Press, 1981.

Proshansky, H., & Altman, I. Overview of the field. In W. P. White (Ed.), *Resources in environment and behavior.* Washington, D.C.: American Psychological Association, 1979. Pp. 3–36.

Riegel, K. F. From traits and equilibrium toward developmental dialectics. In W. J. Arnold (Ed.), *Nebraska symposium on motivation.* Lincoln, Nebraska: University of Nebraska Press, 1976. Pp. 349–407.

Riegel, K. F. *Foundations of dialectical psychology.* New York: Academic Press, 1979.

Riegel, K. F., & Rosenwald, G. C. *Structure and transformation: Developmental and historical aspects.* New York: Wiley, 1975.

Rogers, C. R. *On becoming a person.* Boston, Massachusetts: Houghton, 1961.

Russett, C. E. *The concept of equilibrium in American social thought.* New Haven, Connecticut: Yale University Press, 1966.

Rychlak, J. F. (Ed.). *Dialectic: Humanistic rationale for behavior and development.* Basel: Karger, 1976.

Rychlak, J. F. *The psychology of rigorous humanism.* New York: Wiley, 1977.

Seligman, M. E. P. *Helplessness: On depression, development and death.* San Francisco, California: Freeman, 1975.

Simmel, G. *The sociology of Georg Simmel.* Translated by K. H. Wolff. New York: Free Press, 1950. (Originally published in 1908.)

Stagner, R. Homeostasis as a unifying concept in personality theory. *Psychological Review,* 1951, **58,** 5–17.

Stagner, R. Homeostasis: Corruptions or misconceptions?—A reply. *Psychological Review,* 1954, **61,** 205–208.

Stagner, R. Homeostasis, need reduction, and motivation. *Merrill-Palmer Quarterly of Behavior and Development,* 1961, **7,** 49–68.

Stagner, R. Homeostasis, discrepancy, dissonance: A theory of motives and motivation. *Motivation and Emotion,* 1977, **1,** 103–138.

Stiefel, T. The heresy of science: A twelfth century conceptual revolution. *ISIS,* 1977, **68,** 347–362.

Stokols, D. Environmental psychology. *Annual Review of Psychology,* 1978, **29,** 253–295.

Sundstrom, E., & Altman, I. Field study of dominance and territoriality. *Journal of Personality and Social Psychology,* 1974, **30,** 115–125.

Taylor, D. A. Some aspects of the development of interpersonal relationships: Social penetration processes. *Journal of Social Psychology,* 1968, **75,** 79–90.

Taylor, D. A., & Altman, I. Self-disclosure as a function of reward-cost outcomes. *Sociometry,* 1975, **38,** 18–31.

Taylor, D. A., Altman, I., & Sorrentino, R. Interpersonal exchange as a function of rewards and costs and situational factors: Expectancy confirmation-disconfirmation. *Journal of Experimental Social Psychology,* 1969, **5,** 324–339.

Turner, V. *The ritual process.* Chicago, Illinois: Aldine, 1969.

White, R. W. Motivation reconsidered: The concept of competence. *Psychological Review,* 1959, **66,** 297–333.

Wilhelm, R., & Baynes, C. F. *I Ching or book of changes.* Princeton, New Jersey: Princeton University Press, 1950.

Zimbardo, P. G. *Shyness.* Reading, Massachusetts: Addison Wesley, 1977.

DIRECT EXPERIENCE AND ATTITUDE-BEHAVIOR CONSISTENCY[1]

Russell H. Fazio

DEPARTMENT OF PSYCHOLOGY
INDIANA UNIVERSITY
BLOOMINGTON, INDIANA

Mark P. Zanna

DEPARTMENT OF PSYCHOLOGY
UNIVERSITY OF WATERLOO
WATERLOO, ONTARIO, CANADA

[1]A preliminary report of some of this research program was presented at a symposium on "Recent Approaches to Attitude-Behavior Consistency" at the American Psychological Association Convention, San Francisco, 1977 (Zanna & Fazio, 1977). Some of the reported research was supported by Canada Council Grant S76-0344 to Mark P. Zanna. The authors wish to thank Jerome M. Chertkoff, Michael Ross, and Steven J. Sherman for their helpful comments on an earlier version of this manuscript.

161

I. Overview of the Attitude–Behavior Consistency Problem

To what extent, if at all, are people's attitudes predictive of their behavior? In recent years, this question has been the focus of an increasingly large number of empirical investigations. That the question has been so widely asked itself represents a profound shift in the perspective of social psychology toward the concept of attitude. Early conceptions of attitudes at least implicitly assumed that understanding a person's attitude was tantamount to accurately predicting his or her behavior. This notion that behavior follows from attitudes is reflected in some of the early definitions of attitude. Allport (1935) conceived of an attitude as "a mental and neural state of readiness, organized through experience, *exerting a directive or dynamic influence upon the individual's response* to all objects and situations with which it is related" (p. 810). Campbell (1950) asserted that "an individual's social attitude is a syndrome of *response consistency* with regard to social objects" (p. 31). Similarly, Green (1954) maintained that "the concept of attitude implies a *consistency or predictability of responses*" (p. 336). The directive function of attitudes is also evident in Doob's (1947) suggestion that an "attitude is an implicit response with drive strength which occurs within the individual as a reaction to stimulus patterns and which *affects subsequent overt responses*" (p. 136, emphasis ours in all quotations).

As this discussion implies, numerous and varied definitions of attitudes have been offered. For the present purposes, we shall consider an attitude to be simply the categorization of an object along an evaluative dimension (see Thurstone, 1946; Fishbein, 1963, 1966; Jones & Gerard, 1967). In other words, an attitude is the evaluative feeling that is evoked by a given object.

Although some early skeptics challenged the notion of one-to-one correspondence between attitudes and behavior (e.g., Corey, 1937; La Piere, 1934), it was not until the mid- and late-1960s that a substantial body of social psychologists began to examine seriously the consistency concept. Wicker's (1969) extensive review of the literature represents what is probably the most frequently cited analysis of the strength of the attitude–behavior relationship (see also Calder & Ross, 1973; Deutscher, 1973; Schuman & Johnson, 1976). Wicker concluded that "taken as a whole, these studies suggest that it is considerably more likely that attitudes will be unrelated or only slightly related to overt behaviors than that attitudes will be closely related to actions" (p. 65). Five years earlier, Festinger

(1964) had observed a similarly dismal lack of evidence to support the proposition that attitude change produced corresponding behavior change.

Such careful scrutiny and review led some to suggest that "it may be desirable to abandon the attitude concept" (Wicker, 1971, p. 29). This increased pessimism concerning the predictive validity of attitudes was further fostered by concurrent developments in the areas of personality and attitude change. In the first of these, just as social psychologists were beginning to question the strength of the attitude–behavior relationship, writers in the area of personality were seeking to determine the degree to which trait measures were at all predictive of behavior (Mischel, 1968, 1973). In an article entitled "Are Attitudes Necessary?" Abelson (1972) noted that his title "has its skeptical parallel in the personality field where one might ask, 'Is personality necessary?' "

Although the attitude and personality literatures have tended to retain separate identities and to progress independently, there does exist a clear conceptual parallel in that both attitudes and traits are presumed to bear some relation to overt behavior. Furthermore, we might even regard some traits as attitudes; when individuals attribute certain traits that have evaluative connotations to themselves, they are simply making an evaluative assessment of themselves rather than of some external social object. The notion that traits are unpredictive of cross-situational behavior is, then, an equivalently skeptical statement about the predictive power of attitudes.

A second development which contributed to the questioning of the utility of the attitude concept was the rather rapid emergence of a large body of data which demonstrated that under certain conditions attitudes follow from, rather than direct, behavior. Derived from both Festinger's (1957) cognitive dissonance theory and Bem's (1967) self-perception theory, the notion that attitude change can follow from freely performed behavior has been empirically demonstrated many times (e.g., Festinger & Carlsmith, 1959; Kiesler, Nisbett, & Zanna, 1969). These findings, particularly when viewed from the perspective of self-perception theory, can be interpreted as implying that attitudes may be mere epiphenomena, that is, momentary after-the-fact explanations of past behavior that are not internalized. Viewed as epiphenomena, attitudes cannot be expected to bear any directive influence on behavior.

Given the apparent lack of evidence to support the assumption of attitude–behavior consistency in the context of (a) a conceptually parallel and concurrent controversy regarding the relation between traits and behavior and (b) the emergence of a theoretical perspective that regarded attitudes as epiphenomena, it is no wonder that the notion of attitudes as predictors of behavior began to meet such skepticism. Nonetheless, this skepticism does not appear to have been fully warranted. Moderately strong, if not impressive, relationships between attitude and behavior have been observed and have prompted a more optimistic outlook on the predictive utility of attitudes in recent reviews of the literature (Schuman & Johnson, 1976).

Voting behavior is an excellent case in point (Campbell, Converse, Miller, & Stokes, 1960; Fishbein & Coombs, 1974). For example, Kelley and Mirer's (1974) analysis of the four presidential elections from 1952 to 1964 indicates that preelection attitudes accurately predicted voting behavior for 85% of the respondents. This nearly perfect attitude–behavior relation contrasts markedly with the much lower correlations reported by Wicker (1969) and others. Yet, it is not only in the context of voting behavior that strong relations have been found. As Schuman and Johnson (1976) point out, a rarely mentioned but early report of strong attitude–behavior consistency can be found in Stouffer *et al.* (1949). Self-reports from army trainees about eagerness for combat were found to predict significantly performance in combat several months later. Goodmonson and Glaudin (1971) obtained a correlation of .58 between a measure of attitude toward organ transplantation and a Guttman scale of behavior which had as its most extreme point the actual signing of a legal document providing for posthumous organ donation. Seligman, Kriss, Darley, Fazio, Becker, and Pryor (1979) found a measure of homeowners' attitudes regarding the necessity of air conditioning for the maintenance of their comfort and actual energy consumption to correlate at a level of .65. These two correlations are far above the ostensible .30 ceiling in attitude–behavior relations claimed by Wicker (1969). Similarly, movie attendance (Crespi, 1971) and the purchase of various commercial products (Juster, 1964; Ryan & Bonfield, 1975) have been predicted reasonably well by attitude measures. In the area of race relations, DeFleur and Westie (1958) found that over ⅔ of their subjects who had scored in the upper and lower quartiles on a measure of racial prejudice displayed attitude–behavior correspondence when asked to commit themselves to posing for an interracial photograph for a variety of purposes. Similarly, a large-scale survey of metropolitan Detroit whites revealed a very strong association between survey responses on the issue of open housing and the actual signing of a relevant petition 3 months later (Brannon, Cyphers, Hesse, Hesselbart, Keane, Schuman, Vicarro, & Wright, 1973). Of the survey respondents who supported open housing, 70% signed a petition calling for an open housing policy compared to only 22% of those who had earlier said that they were opposed. Of a separate group of opponents to open housing, 85% signed a petition calling for ''owners' rights.''

This sampling of positive results suggests that calls for the abandonment of the attitude concept were premature. The blanket statement that attitudes have little to do with subsequent behavior is often contradicted by evidence in the attitude–behavior literature. Research has revealed everything from findings of no relation between attitudes and behavior whatsoever [e.g., Corey's (1937) finding of a correlation of .02 between attitudes toward cheating and overt cheating behavior] to the nearly perfect relation observed in the context of voting behavior. Given this range of outcomes, it appears that the question of attitude–behavior consistency has to be approached differently. Rather than asking whether attitudes relate to behavior, we have to ask "Under what conditions do what kinds of attitudes held by what kinds of individuals predict what kinds of behavior?" Instead of assessing whether a given correlation coefficient between an attitude and a behavior measure is statistically significant and/or practically substantial, we need to treat the strength of the attitude–behavior relation as we would treat virtually any other dependent variable and determine what factors affect it.

We shall present data from a program of research that demonstrates the feasibility of such an approach and suggests that abandonment of the attitude concept is unwarranted. The research focuses on what kinds of attitudes relate to behavior. Some potentially specifiable attitudes, as we shall see, are more predictive of later behavior than are other attitudes.

II. The Effect of the Manner of Attitude Formation

The basic issue that our research has addressed is one that considers the role of the manner of attitude formation. Specifically, we have focused on the development of an attitude through direct behavioral experience with the attitude object and investigated whether such attitudes better predict subsequent behavior than attitudes formed without behavioral experience. In other words, will the attitude-to-behavior relation be stronger if it is embedded in a behavior-to-attitude-to-behavior sequence than if it is not?

Of course, if attitudes derived from behavior are to be considered epiphenomena, that is, momentary, after-the-fact explanations of that behavior, then one could not consider the answer to the above question to be positive. There would be no reason to expect such attitudes to be any more predictive of later behavior than attitudes formed without behavioral experience. However, as Kelman (1974) has argued, there does not appear to be any necessary reason to regard attitudes based on behavior as ephemeral. Attitudes may guide future behavior in the same way that judgments about another person guide behavior toward that person. It is now well documented that our impressions and expectations of others tend to affect our mode of behavior with them (e.g., Meichenbaum, Bowers, & Ross, 1969; Word, Zanna, & Cooper, 1974; Snyder & Swann, 1978). Similarly, judgments that we draw concerning our evaluations of an object may influence future behavior toward that object.

The critical question is whether attitudes derived from behavior are any more predictive of later behavior than are attitudes formed on the basis of nonbehavioral information. Do the underlying attitudes of two individuals with identical attitude scale scores differ in their predictive validity if one person's attitude is based on prior behavior and the other person's attitude is not so based? We shall present a series of studies which were conducted in order to examine whether attitudes formed through direct behavioral experience with the attitude object are more predictive of subsequent behavior than are attitudes developed via more indirect nonbehavioral experience.

It should be made clear from the outset that the distinction we are drawing between direct and indirect experience represents a continuum. Toward one end of the continuum is attitude formation through direct experience, which refers to the individual basing an attitude on prior behavior toward the attitude object. In the case of a tangible, physical object, such direct experience would involve actual interaction with, or manipulation of, the object in question. However, in the case of an issue or some attitude object which possesses only a social reality (Festinger, 1954), the term direct experience is used to refer to prior behavior of a committing nature from which the individual can infer the attitude. The other end of the continuum, indirect experience, represents attitude formation on the basis of nonbehavioral information, for example, reading or being told about the attitude object.

To employ an example which we have frequently found to be useful, a child may form an attitude toward a toy in two very different manners. The child may play with the toy (direct experience) or develop an attitude toward the toy on the basis of a friend's or an advertisement's description of that toy (indirect experience). Even if these two attitudes were of equal favorability, it seems reasonable to suggest that they may differ on some dimensions—simply because they were developed in such radically different manners. In particular, because they differ in their immediacy to past behavior, the two attitudes may be differentially successful in the prediction of subsequent behavior.

A. THE "HOUSING" STUDY

The early investigations, aimed at demonstrating that the manner of attitude formation does affect attitude-behavior consistency, proved fruitful. The hypothesis was first examined in a field study by Regan and Fazio (1977). Due to a campus housing shortage, many freshmen at Cornell University spent the first few weeks of the fall semester in temporary housing. Typically, these accommodations consisted of a cot in the lounge of a dormitory. Relative to freshmen who had been assigned immediately to permanent housing, those in temporary quarters had much more direct experience with the housing crisis. The students who had been assigned dormitory rooms, on the other hand, had learned about, and formed their attitudes toward, the housing shortage only through discussions with others and frequent articles appearing in the campus newspaper. This latter group, then, knew about the housing crisis but had no direct experience with it. Thus, a naturally occurring event led to the creation of two identifiable groups of individuals who clearly differed in the manner of their attitude formation. The investigators were able to take advantage of this situation in order to examine the hypothesis in a real-world setting.

Packets from the "Research Group on Campus Housing" were mailed to those students who had been assigned to temporary housing and to a randomly selected group of freshmen who had received permanent accommodations (hereafter referred to as the temporary and permanent groups, respectively). The first half of the packet consisted largely of a questionnaire designed to assess attitudes toward the housing shortage. For example, subjects were asked to indicate how intolerable they found the housing crisis, how much students had suffered because of it, and how adequate they found the administration's efforts to alleviate the crisis. The second half of the packet provided the opportunity for a number of actions the students "might want to take," any and all of which were to be forwarded to the university's Housing Office. Six behavioral opportunities were provided. The students could (1) sign a petition, including their addresses, asking the administration to take several concrete actions to alleviate the housing crisis; (2) get other students to sign this petition; (3) indicate interest in attending a meeting of the research group in the near future to discuss various proposals with dorm residents; (4) indicate interest in joining a committee of dorm residents to investigate the housing situation and make recommendations; (5) list in writing recommendations or suggestions for solving the housing crisis; and (6) write a letter expressing opinions which the research group would forward to the Housing Office.

Included in the questionnaire were two items designed to check whether the temporary and permanent groups differed, as had been presumed, in the degree to which they had engaged in prior relevant behaviors. The results showed that the two groups did differ with respect to their direct experience with the housing crisis. Temporary subjects reported having had significantly more contact with administration officials about the crisis and having made significantly more attempts to pressure the administration to change housing policies than did permanent subjects. In short, the naturally occurring groups differed as expected on the relevant dimension of direct behavioral experience. This difference did not, however, lead to a corresponding difference in the attitudes of the two groups. Generally speaking, temporary and permanent subjects held equivalently negative attitudes regarding the housing crisis. On only one of the seven attitudinal items was there a significant difference in the scores of the two groups, and even this single difference was rather small in magnitude (a difference of 0.23 units on a 5-point scale). Thus, the two groups appear to be characterized by generally equivalent attitudes, yet the attitudes were based on differing amounts of direct experience. The hypothesis asserts that this difference will be associated with a corresponding difference in the strength of the attitude-behavior relation.

A variety of data analyses were performed, all of which supported the hypothesis of greater attitude–behavior consistency among the temporary than among the permanent subjects. For example, multiple regression analyses in which the number of behavioral items completed was employed as the dependent measure revealed that attitudes in the temporary group were more predictive of behavior than those in the permanent group. Attitudinal variables accounted for 31% of the behavioral variance among the temporary subjects but a mere 7% among the permanent subjects. Additional analyses were conducted with the behavioral items constructed so as to form a Guttman scale. With this behavioral measure, differences were again observed between the two groups. For example, the correlation between behavior scores and the sum of the five attitudinal items involving the severity of the housing crisis was .421 in the temporary group and only .037 in the permanent group.[2]

The findings, then, were supportive of the hypothesis; the strength of the attitude–behavior relationship differed in the two groups. The implication is that this difference in consistency is due to the fact that the temporary group had a greater amount of direct behavioral experience with the housing shortage. The correlational nature of the investigation prohibits characterization of the data as anything more than suggestive. Nevertheless, it is encouraging to note that data consistent with the hypothesis were obtained in a natural setting involving a relatively important attitudinal issue.

B. THE "PUZZLE" EXPERIMENT

In order to examine the causal relation between direct experience and attitude–behavior consistency, Regan and Fazio (1977) also conducted a laboratory experiment which can be characterized as a conceptual replication of the housing study. The experiment involved attitudes and behavior with respect to a set of five types of intellectual puzzles. The manner of attitude formation was manipulated by varying the way in which subjects were introduced to the puzzles at the beginning of the experiment. Half of the subjects were presented previously solved examples of each puzzle by the experimenter, who described the puzzle, the directions, and the solution (indirect experience condition). The other subjects were given an opportunity to work the very same example puzzles,

---

[2]In all of our research reported in this article, the variance of the attitudinal and behavioral scores in the various groups or conditions were examined for equivalence. With one exception, the variances were never found to differ between groups. Thus, differences in the range of scores cannot generally account for the differences we observe in the magnitude of correlations. The one exception is the Regan and Fazio (1977) "housing" study in which the variance of behavior scores was greater in the temporary than in the permanent group, and, even in this study, a further analysis involving a matching of the distributions of behavior scores in the two groups revealed some support for the hypothesis. The reader is referred to the original research reports for details concerning the equivalence of distributions in the various studies.

TABLE I
AVERAGE ATTITUDE–BEHAVIOR CORRELATIONS[a]

Correlation	Experience condition	
	Direct	Indirect
Attitude, order of problems attempted	.51	.22
Attitude, proportion of problems attempted	.54	.20

[a] Taken from Regan and Fazio (1977, Experiment 2). Copyright 1977 by Academic Press, adapted by permission.

thus forming their attitudes toward each puzzle type through direct behavioral experience with the attitude objects. After this introduction, all subjects rated the interest value of each of the five types of puzzles. A 15-min "free-play" situation followed, during which the subjects could work on any of the five types of puzzles they wished. The free nature of this time period was emphasized. Three pages of each of the five types of puzzles were available to each subject, who was instructed to number each particular problem as he or she attempted to solve it. From this information, two behavioral measures could be assessed: the order in which the types of problems were attempted and the proportion of available problems of each type which were attempted.

For each subject, rank-order correlations between the interest ratings and the order measure and between the interest ratings and the proportion measure were computed. These two correlations served as measures of the degree to which an individual subject exhibited attitude–behavior consistency. Table I presents the mean correlations in each condition. The prediction that attitude–behavior correspondence would be greater in the direct than in the indirect experience condition was confirmed for both measures. Subjects who had formed their attitudes on the basis of direct behavioral experience with the puzzles displayed significantly greater attitude–behavior consistency than did subjects who formed their attitudes more indirectly on the basis of the experimenter's description of the puzzles. The manipulation had no effect on the amount of interest expressed in any of the puzzles but strongly affected the extent to which that expressed interest was reflected in later behavior.

C. THE "SUBJECT POOL" STUDY

A third investigation was also aimed, at least in part, at examining the strength of the attitude–behavior relationship as a function of direct experience. Fazio and Zanna (1978a) conducted a correlational study in which it was possible to measure direct experience as a continuous variable. The relation between students' attitudes toward participating in psychological experiments and their willingness to commit themselves to joining a departmental subject pool was examined as a function of the number of psychology experiments in which they had previously participated. The strength of the attitude–behavior relationship was expected to vary positively with the number of past experiences the student had with respect to experimental participation.

The sample students for this study was intentionally chosen on the basis that they would be likely to (and in fact did) display a distribution concerning the number of experiments in which they had previously participated. Students enrolled in an introductory social psychology course were asked by their discussion section instructor to complete a general survey on psychology experiments. By the time of the survey, approximately 6 weeks into the semester, students had read and heard descriptions of numerous psychology experiments and were fully aware of what volunteering to participate in psychological research might entail. Furthermore, the class consisted largely of sophomores, who were likely to have had the opportunity during their freshman year to participate in psychological research.

The relevant parts of the questionnaire included an item which asked the students to indicate the number of psychology experiments in which they had previously participated. This item served as the measure of the amount of direct experience the subjects had. The attitude measurement portion of the questionnaire was modeled after one used by Norman (1975). As an affective measure, students completed a 10-item semantic differential scale (e.g., approve–disapprove, valuable–worthless) in which the object of evaluation was volunteering to serve as a subject. As a more cognitive measure, students indicated the extent to which volunteering to serve as a subject would achieve or block the attainment of each of ten relevant goals (e.g., earning money, advancing knowledge about human behavior, obtaining a sense of accomplishment). Affective and cognitive scores were obtained by summing the relevant items. Overall attitude scores were calculated by summing each subject's standardized affective and standardized cognitive scores.

The last page of the questionnaire presented the behavior measure. The student was informed that the Psychology Department was establishing a pool of students who would be contacted and asked to participate in specific experiments as the need for subjects arose. If the student was interested in becoming a member of the subject pool, he or she was to give name and phone number and to indicate the number of experiments in which he or she would be willing to participate. This number served as the subject's behavior score.

Overall, attitude and behavior scores correlated significantly ($r = .322$). However, analyses revealed that the magnitude of this association related as expected to direct experience. A regression analysis showed a statistically significant interaction between direct experience and attitude in the prediction of behavior, indicating that the attitude–behavior relation depended on the

TABLE II

ATTITUDE–BEHAVIOR CORRELATIONS AS A FUNCTION
OF VARIOUS ATTITUDINAL QUALITIES[a]

Attitudinal quality	Amount of attitudinal quality[b]		
	High	Moderate	Low
Direct experience[c]	.42	.36	−.03
Certainty[d]	.38	.40	.08
Latitude of rejection[e]	.52	.26	.19

[a] Adapted from Fazio and Zanna (1978a).

[b] Refers to subjects who had high, moderate, and low direct experience with the attitude object (first row), subjects who reported high, moderate, and low certainty of their attitude (second row), and subjects with wide, intermediate, and narrow latitudes of rejection (third row).

[c] Refers to the number of past participatory experiences with the attitude object (in this case, psychology experiments).

[d] Refers to how certain subjects felt about their attitude (in this case, toward volunteering to act as a subject).

[e] Refers to the number of attitudinal positions subjects found objectionable.

magnitude of direct experience. As the number of direct experiences increased, the correspondence between attitude and behavior increased. This effect is readily observable when attitude–behavior correlations from the three tertiles of the sample on direct experience are examined (see first row of Table II).

A Note about Measurement Reliability

The Fazio and Zanna (1978a) investigation represents the first study conducted in this research program in which an *a priori,* multi-item scale was employed to measure attitudes. Attitude scores were represented by a combination of an affective and a cognitive measure, each of which involved the sum of ten items. The nature of this attitude scale allows us to examine the viability of an alternative explanation for the findings. It is conceivable that differences in measurement reliability account for the observed differences in attitude–behavior consistency. That is, subjects whose attitudes are characterized by indirect experience may have so little attitudinal knowledge that their attitude scores are not very reliable.[3]

[3] We wish to thank Robert Abelson for bringing this important issue to our attention.

TABLE III

RELIABILITY COEFFICIENTS AS A FUNCTION OF
DIRECT EXPERIENCE AND ATTITUDINAL MEASURE

Direct experience[a]	Attitudinal measure		
	Affective	Cognitive	Overall (affective and cognitive)
Low	.86	.72	.82
Moderate	.93	.74	.89
High	.88	.58	.74

[a] Refers to subjects who had a low, moderate, and high number of past participatory experiences with the attitude object (in this case, psychology experiments).

In order to examine this possibility, the sample was divided into three tertiles on the basis of the direct-experience measure, and α coefficients for the affective and cognitive measures in each tertile were computed (Nunnally, 1967). These coefficients, along with the internal reliabilities of the overall attitude measure (i.e., the sum of the standardized affective and standardized cognitive scores), are presented in Table III. Reliability, even within the tertile low in direct experience, is quite high. Furthermore, there is no evidence of differential reliability as a function of the amount of direct experience. Thus, we can be confident that the differences in attitude–behavior consistency are not simply due to a measurement problem.

To summarize, support has been found for the notion that attitudes based on direct, behavioral experience with an attitude object are more predictive of later behavior than are attitudes based on indirect, nonbehavioral experience. The effect has now been observed in studies where direct experience was assessed in two naturally occurring groups, manipulated experimentally, and measured as a continuous variable. Furthermore, these investigations involved different attitude objects and different behaviors, thus attesting to the generalizability of the effect.

A recent experiment by Songer-Nocks (1976) provides yet another conceptual replication regarding the effects of the manner of attitude formation. The experimenter examined the strength of the association between attitudes toward cooperative behavior in a modified Prisoner's Dilemma game and later actual game behavior. Subjects in a prior-experience condition participated in eight preliminary game trials before indicating their attitudes, whereas control subjects did not. Attitudes were significantly more predictive of later behavior given prior experience with the game. Thus, direct experience was again found to affect attitude–behavior consistency.

Attitudes derived from prior behavioral experiences, rather than being ephemeral, appear to guide subsequent behavior to a greater extent than do attitudes based on indirect, nonbehavioral information. Even though a person with only indirect experience with the attitude object may indicate a reliably measured attitude in response to scale items, his or her attitude appears to differ from the attitude of an individual who has had behavioral experience. We shall have more to say about what some of these differences might be at a later point.

The task that remains is to determine and understand how and why this effect of direct experience occurs. We have approached this task in two ways, pursuing what appear to be two processes by which attitude–behavior consistency may occur. On the one hand, a strong attitude–behavior relation may result from the common dependence of both attitude and behavior on prior behavior. If prior and later behavior tend to be consistent (as is likely to be the case if situational forces remain relatively constant), then attitude will be predictive of this later behavior to the extent that it, too, relates to past behavior. Thus, the key to understanding attitude–behavior consistency from this perspective can be found in a determination of the degree to which the attitude reflects past behavior. If the individual's attitudinal expression is inferred from past behavior, then the attitude will be predictive of later behavior because of the strong prior-to-later behavior relation.

On the other hand, attitude–behavior consistency may occur because the individual tends to consider the object in attitudinal terms when he or she encounters an opportunity to behave toward the object. This explanation centers on the likelihood that an individual's behavioral decision will be influenced by attitudinal considerations and suggests that this likelihood will depend on the extent to which the individual's attitude is evoked by observation of the attitude object. Direct- and indirect-experience attitudes may differ on some fundamental dimensions that relate to the likelihood of evocation of the attitude and, hence, to the likelihood that the attitude will influence behavior. We shall present data relevant to each of these two approaches to the question of attitude–behavior consistency.

III. The Prior-to-Later Behavior Relation

In any given situation, a person's past behavior is likely to be the best predictor, in an actuarial sense, of future behavior in that situation. Hence, any measure which reflects that past behavior will also predict future behavior. An attitude inferred from prior behavior does exactly that. The attitude represents a summary of relevant past behaviors, and, as a result, may be more predictive of subsequent behavior than an attitude formed outside the behavioral arena.

A. THE SELF-PERCEPTION OF PAST RELIGIOUS BEHAVIORS

The above notion is perhaps best illustrated by an experiment in which half the subjects were given an opportunity to review, and infer an attitude from, their past religious behaviors (Fazio & Zanna, 1976). These subjects (the self-perception condition) first indicated which of an extensive list of behaviors relevant to religion they had performed in the past. Control subjects did not complete this prior-behavior inventory. Thus, the self-perception subjects had an extended opportunity to review and evaluate their relevant past behaviors, whereas the control subjects did not. All subjects then indicated their attitudes toward being religious and, finally, completed a behavioral intentions inventory which asked them to indicate which of a list of behaviors they intended to perform in the future. Hence, the experiment involved an examination of the attitude–behavior intent relation when it does or does not occur in the context of a prior behavior-to-attitude-to-behavior intent sequence.

As expected, subjects in the self-perception condition were found to express attitudes which were significantly more predictive of their behavioral intentions than did subjects in the control condition (see first row of Table IV). The extremely high correlation between attitude and behavioral intent in the self-perception condition appears to be due, as suggested earlier, to the common dependence of these two variables on prior behavior. Within this condition, scores from the inventories of prior behavior and behavioral intent were found to correlate very highly ($r = .78$). Furthermore, attitudes in this condition appear to have been inferred largely from prior behavior; the correlation between attitude and prior behavior inventory scores was .70. Thus, an attitude which summarized relevant past behaviors was highly predictive of subsequent behavioral intentions.

In contrast, subjects in the control condition, not having been given an opportunity to review extensively their performance of behavior related to religion, appear to have based their attitudes largely on information regarding their family and social backgrounds. The correlation between attitude and a measure which asked subjects to indicate the extent of their religious upbringing tended to be higher in this condition than in the self-perception condition (see second row of Table IV). Reliance on such nonbehavioral information led to the expression of an attitude which was not, relative to the self-perception condition, predictive of behavioral intentions.

TABLE IV
WITHIN-CONDITION CORRELATIONS[a]

	Experimental condition	
Correlation	Self-perception	Control
Attitude, behavioral intention	.78	.52
Attitude, religious upbringing	.42	.70

[a] Adapted from Fazio and Zanna (1976).

Thus, an opportunity to review and evaluate past relevant behaviors had a strong effect on the degree to which attitudes predicted behavioral intentions. Two points should be noted about this result. First, the finding is not attributable to improved reliability of the intentions measure when it is preceded by the prior-behavior measure. Internal consistency coefficients for the behavioral intentions inventory were .824 and .808 in the self-perception and control conditions, respectively. Second, consistency in this study was examined at the level of behavioral intentions, not behavior. This limitation should be kept in mind. Nonetheless, it might be argued that whatever decrease in consistency results from the movement from the intention to perform a behavior to actual performance should affect both conditions equally. Hence, a consistency difference found at the level of behavioral intentions may very well manifest itself with actual behavior.

B. ATTITUDES AND SELF-REPORTS OF SUBSEQUENT BEHAVIOR

A study by Zanna, Olson, and Fazio (1981) is relevant to the second point raised above. Rather than involving behavioral intentions, the investigators measured self-reports of subsequent behavior. Subjects indicated their attitude toward being religious either before or after completing a prior-behavior inventory. Thus, in the self-perception condition, subjects reviewed their past behavior before indicating an attitude, whereas, in the control condition, the review did not occur until after the attitude assessment. Approximately 1 month later, all subjects returned for a second session during which three self-report measures of their actual behaviors pertaining to religion since the first session were assessed. One measure consisted of the same behavior checklist completed during the first session. In addition, subjects were asked to indicate the number of times since the first session that they had (a) attended a religious service and (b) prayed in private.

Actually two replications of the study were conducted. For each replication the correlations between attitudes toward religion and each of the measures of religious behavior were computed within each condition. On the two single-act criterion measures (the "attended services" and "prayed" measures) these correlations were larger in the self-perception than in the control condition.[4] In the control condition, the correlations ranged from .21 to .38, averaging around the traditional .30 mark. However, in the self-perception condition, the correlations were much higher, averaging around .50 (the correlations ranged from .39 to .59).

[4]The expected difference was not observed on the multiple-act, "behavior checklist" measure. Perhaps subjects, who were completing the measure for a second time, attempted to appear consistent with their earlier responses to the items. In any event, the fact that the correlations were extremely high in the control condition (averaging .53 across replications) may have precluded obtaining more substantial relationships in the self-perception condition.

C. AN INDIVIDUAL DIFFERENCE PERSPECTIVE

The findings from these two studies concerning religious attitudes and behavior suggest that the more an attitude represents a summary of relevant past behaviors, the more that attitude will be predictive of future behavior. Two requirements appear necessary for an attitude to constitute such a summary. First, past behavior must have been sufficiently consistent that an accurate summary is possible. If past behavior were highly variable, no single attitudinal statement could be considered to summarize the behavior. Second, the individual must regard the past behavior as an indication of his or her attitude and must infer an attitude from that behavior.

The individual who is most apt, then, to express an attitude which is a summary of past behavior, and, hence, predictive of future behavior, is one whose past behavior toward the attitude object has been relatively consistent and who also bases attitudinal statements on that consistent past behavior. Individual differences on two dimensions appear to be relevant. A direct parallel of that first dimension has been discussed in the personality trait literature. Bem and Allen (1974) have shown that individuals who identify themselves as invariant on a particular trait dimension will, in fact, behave less variably across situations than those who identify themselves as highly variable on that trait. This same individual difference, we have argued, is relevant to the attitude–behavior consistency problem. Thus, it should be possible to ask individuals how much they vary from one situation to another in their behavioral manifestations of a particular attitude, and these self-reports should reflect actual behavioral variability.

However, low variability can be expected to lead to attitude–behavior consistency only if the individual employs the consistent past behavior as critical input from which to infer an attitude. This latter individual-difference dimension is reflected in the construct of self-monitoring (Snyder, 1974, 1976). As defined by Snyder's classification scheme, high self-monitors report being sensitive to situational cues. They closely attend to such cues and monitor and modify their own behavior so as to ensure that it is situation-appropriate. Low self-monitors, on the other hand, report less concern about whether their behavior fulfills the expectations of others or about what impressions others have of them. Instead, they view their behavior as being guided largely by relevant inner dispositions. [See Snyder (1979) for a full and detailed discussion of the self-monitoring construct.] Snyder and Tanke (1976) have demonstrated that this self-monitoring construct is related to attitude change in an induced-compliance situation. After choosing to perform a counterattitudinal behavior, low self-monitors displayed attitude change in the direction of their advocacy, whereas high self-monitors were unaffected by their attitude-discrepant behavior. Thus, only low self-monitors considered their behavior to be reflective of their attitudes, and only they appeared to infer attitudes from that behavior.

If attitudes which represent summaries of past behavior are more predictive of future behavior, then the present individual-difference perspective leads one to expect relatively greater attitude–behavior consistency among low self-monitoring individuals who report themselves to vary little in their behavior toward a particular attitude object than among any other classification of individuals. In a test of this reasoning, Zanna, Olson, and Fazio (1980) examined the consistency between religious attitudes and behavior. In a first session, the subjects (a) indicated their attitudes toward being religious, (b) indicated the degree to which they varied from one situation to another in how religious they were, and (c) completed Snyder's (1974) self-monitoring scale. In a second session, approximately 1 month later, subjects were asked to indicate the frequency with which they had performed several actions since the first sessions. Included among the acts were becoming intoxicated on alcohol, using illegal drugs, attending a religious service, and praying in private.

Each subject was classified as either a high or low self-monitor and as either a high or low variability subject, producing a 2×2 classification matrix. The former classification was performed by a median split of the distribution of self-monitoring scores. Following Bem and Allen (1974), the classification into high and low variability subjects was performed by a median split of the distribution of variability scores at each score of the 11-point attitude scale. This technique removes any possible confound of attitude extremity and variability. Self-monitoring and variability did not correlate ($r = -.01$); as a result, the number of subjects classified into each cell of the matrix was roughly equivalent.

Since attending religious services and praying in private were both conceptually and empirically related, standardized scores on each dimension were summed to form one behavior measure. The alcohol and drug usage data (which also correlated significantly) were similarly treated to form a second behavior measure.

Correlations between attitudes and each of these measures of behavior were computed within each of the four cells produced by the classification scheme and are displayed in Table V. On each measure, correlations tended to be of a higher magnitude in the low self-monitoring–low variability cell than in any of the other cells. The low–low cell represents that group of people whom we could expect to have relatively consistent prior behavior and who are also likely to infer an attitudinal disposition from that behavior. For these people, more so than for any others, attitude represents a meaningful summary of past behavior and, consequently, accurately predicts future behavior.

D. A PARTIAL CORRELATION ANALYSIS

Taken together, these studies all lead to the suggestion that the superior predictive utility of an attitude in a behavior-to-attitude-to-behavior sequence is due, at least in part, to the relationship between prior and subsequent behavior. Attitude and later behavior have a common dependence on prior behavior.

TABLE V
ATTITUDE–BEHAVIOR CORRELATIONS WITHIN A LOW–HIGH SELF-MONITORING × LOW–HIGH
VARIABILITY CLASSIFICATION SCHEME[a]

	Low self-monitoring		High self-monitoring	
Correlation	Low variability	High variability	Low variability	High variability
Attitude, attended services/prayed	.52*	.38*	.34	.29
Attitude, alcohol/drugs	−.59**	−.06	−.21	.18

[a] Adapted from Zanna et al. (1980). Copyright 1980 by the American Psychological Association. Adapted by permission.
*p < .05.
**p < .01.

Whether the prior-behavior–later-behavior relation totally accounts for the attitude–behavior consistency differences can, of course, be examined by analyses of partial correlations. Such an examination constituted an additional aim of the earlier described study by Zanna et al. (1981). Recall that, in this investigation, both self-perception and control subjects completed the prior-behavior inventory. Self-perception subjects did so prior to the attitude assessment, whereas control subjects did so after indicating their attitude. One month later, subjects indicated the extent to which they behaved religiously during the interim period. Among other questions, they were asked the number of times they had attended services and prayed in private. At the simple correlation level, significant differences were found between the two conditions in the magnitude of the various attitude–behavior relationships. If this difference is due entirely to the prior-behavior–later-behavior and prior-behavior–attitude relations, then partialling out the effects of prior behavior should eliminate the difference between the two conditions. Attitude–behavior correlations partialling out prior behavior were computed in each condition. Significant differences between the conditions still remained. Even these partial correlations were of a higher magnitude in the self-perception (overall mean of .35; range from .26 to .45) than in the control condition (overall mean of .09; range of .03 to .22).

The finding suggests that, although the prior-behavior–later-behavior relation undoubtedly plays a role in the phenomenon under consideration, it does not totally account for the effect. In other words, both of the processes that we described earlier by which attitude–behavior consistency may occur appear to be operating.[5] First, the common dependence of attitude and later behavior on prior

[5] The "subject pool" study described earlier (Fazio & Zanna, 1978a) is also of relevance to the dual processes by which attitude–behavior consistency may occur. Like the Zanna et al. (1981) findings, the data from this study point to the insufficiency of the prior–later behavior relation as a

behavior leads attitudes inferred from prior behavior to be predictive of later behavior. But, in addition, the attitude based on behavioral experience may be characterized by certain qualities that make it relatively likely to be evoked on observation of the attitude object and, hence, likely to influence behavior toward the object. It is to this second approach to the question of attitude–behavior consistency, and to its relation to the distinction between direct- and indirect-experience attitudes, that we now turn.

IV. Attitudinal Qualities

An attitude inferred from prior behavior may be characterized by various qualities, not characteristic of an indirect-experience attitude, which make the direct-experience attitude more likely to influence later behavior. Direct- and indirect-experience attitudes apparently differ on some other fundamental dimensions, in addition to differing in the information on which they are based. Differences on these dimensions may mediate the effect of direct experience on attitude–behavior consistency.

A. CONFIDENCE AND CLARITY

Like Bem (1972), we believe that individuals have difficulty assessing their attitudes and feelings unless they have engaged in some freely performed behavior toward the attitude object. Such behavior[6] is generally perceived to be

---

sole explanation of the effects of behavioral experience on attitude–behavior consistency. The analysis involved in this study entailed the prediction of the number of experiments for which the subject had volunteered by a regression equation in which the first entry was attitude, the second entry was the number of experiments in which the subject had participated in the past, and the final entry was the interaction term (i.e., the attitude × number of past experiments cross-product). This last term significantly improved the prediction of the behavior measure over and above the proportion of variance explained by the earlier entries. Thus, even when prior behavior was partialled out of the attitude–behavior relation, the strength of this relation varied positively with the number of experiments in which the subject had participated in the past.

[6]In self-perception theory, as in attribution theories in general, behavior that appears to be under the control of environmental forces is distinguished from behavior under the control of personal forces. In his original proposal, Bem (1967) draws on the behavioristic concept of *mand* to make this distinction. Manded behavior refers to behavior elicited by environmental forces and in laboratory settings is often operationalized by the experimenter's offering the subject no choice but to perform a given behavior. However, the term *manded behavior* also refers to such actions as performing a behavior in return for a relatively large monetary payment. Since behaviors other than those "forced" by an authority figure can be of a manded nature, we shall use the terms *manded* and *unmanded* to refer, respectively, to behaviors that are or are not attributable to an environmental force. These terms are more reflective of the critical distinction than such terms as chosen versus forced behaviors. It is unmanded behavior that is generally perceived as indicative of one's attitude.

more reflective of an internal disposition than is other information. Without the benefit of prior behavior and without the opportunity to infer an attitude from that behavior, an individual is forced to, in some sense, "guess" his or her attitude from other less attitudinally reflective information. The individual may not be able to make as clear and as confident an assessment of his or her attitude as can the individual who infers his or her attitude from behavior and the circumstances surrounding that behavior. Thus, an individual whose attitude is based on direct behavioral experience may hold that attitude with greater certainty than will an individual whose attitude is formed on the basis of indirect experience. This attitudinal quality may, in turn, affect the strength of the attitude–behavior relationship. The more certain an individual is of his or her attitude toward some object, the more likely it is that this attitude will guide later behavior toward the object (Sample & Warland, 1973).

In addition to being held with relatively more certainty, a direct-experience attitude may be more clearly focused and well defined than an indirect experience attitude. The clarity of an attitude may be operationally defined as the width of an individual's latitude of rejection (Sherif & Hovland, 1961). The more attitudinal positions an individual finds objectionable, the more well defined the individual's attitude is. On inferring an attitude from prior behavior, an individual may be better able to clearly demarcate those positions which he or she finds acceptable and objectionable. A clear and well-defined attitude may, in turn, influence later behavior to a greater degree than an unfocused attitude (Sherif, Kelly, Rodgers, Sarup, & Tittler, 1973).

1. The "Subject Pool" Study Revisited

We first examined the notion that confidence and clarity may mediate the effect of direct experience on attitude–behavior consistency in the earlier described study concerning volunteering to participate in psychological research (Fazio & Zanna, 1978a). In addition to assessing attitudes and behaviors toward volunteering, we measured various qualities of the attitude. One of these, as mentioned earlier, was the number of direct experiences the subject had with psychological experiments—which we found to relate to attitude–behavior consistency. In addition to this measure, subjects indicated how certain they were of their attitude. They also completed a latitude scale which required them to indicate which of seven statements, varying from "Participating in psychological research is extremely interesting" to "... extremely boring," they found acceptable and which statements they found objectionable.

Regression analyses showed both certainty and the width of the latitude of rejection to relate to attitude–behavior consistency. As certainty in one's attitude increased, attitude–behavior correspondence increased. Similarly, the more well defined the attitude, that is, the wider the latitude of rejection, the greater the consistency between attitudes and behavior. Table II displays attitude–behavior correlations for three tertiles of the sample on each of the two attitudinal qualities (see second and third rows of the table). As is evident from these correlations and from the regression analyses, each of the two attitudinal qualities is related to the utility of the attitude in predicting behavior.

We still need to assess whether direct experience is related to certainty and to width of the latitude of rejection. As Table VI shows, the three attitudinal qualities did correlate significantly. The more direct experience individuals had, the more certainly they held their attitudes. The more behavioral experiences individuals have had with respect to an attitude object, the more opportunity they will have had to assess and infer attitudes from behavior. Apparently, the confidence with which an attitude is held increases with each such behavioral experience. In addition, individuals' feelings toward a particular object appear to become more clearly focused after each behavioral contact with the object. The more direct experience individuals had, the more well defined their attitudes were. People who have never engaged in behavior toward the attitude object apparently find many attitudinal positions acceptable. After direct behavioral experience and the opportunity to infer attitudes from behavior, individuals apparently restrict the number of positions they are willing to accept and expand their latitudes of rejection.

It is interesting to note that, in studies where the Sherifs and their associates have found a positive relationship between the width of subjects' latitudes of rejection and what they term *ego involvement,* the latter variable has typically been measured by how much behavior the individual has engaged in toward the attitude object (Sherif & Hovland, 1961; Sherif, Sherif, & Nebergall, 1965; Beck & Nebergall, 1967). For example, in the Beck and Nebergall study, persons who

TABLE VI
CORRELATION MATRIX OF THE ATTITUDINAL QUALITIES[a]

Attitudinal qualities	Direct experience	Certainty	Latitude of rejection
Direct experience[b]	—		
Certainty[c]	.23**	—	
Latitude of rejection[d]	.19*	.27**	—

[a] Adapted from Fazio and Zanna (1978a). Copyright 1978 by Academic Press, adapted by permission.

[b] Refers to the number of past participatory experiences with the attitude object (in this case, psychology experiments).

[c] Refers to how certain subjects felt about their attitudes (in this case, toward volunteering to act as a subject).

[d] Refers to the number of attitudinal positions subjects found objectionable.

*$p < .05$.
**$p < .01$.

actively campaigned for a senatorial candidate exhibited wider latitudes of rejection concerning the two candidates than persons who held approximately the same attitude toward the candidate but who were politically inactive. Thus, direct experience may be the critical indicator of what has been called ego involvement. Having engaged in behavior toward the attitude object, the "involved" individual may infer a well-defined attitude characterized by a wide latitude of rejection.

The relationships observed in the "subject pool" study suggest a model of the manner in which direct experience may affect attitude–behavior consistency. Direct experience may produce an attitude that is better defined and more confidently held than an attitude formed through more indirect means. Characterized by these qualities, the attitude based on direct experience may, as a result, better predict later behavior. The correlational nature of this investigation, of course, prohibits any firm conclusions. Nevertheless, the data are consistent with the model we are proposing.

2. Confidence within the Puzzle Paradigm

In order to examine the postulated model in a causal manner, we conducted two laboratory experiments (Fazio & Zanna, 1978b). We first conducted a replication of the earlier described "puzzle" experiment with the addition of confidence as another dependent variable. As before, subjects indicated their attitudes toward a variety of types of puzzles to which they had been introduced via direct or indirect experience. Subjects also indicated, however, how confident they were in each of the attitude ratings they had made. Following these measures, subjects participated in a 15-min "free-play" situation. As before, rank-order correlations were computed between each subject's interest ratings and the order in which he or she worked the problems and between the interest ratings and the proportion of available problems of each type he or she attempted to solve. For each subject, these two correlations were averaged to produce a single score of attitude–behavior consistency. As can be seen from the first row of Table VII, the effect of the manner of attitude formation on consistency was replicated.

TABLE VII
MEAN CONSISTENCY AND CONFIDENCE SCORES[a]

Dependent measure	Experience condition	
	Direct	Indirect
Attitude–behavior consistency	.52	.26
Confidence in attitude	7.90	7.04

[a] Adapted from Fazio and Zanna (1978b, Experiment 1).

Direct experience subjects displayed greater attitude–behavior correspondence than indirect experience subjects.

The mean of each subject's confidence ratings was also computed. As our model predicts, confidence was greater in the direct-experience condition than in the indirect experience condition (see second row of Table VII). Thus, direct and indirect experience attitudes do differ with regard to how confidently they are held. The question that remains, however, is whether confidence causally affects attitude–behavior consistency.

We explored this question in a second experiment which employed the usual puzzle procedure. After subjects were provided direct or indirect experience with a set of puzzles, they rated their interest in each type of puzzle. While the subjects were making these judgments, electrodes attached to their fingertips were supposedly monitoring various physiological functions. Subjects were led to believe that these physiological readings were indicative of how confidently they held their attitudes toward each type of puzzle. For half the subjects, the bogus physiological feedback indicated that they held their attitudes with a high degree of confidence. The other half were led to believe that they held their attitudes with little confidence. After the confidence manipulation, the 15-min free-play situation began. Again, the order in which the subjects attempted to solve the types of puzzles and the proportion of each type attempted served as behavior measures. In addition, the experimenter, located behind a one-way mirror, timed how long each subject spent working on each type of problem.

For each subject, rank-order correlations between interest ratings and each of the three behavior measures were computed. The average of these three correlations served as the subject's attitude–behavior consistency score. An analysis of variance on these data revealed two significant main effects. Replicating the previous findings, direct experience subjects displayed greater consistency than indirect experience subjects. In addition, subjects who had been led to believe that they held their attitudes with high confidence behaved more consistently with their attitudes than those who had been led to believe that they held their attitudes with low confidence (Table VIII).

TABLE VIII

MEAN ATTITUDE-BEHAVIOR CONSISTENCY SCORES[a]

Experience condition	Confidence condition	
	High	Low
Direct	.68	.50
Indirect	.51	.37

[a] Adapted from Fazio and Zanna (1978b, Experiment 2). Copyright 1978 by Duke University Press, reprinted by permission.

Taken together, these two experiments on confidence suggest that an individual may behave more consistently with an attitude based on direct experience than one based on indirect experience because the manner of attitude formation affects the degree of confidence with which that attitude is held. Having greater confidence in an attitude formed via direct experience, an individual is apt to behave more consistently with that attitude. The data provide experimental support for the model proposed earlier and suggest that the relative "strength" of direct experience attitudes is responsible, at least in part, for the effect of direct experience on attitude–behavior consistency.

Since confidence may be fostered by many sources other than direct experience, it should be noted that an attitude formed by indirect means could conceivably also be held with extreme confidence and, hence, be more predictive of behavior than a direct experience attitude. For example, a child's attitude toward members of a given ethnic or racial group may be held with great confidence, even though formed indirectly, because of his or her parents' extreme credibility. In such a case, the predictive validity of an indirect experience attitude may equal, or possibly even surpass, the validity of an attitude formed more directly.

B. PERSISTENCE OF THE ATTITUDE

Some evidence exists in the literature which suggests that attitudes based on direct behavioral experience may be more persistent over time than attitudes based on indirect experience. An intriguing study by Watts (1967) permits a comparison of the persistence over time of equivalent amounts of attitude change produced via direct or indirect means. Watts had subjects in what he termed an active-participation condition write counterattitudinal essays. Subjects in a passive participation condition read a persuasive communication which had been carefully constructed to produce an amount of attitude change equivalent to that produced by essay writing. Immediately after writing or reading, significant attitude change in each of the two conditions was observed, and the average attitude change in the two groups was equal. However, when attitudes were reassessed 6 weeks later, a significant difference between the two conditions was found. Initially induced attitude change among subjects in the active-participation condition persisted such that their attitudes still differed from those of control subjects. The attitudes of subjects in the passive-communication condition, on the other hand, regressed over time to the control level. The findings suggest a substantial difference in attitudinal stability between attitudes formed (or, as in this experiment, changed) on the basis of active, behavioral experience and those formed via more passive, indirect means. This finding of persistence with regard to attitudes based on behavior is in striking contrast to the more typical short-lived nature of attitude change [see Cook & Flay (1978) for an excellent review and analysis of the persistence literature].

The differential stability of attitudes based on direct versus indirect experience may be an important mediator of the effect of the manner of attitude formation on the attitude-behavior relationship. Numerous theorists have suggested that the temporal stability of an attitude moderates the attitude–behavior relationship (e.g., Fishbein, 1967; Schuman & Johnson, 1976). In a recent study, Schwartz (1978) has documented the role of temporal stability. He found that attitude toward tutoring blind children and volunteering to do so correlated more strongly among those subjects whose general set of altruistic attitudes showed temporal stability than among those whose attitudes were marked by relative instability.

C. RESISTANCE TO ATTACK

The work of Kiesler and his colleagues (Kiesler, 1971) suggests yet another dimension on which direct versus indirect experience attitudes might differ. In a program of research on "commitment," Kiesler found that the more committed an individual was to a given attitudinal position, the more resistant to influence that attitude was when he or she was later exposed to a countercommunication. Interestingly, commitment was sometimes manipulated by providing experimental subjects with unmanded behavior from which they could infer an attitude. In various studies, the unmanded behavior consisted of signing a petition (Kiesler, 1971), delivering a speech for little monetary payment (Kiesler & Sakumura, 1966), or repeatedly adopting a particular game strategy (Kiesler, 1971). In each study, control subjects engaged in either manded behavior (e.g., delivering a speech for a relatively large payment) or no behavior at all. Although the manipulations produced no effect on attitude scores in the two conditions, they did affect the "strength" of the attitude. In each investigation, when subjects were exposed to a communication which argued against their attitude, experimental subjects changed their attitudes significantly less than control subjects.

The experimental manipulations employed in the above studies fit neatly into our distinction between attitudes inferred from direct behavioral experience and attitudes based on indirect, nonbehavioral information. Although the research was not designed for the purpose of examining differences between direct and indirect experience attitudes, the data are consistent with our conceptual framework. The findings suggest that direct experience attitudes may be more resistant to attack from external sources.

Generally speaking, the picture that emerges is that attitudes formed through direct experience are stronger than those formed through indirect experience. There is evidence to suggest that direct experience attitudes are more clearly defined, held with greater certainty, more stable over time, and more resistant to counterinfluence. These various qualities are undoubtedly related to some degree and they all reflect what might be considered the strength of the attitude. Due to this relative strength, attitudes based on direct experience are more likely to serve as guides to behavior than are attitudes based on indirect experience.

The importance of these attitudinal qualities lies not only in the fact that they are affected by direct experience but also in what they imply about the determinants of attitude–behavior consistency. Confidence, clarity, and temporal stability have each been found to relate to consistency. Many variables in addition to direct experience may affect these qualities and, hence, affect attitude–behavior consistency. Future research should focus on examining the various antecedents and consequents of these attitudinal qualities.

V.   Reasons for the Differential Strength

A.   AMOUNT OF INFORMATION AVAILABLE

The increased ''strength'' of attitudes based on direct experience is thought to derive from three related sources. First, a direct experience may make more information about the object available to the individual than an indirect experience. For example, it is possible that subjects in the puzzle experiments had more information about the various problems following a direct experience than after an indirect experience. It is not clear that differential amounts of available information necessarily result from a direct versus an indirect experience. A well-written and thoroughly researched newspaper article can provide a reader with much more information than an actual behavioral experience with the object in question. Nevertheless, if more information is available after certain direct experiences, the differential amount of information seems likely to affect attitude–behavior consistency. Having more information at hand after a direct experience, the individual could more easily evaluate the object in a clear, confident, and meaningful way. The resultant attitude would then be more likely to influence subsequent behavior.

B.   INFORMATION PROCESSING

More interestingly, a crucial information processing difference may also exist between direct and indirect experience. Since a direct experience involves behavior toward the attitude object, the behavior itself ought to be salient to the individual. In contrast, since indirect experience involves some medium (e.g., another person or printed matter) describing the attitude object, the medium and the description may be salient. For example, to a child listening to a friend describe a new toy, presumably it is that friend and that description which are salient. To a child playing with a new toy, however, the toy and his or her manipulation of the toy are most likely salient.

The present argument closely parallels the form of Jones and Nisbett's (1971) argument that actors typically attribute their own behavior to relatively more situational and fewer dispositional causes than an observer of that behavior does. These authors postulated that both the amount of information available to actors and observers and how that information is processed by actors and observers differ. This latter explanation was recently tested by Regan and Totten (1975) in an experiment where the perspective of some observers was altered without making available any additional information. All subjects watched a videotape of a get-acquainted conversation between two females. The perspective of some subjects was altered by instructing them to empathize with one of the conversants. As a result, these subjects made relatively more situational and fewer dispositional attributions than subjects who merely observed.

The procedure employed by Regan and Totten (1975) suggests a strategy to determine whether possible information processing differences between direct and indirect experience were responsible, in part, for the superior predictive power of direct experience attitudes. If instructions to empathize with someone lead an individual to take the perspective of that person, then empathizing with someone having a direct experience with an attitude object should make salient to the empathizing observer those same aspects of the situation that are salient to the target person. Hence, just as individuals who have had direct experience with an attitude object display greater attitude-behavior consistency than do individuals who have had indirect experience, empathizing observers should behave more consistently with their own attitudes than observers not instructed to empathize.

In a test of the notion that an information processing difference exists between direct and indirect experience, Fazio, Zanna, and Cooper (1978) had subjects view a videotape of an individual in an actual, unrehearsed direct experience with a set of puzzles. The audio track consisted of a narrative description of the puzzles, the directions, and the solutions. Subjects in the control condition were instructed to listen and watch carefully. The other half of the subjects were told to try to empathize with the person on the videotape and to imagine how they would feel in her position. Following the videotape presentation, all subjects indicated how interesting they found each type of puzzle. The 15-min free-play situation then began.

As before, two rank-order correlations were computed: one between the subject's interest ratings and the order in which she worked the types of problems and one between her interest ratings and the proportion of each type she attempted. The average of these two within-subject correlations was employed as the subject's consistency score. As predicted, attitude-behavior consistency was greater in the empathy condition ($M = .68$) than in the control condition ($M = .35$).

The findings suggest that an information processing difference between direct and indirect experience does exist. Subjects watched the same videotape and thus had the same information available to them.[7] However, the change in

---

[7] Two control conditions were run to ensure that the empathy manipulation did not alter the amount of information available to the subjects by prompting differential attentiveness to the videotape. After having viewed the tape under empathy or control instructions, the subjects were

perspective created by the empathy instructions resulted in greater consistency for the observers.

Focusing on one's behavior (or in the case of the empathy subjects, on imagined behavior) may produce a strong attitude which is likely to predict later behavior. Such behavioral information may be considered a more reliable guide to one's reaction to an object than an evaluation of a medium's description. That is, just as an observer considers knowledge of another's behavior to be the most indicative information concerning that individual's internal disposition, so, too, may a person perceive his or her own behavior to be most reflective of his or her attitude. Hence, by focusing on behavior, as an individual does during a direct experience, an individual may form an attitude that is clear and well defined and that is held confidently.

The importance of the salience of behavioral information is also evident from research on the effects of objective self-awareness on attitude–behavior consistency (Pryor, Gibbons, Wicklund, Fazio, & Hood, 1977). In a series of experiments, Pryor *et al.* demonstrated that self-focused attention affected both the degree to which self-reports of attitude related to past behavior and the degree to which self-reports predicted future behavior. The interesting aspect of this research from the present viewpoint is that the manipulations of objective self-awareness do not affect the amount of information available but do affect the salience of past behavioral information. One experiment involved a procedure similar to the puzzle paradigm. All subjects were first given an opportunity to behave preferentially toward a variety of types of puzzles in a 10-min free-play situation. In the presence or absence of a mirror, the subjects then indicated their attitudes toward each type of puzzle. Subjects in the mirror condition expressed attitudes which correlated more strongly with their earlier behavior than did subjects in the control condition. For example, when consistency scores were computed in the same manner as in the empathy study, the average correlation in the mirror condition was found to be .69, compared to .13 in the control condition. Thus, the presence of a mirror increased the extent to which the subject inferred an attitude from prior behavior.

In another experiment, Pryor *et al.* (1977) examined predictive validity. Subjects completed a self-description of their sociability in the presence or absence of a mirror. In a second session, while waiting for the experiment to begin, the subject was given an opportunity to behave sociably toward an attractive female confederate. Two indices of behavioral sociability were employed: (1) the confederate's evaluation and (2) the number of words spoken by the subject. On both indices, it was found that the correlation between self-reports and behavior was greater in the mirror than in the control condition. (See Carver, 1975;

---

given a recall test. The two groups recalled equally well the names of the types of problems, the number of examples that were presented of each type, and the answers to a few selected examples. In addition, the accuracy and completeness of the subjects' written descriptions of each type of puzzle were rated equivalently across the two conditions by two blind judges.

Gibbons, 1978; Scheier, Buss, & Buss, 1978, for additional research demonstrating increased consistency between self-reports and later behavior as a consequence of self-awareness.)

Together, these experiments suggest that the presence of a mirror enhances the salience of an individual's relevant past behaviors. This focus on behavior leads to the expression of an attitude or self-description that is relatively likely to predict later behavior.

C. ATTITUDE ACCESSIBILITY

The above research suggests a difference between direct and indirect experience with regard to the manner in which incoming information is processed. Attention may be focused on one's behavior in a direct experience, whereas it may be focused on the medium in an indirect experience. In addition to this differential processing of information, storage and retrieval differences may exist. In particular, attitudes based on direct experience may be more accessible from memory than attitudes based on indirect experience. Such differential accessibility might also account for the relative strength of direct versus indirect experience attitudes and, hence, might play a role in determining the degree to which the attitude affects later behavior. The strength of the attitude–behavior relation in a given situation has been shown to vary as a function of the salience of an attitude (Snyder & Swann, 1976). The more salient or available an attitude is, the more likely it is that the individual will access that attitude on observation of the attitude object. Because of this accessibility, the same attitudinal information is apt to be considered when the individual is contemplating behavior toward the object and when he or she is responding to verbal measures about the object, leading to attitude–behavior consistency.

Fazio and Chen (1979) recently conducted two experiments to examine the accessibility of direct versus indirect experience attitudes. The first experiment involved a standard manipulation within the context of the puzzle paradigm. Following the manipulation of direct versus indirect experience, all subjects participated in a reaction time task. Each of 10 randomly ordered slides presented the name of a type of problem followed by an adjective (e.g., "Letter Series: Interesting?"). Ten different adjectives were employed and each puzzle type was paired with one positive and one negative adjective. The subject's task was to press a "Yes" button if the adjective was descriptive of his or her feelings toward that particular type of puzzle or a "No" button if the adjective was not descriptive. Averaged across the 10 trials, direct-experience subjects were able to respond significantly more quickly to these inquiries about their attitudes than were indirect experience subjects (mean reaction times of 7.14 and 8.50 sec, respectively). Hence, the data clearly indicate differential cognitive processes following behavioral versus nonbehavioral experiences.

The second experiment examined reaction time following performance of behavior more closely by explicitly manipulating two critical factors the level of which could not be ascertained in Experiment 1. First, because self-perception experiments typically manipulate the manded versus unmanded nature of a behavior rather than the presence or absence of behavior, a choice manipulation was employed in Experiment 2. It is unclear whether subjects in the direct experience condition of Experiment 1 perceived that their behavior was or was not freely performed. Certainly, no attempt was made to produce salient perceptions of either freedom or lack of freedom. In Experiment 2, all subjects first listened to an audiotape narration which described the five types of puzzles. Then, all subjects received direct experience with at least some of the puzzles. However, the manded or unmanded nature of the direct experience was manipulated. Subjects in the choice condition were given 15 min of work on any of the five types of puzzles. The free nature of this time period was emphasized. Each subject in a no-choice condition was yoked to a subject in the choice condition and was required to spend the same amount of time with each puzzle type and to work the puzzle types in the same order as his or her yoked partner did. In this way, exposure to the different types of puzzles was equated across the two conditions, but in one condition the behavior was manded and in the other unmanded.

The second factor that was manipulated involved a method of ensuring that at least some subjects would have formed their attitudes prior to, rather than during the reaction time task. Some research (e.g., Wixon & Laird, 1976) suggests that subjects may not draw attitudinal inferences from their behavior until they are prompted to do so by some situational cue.[8] We cannot ascertain whether the cues in Experiment 1 were sufficient to prompt subjects to consolidate their thoughts about each puzzle prior to the reaction time task (in which case the reaction time data would reflect accessibility) or not (in which case the reaction time data would reflect the ease of attitude formation). In Experiment 2, half of the subjects completed a measure of their interest in each type of puzzle immediately after the behavioral exposure (consolidation condition). The need to complete the attitude scales should prompt subjects in the choice condition to infer their attitudes from their behavior. The other half of the subjects were not presented with any attitude measures at this point in the experiment (no-consolidation condition). Following this manipulation, all subjects participated in the same reaction time task as in the first experiment.

[8]The question of when such inferences are drawn has long plagued self-perception theory and attribution theories in general [see Berscheid, Graziano, Monson, & Dermer (1976) for a discussion of this issue in the context of attributions about others]. It is quite clear that individuals engage in self-attribution processes when they are prompted to do so by a request that they express an opinion, either in conversation or via an attitudinal measure of some sort. When individuals spontaneously self-perceive, however, is not at all clear. Since attitudes serve a functional purpose of aiding one to categorize and understand a complex and diverse environment, we would expect self-attribution processes to occur most readily when the attitude object is of importance and relevance to the individual in the sense that future interactions with, or inquiries about, the attitude object are expected. It then becomes useful to understand how one feels about the attitude object.

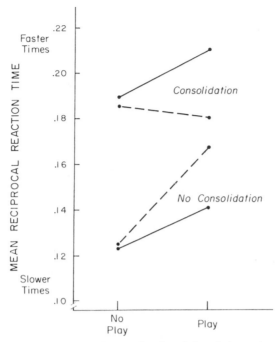

Fig. 1.   Mean reciprocal reaction time as a function of play, choice, and consolidation. (———),
choice; (--), no choice. (Taken from Fazio & Chen, 1979.)

Since each yoked pair did not work on all of the five puzzle types in the
allotted 15 min, the data were analyzed in terms of reaction time to puzzles
played with versus reaction time to puzzles not played with. In effect, this
distinction represents a within-pair comparison of those puzzles on which direct
experience was obtained (i.e., play puzzles) to those on which only indirect
experience occurred (i.e., no-play puzzles; only the information provided in the
narrative description was available to the subject). In each condition, mean
reaction times to the puzzles that were and were not played with are displayed in
Fig. 1. Replicating the earlier experiment, a significant main effect of play versus
no-play was found. Subjects responded more quickly to adjectives paired with
those puzzles on which they had obtained direct experience than to those on
which they had only indirect experience. A main effect of the consolidation
manipulation was also present, such that those subjects who had consolidated
their thoughts and had previously expressed attitudes responded more quickly
than those who had not.
    More interestingly, a three-way interaction was found (see Fig. 1). This
interaction can be described most easily by noting that the general effect of
subjects' responding more quickly to play than to no-play puzzles tended to be
true in each of the four conditions except the no-choice–consolidation condition.
Within the no-consolidation conditions, these data imply that direct experience

(as is obtained on puzzles played with), regardless of whether it involves choice or no choice, appears to facilitate the assessment of one's attitude relative to indirect experience (as with respect to puzzles not played with). Consistent with Bem's (1972) basic assumption that individuals find it difficult to assess their attitudes unless they have engaged in behavior and consistent with a theme that has been expressed throughout this article, it would appear to be easier to decide what one's attitude must be following direct experience than following indirect experience. The ease with which this decision process is accomplished may be one reason that attitudes based on direct experience are more confidently held and more clearly defined than attitudes formed via indirect means.

A second implication of these data concerns accessibility. Once formed, attitudes based on nonchosen behavior are apparently no more accessible than consolidated attitudes based on nonbehavioral experience (the no-choice-consolidation condition). However, increased accessibility does appear to occur in the choice–consolidation condition. Freely performed behavioral experience seems to produce an attitude that can be more readily accessed from memory than does indirect experience. Apparently, unmanded behavior of this sort is considered such a relevant guide to one's attitude that an attitude inferred from that behavior is stored in such a manner that it can be easily retrieved. Rather than being epiphenomena, attitudinal inferences from freely performed behavior appear to be relatively strong, clear, and interpretable internal cues. This greater accessibility relative to indirect experience attitudes is apt to prompt differential attitude–behavior consistency, since consistency will occur only to the extent that the same attitudinal information guides one's response to a verbal measure and to a behavioral decision. The increased accessibility of attitudes based on unmanded direct experience might also account for their greater persistence over time and relative resistance to attack. Being readily accessible, the attitude can serve as a filter through which any counterattitudinal information is interpreted. Such biased perception of the counterinformation is apt to make yielding to an attack unlikely.

The present focus on accessibility is congruent with the recent trend in social psychology to give consideration to the role of cognitive processes. Various social psychologists have discussed the importance of schemas (Markus, 1977), prototypes (Cantor & Mischel, 1977), and scripts (Abelson, 1978), each of which is considered to be a cognitive representation of some object (including the self), person, personality trait, or behavior sequence. Much of the research from this cognitive–social perspective has focused on the issue of personality traits (e.g., Higgins, Rholes, & Jones, 1977; Cantor & Mischel, 1977; Markus, 1977). The present research suggests that it may be useful to adopt a similar orientation with respect to attitudes (see Tesser, 1978). In fact, the procedure employed in the Fazio and Chen experiments closely parallels that used by Markus (1977), who found that reaction time to trait adjectives was related to the degree to which subjects had well-defined self-schemas on a particular personality dimension. Similarly, our findings suggest that reaction time to attitudinal adjectives can vary as a function of the manner in which that attitude was formed.

In summary, we have focused on three factors that appear to be responsible for the differential strength of direct and indirect experience attitudes. (1) Direct experience may make more information about the object available to the person. (2) Direct experience may lead one to focus on incoming behavioral information, which tends to facilitate the ease with which one can decide on one's attitude. (3) Direct experience, at least when it is of an unmanded nature, leads to the formation of an attitude which is readily accessible from memory. These last two factors, in particular, are based on the theoretical assumption that people consider behavioral experiences to be reliable information that is highly reflective of their attitudes toward the given object. As a result, individuals form relatively strong attitudes when they can employ such information as the basis for their attitudes.

We have found this theoretical assumption to be a convenient heuristic for considering our research. However, it is important to recognize that other processes, in addition to the notion that people assume behavior to be dispositionally reflective, may contribute to the relative strength of direct experience attitudes. These additional mechanisms are not necessarily competing interpretations; multiple processes might contribute to the effect or be at work in different situations. If one were to postulate the existence of a general striving for self-consistency, as, for example, is done by self-awareness theory (Wicklund, 1975), then individuals may be motivated to form an unusually strong attitude so as to justify past behavior as sufficiently as possible. For example, an individual may be motivated to believe that he or she holds the attitude with great confidence. As a result, the attitude is likely to be evoked on observation of the object and to guide behavior toward that object. Such a motivated process may be particularly likely to occur in the case of initial behavior that is sufficiently extreme to be considered counterattitudinal (Fazio, Zanna, & Cooper, 1977). In such a case, a process of motivated dissonance reduction may lead to the development of a new strong attitude so as to justify the performance of counterattitudinal behavior.

Yet another process that may contribute to the relative strength of attitudes based on prior behavior concerns the elimination of competing responses (Harrison, 1968; Matlin, 1971). Frequently discussed in the context of Zajonc's (1968) mere-exposure hypothesis, this notion would argue that a consequence of behavioral experience is the extinction of any alternative reactions to the attitude object that might weaken or detract from the strength of the attitude. Thus, direct experience may result in the object evoking fewer and weaker alternative responses on subsequent observation.

Each of these mechanisms may contribute to the relative strength of attitudes based on prior behavior. In any given situation, any or all of the processes may be involved. Or, a given process may be more likely to operate in a given situation. Regardless, future research needs to address and clarify these possible mechanisms by which attitudes based upon direct experience attain increased accessibility, confidence, clarity, and stability.

The other question that remains about the relative strength of attitudes based upon direct behavioral experience concerns its consequences for behavior. How is it that such strong attitudes are "translated" into behavior which corresponds to the attitude? Social psychologists have paid little attention to the process or processes by which attitude–behavior consistency might occur. Throughout the literature (as in the present report), mention is made of attitudes "guiding" or "influencing" behavior with little or no accompanying explanation as to how this might occur.

Given the lack of relevant research, we can only speculate about the manner in which attitudes guide behavior. One possibility is a very deliberate, conscious process in which the individual strives for self-consistency. In other words, the individual may attempt to live up to his or her conception and evaluation of the attitude object, if and when the attitude is activated upon encountering the attitude object. Such a process may be particularly likely to operate in contexts where individuals experience objective self-awareness or for particular kinds of people, such as those high in private self-consciousness (Wicklund, in press). Certainly, some forms of human action (e.g., voting behavior, a domain, as mentioned earlier, in which strong attitude–behavior relations are typically observed) are very much characterized by this type of deliberate decision process. Via such a process, attitudes based upon direct experience would be more likely to prompt correspondent behaviors than attitudes based upon indirect experience because they are more likely to be accessed upon observation of the attitude object. Furthermore, since attitudes based on direct experience are held with greater confidence and clarity, individuals who have formed their attitudes in this manner may feel a stronger desire to behave consistently with their attitudes than individuals who have formed relatively weak attitudes through indirect experience.

Another possible process by which attitudes might guide behavior is much less deliberate on the part of the person involved and assumes that the individual's behavior is determined by his or her immediate perceptions of the attitude object. If an attitude is activated upon encountering the attitude object, the attitude may bias the individual's immediate perceptions of the object through a process of selective perception. Much evidence exists to suggest that attitudes can affect perceptions. For example, Proshansky (1943) found that individuals' attitudes toward organized labor related to their descriptions of what they had "seen" in an ambiguous, but labor relevant picture. More recently, it has been observed that attitudes toward another person affect the causal interpretations that are offered for that person's behavior (e.g., Regan, Straus, & Fazio, 1974). Since attitudes based upon direct experience seem to be characterized by relative accessibility, such an attitude may be activated when the individual interacts with the attitude object and, hence, may influence the person's immediate perceptions of the object. These perceptions, filtered as they are through the attitude, then influence the individual's behavioral response, prompting attitude–behavior consistency. Since the relatively weak attitudes formed through indirect experience are not as likely to be evoked when the attitude object is encountered, the immediate perceptions of the object and the ultimate behavior may not be as strongly affected by the attitude in this case. Future research needs to assess the relation between the manner of attitude formation and selective perception in order to examine this possibility. Furthermore, the conditions under which each of these two processes might operate needs to be addressed empirically.

VI. The Attitude–Behavior Relationship

The findings from the present program of research suggest that, in attempting to predict behavior, it will be useful to ascertain the extent to which the given sample of individuals have formed their attitudes from direct behavioral experience with the attitude object. Attitudes formed in such a manner can account for a reasonable proportion of the behavioral variance, and they appear to do so for two reasons. First, the predictive capability of direct experience attitudes is enhanced to the extent that a strong prior-to-later behavior relation exists. By sharing a common dependence on prior behavior, the attitude can predict later behavior. Second, individuals appear to form, for a number of possible reasons, relatively stronger attitudes following direct, as opposed to indirect, experiences. These stronger attitudes are more likely to be evoked upon the individual's encountering the object and, hence, are more likely to influence later behavior toward the object.

In general, the research suggests a relatively optimistic view of the nature of the relationship between attitudes and behavior. At least sometimes, attitudes can serve as convenient predictors of behavior. This is not to say that there exists a one-to-one correspondence between direct experience attitudes and behavior, but it does imply that the attitude concept can be useful and need not be abandoned.

Let us return to the question we raised earlier as characteristic of recent approaches to the study of the attitude–behavior relationship: Under what conditions do what kinds of attitudes held by what kinds of individuals predict what kinds of behaviors? Considerable progress has been made in recent years in specifying the situational variables, attitudinal qualities, and personality factors which affect the strength of the attitude–behavior relation. With respect to situational factors, much research points to the importance of normative constraints (e.g., Warner & DeFleur, 1969; Ajzen & Fishbein, 1973). To the extent that powerful situational constraints of a counterattitudinal nature are impinging on an individual, his or her attitude cannot be expected to guide behavior. Norms which are congruent with an individual's attitude, on the other hand, tend to enhance the likelihood that the person will behave in an attitudinally consistent manner (Schofield, 1975).

Various personality factors also appear to be related to attitude–behavior

consistency. The extent to which an individual possesses the self-image of a
"doer" appears to be a determinant of attitude-behavior consistency (McArthur,
Kiesler, & Cook, 1972). Furthermore, low self-monitors (i.e., individuals who
report that their behavior is guided largely by relevant inner states rather than by
situational forces) who also report being situationally invariant with respect to a
given class of behaviors tend to display greater attitude-behavior consistency
than either high self-monitors or low self-monitors who report high variability
(Zanna *et al.*, 1980).

With regard to the question of "what kinds of attitudes," two approaches
are evident in the literature. One approach, which the majority of our own
research has followed, involves the examination of various qualities of the attitude which relate to attitude-behavior consistency. The manner of attitude
formation is of obvious relevance. In pursuing and investigating direct experience further, we have also found that how confidently the attitude is held (see
also Sample & Warland, 1973) and how well defined the attitude is (see also
Sherif *et al.*, 1973) are related to attitude-behavior consistency. The temporal
stability of an attitude also has been found to be relevant (Schwartz, 1978). In
addition, Norman (1975) has suggested that the degree of consistency between
affective and cognitive components of an attitude is related to the strength of the
attitude-behavior relationship. Although Fazio and Zanna (1978a) failed to replicate this finding and found some suggestive evidence that the effect of intra
attitudinal consistency may be limited to attitudes which are based on little or no
direct experience, affective-cognitive consistency may be yet another determinant of the attitude-behavior relationship. At a more cognitive level, the accessibility of an attitude from memory may also play a role in the degree to which an
individual behaves consistently with that attitude. Any attitudinal quality that has
the effect of increasing the likelihood that an attitude will be accessed on observation of the object may be a determinant of attitude-behavior consistency. Future
research should focus on what antecedent variables affect these various attitudinal qualities and, hence, make the attitude more likely to influence later behavior.

A second approach to the question of "what kinds of attitudes" actually
relates to the issue of "what kinds of behaviors." It is now well documented that
the observed attitude-behavior relation is enhanced by employing attitude and
behavior measures of equivalent levels of specificity (Ajzen & Fishbein, 1977).
Specific or single-act behaviors are best predicted by specific attitudes (Fishbein,
1966; Wicker & Pomazol, 1971; Weigel, Vernon, & Tognacci, 1974; Heberlein
& Black, 1976). It has been suggested that an attitude measure which is specific
to the single-act leads the individual to access from memory and consider the
same attitudinal information when the attitude measure and the behavioral opportunity are encountered (Borgida, Swann, & Campbell, 1977). This explanation
again implicates such cognitive factors as storage and retrieval mechanisms as
important determinants of the attitude-behavior relation.

General attitudes, on the other hand, have been found to be predictive of general behavior patterns across multiple acts (Fishbein & Ajzen, 1974; Weigel & Newman, 1976). Since a multiple-act behavior measure by definition involves a variety of relevant single actions and, hence, contains a greater number of observations than a single-act measure, multiple-act measures would tend to be relatively more reliable. This involves nothing more than the well-established measurement theory principle that increasing the number of items included in a measure tends to increase the measure's reliability (Magnusson, 1966; Nunnally, 1967). This increased reliability undoubtedly plays a role in the observation of enhanced attitude–behavior correlations when general attitudes and multiple behaviors are assessed. In addition, as Ajzen (in press) has argued, the improved predictability may derive from increased validity of the behavior measure. Any given single action may be unrepresentative of an individual's general behavior pattern toward an object. Since a multiple-act measure involves a large set of relevant behaviors varying across situations, the overall behavioral trend more closely parallels a global attitude measure than does any single action.

Especially when considered as a whole, the accumulating research suggests that the skepticism surrounding the predictive utility of attitudes may not be warranted. It is very clear that no general cross-situational one-to-one correspondence exists between attitudes and behavior. However, some kinds of attitudes for some kinds of people in some situations are predictive of some kinds of later behavior. In retrospect, as Schuman and Johnson (1976) have noted, it appears rather naive to have ever expected more.

Personality Traits and Behavior

Throughout this report, we have noted a parallel between the attitude–behavior issue and the personality-trait–behavior issue. Researchers in each area at first questioned the existence of a relation between the construct of interest and behavior. In both areas, progress has been made toward specifying factors which affect the relationship at issue (e.g., Bem & Allen, 1974; Bem & Funder, 1978). In both areas, the question of the predictive utility of the construct is now approached with considerably more optimism. More specific parallels also exist. In examining the attitude–behavior issue from an individual-difference perspective, Zanna et al. (1980b) relied heavily on work done in the personality domain. In examining attitude accessibility, Fazio and Chen (1979) employed a methodology similar to that used by Markus (1977) with respect to personality traits. In examining the predictive utility of traits, Epstein (1979) has demonstrated the importance of the distinction between single- versus multiple-act behaviors that has proved so useful in the attitude literature. Specifically, Epstein argued that, since traits are general, global constructs, they can be expected to predict only general behavioral tendencies, not single instances of behavior. He found that traits were reasonably valid predictors of behavior when the behavior measure involved a large number of observations of single instances of behavior.

What these numerous parallels suggest is that the two areas need not operate independently. Constructs found to be relevant to the trait issue may also be relevant to the attitude issue and vice versa. For example, it might be fruitful to examine the extent to which individuals ascribe traits to themselves on the basis of prior behavioral evidence. Trait self-ascriptions grounded in past behavior may be relatively more predictive of later behaviors than self-ascriptions based on nonbehavioral information. Some suggestive evidence to support this possibility is provided by Comer and Laird (1975), who examined the impact of naturally occurring self-inferences on subsequent behavior. From their agreement to perform an unpleasant task (eating a worm), subjects tended to make one of three inferences: (1) that eating a worm was not actually all that unpleasant, as indicated by a measure of attractiveness; (2) that they were brave individuals, as indicated by a self-rating change from a preexperimental measure; or (3) that they deserved to suffer, again a change score. After arriving at one of these conclusions, subjects were asked to choose between a task in which shocks were to be administered and a neutral task. A greater number of those subjects who modified their self-conceptions (i.e., subjects who made the second or third of the preceding inferences) chose the shock task than did subjects who changed their conception of the worm (i.e., the first inference). Thus, trait self-ascriptions (self-concept changes) based on prior behavior tended to guide a later, relevant decision.

Clearly, further research is necessary to examine whether the basis (behavioral versus nonbehavioral) on which people describe themselves as possessing a given trait determines the predictive utility of that trait. Nevertheless, this possibility is yet another example of the many interfaces between trait and attitude research. A vigorous exchange of hypotheses, constructs, and methodologies between personality and attitude researchers would appear to benefit progress in both domains. Hopefully, the two areas can progress jointly toward an understanding of how and when traits and attitudes can be useful in the prediction of behavior.

REFERENCES

Abelson, R. Are attitudes necessary? In B. T. King & E. McGinnies (Eds.), *Attitudes, conflict, and social change*. New York: Academic Press, 1972.

Abelson, R. P. *Scripts*. Invited address to the Midwestern Psychological Association, Chicago, 1978.

Ajzen, I. On behaving in accordance with one's attitude. In M. P. Zanna, E. T. Higgins, & C. P. Herman (Eds.), *Consistency in social behavior: The Ontario symposium* (Vol. 2). Hillsdale, N.J.: Erlbaum, in press.

Ajzen, I., & Fishbein, M. Attitudinal and normative variables as predictors of specific behaviors. *Journal of Personality and Social Psychology*, 1973, **27**, 41-57.

Ajzen, I., & Fishbein, M. Attitude-behavior relations: A theoretical analysis and review of empirical research. *Psychological Bulletin*, 1977, **84**, 888-918.

Allport, G. W. Attitudes. In C. Murchison (Ed.), *Handbook of social psychology*. Worcester, Massachusetts: Clark Univ. Press, 1935.

Beck, D., & Nebergall, R. E. *Relationship between attitude neutrality and involvement*. Paper presented to the annual meeting of the Speech Association of America, Los Angeles, 1967. (Data reported in Sherif, M., & Sherif, C. W. *Social psychology.* New York: Harper, 1969.)

Bem, D. J. Self-perception: An alternative interpretation of cognitive dissonance phenomena. *Psychological Review,* 1967, **74,** 183–200.

Bem, D. J. Self-perception theory. In L. Berkowitz, (Ed.), *Advances in experimental social psychology* (Vol. 6). New York: Academic Press, 1972.

Bem, D. J., & Allen, A. On predicting some of the people some of the time: The search for cross-situational consistencies in behavior. *Psychological Review,* 1974, **81,** 506–520.

Bem, D. J., & Funder, D. C. Predicting more of the people more of the time: Assessing the personality of situations. *Psychological Review,* 1978, **85,** 485–501.

Berscheid, E., Graziano, W., Monson, T., & Dermer, M. Outcome dependency: Attention, attribution, and attraction. *Journal of Personality and Social Psychology,* 1976, **34,** 978–989.

Borgida, E., Swann, W. B., & Campbell, B. *Attitudes and behavior: The specificity hypothesis revisited.* Paper presented at a symposium on "Recent Approaches to Attitude-Behavior Consistency" at the American Psychological Convention, San Francisco, 1977.

Brannon, R., Cyphers, G., Hesse, S., Hesselbart, S., Keane, R., Schuman, H., Vicarro, T., & Wright, D. Attitude and action: A field experiment joined to a general population survey. *American Sociological Review,* 1973, **38,** 625–636.

Calder, B. J., & Ross, M. *Attitudes and Behavior.* Morristown, New Jersey: General Learning Press, 1973.

Campbell, A., Converse, P. E., Miller, W. E., & Stokes, D. E. *The American voter.* New York: Wiley, 1960.

Campbell, D. T. The indirect assessment of social attitudes. *Psychological Bulletin,* 1950, **47,** 15–38.

Cantor, N., & Mischel, W. Traits as prototypes: Effects on recognition memory. *Journal of Personality and Social Psychology,* 1977, **35,** 38–48.

Carver, C. S. Physical aggression as a function of objective self-awareness and attitudes toward punishment. *Journal of Experimental Social Psychology,* 1975, **11,** 510–519.

Comer, R., & Laird, J. D. Choosing to suffer as a consequence of expecting to suffer: Why do people do it? *Journal of Personality and Social Psychology,* 1975, **32,** 92–101.

Cook, T. D., & Flay, B. R. The persistence of experimentally induced attitude change. In L. Berkowitz (Ed.), *Advances in experimental social psychology* (Vol. 11). New York: Academic Press, 1978.

Corey, S. M. Professed attitudes and actual behavior. *Journal of Educational Psychology,* 1937, **28,** 271–280.

Crespi, I. What kinds of attitude measures are predictive of behavior? *Public Opinion Quarterly,* 1971, **35,** 327–334.

DeFleur, M. L., & Westie, F. R. Verbal attitudes and overt act: An experiment on the salience of attitudes. *American Sociological Review,* 1958, **23,** 667–673.

Deutscher, I. *Why do they say one thing, do another?* Morristown, New Jersey: General Learning Press, 1973.

Doob, L. W. The behavior of attitudes. *Psychological Review,* 1947, **54,** 135–156.

Epstein, S. The stability of behavior: I. On predicting most of the people much of the time. *Journal of Personality and Social Psychology,* 1979, **37,** 1097–1126.

Fazio, R. H., & Chen, J. *Attitude accessibility as a function of direct experience.* Unpublished, Indiana University, 1979.

Fazio, R. H., & Zanna, M. P. *Attitude-behavior consistency as a function of the salience of past behavior.* Paper presented at Eastern Psychological Association Convention, New York, 1976.

Fazio, R. H., & Zanna, M. P. Attitudinal qualities relating to the strength of the attitude-behavior relationship. *Journal of Experimental Social Psychology,* 1978, **14,** 398–408. (a)

Fazio, R. H., & Zanna, M. P. On the predictive validity of attitudes: The roles of direct experience and confidence. *Journal of Personality,* 1978, **46,** 228–243. (b)

Fazio, R. H., Zanna, M. P., & Cooper, J. Dissonance and self-perception: An integrative view of each theory's proper domain of application. *Journal of Experimental Social Psychology,* 1977, **13,** 464–479.

Fazio, R. H., Zanna, M. P., & Cooper, J. Direct experience and attitude-behavior consistency: An information processing analysis. *Personality and Social Psychology Bulletin,* 1978, **4,** 48–52.

Festinger, L. A theory of social comparison processes. *Human Relations,* 1954, **7,** 117–140.

Festinger, L. *A theory of cognitive dissonance.* Stanford, California: Stanford Univ. Press, 1957.

Festinger, L. Behavioral support for opinion change. *Public Opinion Quarterly,* 1964, **28,** 404–417.

Festinger, L., & Carlsmith, J. M. Cognitive consequences of forced compliance. *Journal of Abnormal and Social Psychology,* 1959, **58,** 203–211.

Fishbein, M. An investigation of the relationships between beliefs about an object and attitude toward that object. *Human Relations,* 1963, **16,** 233–240.

Fishbein, M. The relationship between beliefs, attitudes, and behavior. In S. Feldman (Ed.), *Cognitive consistency.* New York: Academic Press, 1966.

Fishbein, M. Attitudes and the prediction of behavior. In M. Fishbein (Ed.), *Readings in attitude theory and measurement.* New York: Wiley, 1967.

Fishbein, M., & Ajzen, I. Attitudes toward objects as predictors of single and multiple behavioral criteria. *Psychological Review,* 1974, **81,** 59–74.

Fishbein, M., & Coombs, F. S. Basis for decision: An attitudinal analysis of voting behavior. *Journal of Applied Social Psychology,* 1974, **4,** 95–124.

Gibbons, F. X. Sexual standards and reactions to pornography: Enhancing behavioral consistency through self-focused attention. *Journal of Personality and Social Psychology,* 1978, **36,** 976–987.

Goodmonson, C., & Glaudin, V. The relationship of commitment-free behavior and commitment behavior: A study of attitude toward organ transplantation. *Journal of Social Issues,* 1971, **27,** 171–183.

Green, B. F. Attitude measurement. In G. Lindzey (Ed.), *Handbook of social psychology* (Vol. 1). Reading, Massachusetts: Addison-Wesley, 1954.

Harrison, A. A. Response competition, frequency, exploratory behavior, and liking. *Journal of Personality and Social Psychology,* 1971, **19,** 295–300.

Heberlein, T. A., & Black, J. S. Attitudinal specificity and the prediction of behavior in a field setting. *Journal of Personality and Social Psychology,* 1976, **33,** 474–479.

Higgins, E. T., Rholes, W. S., & Jones, C. R. Category accessibility and impression formation. *Journal of Experimental Social Psychology,* 1977, **13,** 141–154.

Jones, E. E., & Gerard, H. B. *Foundations of social psychology.* New York: Wiley, 1967.

Jones, E. E., & Nisbett, R. E. *The actor and the observer: Divergent perceptions of the causes of behavior.* Morristown, New Jersey: General Learning Press, 1971.

Juster, F. T. *Anticipations and purchases: An analysis of consumer behavior.* Princeton, New Jersey: Princeton Univ. Press, 1964.

Kelley, S., & Mirer, T. W. The simple act of voting. *American Political Science Review,* 1974, **68,** 572–591.

Kelman, H. C. Attitudes are alive and well and gainfully employed in the sphere of action. *American Psychologist,* 1974, **29,** 310–324.

Kiesler, C. A. *The psychology of commitment.* New York: Academic Press, 1971.

Kiesler, C. A., Nisbett, R. E., & Zanna, M. P. On inferring one's belief from one's behavior. *Journal of Personality and Social Psychology,* 1969, **11,** 321–327.

Kiesler, C. A., & Sakumura, J. A test of a model for commitment. *Journal of Personality and Social Psychology,* 1966, **3,** 349–353.

LaPiere, R. T. Attitudes vs. actions. *Social Forces,* 1934, **13,** 230–237.

McArthur, L. A., Kiesler, C. A., & Cook, B. P. Acting on an attitude as a function of self-percept and inequity. *Journal of Personality and Social Psychology,* 1969, **12,** 295–302.

Magnusson, D. *Test theory*. Reading, Massachusetts: Addison-Wesley, 1966.

Markus, H. Self-schemata and processing information about the self. *Journal of Personality and Social Psychology*, 1977, **35**, 63–78.

Matlin, M. W. Response competition, recognition, and affect. *Journal of Personality and Social Psychology*, 1971, **19**, 295–300.

Meichenbaum, D. H., Bowers, K. S., & Ross, R. R. A behavioral analysis of teacher expectancy effects. *Journal of Personality and Social Psychology*, 1969, **13**, 306–316.

Mischel, W. *Personality and assessment*. New York: Wiley, 1968.

Mischel, W. Toward a cognitive social learning reconceptualization of personality. *Psychological Review*, 1973, **80**, 252–283.

Norman, R. Affective–cognitive consistency, attitudes, conformity, and behavior. *Journal of Personality and Social Psychology*, 1975, **32**, 83–91.

Nunnally, J. C. *Psychometric theory*. New York: McGraw-Hill, 1967.

Proshansky, H. M. A projective method for the study of attitudes. *Journal of Abnormal and Social Psychology*, 1943, **38**, 393–395.

Pryor, J. B., Gibbons, F. X., Wicklund, R. A., Fazio, R. H., & Hood, R. Self-focused attention and self-report validity. *Journal of Personality*, 1977, **45**, 514–527.

Regan, D. T., & Fazio, R. H. On the consistency between attitudes and behavior: Look to the method of attitude formation. *Journal of Experimental Social Psychology*, 1977, **13**, 38–45.

Regan, D. T., & Totten, J. Empathy and attribution: Turning observers into actors. *Journal of Personality and Social Psychology*, 1975, **32**, 850–856.

Regan, D. T., Straus, E., & Fazio, R. H. Liking and the attribution process. *Journal of Experimental Social Psychology*, 1974, **10**, 385–397.

Ryan, M. J., & Bonfield, E. H. The Fishbein extended model and consumer behavior. *Journal of Consumer Research*, 1975, **2**, 118–136.

Sample, J., & Warland, R. Attitude and prediction of behavior. *Social Forces*, 1973, **51**, 292–304.

Scheier, M. F., Buss, A. H., & Buss, D. M. Self-consciousness, self-report of aggressiveness, and aggression. *Journal of Research in Personality*, 1978, **12**, 133–140.

Schofield, J. W. Effect of norms, public disclosure, and need for approval on volunteering behavior consistent with attitudes. *Journal of Personality and Social Psychology*, 1975, **31**, 1126–1133.

Schuman, H., & Johnson, M. P. Attitudes and behavior. *Annual Review of Sociology*, 1976, **2**, 161–207.

Schwartz, S. H. Temporal instability as a moderator of the attitude-behavior relationship. *Journal of Personality and Social Psychology*, 1978, **36**, 715–724.

Seligman, C., Kriss, M., Darley, J. M., Fazio, R. H., Becker, L. J., & Pryor, J. B. Predicting summer energy consumption from homeowners' attitudes. *Journal of Applied Social Psychology*, 1979, **9**, 70–90.

Sherif, C. W., Sherif, M., & Nebergall, R. E. *Attitude and attitude change: The social judgment-involvement approach*. Philadelphia: Saunders, 1965.

Sherif, C. W., Kelly, M., Rodgers, H. L., Sarup, G., & Tittler, B. I. Personal involvement, social judgment, and action. *Journal of Personality and Social Psychology*, 1973, **27**, 311–328.

Sherif, M., & Hovland, C. I. *Social judgment: Assimilation and contrast effects in communication and attitude change*. New Haven, Connecticut: Yale University Press, 1961.

Snyder, M. The self-monitoring of expressive behavior. *Journal of Personality and Social Psychology*, 1974, **30**, 526–537.

Snyder, M. Attitude and behavior: Social perception and social causation. In J. H. Harvey, W. J. Ickes, & R. F. Kidd (Eds.), *New direction in attribution research* (Vol. 1). Hillsdale, New Jersey: Erlbaum, 1976.

Snyder, M. Self-monitoring processes. In L. Berkowitz (Ed.), *Advances in experimental social psychology* (Vol. 12). New York: Academic Press, 1979.

Snyder, M., & Monson, T. C. Persons, situations, and the control of social behavior. *Journal of Personality and Social Psychology*, 1975, **32**, 637–644.

Snyder, M., & Swann, W. B. When actions reflect attitudes: The politics of impression management. *Journal of Personality and Social Psychology,* 1976, **34**, 1034–1042.

Snyder, M., & Swann, W. B. Behavioral confirmation in social interaction: From social perception to social reality. *Journal of Experimental Social Psychology,* 1978, **14**, 148–162.

Snyder, M., & Tanke, E. D. Behavior and attitude: Some people are more consistent than others. *Journal of Personality,* 1976, **44**, 501–517.

Songer-Nocks, E. Situational factors affecting the weighting of predictor components in the Fishbein model. *Journal of Experimental Social Psychology,* 1976, **12**, 56–59.

Stouffer, S. A., Lumsdaine, A. A., Lumsdaine, M. H., Williams, R. M., Smith, M. B., Janis, I. L., Star, S. A., & Cottrell, L. S. *The American soldier* (Vol. II), *Combat and its aftermath.* Princeton, New Jersey: Princeton Univ. Press, 1949.

Tesser, A. Self-generated attitude change. In L. Berkowitz (Ed.), *Advances in experimental social psychology* (Vol. 11). New York: Academic Press, 1978.

Thurstone, L. L. Comment. *American Journal of Sociology,* 1946, **52**, 39–40.

Warner, L. G., & DeFleur, M. L. Attitude as an interactional concept: Social constraint and social distance as intervening variables between attitudes and action. *American Sociological Review,* 1969, **34**, 153–169.

Watts, W. A. Relative persistence of opinion change induced by active compared to passive participation. *Journal of Personality and Social Psychology,* 1967, **5**, 4–15.

Weigel, R. H., & Newman, L. S. Increasing attitude-behavior correspondence by broadening the scope of the behavioral measure. *Journal of Personality and Social Psychology,* 1976, **33**, 793–802.

Weigel, R. H., Vernon, D. T. A., & Tognacci, L. N. The specificity of the attitude as a determinant of attitude-behavior congruence. *Journal of Personality and Social Psychology,* 1974, **30**, 724–728.

Wicker, A. W. Attitudes versus actions: The relationship of verbal and overt behavioral responses to attitude objects. *Journal of Social Issues,* 1969, **25**, 41–78.

Wicker, A. W. An examination of the ''other variables'' explanation of attitude-behavior inconsistency. *Journal of Personality and Social Psychology,* 1971, **19**, 18–30.

Wicker, A. W., & Pomazal, R. J. The relationship between attitudes and behavior as a function of specificity of attitude object and presence of significant others during assessment conditions. *Representative Research in Social Psychology,* 1971, **2**, 26–31.

Wicklund, R. A. Objective self-awareness. In L. Berkowitz (Ed.), *Advances in experimental social psychology* (Vol. 8). New York: Academic Press, 1975.

Wicklund, R. A. Self-focused attention and the validity of self-reports. In M. P. Zanna, C. P. Herman, & E. T. Higgins (Eds.), *Consistency in social behavior: The Ontario symposium.* Hillsdale, New Jersey: Erlbaum, in press.

Wixon, D. R., & Laird, J. D. Awareness and attitude change in the forced-compliance paradigm: The importance of when. *Journal of Personality and Social Psychology,* 1976, **34**, 376–384.

Word, C. O., Zanna, M. P., & Cooper, J. The nonverbal meditation of self-fulfilling prophecies in interracial interaction. *Journal of Experimental Social Psychology,* 1974, **10**, 109–120.

Zajonc, R. B. The attitudinal effects of mere exposure. *Journal of Personality and Social Psychology Monograph Supplement,* 1968, **9** (2), 1–27.

Zanna, M. P., & Fazio, R. H. *Direct experience and attitude-behavior consistency.* Paper presented at a symposium on ''Recent Approaches to Attitude-Behavior Consistency'' at the American Psychological Association Convention, San Francisco, 1977.

Zanna, M. P., Olson, J. M., & Fazio, R. H. Attitude-behavior consistency: An individual difference perspective. *Journal of Personality and Social Psychology,* 1980, **38**, 432–440.

Zanna, M. P., Olson, J. M., & Fazio, R. H. Self-perception and attitude-behavior consistency. *Personality and Social Psychology Bulletin,* 1981, **7**, 252–256.

PREDICTABILITY AND HUMAN STRESS: TOWARD A CLARIFICATION OF EVIDENCE AND THEORY

Suzanne M. Miller

DEPARTMENT OF PSYCHOLOGY
TEMPLE UNIVERSITY
PHILADELPHIA, PENNSYLVANIA

ADVANCES IN EXPERIMENTAL SOCIAL
PSYCHOLOGY, VOL. 14

I. Introduction

Individuals are continually faced with aversive events as they go through life, such as the prospect of undergoing a surgical operation, contracting cancer, losing a job, or being rejected by a loved one. These events can either be predictable or unpredictable. That is, sometimes one can know beforehand when and under what circumstances an event will occur, and what it will be like (predictability), and sometimes one has no information about the event (unpredictability). How "stressful" is such an event when it is predictable as opposed to unpredictable?

The literature on predictability and human stress is as confused as it is voluminous, with a morass of studies yielding conflicting results and with diverse theories offering only partially satisfactory explanations at best. There appear to be three basic reasons for this confusion: (a) Different experimenters use different conceptions of predictability; (b) different levels of analysis have been used to measure "stress" reactions; and (c) despite a proliferation of theories, no one theory satisfactorily explains most of the data. This article attempts to move toward a clarification of the issues and a coherent integration of the total results.

As a first step it will be necessary to specify the notion of *predictability*. Two nonoverlapping classes of predictability will be defined: knowing the conditions under which the event will occur (contingency predictability) and knowing what the event will be like (what-kind-of-event predictability). Second, the major concepts and measures of stress will be reviewed briefly, and then the five major existing theories of predictability and human stress will be presented. These theories generally share the view that predictable aversive events are less stressful than unpredictable aversive events. Although this is often true, there is considerable evidence showing that predictability can sometimes increase, as well as decrease, stress and arousal. To specify the conditions under which predictability has stress-reducing effects and when it does not, I consider four new hypotheses which attempt to organize the sweep of data.

Next, the available evidence is reviewed and its fit to the theories and hypotheses is examined. Methodological and conceptual inadequacies in existing studies are outlined, revealing empirical gaps in the literature. Finally, I suggest priorities and directions for future research efforts and offer some degree of integration between the existing theoretical explanations.

II. Definitions of Predictability

A. CONTINGENCY PREDICTABILITY

Contingency predictability exists when the individual knows *when and under what circumstances an event will occur*. More rigorously, an event is predictable when its probability of occurrence is greater under one given set of conditions than under other conditions. For example, if an event only occurs when a tone is on and never occurs when the tone is off, then it is predictable. When the event is equally likely to occur under all conditions (i.e., during tone on and tone off), then the presence of the tone provides the individual with no more information about the event's occurrence than does the absence of the tone (see Rescorla, 1967; Seligman, Maier, & Solomon, 1971). Hence the event is unpredictable.

A real-life example of an aversive event should help to make these differences more concrete. Consider two individuals, both of whom must undergo an aversive dental procedure. Individual A always receives a warning tap on the shoulder just before the dentist is about to begin drilling. The dentist never taps the person at any other time. Individual B, on the other hand, receives no taps from the dentist. Instead, the drill goes on and off without any warning. So the first individual knows when to expect the drill (contingency predictability), whereas the second individual does not (unpredictability).

There are three main procedures for operationalizing contingency predictability in the laboratory:

1. By far the simplest and most common procedure involves the presentation of a stimulus (usually a tone) to signal the occurrence of an aversive event (usually electric shock). In the predictability group, the event never occurs in the absence of the signal (i.e., during tone off). In the unpredictability group, the shock occurs randomly with respect to the tone (e.g., Averill & Rosenn, 1972; Geer & Maisel, 1972).

2. One inconvenience of this paradigm is that reactivity to the event may be dampened not because "stress" is really reduced but merely because physiological response systems do not have time to recover when an event immediately follows a signal (Grings, 1960). One way of circumventing this problem is by comparing temporally random delivery of the event with nonrandom delivery of the event (e.g., Furedy & Chan, 1971; Glass, Singer, & Friedman, 1969; Lovibond, 1968). In the nonrandom (predictability) condition, the passage of a given period of time serves as the signal, so that the event is more likely during some specified slots of time than during others. Merely substitute the specified time slot for the signal and the logic detailed above remains the same. With random delivery, the event is unpredictable because it is equally likely in all time slots.

3. The random–nonrandom paradigm, although it avoids an explicit signal, poses a further procedural problem. Unless the interval between presentations of the event is relatively short, subjects cannot keep track of the time well enough to know exactly when to expect the next event. Therefore, the occurrence of the event becomes subjectively random. An alternative method is to use a "countdown" procedure (e.g., Bowers, 1971a,b). The predictability subject is

told that the event will occur at the count of zero, whereas the unpredictability subject is told that the event can occur at any number in the countdown. Alternatively, subjects can be provided with a clock; in the predictability condition, the event is delivered at a specified time, whereas, in the unpredictability condition, the event can occur at any time (e.g., Monat, Averill, & Lazarus, 1972). In some procedures, all subjects are given information about when the event will occur (e.g., "in six minutes"), but only the predictability group is given a clock to accurately track the passage of time (e.g., Gaebelein, Taylor, & Borden, 1974; Mansueto & Desiderato, 1971).

B.   WHAT-KIND-OF-EVENT PREDICTABILITY

What-kind-of-event predictability refers to *what the event will be like and what effects it will have*. This category is intuitively straightforward and requires little elaboration. It has been investigated in both laboratory and field (i.e., hospital) settings. Generally, laboratory research has concentrated on giving predictability subjects *stimulus information,* that is, information about the physical characteristics of a prospective event (e.g., its quality, intensity, and properties). So, for example, the predictability group is told to expect high shock versus low shock or punishment versus reward (Elliott, 1966; Jones, Bentler, & Petry, 1966; Lanzetta & Driscoll, 1966). The unpredictability group is given a much lower level of what-kind-of-event predictability, although it is not held at zero. Here the subject is told to expect shock but does not know its intensity, or is told to expect punishment or reward but does not know which.

In addition to stimulus information, an individual can have *response information*. That is, one can know something about the effects which the aversive event is likely to have. For example, the predictability subject is informed that shock will have a tingling or burning sensation, whereas the unpredictability subject is uninformed about what shock will feel like (e.g., Staub & Kellett, 1972). A subset of response information is *arousal information,* where only the predictability subject receives information about the emotional effects of the event (e.g., "You will have a rapid heart rate, sweaty palms, etc.").

Most studies, particularly the field-oriented ones, have tended to confound stimulus and response information together, comparing a predictability group that has both types with an unpredictability group that has neither type. This is unfortunate, since some of the most promising hypotheses make differential predictions for these two types of information.

C.   INTERACTIONS OF THE TWO CLASSES OF PREDICTABILITY

What-kind-of-event predictability is, in principle, independent of contingency predictability. That is, whenever contingency predictability is increased or decreased, what-kind-of-event predictability remains unchanged. For example, an individual who knows when to expect the dentist's drill (contingency predictability) has no more information about what it will be like than an individual who does not know when to expect it (contingency unpredictability).

Similarly, variations in what-kind-of-event predictability do not affect contingency predictability. Consider two subjects who are threatened with electric shock and who do not know when to expect the event (contingency unpredictability). If one subject is then told what the intensity of shock will be and what it will feel like, he has more what-kind-of-event predictability than the other subject. However, this information has not provided a signal for the occurrence of shock, so the event is still unpredictable in the contingency sense.

In practice, however, what-kind-of-event predictability is often operationalized in a way that alters contingency predictability. This is particularly the case for hospital field studies. For example, by supplying detailed information about a forthcoming surgical procedure, contingency predictability is often increased by specifying the conditions under which the aversive event will occur (e.g., "If your diagnostic tests show that . . . , then we will have to operate; if your diagnostic tests do not show that . . . , then we will not have to operate"). The most viable hypotheses do not always predict identical effects for the two classes of predictability. Therefore, care should be taken to eliminate this possible source of confounding in any studies of theoretical interest.

D. CONTROLLABILITY

Not only have the two classes of predictability been confused in the literature, but predictability has often been collapsed with controllability. A response *controls* an event if, and only if, the probability of the event given the response differs from the probability of the event in the absence of the response (Seligman, 1975). The event is *uncontrollable* if the probability of the event given a particular response is the same as the probability of the event in the absence of that response, and this is so for all responses. Thus, if the aversive event is controllable, the individual can make an instrumental response which somehow modifies it. To say that it is predictable implies only that the individual can *know* something about the event, whether or not the person can *do* anything to change it. Evidently, controllable events are predictable (when control is exercised), since the controlling response predicts the occurrence and/or nature of the event: if you can escape a shock by pressing a button, by controlling it one can know exactly when it is going to stop. However, a predictable event may or may not be controllable. For example, shock duration can be made *predictable* by providing the noncontrolling subject with an external signal (such as a tone) that tells when shock will stop. By itself, such information (predictability) does not enable the individual to shorten the duration of shock (controllability).

Recent reviews of the controllability literature (Averill, 1973; Bandura, 1977; Gal & Lazarus, 1975; Miller, 1979a, 1980a) generally agree that individuals prefer and experience less stress when they can instrumentally control an aversive event (e.g., Bowers, 1968; Elliott, 1969; Gatchel, McKinney, & Koebernick, 1977; Gatchel & Proctor, 1976; Houston, 1972; Sandman, 1975; Szpiler & Epstein, 1976). Traditional theories explain this result in terms of the extra predictability that control provides. That is, control is alleged to be stress reducing only because it provides an individual with increased predictability. However, control still reduces stress, even in contrast with groups without control which are provided with external signals that give them equal predictability. In addition, control is less stressful even when the controlling individual does not actually execute the instrumental response (''potential'' control), and so has no opportunity to obtain increased predictability (Corah & Boffa, 1970; Glass, Reim, & Singer, 1971; Glass et al., 1969; Miller, 1979e). Therefore, the beneficial effects of controllability do not derive simply from the increase in predictability.

A more viable theoretical account is that control reduces stress because the controlling individual expects a less aversive outcome than the noncontrolling individual. This can be for one of two reasons. First, individuals with control have a guaranteed upper limit on how bad an aversive situation can become, since they attribute the cause of relief to an internal, stable factor (their own response). For example, when individuals can escape shock, they know that it will not last longer than their reaction time required to turn it off. Therefore, they expect a short duration shock. In contrast, individuals without control have no guarantee that shock will end quickly, since they attribute the cause of relief to an external, more unstable factor (e.g., the experimenter). Therefore, they expect a (potentially) longer duration shock.

Alternatively, control may enable an individual to present aversive stimuli to himself to suit fluctuations in internal mood and sensitivity (e.g., ''Right now, I feel particularly vulnerable, so I will turn the shock off quickly''). Therefore, the person never receives a subjectively intolerable shock of long duration. In contrast, when shock is uncontrollable, it comes and goes without regard to fluctuations in the individual's internal state. Thus, the shock feels worse since the individual is bound to receive, at some point, a subjectively intolerable shock of long duration. (See Miller, 1979a, 1980a, for a thorough review.)

It is thus virtually impossible that controllability reduces to predictability. However, it is still possible that predictability reduces to controllability. That is, having information about an aversive event may decrease stress only when such information makes the aversive event more controllable. As will be seen, however, those theories which attempt to account for predictability effects in terms of control do not fit well with the existing data. Therefore, the stress effects of predictability appear to be clearly distinguishable from the stress effects of controllability. As this is a paper about predictability, not controllability, all of the studies reviewed here vary predictability while holding controllability constant (usually by making the event uncontrollable).

III.   Measurement of Stress

Stress is a hypothetical construct which can be measured at several different levels of analysis. In the predictability literature, stress has been operationalized in the following three main ways:

1. *Preference.* Do individuals prefer to experience a predictable or an unpredictable aversive event?
2. *Anticipatory arousal.* Are individuals more aroused and anxious while waiting for a predictable or an unpredictable aversive event?
3. *Impact arousal.* Does a predictable aversive event hurt less than an equivalent, but unpredictable, aversive event?

Preference can be accessed subjectively, by exposing individuals to predictability and unpredictability and asking them to state their preference, or behaviorally, by actually allowing individuals to choose for themselves whether the event will be predictable or unpredictable. Anticipatory and impact arousal can be accessed physiologically (via electrodermal and cardiovascular measures), subjectively (via self-reports of anxiety and pain), and behaviorally (via performance on proofreading tasks, etc.).

The preference–anticipatory–impact distinctions are important, because the various theories often do not make identical predictions for the three measures of stress. Moreover, the experimental evidence shows that these stress measures are not uniformly affected by predictability manipulations. Indeed, research in a variety of other contexts indicates that it is the exception rather than the rule for the stress measures to covary together (cf. Lang, 1970; Rachman, 1974). Therefore, the measures cannot be collapsed together, nor can any *one* measure can be viewed as representing the stress response. Rather, the convergence of evidence from all three measures provides an integrated index of overall level of stress.

IV.   Traditional Theories of Predictability and Stress

There are five traditional classes of theories which bear on predictability and stress: information seeking, preparatory response, preparatory set, uncontrollability, and safety signal. Although the list is not exhaustive, and other theoretical accounts exist which could be extended to the issue of predictability and human stress, these five primary theories have generated the bulk of experimentation in the field and are most closely tied to the data. For the sake of simplicity, the theories have been purified by boiling them down to their essential propositions. Several of the theories have never been formulated in an explicit fashion that would allow for clear-cut differential predictions. Moreover, some of the theories have added extra premises and major qualifications as inconvenient evidence has accumulated. Purifying them will allow for cleaner prediction, disconfirmation, and comparison and will emphasize the distinctive premises of each theory. On the other hand, no given theorist can be burdened with the responsibility for the simplified versions.

A. INFORMATION SEEKING

People and animals seek information. When faced with uncertainty, they strive for certainty (Berlyne, 1960). Uncertainty (or that subclass of uncertainty defined here as unpredictability) causes conflict and therefore increases arousal. Certainty (predictability) resolves conflict and reduces arousal. Alternatively, predictability allows the growth of a neuronal model which facilitates habituation, whereas unpredictability retards habituation (Sokolov, 1963).

Here is a more detailed account. When a sequence of aversive events is predictable, the properties of the sequence are stored in a neuronal model. A neuronal model is a hypothetical organization of neurons which stores information about the parameters of an event. The development of such a model reduces the level of activation in the reticular activating system. This, in turn, reduces the aversiveness of the total situation and habituation can proceed more rapidly. In contrast, when the event is unpredictable, the development of a neuronal model is retarded and arousal is maintained in the reticular activating system. This augments the aversiveness of the total situation and habituation proceeds more slowly.

Consider an individual at the dentist's office. When the dentist explains what is going to happen ("I will be drilling rather than filing and it will sting") and/or explains the conditions under which it will occur ("I will tap you just beforehand"), the individual develops a neuronal model of the situation, which reduces conflict. This individual will habituate more rapidly and be less aroused and surprised than an individual who is not provided with such information.

These theories imply (1) choice of a predictable over an unpredictable aversive event because the individual seeks to avoid uncertainty, (2) higher anticipatory arousal with an unpredictable event because the uncertain individual is in more conflict, and (3) greater impact with an unpredictable aversive event because the event is more surprising.

B. PREPARATORY RESPONSE

This theory focuses on contingency predictability. When an aversive event is predictable, individuals are capable of making a well-timed response which lessens the impact of the event. When the event occurs without warning (unpredictability) a well-timed preparatory response cannot be made (Perkins, 1955, 1968). Thus, in the dental example, an individual who knows when to expect the drill (contingency predictability) can, at the appropriate moment, somehow tense his muscles or set his jaw in a way that makes the drilling hurt less. This view can also be extended to what-kind-of-event predictability. An individual who knows what to expect (e.g., drilling vs. filing or stinging vs. burning) can select the most appropriate response for reducing the impact of the drill.

The theory implies (1) choice of a predictable over an unpredictable aversive event since predictable events are lessened in their intensity and (2) greater impact with an unpredictable event since the event is actually more intense. The theory is equivocal about anticipatory stress. Unpredictability may be expected to result in more anticipatory stress, since the individual is waiting for a more aversive event. On the other hand, engaging in the preparatory response during predictability might in itself increase other indices of anticipatory arousal. This can be for one of two reasons. First, feedback from and perception of muscular tension may, in turn, increase subjective feelings of anxiety (and perhaps, as a further consequence, increase autonomic arousal). Second, increased muscular effort and expenditure may, in and of itself, be reflected in increased autonomic activity (particularly in the cardiovascular system) (Obrist, Webb, & Sutterer, 1969; Obrist, Webb, Sutterer, & Howard, 1970a,b).

C. PREPARATORY SET

When individuals learn that an aversive event is predictable, they adopt a preparatory set which produces large anticipatory arousal in the form of higher skin conductance or increased heart rate. These responses (CRs), in turn, decrease or dampen the impact of the event itself (URs) (Grings, 1960, 1969). For instance, an individual who has contingency predictability learns to form a preparatory set whenever the dentist says "I'm going to start drilling." This set increases anticipatory autonomic arousal, which then inhibits impact arousal once the drilling occurs.

There is a second premise of preparatory set theory which is relevant to what-kind-of-event predictability. As stated, individuals form a preparatory set when they know the conditions under which an aversive event will occur. This set only reduces impact arousal to the extent that (1) the individual knows *what* to expect and (2) these expectations are *confirmed*. So, if the individual expects a moderately painful drill and receives same, then his anticipatory responses swamp and reduce his impact responses. If, on the other hand, drilling turns out to be intensely painful, then impact reduction does not occur.

Unlike the preparatory response view, this theory explicitly implies (1) higher anticipatory arousal with a predictable event since this arousal is the mechanism by which the aversive event is to be reduced and (2) greater impact with an unpredictable event. The theory is somewhat flexible about choice. If the added arousal to the signal outweighs the lessened impact of the event, unpredictability should be chosen. Conversely, if the lessened impact of the event outweighs the added arousal to the signal, predictability should be chosen. This latter possibility seems most reasonable since the strategy is alleged to be adaptive, that is, the net result of a higher anticipatory response and a lower impact response should be less total arousal.

D. UNCONTROLLABILITY

This theory is similar to preparatory response theory but primarily addresses what-kind-of-event predictability. Unpredictability undermines direct coping with the aversive event because the source of the event cannot be identified. Inability to cope with an event (uncontrollability) increases anticipatory anxiety (Lazarus, 1966) and maintains a state of undirected arousal and unresolved fear (Epstein, 1972). For example, suppose that individuals respond to drilling by setting their jaws and to tooth extraction by pursing their lips. Individuals who know that the dentist will be drilling (what-kind-of-event predictability) then know how to respond—by setting their jaws. This directs arousal, resolves fear, and reduces stress. It should also make the drilling hurt less. If, on the other hand, individuals do not know whether the dentist will be drilling or extracting teeth (unpredictability), they do not know which response to select and arousal remains high.

Extended to contingency predictability, an individual who expects the drill but does not know when to expect it maintains arousal because coping tendencies that have been activated cannot be expressed. Moreover, since the individual does not know when to execute the response, the impact of the event actually is worse. The theory implies (1) choice of a predictable aversive event in order to choose an appropriate coping response and so direct arousal, (2) greater anticipatory arousal with an unpredictable event because the individual perceives less control, and (3) greater impact with an unpredictable event since an appropriate coping strategy cannot be selected.

E. SAFETY SIGNAL

When a danger signal reliably predicts an aversive event, the absence of the signal reliably predicts safety or the absence of the event. Therefore, the individual can relax when the signal is not on (i.e., during safety periods). In contrast, when the event is unpredictable, no signal predicts danger and so no signal predicts safety. Therefore, the individual remains in constant fear and can never relax (Seligman, 1968; Weiss, 1970). To illustrate, if the dentist always gives a warning before turning on the drill (contingency predictability), then the patient knows that the drill will never come on in the absence of such a warning and can relax as long as the dentist is quiet. Conversely, if the dentist provides no warning (unpredictability), then the patient can never relax because the drilling could begin at any moment.

In the case of what-kind-of-event predictability, predictability will be stress reducing because the individual is informed that the aversive event will be less intense than the maximum possible. When individuals know that the dentist will be drilling, they also know that the dentist will not be doing root canal work or extracting teeth. This person relaxes more than someone who does not know what to expect and so has no safety signals that the person will not be subjected to even more intense pain and discomfort. So, predictability provides an individual with relative safety, which in turn reduces the level of anticipatory arousal.

This theory (1) implies choice of a predictable over an unpredictable aversive event because predictable aversive events provide more safety and (2) makes two predictions about anticipatory arousal. Greater arousal should occur with predictability during the danger signal than during an equivalent period of unpredictability, since the probability of the event at any moment is higher during the danger signal. If anticipatory arousal is measured during a period that includes both danger signals and substantial periods of safety signal, however, net arousal should be lower in predictability. This is because the individual with predictability has more safety signals than the individual without predictability. The theory is silent about impact. That is, it makes no prediction about whether or not a predictable aversive event should actually hurt less than an unpredictable aversive event.

F. SUMMARY

Overall, the traditional theories emphasize the stress-reducing role of predictability. Individuals prefer predictability over unpredictability (information seeking, preparatory response, uncontrollability, safety signal) and show less anticipatory arousal with predictability (information seeking, uncontrollability, safety signal) and show less impact arousal with predictability (information seeking, preparatory response, preparatory set, uncontrollability). Two major themes emerge which account for these stress-reducing effects. The first theme is common to the preparatory response, preparatory set, and uncontrollability views. Predictability reduces stress because it enables the individual to make some overt response which actually reduces or alters the impact of the event. Such a response can take the form of a preparatory musculature adjustment (such as tensing or freezing), a preparatory set (such as large anticipatory electrodermal or heart rate responses), or a more general coping response (such as executing avoidance or escape responses).

The second, and more psychologically interesting, theme is implicit in the information-seeking and safety signal views. These theories are concerned with the situation where the individual does not or cannot make an overt response to reduce the aversive event. Predictability is still held to be stress reducing, because an individual who knows what to expect attends less to danger than an individual who does not know what to expect.

From the information-seeking perspective, an individual shows high anticipatory and impact arousal to an aversive event if he remains in a state of sustained conflict and surprise. Conflict and surprise are reduced when an individual is able to form a neuronal model or schema which accurately represents the aversive situation. This facilitates habituation, which is the process by which events gradually lose their power to stimulate attentional and orienting responses. Predictability allows an individual to develop a neuronal model of the situation such that he or she attends less and less to the aversive event over time (i.e., habituates). This reduces conflict and surprise and, correspondingly, anticipatory and impact arousal.

In contrast, unpredictability does not allow the growth of a neuronal model, so the individual continues to attend and orient to the event (i.e., does not habituate). The individual is conflicted and surprised by it, and this maintains anticipatory and impact arousal.

Safety signal does not rely on the process of habituation and decreased attention to the aversive event to explain the arousal-reducing effects of predictability. Rather, it postulates that predictability pulls an individual's attention toward external safety signals. Anticipatory arousal is held to be proportional to the perceived momentary probability of the aversive event. When an individual has a signal that predicts the onset of danger, the absence of the signal predicts the absence of danger or the onset of safety. So the individual spends a considerable amount of time attending to safety signals (i.e., during tone off), where the perceived momentary probability of the event is low, and only part of the time attending to danger signals (i.e., during tone on), where the perceived momentary probability of the event is high. This reduces anticipatory arousal and promotes relaxation. Conversely, the individual without a warning signal (unpredictability) has no safety signal that reduces the perceived momentary probability of the aversive event. He or she is in perpetual danger and is constantly vigilant for the aversive event. This maintains heightened arousal.

Unfortunately, the relation between predictability and human stress is more complex than the traditional theories imply. While it is true that predictability sometimes decreases stress, it can also have the reverse effect (Bandura, 1979, 1981). Any satisfactory theoretical account must therefore spell out the conditions under which predictability is stress enhancing as well as the conditions under which it is stress reducing. The next class of theory seeks to accomplish this. It is basically an extension of the attention deployment theme and broadens this framework by emphasizing the way in which individuals cognitively process information about aversive events to reduce concomitant stress reactions.

V. Information-Processing Hypotheses of Predictability and Stress

Recent advances in cognitive and personality psychology have emphasized that in any given situation there is a large pool of information available to and impinging on the individual. In seeking to reduce and simplify this load, the individual processes information in a way that both organizes and categorizes it (Mischel, 1979). Extended to aversive situations, how an individual goes about the process of encoding, evaluating, and attending to information should determine the level of stress and anxiety experienced. When information is encoded in a way that attenuates or blunts the psychological impact of aversive events, concomitant stress is lowered. When information is encoded in a way that psychologically augments external threat or focuses the individual's thoughts on it, concomitant stress remains high. Predictability should only be stress reducing to the extent that it enables the individual to attenuate or turn down the psychological impact of threat. In contrast, it should be stress inducing whenever it sensitizes or turns up the psychological impact of threat.

There are four undeveloped but potentially useful versions of the encoding approach. These theories spell out the conditions under which predictability facilitates the use of stress-reducing cognitive strategies, and when it does not.

A. THE BLUNTING HYPOTHESIS

There are two main modes for coping with aversive events. The first mode, *monitoring,* is to be alert for and sensitized to threat-relevant information. A second mode, *blunting,* is to cognitively avoid or transform threat-relevant information; it is called blunting because it helps individuals to blunt the psychological impact of objective sources of danger. The main premises of the blunting hypothesis attempt to specify when each coping mode is engaged and when each is stress reducing.

Consider first the case of contingency predictability. Arousal remains high in aversive situations to the extent that an individual is tuned into and monitors the negative aspects of the event. When an aversive event is controllable, monitoring is the main coping modality. Although it heightens arousal, this tactic enables the individual to execute controlling actions. When an aversive event is uncontrollable, however, monitoring (which heightens arousal) has no instrumental value. Therefore, blunting becomes the main coping mode on these occasions since an individual without controlling actions can most effectively ''tune out'' and reduce stress by engaging in distraction and similar psychological techniques. Here, contingency predictability will not be preferred and is

arousal inducing since it forces the individual back into the psychological presence of danger. To illustrate, consider a dental patient whose dentist warns him
or her every time the drill goes on (predictability). The individual will be listening for the dentist's warning; and the dentist's voice itself is invasive and intrusive, even if the individual is trying to block it out. In contrast, if a patient
receives no warning (unpredictability), threat-relevant information is more di-
luted and less psychologically invasive and intrusive. This makes it easier for the
individual to be distracted.

Two main considerations may make it difficult or inappropriate for the
individuals to distract themselves. The first is situational; that is, threat conditions may be too intense to allow distraction. The second is individual variability
in the ability and inclination to distract oneself; that is, some people may find it
undesirable or difficult to distract themselves, even when situational factors
support distraction. Under these two circumstances, which are discussed in detail
below, predictability will be preferred and stress reducing. This can be for safety
signal reasons (i.e., predictability provides the individual with external safety
signals which allow at least some time to be spent attending to safety) or for
information-seeking reasons (i.e., predictability eventually allows the growth of
a neuronal model which enables the individual to habituate and attend less to
danger over time).

Now let us consider what-kind-of-event predictability. Like contingency
predictability, this will be preferred under uncontrollable threat conditions which
do not support blunting, either for safety signal reasons or for information-
seeking reasons. Conversely, unpredictability will be preferred whenever situational or individual factors *do* support distraction, with one exception. When the
information provided facilitates blunting, then predictability will be preferred,
even under conditions which do support distraction. For example, predictability
should have beneficial effects when it puts an upper limit on how bad the
situation can become. If an individual is informed that the dentist will be drilling
(stimulus information), then he or she does not anticipate a more aversive procedure, such as root canal work. If the individual is told to expect moderate sensations (response information), then he or she does not anticipate intense sensations.
This reduces the threatening aspects of the event and makes it easier for the individual to tune out. What-kind-of-event predictability will also be preferred when it
focuses the individual on the nonthreatening aspects of the event. The dentist who
says "Remember that pain is just a protective sensory mechanism" or "Remember
that with every touch of the drill your teeth get healthier" shifts the individual's
negative perceptions of the event to more neutral or even positive ones. This, in
turn, is stress reducing.

The monitoring–blunting difference in coping modalities has not escaped
the interest of clinicians. Beginning with Freud, the notion of repression and
defense mechanisms has been the bedrock of psychoanalytic theorizing. However, it has been a peculiarity of psychodynamic research in personality that it

has focused on trying to demonstrate the unconscious qualities of this mechanism but has paid little attention to the larger questions of informational preferences under threat and the consequences for coping with stress.

Theorizing has also been inadequate in the experimental literature. The main problem is that these models stem primarily from the animal laboratory and so have obscured the role of cognitive avoidance and transformations with human beings. Instead, these theories have assumed a perfect isomorphism between the objective and perceived aspects of danger. If subjects are faced with an objective danger, they have to be perceiving the danger. Thus, these models have focused on the objective arrangements of events without considering that such events may be psychologically transformed by the individual. With this focus, it follows that predictability should be stress reducing, since it at least provides external safety signals or facilitates habituation.

What people do in their heads is not always related to what faces them in the objective world. One way of conceptualizing the threat process is in terms of the objective presence or absence of threat and the perceived presence or absence of threat (see Table I). To the extent that the individual perceives, attends to, and monitors objective danger (cell A), the result is realistic fear and heightened arousal. Contingency predictability and what-kind-of-event predictability reduce such arousal by providing external safety signals or by facilitating habituation. In cell D, the individual neither perceives nor faces objective danger. This individual is attending to safety and should be relaxed.

The psychologically more interesting, and more complex, cells are the remaining two. In cell B, the danger signal is objectively present but not perceived (i.e., it is psychologically blunted or absent). When this is so, the individual is either unaware of the danger or, more interestingly, is engaged in a cognitive blunting strategy that tunes out the danger. For example, the individual can distract him- or herself by thinking about other events, can relax by calming self-talk, or can reinterpret the event as a positive, beneficial experience. This individual should show less arousal than an individual who is monitoring danger.

TABLE I
RELATIONSHIP BETWEEN PERCEIVED THREAT AND OBJECTIVE THREAT

Perceived threat	Objective threat	
	Present	Absent
Present	A. Attending to danger cues	C. Brooding, worrying, ruminating, rehearsing
Absent	B. Distraction; also, self-relaxation, detachment, reinterpretation, intellectualization, denial	D. Attending to safety cues

Predictability will generally be dispreferred, since it interferes with adopting a blunting mode. Certain types of what-kind-of-event predictability may be preferred, as detailed above. Cell B will be discussed further below. Finally, the individual can perceive danger even though not objectively confronted by it (cell C). When this is so, we say the person is brooding, ruminating, rehearsing about the event, or worrying. This cell has important clinical implications which have been discussed elsewhere (see Miller & Grant, 1979).

What are the different blunting strategies that allow one to absent oneself psychologically from an objectively present danger signal? Foremost among them is distraction. This can occur through covert activity inside a subject's head or through external means. For example, in an experiment by Miller (1979b), subjects were threatened with electric shock and were given a choice between listening for a signal that predicted the occurrence of shock (predictability) or listening instead to music with no signal for shock (distraction). Preference for distraction from the threat-relevant information was indexed by the amount of time each subject spent listening to the music (see also Averill & Rosenn, 1972; Miller, 1979d). Similarly, in an experiment by Miller (1979c), subjects worked on a stressful cognitive task, but could attend as often as they wished to a clock that signaled how much time had passed and/or a light that signaled how well they were performing. Less time spent looking at the clock and/or light was taken as indicating greater preference for distraction. Finally, in a related vein, subjects who have undergone or who are about to undergo failure experiences can choose to attend to negative or positive personality information about themselves rather than to information about the stressor itself. Less time spent scanning for personality liabilities (negative information) was seen as demonstrating greater preference to distract oneself from ego-threatening information (Mischel, Ebbesen, & Zeiss, 1973, 1976).

Distraction has at least two properties other than choice which make it measurable: It should reduce emotional arousal and it should reduce processing of external threat-relevant information. That is, the distracting individual should both show less stress and input less information about the event. Many studies have looked at reduced arousal, most commonly by psychophysiological measurement. Yet these indices can be ambiguous, confounding attentional and emotional processes (e.g., Kilpatrick, 1972). Do distracting individuals show reduced autonomic activity because they are less emotional about the event or because they are less vigilant for threat-relevant cues? Or, as some views postulate, does a decrease in autonomic activity with unpredictability reflect increased vigilance for threat-relevant cues? To date, no study has taken advantage of the convenient property of reduced information processing to tease these processes apart (e.g., Wachtel, 1968). In principle, effectiveness of distraction should be proportional to both reduced arousal and independently measured reduced processing of external threatening information.

Other blunting strategies, for the moment less conveniently measurable and operationalizable, can also accomplish psychological withdrawal from danger signals. Subjects can be encouraged to engage in denial or detachment (e.g., "Remember the gory film consists only of actors and red dye, not real people and blood") (Lazarus, Opton, Nomikos, & Rankin, 1965). These strategies should reduce emotional arousal and might reduce processing of external information. The subjects can be encouraged to engage in intellectualization or reinterpretation (e.g., "Concentrate on the interesting tingling response that electric shock induces") (Holmes & Houston, 1974). This should reduce emotional arousal but possibly not reduce processing of all threat-relevant information. For example, information related to the negative aspects of the event may be suppressed but not information related to its neutral or positive aspects (see Meichenbaum, 1977).

The evidence so far bears only on arousal measures and indicates that individuals who are induced to engage in blunting strategies, or who spontaneously engage in such strategies, show reduced stress to threatening films (Lazarus and Alfert, 1966; Lazarus et al., 1965; Speisman, Lazarus, Mordkoff, & Davison, 1964), to physical stressors in the laboratory (Barber & Hahn, 1962; Blitz & Dinnerstein, 1971; Bloom, Houston, Holmes, & Burish, 1977; Holmes & Houston, 1974; Neufeld, 1970), and to aversive medical and surgical procedures (Langer, Janis, & Wolfer, 1975; Mead, 1970; Miller, 1979f, 1980; Miller & Wagner, 1980). A thorough review of this literature falls outside the domain of this contribution (see Lazarus, 1966).

Some laboratory and real-life conditions should facilitate distraction more than others (see Table II). First, low-frequency, low-intensity, and short-duration aversive events should support distraction more than high-frequency, high-intensity, and long-duration events, as should the temporal remoteness of the aversive event (see, e.g., Averill & Rosenn, 1972; Monat, 1976; Monat et al., 1972). In addition, in the laboratory, explicit instructions that subjects should, or are allowed to, distract themselves or the availability of external distractors should enhance distraction. Finally, uncontrollable aversive events should sup-

TABLE II
PREDICTIONS OF BLUNTING HYPOTHESIS FOR STIMULUS
CONDITIONS WHICH DO AND DO NOT SUPPORT DISTRACTION

	Supports distraction	Does not support distraction
Predictability	Low	High
Event frequency	Low	High
Event intensity	Low	High
Event duration	Low	High
Anticipatory interval	Long	Short
Controllability	Low	High
External distractors	Available	Unavailable

port distraction better than controllable aversive events because execution of a controlling response of necessity directs attention toward the aversive situation. The harder or more complex the controlling response is to perform, the more difficult it should be to distract. In contrast, with uncontrollable events, the individual is freer to engage in non-threat-related activity, and such activity can enhance diversion of attention and distraction (see Gal & Lazarus, 1975).

The ability to successfully distract oneself from danger signals should be subject to wide individual differences. Some people should find it easy or desirable to distract even under laboratory conditions providing minimal support; others should find it difficult or inappropriate to distract even under conditions providing maximal support. People who believe themselves to be ineffective distractors should tend consistently to choose predictability, especially under conditions which do not support distraction. People who believe themselves to be effective distractors should tend consistently to choose unpredictability, even under conditions which do not support distraction. This means that there should be a consistent minority of subjects choosing unpredictability under conditions apparently not favoring distraction who will show lower arousal and a consistent minority choosing predictability (and showing higher anticipatory arousal) under conditions supporting distraction. If these minorities are forced to their non-preferred condition, they will show higher arousal than they did in their preferred condition (see Miller, 1980b; Miller & Wagner, 1980).

It would seem important, then, to be able to identify independently and in advance those disposed either to distract themselves or to monitor for danger. However, the scales that are currently available for identifying information seekers and information avoiders are based on psychodynamic views of personality (e.g., Byrne, 1961; Goldstein, 1959). They have proven to be of limited validity in predicting who actually seeks out or avoids information in objectively aversive situations and in predicting how aroused individuals become when predictability or unpredictability is imposed on them (Averill & Rosenn, 1972; Cohen & Lazarus, 1973; Miller, 1979f; Miller & Wagner, 1980). They also may be confounded by general response sets.

To circumvent these problems, I devised a new self-report measure which is more closely tailored to the kinds of informational choices under study. So far, this scale accurately predicts preference for information or distraction under laboratory and field conditions. For example, in the laboratory it predicts those who seek out or avoid information about electric shock (Miller, 1979d), those who seek out or avoid information about their performance on a stressful cognitive task (Miller, 1979e), and how individuals respond to a painful stimulus (the cold presser test) when information or distraction is imposed on them (Chorney, Efran, Ascher, & Lukens, 1981). In field studies, it predicts how individuals respond to aversive medical diagnostic procedures as a function of information or distraction (Miller, 1979f; Miller & Wagner, 1980). (For details, see Miller, 1980b).

Having stated the blunting hypothesis, its predictions can now be made explicit:

1. For both contingency and what-kind-of-event predictability, this hypothesis predicts choice of a predictable over an unpredictable aversive event under invasive conditions which do not support distraction. The reasons are identical to those of the safety signal and information-seeking hypotheses above.

2. In contrast, the blunting hypothesis predicts choice of an unpredictable over a predictable event under noninvasive conditions which do not support distraction. This is because a subject can more effectively reduce arousal by ignoring warning signals and engaging in a blunting strategy than by scanning for external signals or by the process of habituation. What-kind-of-event predictability will still be chosen under noninvasive conditions when it focuses the individual away from the negative aspects of the event and so facilitates blunting.

3. It suggests that there is a consistent minority of subjects choosing unpredictability under conditions apparently not favoring distraction who will show lower arousal and also a consistent minority choosing predictability (and showing higher anticipatory arousal) under conditions supporting distraction. If these minorities are forced to their nonpreferred condition, they will show higher arousal than they did in their preferred condition.

4. It generally predicts greater anticipatory arousal with predictability under conditions which support blunting in the unpredictability condition since the blunting individual is not processing threat-relevant information. It also predicts lower anticipatory arousal with what-kind-of-event predictability when the individual can attend to nonnegative aspects and thereby tune out.

5. It is silent about impact arousal but could invoke a premise of increased habituation with predictability under conditions not favoring distraction, or increased habituation with unpredictability and blunting under conditions favoring distraction.

None of the remaining views addresses contingency predictability, but each of them specifies conditions under which what-kind-of-event predictability (information) is stress reducing. Stress reductions occur when information induces an analytical set (e.g., Leventhal, Brown, Sacham, & Engquist, 1979), when it provides a less aversive script to enact (e.g., Langer & Abelson, 1972), and when arousal is misattributed to a neutral source (a logical extension of Schachter, 1964; Schachter & Singer, 1962; Nisbett & Schachter, 1966).

B. THE ANALYTIC HYPOTHESIS

Leventhal's view assumes that inputs about aversive events can either be encoded in an objective, analytical way or can set off an emotional memory schematization. In objective encoding, individuals focus on the concrete, sensory, nonthreatening aspects of the aversive event. This facilitates habituation (and thereby promotes stress reduction). In contrast, emotional encoding interferes with habituation because individuals focus on the anticipatory threat value of the event. Therefore, arousal remains high.

Response information (e.g., "When I drill, you will feel pressure and sensations such as tingling and aching in your gums") prepares individuals with a detailed preview of the tactile, thermal, and visual changes that they will experience during the stress impact. Such information allows for analytic encoding since the information is encoded as a set of objective features, such as coldness, numbness, and pins and needles, rather than the schematization of the impact as pain, fear, and uncertainty as to whether the skin will be damaged, etc. Arousal information ("This will give you butterflies in the stomach") involves descriptions of emotional behaviors such as rapid heart rate, sweaty palms, etc. Such information is incompatible with analytic encoding since it does not assist the individual in forming a schema of the objective stimulus features or help to block out awareness of stimulus sensations. Similarly, stimulus magnitude information (e.g., "This will hurt") is incompatible with analytic encoding since it encourages processing a stimulus as a threatening event.

The analytic hypothesis is thus relevant to a subset of the literature. It predicts (1) choice of predictability when response information is provided because such information facilitates analytic encoding and (2) reduced impact arousal with this type of predictability since an event that is processed in terms of its objective properties loses the power to stimulate emotional responses and so facilitates habituation. It is silent on variations in anticipatory arousal, although it could add a premise that response information decreases anticipatory fear since the individual anticipates a less aversive event.

C. THE SCRIPT HYPOTHESIS

Langer and Abelson's (1972) view emphasizes the role of scripts in the area of interpersonal interactions; this approach can be extended to the predictability domain. A script is a coherent sequence of events expected by the individual, involving the person as a participant or observer. When individuals enter situations, they stereotypically enact prior scripts and, thus, often fail to process new or contradictory information. As applied to predictability, individuals who receive what-kind-of-event predictability are provided with a script (i.e., an expected set of events) which details the appropriate stimuli, responses, and arousal to that event. This script—and not the actual event—then dictates the magnitude of stress responses. If the informational script details an event of lower magnitude than the actual event, an individual will show reduced stress, since his behavior is governed by the prior script and not by the event itself. So, using the dentist example, consider an individual who is about to have his or her teeth drilled. If that individual is told to expect a level of pain and discomfort normally associated with teeth cleaning rather than drilling, the magnitude of the stress reaction will be reduced and will correspond to the cleaning procedure and not to the actual drilling procedure. When preparatory information details an event of the same magnitude as the actual event (i.e., when it is accurate) or when it details an event of greater magnitude than the actual event (i.e., when it is an overestimation) then stress reductions should not occur.

The theory thus predicts (1) choice of what-kind-of-event predictability when such information provides a less aversive script to enact, (2) lower anticipatory arousal with predictability, as long as the script which is to be enacted entails an event of lower magnitude than the upcoming event itself, and (3) lower impact arousal with predictability, as long as the script entails a level of pain lower than that associated with the actual event.

D.   THE AROUSAL HYPOTHESIS

This hypothesis is an extension of cognition-arousal theories of emotion (e.g., Schachter, 1964). According to this view, an emotional state is a joint function of a state of physiological arousal and a cognition appropriate to this state of arousal. That is, individuals label their physiological states in terms of cognitions available to them. Precisely the same state of physiological arousal can be labelled as stressful or nonstressful, depending on how the individual construes the situation. When individuals are led to attribute arousal to a neutral source, they attach a neutral, nonemotional label to their state, which in turn is arousal reducing.

To the extent that arousal information (a form of predictability) enables an individual to attribute arousal to a neutral, nonemotional source, then predictability is stress reducing. If the dental patient can be induced to attribute arousal to some source other than the drill (e.g., to a pill just ingested), the person will show less stress than an individual who does not receive this information and who attributes arousal to the procedure itself.

This view predicts (1) that individuals will prefer what-kind-of-event predictability as long as such information links arousal to a nonthreatening source, (2) lower anticipatory arousal with this type of information since individuals redefine their states in less emotional terms, and (3) lower impact arousal with such information since individuals are less emotional about the event.

VI.   Evidence

Having defined predictability and stress and stated all the theories, let us now examine the fit of the evidence to the theories. Tables III and V present the predictions of each theory, the synopsis of the evidence, and a summary of the evidence for the two classes of predictability.

TABLE III

Summary of Theoretical Predictions and Experimental Evidence for Contingency Predictability

	Stress			
	Preference (no distraction)	Preference (distraction)	Anticipatory arousal	Impact arousal
Theoretical predictions				
Information seeking (predictable event is less surprising)	P/UN		P/UN	P/UN
Preparatory response (response reduces intensity of predictable event)	P/UN	P/UN	P/UN	
Preparatory set (increased anticipatory arousal with predictability reduces impact arousal)	P/UN		0	P/UN
Uncontrollability (predictable event is more controllable)	P/UN	P/UN	UN/P	P/UN
Safety signal (more safety and more relaxation with predictable event)	P/UN	P/UN	P/UN	P/UN
Blunting (psychological withdrawal from danger reduces stress)	P/UN	P/UN	P/UN	0
Summary of the evidence	P/UN clear	UN/P clear	UN/P UN/P probable	0 (P/UN) Most show no difference
Studies in which P/UN	Badia et al., 1966, Exp. I (20)[a] .05[b]		Averill et al., 1977 (80) .05 (SCL)	D'Amato & Gumenik, 1960 (21) .01

224

Cook & ..., 1954

D'Amato & Gumenik, 1960
 (21) .01
Jones et al., 1966
 (32) .01
Lanzetta & Driscoll, 1966
 (24) .025
Maltzman & Wolff, 1970
 (40) .01
Monat et al., 1972, Exp. II
 (40) .001

Studies in which UN/P

Averill et al., 1977
 (80) .001
Averill & Rosenn, 1972
 (80) .005
Miller, 1979b
 (68) .01
Rothbart & Mellinger, 1972
 (88) .01

Averill et al., 1977
 (80) .05 (subjective)
Bowers, 1971a
 (8) .005 (HR)
Bowers, 1971b
 (16) .0001
Elliott, 1969
 (32) .01
Gaebelein et al., 1976
 (20) .001 (HR)
Geer & Maisel, 1972
 (60) .01
Mansueto & Desiderato, 1971
 (80) .001
Miller, 1979b
 (68) .001
Monat, 1976
 (108) .001
Monat et al., 1972
 Exp. I (80) .001
 Exp. II (40) .001

Averill & Rosenn, 1972
 (80) .005 (SCL and HR)
Klemp & Rodin, 1976
 (24) .05

Epstein & Kling, 1973
 (30) .01
Gaebelein et al., 1976
 (20) .01
Lovibond, 1968
 (60) .01
Maltzman & Wolff, 1970
 (40) .01
Peeke & Grings, 1968
 (60) .01
Price & Geer, 1972
 (20) .05 (5 sec)

Averill et al., 1977
 (80) .05

(continued)

TABLE III—*Continued*

	Stress			
	Preference (no distraction)	Preference (distraction)	Anticipatory arousal	Impact arousal
Studies in which P = UN			Averill et al., 1977 (80) ns. (HR)	Averill & Rosenn, 1972 (80) ns.
			Averill & Rosenn, 1972 (80) ns. (subjective)	Cook & Barnes, 1964 (40) ns.
			Elliott, 1966 (60) ns.	Furedy, 1973 (48) ns.
			Gaebelein et al., 1976 (20) ns. (SCL)	Furedy & Chan, 1971 Exp. I (40) ns. Exp. II (60) ns.
			Glass et al., 1969 (48) ns.	Furedy & Ginsberg 1973 (48) ns.
			Rothbart & Mellinger 1972 (88) ns.	Furedy & Klajner, 1972 (28) ns.
				Geer & Maisel, 1972 (60) ns.
				Glass et al., 1969 (48) ns.
				Klemp & Rodin, 1976 (24) ns.
				Lanzetta & Driscoll, 1966 (24) ns.
				Price & Geer, 1972 (20) ns. (10 sec)

NOTE. P/UN, predictability is preferred to unpredictability, predictability produces less anticipatory arousal, predictability produces less impact arousal; UN/P, unpredictability is preferred to predictability, unpredictability produces less anticipatory arousal, unpredictability produces less impact arousal; P = UN, no difference between predictability and unpredictability; 0, no prediction.

[a] Sample size.

A. CONTINGENCY PREDICTABILITY (Table III)

1. Preference

Overall, people prefer to know the conditions under which an uncontrollable aversive event will occur. This is true for studies where subjects experience both predictable and unpredictable events and express their preference between the two alternatives (Monat *et al.*, 1972, Experiment II) and also for studies where subjects actually choose for themselves which condition they want to undergo (Jones *et al.*, 1966).

For example, in a study by Pervin (1963) all subjects were exposed to two relevant experimental conditions. In the predictability condition, the probability of shock following a blue light was 100%, and the probability of shock following a yellow light was 0%. In the unpredictability condition, a white light was sometimes followed by shock and sometimes not. Results showed that the majority of subjects expressed a preference for predictability (blue light) over unpredictability (white light).

In a second study by Lanzetta and Driscoll (1966), all subjects were threatened with a 50% probable electric shock. On each trial, subjects could choose to have information about whether or not shock would actually occur on that trial. As in the Pervin study, most subjects preferred information over no information.

In addition to the above evidence, subjects usually choose aversive events which immediately follow the warning signal (predictability) over events which occur after a longer, more variable delay (unpredictability) (Badia, McBane, Suter, & Lewis, 1966, Experiments I and II; Cook & Barnes, 1964; D'Amato & Gumenik, 1960; Maltzman & Wolff, 1970). Although randomly delayed trauma involves a longer anticipatory interval, which can be aversive in itself (Breznitz, 1967; Folkins, 1970), the delay interval employed in these studies is fairly minimal. So preference for predictability per se, rather than preference for shorter anticipatory intervals, probably accounts for the observed effects.

In sum, subjects clearly prefer predictability to simple unpredictability, and this is consistent with all the traditional theories. Individuals should choose predictability in order to reduce conflict (information seeking), to make a well-timed preparatory response (preparatory response), to form a large anticipatory response and thereby reduce the impact response (preparatory set), to execute a coping response (uncontrollability), or to discriminate safe from unsafe periods (safety signal).

In the above studies, however, there was always a minority of subjects who did not opt for predictability. Moreover, in real-life aversive situations, an individual is not merely faced with a choice of attending to a warning signal or waiting passively for an unpredictable event. Instead, there is almost limitless opportunity for distraction. Recall the dental patient. While sitting in the chair, the person can do mental puzzles, think through his or her schedule, conjure up happy memories, or simply fall asleep. Indeed, at times there may be no alternative but to distract oneself. A man in need of a hernia operation who is on a waiting list for a hospital bed to become available must still perform his job, attend to his family and chores, and maintain his friendships. The relevant analogue studies are therefore those that contrast predictability to unpredictability plus distraction, since such studies mirror real-life stress less artificially than studies which do not allow distraction.

Four studies have investigated preference for predictability versus preference for unpredictability plus distraction. In three of these studies (Averill, O'Brien, & DeWitt, 1977; Averill & Rosenn, 1972; Miller, 1979b), subjects could either distract themselves by listening to music or they could choose to monitor a signal for shock.

For example, in an experiment by Miller (1979b), subjects were threatened with a low probability electric shock and were allowed to choose whether they wanted information about when the shock might occur (predictability) or whether they wanted to distract themselves (unpredictability plus distraction). This meant, in practice, that subjects could listen to a monotone which would be interrupted by a high warning tone that signaled possible shock onset. Alternatively, they could listen to music on another channel, with no warning stimulus. Thus listening to the monotone showed preference for information, whereas listening to music showed preference for distraction. Half of the subjects were told they could avoid shock altogether by pressing a button on those trials where they detected the warning signal (controllability). For the other subjects, avoidance of the shock was not possible (uncontrollability).

As can be seen in Table IV, individuals clearly preferred information when they could use that information to avoid. However, when subjects could not avoid, the preference is reversed, and the majority chose distraction. Among those who could avoid, 71% monitored the signal on the majority of the six trials. Among those who could not avoid, only 32% monitored the signal for the majority of trials. All of the other studies found similar results. Indeed, Averill *et al.* (1977) have shown that preference for distraction systematically increases as the possibility of avoiding shock decreases.

TABLE IV

NUMBER OF SUBJECTS WHO ARE MONITORS (LISTEN FOR THE WARNING SIGNAL) AND DISTRACTORS (LISTEN TO THE MUSIC)

	Monitors	Distractors
Avoidance subjects	24	10
Nonavoidance subjects	11	23

In a related study, Rothbart and Mellinger (1972) had subjects work on an arithmetic task under threat of shock. Subjects could attend as often as they wished to a light that signaled shock onset. Here as well, subjects preferred unpredictability when no avoidance response was available. Obviously, preference for predictability should occur under conditions allowing avoidance, since only by choosing predictability can subjects avoid shock altogether. It is the cases of informational choice, when avoidance is not allowed, that are theoretically interesting and that help to untangle the preference for predictability per se from the desire to control.

The fact that individuals choose unpredictability plus distraction over predictability is contrary to all the traditional theories. However, it is consistent with the view (blunting hypothesis) that subjects prefer unpredictable aversive events when unpredictability allows them to cognitively avoid or tune out from impending danger. This view can also account for the finding that a minority of subjects seem to prefer unpredictability, even when external distractors are not provided. This is because it predicts individual differences in the ability and inclination to engage in distraction. Individuals who are good distractors should typically opt for unpredictability, even when environmental conditions provide minimal support for distraction (e.g., when no external distractors are provided).

2. Anticipatory Arousal

The evidence on anticipatory arousal is conflicting, but most studies indicate that predictability produces greater anticipatory arousal than unpredictability. On the physiological level, this is so with respect to tonic skin conductance level (SCL) (Mansueto & Desiderato, 1971; Miller, 1979b; Monat, 1976; Monat et al., 1972, Experiments I and II), the frequency of phasic nonspecific skin conductance responses (SCRs) (Bowers, 1971b; Geer & Maisel, 1972; Miller, 1979b; Monat, 1976; Monat et al., 1972, Experiments I and II), and heart rate (HR) (Bowers, 1971a,b; Elliott, 1969; Gaebelein et al., 1974; Mansueto & Desiderato, 1971; Monat, 1976; Monat et al., 1972, Experiments I and II). In these studies, unpredictability was associated with lower HR, lower SCL, and fewer SCRs (i.e., less arousal) than predictability.

Other studies have found no difference between predictability and unpredictability for SCRs (Bowers, 1971a), SCL (Gaebelein et al., 1974; Glass et al., 1969), and HR (Averill et al., 1977; Elliott, 1966). In contrast, a few studies report that unpredictability produces greater arousal in terms of SCL (Averill et al., 1977; Averill & Rosenn, 1972) and HR (Averill & Rosenn, 1972).

A good example of a study in this class is one by Geer and Maisel (1972). All subjects were shown a series of slides of dead bodies presented at 60-sec intervals. In the predictability group, each slide was preceded by a 10-sec tone. In the unpredictability group, the slides appeared without prior warning. Subjects who could not predict the occurrence of the slides showed lower electrodermal arousal (i.e., fewer nonspecific SCRs) than subjects who could predict the slides.

It would seem, then, that predictability is generally associated with greater anticipatory physiological arousal than unpredictability. However, some authors, following Lacey (1967), challenge the view that the lower HR associated with unpredictability reflects decreased emotional arousal. Instead, lower HR presumably reflects increased attention. Unpredictability is alleged to increase information seeking for anxiety-reducing cues, with the concomitant physiological effect of lowering HR (e.g., Bowers, 1971a,b). This interpretation seems unlikely, since five of the six studies which measured frequency of nonspecific SCRs found lower arousal with unpredictability. Since the SCR measure more validly unconfounds the effects of emotion and attention and is a "purer" measure of arousal (Katkin, 1965, 1966; Kilpatrick, 1972), we can conclude that unpredictability probably produces more autonomic relaxation.

What about the subjective consequences of predictability? The few studies that obtained self-report measures of anticipatory fear and anxiety show that predictability either leads to increased subjective arousal (Averill *et al.*, 1977; Miller, 1979b; Monat *et al.*, 1972, Experiments I and II; Monat, 1976) or produces no significant differences (Averill & Rosenn, 1972; Rothbart & Mellinger, 1972). Two studies found increased anxiety with unpredictability (Klemp & Rodin, 1976; Pervin, 1963).

In summary, the physiological and subjective data show that predictable aversive events probably cause higher anticipatory arousal than unpredictable events. These results are contrary to information-seeking theory, which says that predictability should reduce conflict and thereby lower arousal. The results are also contrary to uncontrollability theory, which says that predictability should reduce anticipatory anxiety since it enables subjects to select an optimal coping strategy and, thereby, to reduce and direct their arousal. The preparatory response theory is silent on these data and is therefore inconsistent with the observed effects.

The data are, on the surface, consistent with preparatory set theory. The theory predicts increased anticipatory arousal with predictable aversive events as the means by which subsequent impact arousal is to be reduced. However, the *prima facie* appearance of confirmation for the theory is undermined as one considers the argument more closely. This is because the proposed route to the prediction of increased anticipatory arousal with predictability (which is borne out by the evidence) is through an aspect of the theory which is not borne out by the evidence (reduced impact arousal with predictability), as will be discussed later.

Safety signal makes two predictions about anticipatory arousal. First, predictability subjects should show greater anticipatory arousal when the danger signal is on than do unpredictability subjects during an equivalent period. This is because the perceived probability of the event is greater for the predictability subject. The data confirm this prediction (see, e.g., Geer & Maisel, 1972). However, safety signal also makes a second, more critical, prediction. Net anticipatory arousal should be lower with predictability when arousal is measured over a period that includes both danger signals and substantial amounts of safety signal. This is because the predicting subject spends only some of the time in high fear (when the danger signal is on) and most of the time in relaxation (when the danger signal is off). In contrast, the unpredictability subject spends all of the time in moderate fear. The data do not confirm this prediction.

None of the traditional theories accurately predicts the general finding of increased anticipatory arousal with predictability. How then is it possible to account for these data? The results make sense if we invoke the blunting hypothesis premise that arousal is lowest when an individual is distracting himself; and distraction is often easier with unpredictable aversive events than with predictable aversive events. Consider predictability subjects in the Geer and Maisel (1972) study. They will be listening for the tone that signals when the gory photograph will appear. Moreover, the tone itself is invasive and intrusive, even if they are trying not to listen for it. Thus, distraction is difficult. In contrast, for unpredictability subjects, threat-relevant information is less salient and impinges less into their consciousness. This makes it easier to psychologically dampen, tune out, and distract themselves away from thoughts about threat.

If the blunting hypothesis is correct, it should integrate the evidence on anticipatory arousal and predictability. That is, the conflict in results between studies that find decreased arousal with unpredictability and those that find the opposite effect should be reconciled by differences in the effectiveness of distraction. In studies where unpredictability decreases arousal, subjects should be distracting themselves and situational conditions should facilitate distraction. In studies where unpredictability increases arousal, subjects should not be distracting themselves and situational conditions should interfere with distraction.

Unfortunately, many of the studies do not provide evidence that directly bears on this hypothesis. Since they were not conducted with the blunting hypothesis in mind, they did not obtain measures of whether subjects were or were not distracting themselves. Of the five studies that obtained self-reports of distraction, three found that stress was reduced with unpredictability. In all of these three studies, unpredictability subjects reported engaging in fewer thoughts about the experiment and shock than predictability subjects. In the two remaining studies, unpredictability increased stress on some measures, decreased stress on other measures, and made no difference on still other measures. Correspondingly, there was no significant difference in shock-related thoughts among groups.

The three studies that contrasted unpredictability plus an external distractor to predictability present an instructive contrast. One (Miller, 1979b) found lower physiological and subjective arousal during distraction, whereas the other two (Averill & Rosenn, 1972; Averill et al., 1977) found equal or higher arousal during distraction. Differences in ease of distraction with unpredictability may account for these discrepant results. In the Averill and Rosenn (1972) study, moderate to intense shock (an invasive and intrusive event) actually occurred on three of the four trials, with the likely result of jarring subjects out of a distracting, avoidant mode into a monitoring, sensitized mode. In line with this interpretation, Averill's distraction group maintained higher physiological arousal than the predictability group, equivalent subjective arousal, and did not report thinking significantly less about shock over time (see also Averill *et al.*, 1977).

In Miller's study, shock was threatened but never actually occurred. So distracting subjects were never forcefully reminded of the aversive event and showed a pattern of decreasing physiological and subjective arousal over time. Figure 1 shows this effect for the frequency of nonspecific skin conductance responses. Monitors and distractors began with similar levels of arousal on trial 1, but then subjects who distracted themselves showed a rapid decline in frequency of nonspecific responses, whereas those subjects who were monitoring stayed more highly aroused. In addition, there was a clear effect of distracting on reports of shock-related thoughts. As Fig. 2 shows, the two groups thought equally about shock on trial 1, but after the first trial distracting subjects rapidly shifted their attention away from the experiment. Monitoring subjects remained highly aroused.

One final study is worth highlighting, because it demonstrates the interaction between situational factors and ease of distraction (Monat, 1976). Subjects waited 1 min, 3 min, or 12 min for receipt of electric shock under conditions where they knew (predictability) or did not know (unpredictability) when shock would occur. Predictability generally produced a pattern of increasing anticipatory physiological arousal (measured by HR, SCL, and SCR) and subjective arousal (self-reported tension), and was associated with more vigilant thoughts. Unpredictability produced the opposite pattern. The difference observed between

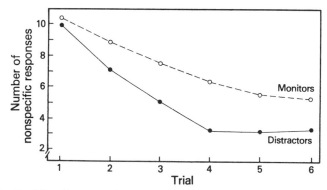

Fig. 1.   Mean frequency of nonspecific electrodermal responses for six trials.

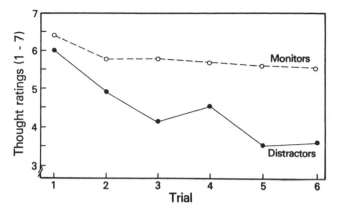

Fig. 2.   Mean ratings of shock-related thoughts (on a 1 to 7 scale, where 0 = "My thoughts were not at all on the shock," and 7 = "My thoughts were completely on the shock") for six trials.

the predictability and unpredictability groups was greater, the longer the anticipatory interval. These results make sense if we assume that it is easier to distract with unpredictable events when the wait is longer rather than shorter. However, distraction may be well-nigh impossible, no matter how long the wait, with psychologically invasive predictable events. Indeed, the only two studies to show higher subjective arousal with unpredictability (Klemp & Rodin, 1976; Pervin, 1963) used extremely short anticipatory intervals.

So the evidence shows that unpredictability is stress reducing, and this may be because subjects are able to distract themselves. In order to confirm this interpretation, further experiments are needed which systematically manipulate ease of distraction during predictable and unpredictable aversive events and simultaneously measure anticipatory arousal and attention deployment.

3.   Impact

Overall, predictability has no consistent effect on the impact of an aversive event. For the electrodermal system, the usual criterion for an impact response is a clearly discernible skin conductance response (SCR) within a specified time after the onset of the event. Some results have shown that the impact SCR (within 5 sec) is smaller for the predictability group (Peeke & Grings, 1968; Price & Geer, 1972) and habituates faster (Maltzman & Wolff, 1970). In contrast, Furedy and Klajner (1972), Geer and Maisel (1972), and Lanzetta and Driscoll (1966) found no impact differences. It has been suggested, however, that with a 5-sec interval between the signal and the event, impact SCRs may be diminished simply as an artifact of having responded to the warning signal. Lovibond (1968), using a longer, 10-sec criterion, found more rapid habituation with predictability. This result has since failed to replicate (Furedy & Chan, 1971), and the results of another study (Price & Geer, 1972) also conflict with it (see also Bowers, 1971a,b). Finally, the electrodermal response to impact has been reported in relation to overall tonic (i.e., base-level) shifts from the period just before the event to the period just after the event. When this criterion is used, one study has found that predictability decreases tonic arousal at impact (Gaebelein et al., 1976).

Three studies have investigated HR impact responses. One study found that predictability facilitates habituation (Epstein & Kling, 1971), whereas the other two found no difference (Furedy & Chan, 1971; Furedy & Klajner, 1972).

On the subjective level, the majority of studies have found that predictability has no effect on the impact of the event. That is, there are no differences in self-reports of pain and discomfort between subjects with predictability and subjects without predictability (Averill & Rosenn, 1972; Furedy, 1973; Furedy & Chan, 1971; Furedy & Ginsberg, 1973; Furedy & Klajner, 1972; Glass et al., 1969). One study found reports of increased painfulness under predictability (Averill et al., 1977). In contrast, four studies found that a predictable aversive event is less painful (D'Amato & Gumenik, 1960; Lovibond, 1968; Maltzman & Wolff, 1970; Pervin, 1963). (See also Furedy, 1970; Furedy & Doob, 1971a,b, 1972; Furedy, Fainstat, Kulin, Lasko, & Nichols, 1972.)

In sum, there are no clear-cut impact differences, either physiological or subjective, between predictable and unpredictable aversive events under contingency predictability. Perhaps this is the case because contingency predictability has no effect on the impact of an aversive event. This conclusion is inconsistent with the preparatory set, preparatory response, uncontrollability, and information-seeking theories. According to these views, a predictable aversive event should hurt less since it allows the subject to form a preparatory set, make a well-timed preparatory response, execute the optimal coping strategy, or reduce surprise and facilitate habituation. Both the safety signal and blunting hypotheses are silent about the effects of predictability on impact and, thus, are consistent with the lack of observed differences.

B.   WHAT-KIND-OF-EVENT PREDICTABILITY (Table V)

1. Preference

Three out of three studies show that subjects prefer predictability over unpredictability. Jones et al. (1966) found that subjects chose information about what intensity of shock they would receive over no information; but the preference for intensity information (what-kind-of-event predictability) was weaker than the preference for time information (contingency predictability). Lanzetta and Driscoll (1966) "threatened" subjects with a shock or reward event, and subjects chose to know what outcome would occur on every trial. Both of these laboratory studies involved only predictability about the nature of the stimulus.

TABLE V

SUMMARY OF THEORETICAL PREDICTIONS AND EXPERIMENTAL EVIDENCE FOR WHAT-KIND-OF-EVENT PREDICTABILITY

| | Preference (no distraction) | Stress | | |
		Anticipatory arousal	Impact arousal	Postimpact arousal (recovery)
Theoretical predictions				
Information seeking (predictable event is less surprising)	P/UN	P/UN	P/UN	P/UN
Preparatory response (response reduces intensity of predictable event)	P/UN	0	P/UN	P/UN
Preparatory set (increased anticipatory arousal with predictability reduces impact arousal)	P/UN	UN/P	P/UN	P/UN
Uncontrollability (predictable event is more controllable)	P/UN	P/UN	P/UN	P/UN
Safety signal (more safety and more relaxation with predictable event)	P/UN	P/UN	0	P/UN
Blunting (psychological withdrawal from danger reduces stress)	P/UN	UN/P	0(P/UN)	UN/P

(continued)

TABLE V—*Continued*

| | Stress | | | |
	Preference (no distraction)	Anticipatory arousal	Impact arousal	Postimpact arousal (recovery)
Analytic (response information facilitates habituation)	P/UN	0	P/UN	P/UN
Script (predictability entails a less aversive script)	P/UN		P/UN	P/UN
Arousal (predictable events misattribute arousal to a neutral source)	P/UN	P/UN	P/UN	P/UN
Summary of the evidence	P/UN probable	Investigated but unknown	P/UN probable	UN/P probable
Studies in which P/UN	Jones *et al.*, 1966 (32)[a] .01[b] Lanzetta & Driscoll, 1966 (24) .005 Vernon, 1971 (500) .05	Elliott, 1966 (60) .001 Staub, 1968 (19) .02 (behavior) Staub & Kellett. 1972 (43) .01	Bobey & Davidson, 1970 (80) .001 Johnson, 1973 Exp. I, (20) .05 Exp. II, (48) .025 (response information) Johnson & Leventhal, 1976 (48) .01	Egbert *et al.*, 1964 (97) .01 Andrew, 1970 (59) .05 (sensitizers and neutrals) Miller, 1979f (40) .01 (monitors, physiological)

	Leventhal et al., 1979 (50) .001 (response information) Miller, 1979f (40) .05 Mills & Krantz, 1979, Exp. I (40) .002 Staub & Kellet, 1972 (43) .02	Sime, 1976 (57) .001 (high fear)
		Cohen & Lazarus, 1973 (61) .01 Miller, 1979f (40) .01 (subjective) Andrew, 1970 (59) .05 (avoiders) Miller, 1979f (40) .01 (blunters, physiological) Sime, 1976 (57) .001 (low fear)
Studies in which UN/P	Langer et al., 1975 (60) .01 (observer) Miller, 1979f (40) .01	
Studies in which P = UN	Langer et al., 1975 (60) ns. (physiological) Vernon & Bigelow, 1974 (40) ns.	Mills & Krantz, 1979, Exp. II (44) ns. (subjective)

NOTE. P/UN, predictability is preferred to unpredictability, predictability produces less anticipatory arousal, predictability produces less impact arousal; UN/P, unpredictability is preferred to predictability, unpredictability produces less anticipatory arousal, unpredictability produced less impact arousal; P = UN, no difference between predictability and unpredictability; 0, no prediction.

[a]Sample size.

[b]Most significant p value.

Preference for response information has not yet been investigated in the laboratory.

The one field study on choice confounds stimulus and response information.
Vernon (1971) compared the information seeking of tuberculosis patients with
informative and noninformative physicians. Those patients with noninformative
physicians (i.e., with more unpredictability) read more books on tuberculosis
(9% vs. 5%). Books on tuberculosis contain both stimulus and response information, of course. Moreover, book reading is probably not the best index of information seeking, since only a minority of the patient population ever used the
hospital library facilities in the first place.

In summary, although the available evidence has to be supplemented, results to date have been highly consistent. Therefore, it seems probable that
individuals prefer predictability, in the what-kind-of-event sense, to unpredictability. All relevant theories predict these results—information seeking, preparatory response, and preparatory set for obvious reasons, uncontrollability because the aversive event is better identified and thus better controlled, safety
signal because information that the aversive event is less intense than the
maximum possible provides relative safety. The results are also consistent with
the information-processing hypotheses. No study has measured choice of what-
kind-of-event predictability when distraction is provided in the unpredictability
condition.

2. Anticipatory Arousal

The data here are conflicting. Elliott (1966) presented one group (predictability) with a sample "anchoring" shock before the actual session began. This
group had lower anticipatory HR and less subjective tension than a group given
no sample shock (unpredictability). Staub (1968) found that subjects who received information about snakes (e.g., flicking of the tongue, characteristics of
skin and movement, description of how fear is acquired and maintained) approached and touched snakes more readily than an uninformed group, although
self-reports of fear were not reduced. Similarly, Staub and Kellett (1972) found
that stimulus information (describing the safety features of the shock apparatus
and laboratory) and response information (describing commonly reported sensations such as tingling and describing general arousal reactions such as accelerated
heart rate and tremor of the arm) each alone reduced self-reported worry about
the effects of electric shock. However, neither stimulus nor response information
reduced self-reported fear about receiving electric shock. Unfortunately, these
self-report measures were obtained retrospectively, after the experiment was
over, rather than during the anticipatory phase itself.

The remaining studies were all conducted in hospital settings. For example,
Williams, Jones, Workhoven, and Williams (1975) divided presurgical therapeutic abortion patients into low and high anxiety groups on the basis of personality

testing. On the eve of the operation, patients were visited either by an informative and supportive anesthesiologist (predictability) or by an uninformative, cursory anesthesiologist (unpredictability). Right before the operation, all subjects were injected with thiopental sodium and the time to disappearance of SCRs was measured. High-anxiety patients with the informative visit showed rapid disappearance of SCRs (less arousal), but there was no such effect for low-anxiety patients. Unfortunately, amount of information was confounded with degree of supportiveness in this study.

Among better controlled field studies, Vernon and Bigelow (1972) found no subjective anticipatory effect of information about surgery. Information centered on a description and rationale of the significant events that would befall a herniorrhaphy patient, including preoperative and postoperative procedures and postoperative discomfort.

Finally, Langer *et al.* (1975) studied patients about to undergo major surgery for such operations as hysterectomies, hernia repairs, cholecystectomies, tubal ligations, etc. Predictability patients were informed about the nature and reasons of the preoperative procedures (such as skin preparation, elimination, anesthesia) and the nature of the probable pains and discomforts they would experience following surgery. Unpredictability patients did not receive this extra information. They found that nurses gave higher anticipatory stress ratings to patients who had received preparatory information, although observer ratings are probably not the most valid index of anxiety. Indeed, the physiological measures (HR, blood pressure) did not differentiate between groups. However, in a recent study (Miller, 1979f), high information increased self-reports of anticipatory anxiety and depression for female gynecological patients about to undergo an aversive diagnostic procedure.

Thus the anticipatory arousal effects of what-kind-of-event predictability are contradictory. Unfortunately, many of the studies suffer from methodological confusions (e.g., contaminating information and reassurance, obtaining retrospective self-ratings, etc.) which make interpretations difficult. The laboratory studies suggest minimal arousal reduction or no effects as a function of what-kind-of-event predictability. The better controlled field studies suggest arousal increments or no effect as a function of predictability. The data are too inconclusive to be brought to bear on the theories, and future studies should more systematically investigate the interacting effects of individual differences and types of information on anticipatory arousal.

3. Impact

Overall, predictable aversive events seem to have less impact than unpredictable aversive events in both laboratory and field studies. In contrast, predictability may retard the recovery process, at least for some individuals.

For example, Neufeld and Davidson (1971) gave one group of subjects a detailed verbal account of the radiant heat pain they were about to experience, describing the heat apparatus, the procedure involved in heat administration, and sensations associated with the radiant heat stimulus. A second group received an account of an irrelevant stimulus. (Two additional groups watched a model undergoing the relevant or irrelevant event, with no apparent discomfort.) The groups that received relevant verbal or vicarious information demonstrated more pain tolerance during radiant heat. Similarly, Bobey and Davidson (1970) found that subjects exposed to information exhibited increased pain tolerance. Finally, in a blood bank setting, subjects receiving a combination of response (e.g., "feel a slight numbness or tingling") and stimulus information (e.g., "blood will flow into the collection bag") required less nurse intervention and retrospectively reported that they felt less discomfort during the procedure than subjects not receiving information (Mills & Krantz, 1979). The results of a follow-up study showed that response information about ice water immersion of the hand reduced behavioral aftereffects (as measured by proofreading), although no self-report differences of discomfort emerged between groups.

Among more comprehensive studies, Staub and Kellett (1972) assessed the importance of stimulus and response information, separately and combined, on impact reactions to shock. As noted, subjects were divided into four groups that either received response information (detailing the sensations and somatic consequences of electric shock), stimulus information (describing shock apparatus and principles of its operation), both types of information, or neither type. With regard to impact, subjects given both types of information exhibited higher tolerance levels and accepted more shocks before they reported that the shocks were painful, but neither type of information by itself was sufficient to produce these effects.

In a similar set of experiments, Johnson (1973, Experiments I, II, and III) gave subjects brief information about the response sensations of ischemic pain (e.g., "you can expect to feel . . . tingling and aching, followed by numbness") or a control message about the stimulus properties of the ischemic pain procedure (e.g., "A tourniquet filled with air will cause high pressure on your arm"). Subjects given response information reported less emotional distress during the procedure than subjects given stimulus information, although they did not give lower ratings of stimulus intensity (Experiments I and II). Prior to impact, subjects also rated how intense and distressing they thought the pain would be (Experiment III). No difference emerged between the two information groups on this measure.

In a follow-up experiment by Leventhal et al. (1979), subjects given information about the response sensations produced by ice-water immersion of the hand reported less distress and gave lower ratings of stimulus intensity than subjects given a control stimulus-property message or a message about bodily arousal. However, reduced impact did not occur for the response sensation group when they also received additional stimulus information that the immersion procedure would be painful.

So, overall, the laboratory studies show that what-kind-of-event predictability probably reduces impact arousal and that response information may be a more potent stress reducer than other types of information. Several field studies, conducted in hospital settings, have also investigated the effects of preparatory information, particularly on the recovery process (i.e., on postimpact arousal). In the pioneer study, Janis (1958) found that individuals who showed a moderate amount of anticipatory anxiety before surgery had the easiest convalescence. In contrast, individuals with extreme anticipatory anxiety were highly anxious during convalescence, and individuals with minimal anxiety were angry and resentful following surgery. Janis inferred that moderately anxious patients actively sought information about the impending harm and used this knowledge to worry "usefully" about the forthcoming surgery. Highly anxious patients also sought information but then concentrated on terrifying aspects and so were oversensitized to surgery. Low-anxiety patients did not seek information and had overoptimistic estimates about the effects of surgery.

Follow-up work has failed to confirm the presumed curvilinear relationship between level of preoperative anxiety and recovery, yielding either no relation or a linear relation (i.e., the more anticipatory fear, the worse the recovery) (e.g., Cohen & Lazarus, 1973; Johnson et al., 1973; Sime, 1976; Wolfer & Davis, 1970). Results of studies on the relationship between level of preparatory information and recovery have been mixed. Some support for Janis's findings was provided by Egbert, Battit, Welch, and Bartlett (1964). They externalized Janis's inferred information and showed that patients explicitly exposed to information about postoperative effects took less medication after surgery and recovered more speedily than unprepared patients. Unfortunately, information was contaminated both with reassurance and with instructions on how to take controlling actions to reduce pain.

Further studies have had trouble replicating Janis's original results. For example, in a recent study by Langer et al. (1975), where information was uncontaminated by any of the preceding factors, no relation emerged between preparatory information and the postoperative use of medication. Similarly, Vernon and Bigelow (1974) reported that, although preparatory preoperative information resulted in less postoperative anger, it was unrelated to postoperative fear and depression. Moreover, prior to the operation, informed patients seemed more sensitized to the negative aspects of the experience and were more likely to mention pain and possible complications, whereas the uninformed patients were more likely to mention benefits, to deny thoughts about the operation, or to focus their concern on their jobs and families.

The remaining studies all looked at how individual personality characteristics interact with and determine the impact of information. For example, on the basis of a personality questionnaire, Andrew (1970) divided a patient sample into sensitizers (those who typically seek information), avoiders (those who avoid information), and neutrals (those who fall in the middle). One-half of each group was exposed to a tape recording that detailed the surgical procedure. Less medication was taken and earlier discharge occurred for the prepared neutral coping group only. There were no differences between prepared and unprepared sensitizers, perhaps because all these patients had already sought out information about the surgery. For the avoiders, preparation increased the amount of medication used. So different personality traits may influence the effect of what-kind-of-event predictability on recovery.

Cohen and Lazarus (1973) obtained self-report measures of the extent to which patients actually sought information (predictability) or avoided information (unpredictability) prior to surgery. It was found that those who avoided information or who adopted an intermediate strategy spent fewer days in the hospital and had fewer postsurgical complications than those who sought out information. There was a strong correlation between self-reported ratings of anxiety and self-reported ratings of information seeking, but the nature of this relationship was unclear. Information seekers may have sought out more information because they were more anxious, or they may have been made more anxious by the information they obtained.

Patients were also divided into sensitizers, avoiders, and neutrals on the basis of a personality questionnaire as in Andrew's (1970) study, and patients classified as sensitizers took more pain medications. No relation emerged between personality-based ratings of sensitization avoidance and self-report ratings of actual information seeking. This calls into question the validity of Andrew's personality-based categorization.

In a follow-up study by Sime (1976), self-report ratings of presurgical fear, information seeking, and information received from the staff were obtained. There was no relation between self-reported information seeking and recovery measures. However, high-fear subjects who reported receiving little information from the staff showed the poorest recovery. In contrast, increased information slightly retarded the recovery of moderate-fear subjects.

All the above studies show that information can enhance the recovery process for some individuals. Andrew found that sensitizers and neutrals benefited from information and did better than avoiders, who were harmed by information; Cohen and Lazarus found that information avoiders and neutrals did better than information seekers and sensitizers; Sime found that high-fear patients benefited from information but low-fear patients were harmed by information. It is difficult to reconcile the inconsistencies between the three studies because of differences in the nature of measures obtained. Andrew did not obtain a measure of the amount of information actually sought by patients, Cohen and Lazarus did not control the amount of information received by patients, and Sime did not obtain personality-based ratings of sensitization–avoidance.

The results of a recent study help to clarify the effects of information (Miller, 1979f). The sample consisted of 40 gynecological patients about to undergo colposcopy, which is a standardized diagnostic procedure to check for the presence of abnormal (cancerous) cells in the uterus. Patients were first divided into monitors (information seekers) or blunters (information avoiders) based on a recently validated scale that has been shown to predict actual information seeking (e.g., Miller, 1979d,e). Half of each group was then given voluminous information about the procedure and its effects (predictability), and half was given (the usual) minimal information (unpredictability). Information patients heard and viewed such things as what the examination room looked like, how they would be placed on the table, how the doctor would perform the colposcopy (e.g., "The doctor will then pull over the colposcope, turn it on and look through it at your cervix. He may move the speculum slightly, which will cause you to feel some minor pressure"), and what the patient could expect to experience and feel during the days following the procedure (e.g., "You may observe a brownish discharge. This is from the stiptic solution").

For psychophysiological measures, the degree of consistency between a patient's coping style and the level of preparatory information she receives strongly determines her level of arousal. This effect can be seen in Fig. 3. There were initially no pulse rate differences between groups on arrival at the hospital.

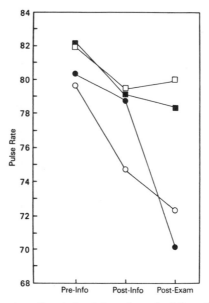

Fig. 3. Mean pulse rate readings before information, after information, and after the examination. (●), Monitors, high information; (■), monitors, low information; (○), blunters, low information; (□), blunters, high information.

The only group to show a decrease in pulse rate immediately prior to the exam were blunters who had been given low information, and they maintained this low pulse rate throughout. By the end of the exam, monitors who had been given high information also showed reduced pulse rate, but low-information monitors and high-information blunters showed sustained higher pulse rates.

Information per se had an effect, with patients exposed to high information showing increased self-reports of anxiety, depression, and discomfort before, immediately after, and in the days following the procedure, irrespective of whether patients were monitors or blunters. However, despite the subjectively arousing cost of information before and after the procedure, it is possible that information may marginally reduce impact. High-information patients engaged in slightly less hand clenching and cried out slightly less during the procedure itself than did low-information patients.

Being a monitor or a blunter was unrelated to the repression–sensitization dimension, which, like the Cohen and Lazarus study, calls into question the meaningfulness of Andrew's results. However, the monitor–blunter coping dimension had an effect on subjective arousal. Monitoring was associated with more anxiety before, during, and after the procedure than blunting, irrespective of level of information. Moreover, during the exam itself, the doctor rated monitors as more anxious than blunters, as indexed by muscular tension in the vaginal area. This is shown in Fig. 4.

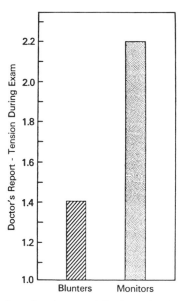

Fig. 4.   Mean doctor ratings of tension (on a 3.0 point scale, where 0.0 = no tension and 3.0 = extreme tension) during the examination.

So, overall, high information was more arousing than low information and monitoring was more arousing than blunting. In addition, arousal was reduced when there was consistency between a patient's coping style and her level of information.

One further field study is worth mentioning because it focused on impact measures obtained during surgery rather than on measures obtained during recovery. In this study (Johnson & Leventhal, 1974), patients about to undergo an endoscopic examination received either sensory preparation (i.e., information composed of both the stimulus and response properties of the procedure) or behavioral preparation (i.e., information relevant to reducing the impact of the procedure). A third group received both types of information, and an additional control group received no information. Combined preparation reduced amount of sedation and amount of gagging. Sensory preparation alone produced both of these effects, and also maintained stable heart rate. Behavioral preparation alone had little effect.

The first basic conclusion to emerge is that what-kind-of-event predictability seems to reduce the impact effects of aversive events, both in the laboratory and under real-life stress conditions. Among the traditional views, these results are contrary to safety signal, which makes no prediction regarding impact. They are consistent with the information seeking, preparatory response, preparatory set, and uncontrollability theories.

The second conclusion has to do with what types of predictability most effectively reduce impact. Although most of the studies collapse all types of information together, there is some indication that response information does reduce impact arousal more effectively than do other types of information (e.g., Johnson, 1973; Leventhal et al., 1979). None of the traditional theories can account for this effect, because they predict that stress reduction should occur with information per se and should not be limited to selected types of information.

The newer theories, which denote conditions under which stress reduction should occur, are more articulate about these results. For example, the data are entirely consistent with Leventhal's view, which explicitly states that only response (sensory) information should reduce stress since only it induces analytical encoding. In contrast, other types of information (e.g., stimulus and arousal) induce emotional encoding and should not reduce stress. These results are also compatible with the blunting view, which predicts that when information facilitates blunting it should reduce stress generally, including perhaps impact arousal. Response information, which focuses on the nonthreatening aspects of an event, enables the individual to avoid and transform threat-relevant cues cognitively. Other types of information (e.g., "This will hurt") sensitize the individual to the threatening aspects of the procedure and interfere with cognitive avoidance and transformation.

The results are also consistent with the script hypothesis, which predicts that predictability reduces stress when it entails a less aversive script to enact. Response information decreases the magnitude of the event (e.g., "This will tingle" as opposed to "This is painful") and so details a less aversive script than other types of information. Finally, according to the arousal view, stress reduction occurs when individuals misattribute their arousal to a neutral source. Calvert-Boyanowky and Leventhal (1975) have shown that arousal information per se seems to reduce *avoidance* behavior, even if the arousal is not misattributed to a neutral source. However, arousal information does not actually reduce the level of arousal associated with an aversive event (Leventhal *et al.*, 1979).

The third conclusion is that the recovery process may be retarded with a combination of stimulus and response information, at least for some individuals. None of the theories makes explicit predictions for recovery. However, any theory that predicts increased anticipatory or impact arousal with predictability can also predict increased postimpact effects if the anticipatory or impact arousal perseveres. The results showing retarded recovery with information are inconsistent with the traditional views, since they all predict beneficial effects or no effects of information on anticipatory and impact arousal. The results are consistent with the information-processing views. Unselected information increases arousal generally and therefore retards recovery to the extent that it prevents a blunting mode from being engaged (blunting hypothesis), induces emotional encoding (analytic encoding hypothesis), or provides an aversive script to enact (script hypothesis). Future work should more directly and systematically investigate the validity of the information-processing views, with experiments designed to differentially test among the competing hypotheses.

Finally, the stress effects of what-kind-of-event predictability are moderated by individual difference variables, with some individuals benefiting more from information and others benefiting more from distraction. These data are consistent with the information-processing views, which link stress reduction to the ability to cognitively avoid, analytically encode, or enact scripts. The blunting hypothesis explicitly predicts individual differences in the ability and inclination to engage in a blunting mode of cognitive processing and the other hypotheses could make a similar prediction.

VII. Summary and Evaluation of the Evidence

As can be seen in the summary of the evidence in Tables III and V, a few issues have been thoroughly researched and adequately resolved, requiring little further empirical work. Conversely, some issues have never been addressed experimentally, and so the crucial data are absent. And the majority of issues have been only partially resolved, with the relevant evidence being suggestive but inconclusive. Future studies that have been pointed out as useful should help to remedy the gaps and confusions.

The choice data under no distraction are very consistent. Here the evidence clearly shows that contingency predictability is preferred to unpredictability. Similarly, subjects probably prefer what-kind-of-event predictability to unpredictability. When the choice is between predictability and unpredictability with distraction, the data for contingency predictability are clear-cut—that is, the preference reverses, and subjects clearly prefer unpredictability. No study has yet investigated either the effects of distraction or response versus stimulus information on preference for what-kind-of-event predictability.

With regard to anticipatory arousal, the existing data are highly consistent for contingency predictability. That is, predictable aversive events probably increase anticipatory arousal, particularly under conditions that support distraction with unpredictability. It is not yet clear whether the same relation holds between anticipatory arousal and what-kind-of-event predictability. However, what-kind-of-event predictability probably increases arousal during the postimpact or recovery phase.

Finally, the data on impact arousal are the least conclusive and the most incoherent and puzzling. In the contingency predictability case, the majority of studies show that predictable aversive events have no apparent effect on impact. On the other hand, the data on what-kind-of-event predictability suggest that impact may be reduced with predictable aversive events, although recovery may be impeded.

VIII.   Final Evaluation of the Theories

Referring again to Tables III and V, it can be seen that no one theory by itself adequately accounts for all the data. Among the traditional views, all the theories fare about the same.

1. Preparatory response relies on making an appropriate response under predictability that reduces the impact of the aversive event. It handles the what-kind-of-event predictability data on choice and impact reasonably well, except for increased postimpact arousal with predictability and the differential effectiveness of stimulus and response information. It fares very badly in contingency predictability, where the clearest evidence exists. Here, it fails to handle impact, is silent on anticipatory arousal, and fails to handle distraction. It is a nicely flexible theory inasmuch as it does not specify or measure the preparatory response; rather it infers its existence.

2. Uncontrollability relies on prediction to better identify the aversive event and thereby to allow selection of an optimal coping strategy. It is strong on the what-kind-of-event data, since the prediction literally identifies the nature of the

event, but provides no account of the superiority of response information or of increased postimpact arousal with predictability. It is hopelessly weak on the contingency predictability data, where the clearest evidence emerges, making incorrect predictions for choice under distraction, anticipatory arousal, and impact. The theory is also rather vague.

3. Preparatory set relies on the occurrence of a large anticipatory response with predictability to diminish the impact response to the aversive event. It does not do particularly well under any class of predictability. It handles the impact data for what-kind-of-event predictability nicely, but is embarrassed by the lack of reduced impact with contingency predictability. It is silent on choice and does not account for the distraction data or the data on response information. It is not at all vague, and this is part of the problem. This theory may be too much tied to the vagaries of electrodermal measurement, confusing underlying phenomena with the electrodermal index of the phenomena. It seems a shallow fact of electrodermal measurement that only a reduced skin conductance response can be elicited right after a substantial response. This does not imply that the whole impact response (including pain) is reduced by the preparatory skin conductance response.

4. Information seeking relies on predictability resolving conflict, thereby reducing arousal and allowing habituation more readily than unpredictability. It handles the what-kind-of-event predictability data adequately, except for greater postimpact arousal with what-kind-of-event predictability. However, it handles all the higher quality contingency predictability data badly. It is embarrassed by the lack of reduced impact under contingency predictability and fails to account for greater anticipatory arousal with contingency predictability. It could add a premise invoking greater fear to a signal that reliably and certainly predicts shock and say that the greater fear swamps the reduced arousal of certainty per se. It fails to account for the distraction data and the response information data but could add another premise like that which is the cornerstone of the blunting hypothesis or the analytic hypothesis. The new theory would be a bit unwieldy, but so are the data. There seems to be something essentially true about information-seeking theory, but it may be more at home in the domain of neutral and positive events than in that of highly aversive events. With neutral and positive events, arousal produced by curiosity and lack of habituation accounts for more of the variance than it does with highly aversive events, where such arousal is swamped by fear and even terror. The theory is also too wedded to electrodermal vagaries, tending to assimilate tonic skin conductance shifts produced by attention and vigilance with phasic skin conductance responses produced by fear.

5. Safety signal theory relies on inhibition of fear produced by the signals for no aversive event. This theory does quite well on choice for contingency predictability and what-kind-of-event predictability, except for choice under dis-

traction. It does not account for the relationship between effectiveness of distraction and anticipatory arousal under contingency predictability or for the relationship between postimpact arousal and what-kind-of-event predictability. Because it is silent on impact, it fails to predict the reduced impact under what-kind-of-event predictability, although it is not inconsistent with the lack of reduced impact under contingency predictability. This theory is too wedded to Pavlovian experiments, particularly infrahuman experiments, and so ignores the fact that humans can engage in cognitive strategies, such as distraction, or form analytic sets. Finally, the theory is sometimes difficult to apply, since one must attempt to identify which periods subjects were likely to have construed as dangerous and which safe in studies that did not make this distinction by design.

It can be seen in the discussion of the theories that each was able to add extra premises from alternative theories to better account for all the data. The views are not mutually exclusive. The safety signal hypothesis does not deny that habituation might reduce impact, information seeking does not deny that humans might prefer to distract under certain conditions, preparatory set does not deny that subjects might relax in the presence of safety signals, etc. As the data stand, any complete account will probably have to rely on the acceptance of more than one set of premises, although the theories become more unwieldy.

Some new hypotheses combine several premises and emphasize the facts that individuals cognitively process information so as to reduce stress and that predictability can facilitate or retard such processing.

1. The blunting hypothesis combines the traditional premises with the premise that humans will distract themselves from danger-related cues, when circumstances permit, and so reduce arousal. The hypothesis handles all the choice data for contingency and what-kind-of-event predictability and is unsurprisingly uniquely strong on the choice data under distraction. It is also uniquely strong on anticipatory arousal with contingency predictability, accounting for the variations in anticipatory arousal that seem to occur with variations in the ease of distraction with unpredictability. It also accounts for greater postimpact arousal with what-kind-of-event predictability. Like safety signal, the hypothesis is not inconsistent with the lack of reduced impact under contingency predictability but needs a premise like habituation to account for impact reduction with what-kind-of-event predictability.

It must be remarked that the blunting hypothesis, like every other view, cannot be reconciled to the pattern of the existing impact data. Why should contingency predictability show no reduced impact but what-kind-of-event predictability show reduced impact? Each theory makes the same prediction for impact under the two classes of predictability. Perhaps it is not the theories that should be embarrassed but the data; this is an area in which more research is clearly called for.

As it stands, the blunting hypothesis is too flexible. However, future research should pin it down empirically since engaging in distraction has empirical consequences. It should not only reduce arousal but also concomitantly reduce processing of external threat-relevant information, and it should occur most effectively under a specified set of facilitating operations and for a specified set of individuals.

2. The analytic encoding hypothesis relies on response information with what-kind-of-event predictability producing an analytic set and thereby allowing habituation. It is expectedly strong on what-kind-of-event predictability, predicting choice and reduced impact (particularly with response information). However, it makes no predictions about contingency predictability.

3. The script hypothesis relies on what-kind-of-event predictability providing subjects with a less aversive script to enact and handles the choice and impact data well. But, like the analytic view, it is silent on contingency predictability.

4. The arousal hypothesis relies on subjects misattributing their arousal to a neutral source under what-kind-of-event predictability, but the evidence does not appear to support this view.

In conclusion, a review of the evidence suggests that humans generally prefer predictable over unpredictable aversive events. There is one exception, however. When individuals can distract themselves from danger-related information, they prefer unpredictable aversive events. The evidence is less clear about anticipatory arousal. Predictable aversive events are more arousing under contingency predictability, particularly when individuals can distract themselves with unpredictability, but the evidence on what-kind-of-event predictability is too inconclusive to draw any conclusions. The evidence on impact is least clear of all. With contingency predictability impact is not reduced. In contrast, with what-kind-of-event predictability, impact seems reduced. A new perspective was advanced that views individuals as information processors who benefit from unpredictability to the extent that they can cognitively avoid or transform threat-relevant information. Otherwise, they prefer and benefit from predictability. Although this is a multifactor framework, it handles the data more adequately than traditional single-factor views.

ACKNOWLEDGMENTS

I am indebted to I. Martin and H. Eysenck, with whom initial discussion of this topic began. I also thank A. Bandura, P. Benacerraf, P. Eelen, R. Grant, H. Lief, W. Miller, W. Mischel, M. Seligman, and J. Volpicelli for their comments and suggestions. The work was partially supported by US PHS Grant MH 19604-07 from the National Institute of Mental Health, Grant RR-09069 from the National Institute of Health, and Temple University Grant-in-Aid of Research 700-053-15.

REFERENCES

Andrew, J. M. Recovery from surgery, with and without preparatory instruction, for three coping styles. *Journal of Personality and Social Psychology,* 1970, **15,** 223–226.

Averill, J. R. Personal control over aversive stimuli and its relationship to stress. *Psychological Bulletin*, 1973, **80**, 286-303.

Averill, J. R., O'Brien, L., & DeWitt, G. W. The influence of response effectiveness on the preference for warning and on psychophysiological stress reactions. *Journal of Personality*, 1977, **45**, 396-418.

Averill, J. R., & Rosenn, M. Vigilant and nonvigilant coping strategies and psychophysiological stress reactions during the anticipation of an electric shock. *Journal of Personality and Social Psychology*, 1972, **23**, 128-141.

Badia, P., McBane, B., Suter, S., & Lewis, P. Preference behavior in an immediate versus variably delayed shock situation with and without a warning signal. *Journal of Experimental Psychology*, 1966, **72**, 847-852.

Bandura, A. Self-efficacy: Toward a unifying theory of behavior change. *Psychological Review*, 1977, **84**, 191-215.

Bandura, A. *Self-efficacy: An integrative construct*. Invited address presented at the Western Psychological Association, San Diego, April 1979.

Bandura, A. Self-referent thought: A developmental analysis of self-efficacy. In J. H. Flavell & L. D. Ross (Eds.). *Social cognitive development: Frontiers and possible futures*. London and New York: Cambridge University Press, 1981.

Barber, T. X., & Hahn, K. W. Physiological and subjective response to pain-producing stimulation under hypnotically-suggested and working-imagined "analgesia." *Journal of Abnormal and Social Psychology*, 1962, **65**, 411-418.

Berlyne, D. E. *Conflict, arousal and curiosity*. New York: McGraw-Hill, 1960.

Blitz, B., & Dinnerstein, A. J. Role of attentional focus in pain perception: Manipulation of response to noxious stimulation by instructions. *Journal of Abnormal Psychology*, 1971, **77**, 42-45.

Bloom, L. J., Houston, B. K., Holmes, D. J., & Burish, T. S. The effectiveness of attention diversion and situational redefinition for reducing stress to a nonambiguous threat. *Journal of Research in Personality*, 1977, **11**, 83-96.

Bobey, M. J., & Davidson, P. O. Psychological factors affecting pain tolerance. *Journal of Psychosomatic Research*, 1970, **14**, 371-376.

Bowers, K. S. Pain, anxiety, and perceived control. *Journal of Consulting and Clinical Psychology*, 1968, **32**, 596-602.

Bowers, K. S. The effects of UCS temporal uncertainty on heart rate and pain. *Psychophysiology*, 1971, **8**, 382-389. (a)

Bowers, K. S. Heart rate and GSR concomitants of vigilance and arousal. *Canadian Journal of Psychology*, 1971, **25**, 175-184. (b)

Breznitz, S. Incubation of threat: Duration of anticipation and false alarm as determinants of the fear reaction to an unavoidable frightening event. *Journal of Research in Personality*, 1967, **2**, 173-179.

Byrne, D. The repression-sensitization scale: Rationale, reliability, and validity. *Journal of Personality*, 1961, **29**, 334-349.

Calvert-Boyanowsky, J., & Leventhal, H. The role of information in attenuating behavioral responses to stress: A reinterpretation of the misattribution phenomenon. *Journal of Personality and Social Psychology*, 1975, **32**, 214-221.

Chorney, R. L., Efran, J., Ascher, L. M., & Lukens, M. D. *The performance of monitors and blunters during painful stimulation*. Paper presented at the Eastern Psychological Association, New York, April 1981.

Cohen, F., & Lazarus, R. S. Active coping processes, coping dispositions, and recovery from surgery. *Psychosomatic Medicine*, 1973, **35**, 375-389.

Cook, J. O., & Barnes, L. W., Jr. Choice of delay of inevitable shock. *Journal of Abnormal and Social Psychology*, 1964, **68**, 669-672.

Corah, N. J., & Boffa, J. Perceived control, self-observation, and response to aversive stimulation. *Journal of Personality and Social Psychology*, 1970, **16**, 1–4.

D'Amato, M. R., & Gumenik, W. E. Some effects of immediate versus randomly delayed shock on an instrumental response and cognitive processes. *Journal of Abnormal and Social Psychology*, 1960, **60**, 64–67.

Egbert, L. D., Battit, G. E., Welch, C. E., & Bartlett, M. K. Reduction of postoperative pain by encouragement and instruction of patients. A study of doctor-patient rapport. *The New England Journal of Medicine*, 1964, **270**, 825–827.

Elliott, R. Effects of uncertainty about the nature and advent of a noxious stimulus (shock) upon heart rate. *Journal of Personality and Social Psychology*, 1966, **3**, 353–356.

Elliot, R. Tonic heart rate: Experiments on the effects of collative variables lead to a hypothesis about its motivational significance. *Journal of Personality and Social Psychology*, 1969, **12**, 211–228.

Epstein, S. The nature of anxiety with emphasis upon its relationship with expectancy. In S. D. Spielberger (Ed.), *Anxiety: Current trends in theory and research* (Vol. II). New York: Academic Press, 1972.

Epstein, S. Expectancy and magnitude of reaction to a noxious UCS. *Psychophysiology*, 1973, **10**, 100–107.

Epstein, S., Breitner, L., & Hoobler, R. *The influence of hope versus resignation on anticipatory arousal and reaction to the impact of an unavoidable noxious stimulus.* Paper presented at the meeting of the Society for Psychophysiological Research, New Orleans, October 1970.

Epstein, S., & Clarke, S. Heart rate and skin conductance during experimentally induced anxiety: Effects of anticipated intensity of noxious stimulation and experience. *Journal of Experimental Psychology*, 1970, **84**, 105–112.

Epstein, S., & Kling, J. S. Reactivity during anticipation and impact of an unavoidable noxious stimulus as a function of time uncertainty. Unpublished study, 1971. Cited in S. Epstein, Expectancy and magnitude of reaction to a noxious UCS, *Psychophysiology*, 1973, **10**, 100–107.

Epstein, S., & Roupenian, A. Heart rate and skin conductance during experimentally induced anxiety: The effect of uncertainty about receiving a noxious stimulus. *Journal of Personality and Social Psychology*, 1970, **16**, 20–28.

Folkins, C. H. Temporal factors and the cognitive mediators of stress reaction. *Journal of Personality and Social Psychology*, 1970, **14**, 173–184.

Furedy, J. J. Test of the preparatory adaptive response interpretation of aversive classical autonomic conditioning. *Journal of Experimental Psychology*, 1970, **84**, 301–307.

Furedy, J. J. Auditory and autonomic tests of the preparatory-adaptive-response interpretation of classical aversive conditioning. *Journal of Experimental Psychology*, 1973, **99**, 280–283.

Furedy, J. J. An integrative progress report on informational control in humans: Some laboratory findings and methodological claims. *Australian Journal of Psychology*, 1975, **27**, 61–83.

Furedy, J. J., & Chan, R. M. Failures of information to reduce rated aversiveness of unmodifiable shock. *Australian Journal of Psychology*, 1971, **23**, 85–94.

Furedy, J. J., & Doob, A. N. Autonomic responses and verbal reports in further tests of the preparatory-adaptive-response interpretation of reinforcement. *Journal of Experimental Psychology*, 1971, **89**, 258–264. (a)

Furedy, J. J., & Doob, A. N. Classical aversive conditioning of human digital volume-pulse change and tests of the preparatory-adaptive response interpretation of reinforcement. *Journal of Experimental Psychology*, 1971, **89**, 403–407. (b)

Furedy, J. J., & Doob, A. N. Signalling unmodifiable shocks: Limits on human informational cognitive control. *Journal of Personality and Social Psychology*, 1972, **21**, 111–115.

Furedy, J. J., Fainstat, D., Kulin, P., Lasko, L., & Nichols, S. Preparatory-response versus information-seeking interpretations of preference for signalled loud noise: Further limits on human informational cognitive control. *Psychonomic Science*, 1972, **27**, 108–110.

Furedy, J. J., & Ginsberg, S. Effects of varying signalling and intensity of shock on an unconfounded and novel electrodermal autonomic index in a variable and long-interval classical trace conditioning paradigm. *Psychophysiology,* 1973, **10,** 328-334.

Furedy, J. J., & Klajner, F. Unconfounded autonomic indexes of the aversiveness of signalled and unsignalled shocks. *Journal of Experimental Psychology,* 1972, **93,** 313-318.

Gaebelein, J., Taylor, S. P., & Borden, R. Effects of an external cue on psychophysiological reactions to an external event. *Psychophysiology,* 1974, **11,** 315-320.

Gal, R., & Lazarus, R. S. The role of activity in anticipating and confronting stressful situations. *Journal of Human Stress,* 1975, **1,** 4-20.

Gatchel, R. J. & Proctor, J. D. Physiological correlates of learned helplessness in man. *Journal of Abnormal Psychology,* 1976, **85,** 27-34.

Gatchel, R. J., McKinney, M. E., & Koebernick, L. F. Learned helplessness, depression, and physiological responding. *Psychophysiology,* 1977, **14,** 25-31.

Geer, J. H., Davison, G. C., & Gatchel, R. J. Reduction of stress in humans through nonveridical perceived control of aversive stimulation. *Journal of Personality and Social Psychology,* 1970, **16,** 731-738.

Geer, J. H., & Maisel, E. Evaluating the effects of the prediction-control confound. *Journal of Personality and Social Psychology,* 1972, **23,** 314-319.

Glass, D. C., Reim, B., & Singer, J. E. Behavioral consequences of adaptation to controllable and uncontrollable noise. *Journal of Experimental Social Psychology,* 1971, **7,** 244-257.

Glass, D. C., & Singer, J. E. *Urban stress: Experiments on noise and social stressors.* New York: Academic Press, 1972.

Glass, D. C., Singer, J. E., & Friedman, L. N. Psychic cost of adaptation to an environmental stressor. *Journal of Personality and Social Psychology,* 1969, **12,** 200-210.

Glass, D. C., Snyder, M. L., & Singer, J. E. Periodic and aperiodic noise: The safety signal hypothesis and noise aftereffects. *Physiological Psychology,* 1978, **1,** 361-363.

Goldstein, M. J. The relationship between coping and avoidance behavior and response to fear-arousing propaganda. *Journal of Abnormal and Social Psychology,* 1959, **58,** 247-252.

Grings, W. W. Preparatory set variables related to classical conditioning of autonomic responses. *Psychological Review,* 1960, **67,** 243-250.

Grings, W. W. Anticipatory and preparatory electrodermal behavior in paired stimulus situations. *Psychophysiology,* 1969, **5,** 597-611.

Grings, W. W. Cognitive factors in electrodermal conditioning. *Psychological Bulletin,* 1973, **79,** 200-210.

Grings, W. W., & Sukoneck, H. I. Prediction probability as a determiner of anticipatory and preparatory electrodermal behavior. *Journal of Experimental Psychology,* 1971, **91,** 310-317.

Holmes, D. S., & Houston, B. K. Effectiveness of situation redefinition and affective isolation in coping with stress. *Journal of Personality and Social Psychology,* 1974, **29,** 212-218.

Houston, B. K. Control over stress, locus of control, and response to stress. *Journal of Personality and Social Psychology,* 1972, **21,** 249-255.

Janis, I. L. *Psychological stress.* New York: Wiley, 1958.

Johnson, J. E. Effects of accurate expectations about sensations on the sensory and distress components of pain. *Journal of Personality and Social Psychology,* 1973, **27,** 261-275.

Johnson, J. E., & Leventhal, H. Effects of accurate expectations and behavioral instructions on reactions during a noxious medical examination. *Journal of Personality and Social Psychology,* 1974, **29,** 710-718.

Jones, A., Bentler, P. M., & Petry, G. The reduction of uncertainty concerning future pain. *Journal of Abnormal Psychology,* 1966, **71,** 87-94.

Katkin, E. S. Relationship between manifest anxiety and two indices of autonomic response to stress. *Journal of Personality and Social Psychology,* 1965, **2,** 324-333.

Katkin, E. S. The relationship between a measure of transitory anxiety and spontaneous autonomic activity. *Journal of Abnormal Psychology*, 1966, **71**, 142-146.

Kilpatrick, D. G. Differential responsiveness of two electrodermal indices to psychological stress and performance of a complex cognitive task. *Psychophysiology*, 1972, **9**, 218-226.

Klemp, G. O., & Rodin, J. Effects of uncertainty, delay, and focus of attention on reactions to an aversive situation. *Journal of Experimental Social Psychology*, 1976, **12**, 416-421.

Lacey, J. L. Somatic response patterning and stress: Some revisions of activation theory. In M. H. Appley and R. Trumbel (Eds.), *Psychological stress: Issues in research*. New York: Appleton, 1967.

Lang, P. J. Stimulus control, response control and desensitization of fear. In D. Levis (Ed.), *Learning approaches to therapeutic behavior change*. Chicago, Illinois: Aldine Press, 1970.

Langer, E. J., & Abelson, R. P. The semantics of asking a favor: How to get help without really dying. *Journal of Personality and Social Psychology*, 1972, **24**, 26-32.

Langer, E. S., Janis, I. L., & Wolfer, J. A. Reduction of psychological stress in surgical patients. *Journal of Experimental Social Psychology*, 1975, **11**, 155-165.

Lanzetta, J. T., & Driscoll, J. M. Preference for information about an uncertain but unavoidable outcome. *Journal of Personality and Social Psychology*, 1966, **3**, 96-102.

Lazarus, R. S. *Psychological stress and the coping process*. New York: McGraw-Hill, 1966.

Lazarus, R. S., & Alfert, E. Short-circuiting of threat by experimentally altering cognitive appraisal. *Journal of Abnormal and Social Psychology*, 1966, **69**, 195-205.

Lazarus, R. S., Opton, E. M., Nomikos, M. S., & Rankin, N. O. The principle of short-circuiting of threat: Further evidence. *Journal of Personality*, 1965, **33**, 622-635.

Leventhal, H., Brown, D., Shacham, S., & Engquist, G. Effects of preparatory information about sensations, threat of pain, attention on cold pressor distress. *Journal of Personality and Social Psychology*, 1979, **37**, 688-714.

Lovibond, S. H. The aversiveness of uncertainty: An analysis in terms of activation and information theory. *Australian Journal of Psychology*, 1968, **20**, 85-91.

Maltzman, I., & Wolff, C. Preference for immediate versus delayed noxious stimulation and the concomitant G.S.R. *Journal of Experimental Psychology*, 1970, **83**, 76-79.

Mansueto, C. S., & Desiderato, O. External versus self-produced determinants of fear reaction after shock threat. *Journal of Research in Personality*, 1971, **5**, 30-36.

Mead, P. G. The effect of orientation passages on patient stress prior to dentistry. *The Psychological Record*, 1970, **20**, 479-480.

Meichenbaum, D. *Cognitive-behavior modification: An integrative approach*. New York: Plenum, 1977.

Miller, S. M. Controllability and human stress: Method, evidence and theory. *Behavior Research and Therapy*, 1979, **17**, 287-304. (a)

Miller, S. M. Coping with impending stress: Psychophysiological and cognitive correlates of choice. *Psychophysiology*, 1979, **16**, 572-581. (b)

Miller, S. M. *A laboratory investigation of potential control under conditions of threat: Effects on choice and arousal*. Unpublished, Temple University, 1979. (c)

Miller, S. M. *Monitors vs. blunters: Validation of a questionnaire to assess two cognitive styles for coping with threat*. Unpublished, Temple University, 1979. (d)

Miller, S. M. *Coping with psychological threat by monitoring vs. blunting*. Unpublished, Temple University, 1979. (e)

Miller, S. M. *The interacting effects of information and coping style in adapting to gynecologic stress: When the doctor should tell all*. Unpublished, Temple University, 1979. (f)

Miller, S. M. Why having control reduces stress: If I can stop the roller coaster I don't want to get off. In J. Garber & M. E. P. Seligman (Eds.), *Human helplessness: Theory and applications*. New York: Academic Press, 1980. (a)

Miller, S. M. When is a little information a dangerous thing?: Coping with stressful life-events by monitoring vs. blunting. In S. Levine and H. Ursin (Eds.), *Coping and health*. Proceedings of a NATO conference. New York: Plenum, 1980. (b)

Miller, S. M., & Grant, R. The blunting hypothesis: A view of predictability and human stress. In P. O. Sjöden, S. Bates, & W. S. Dockens (Eds.), *Trends in behavior therapy*. New York: Academic Press, 1979.

Miller, S. M., & Wagner, A. *Individual differences in response to information and choice before an aversive gynecological procedure*. Unpublished, Temple University, 1980.

Mills, R. T., & Krantz, D. S. Information, choice, and reactions to stress: A field experiment in a blood bank with laboratory analogue. *Journal of Personality and Social Psychology*, 1979, **37**, 608-620.

Mischel, W. On the interface of cognition and personality. *American Psychologist*, 1979, **34**, 740-754.

Mischel, W., Ebbesen, E. B., & Zeiss, A. R. Selective attention to the self: Situational and dispositional determinants. *Journal of Personality and Social Psychology*, 1973, **27**, 129-142.

Mischel, W., Ebbesen, E. B., & Zeiss, A. R. Determinants of selective memory about the self. *Journal of Consulting and Clinical Psychology*, 1976, **46**, 92-103.

Monat, A. Temporal uncertainty, anticipation time, and cognitive coping under threat. *Journal of Human Stress*, 1976, **2**, 32-43.

Monat, A., Averill, J. R., & Lazarus, R. S. Anticipatory stress and coping reactions under various conditions of uncertainty. *Journal of Personality and Social Psychology*, 1972, **24**, 237-253.

Neufeld, R. W. J. The effect of experimentally altered cognitive appraisal on pain tolerance. *Psychonomic Science*, 1970, **20**, 106-107.

Neufeld, R. W. J., & Davidson, P. O. The effects of vicarious and cognitive rehearsal on pain tolerance. *Journal of Psychosomatic Research*, 1971, **15**, 329-335.

Niemelä, P. Electrodermal responses as a function of quantified threat. *Scandinavian Journal of Psychology*, 1969, **10**, 49-56.

Nisbett, R. E., & Schachter, S. Cognitive manipulation of pain. *Journal of Experimental Social Psychology*, 1966, **2**, 227-236.

Obrist, P. A., Webb, R. A., & Sutterer, J. R. Heart rate and somatic changes during aversive conditioning and a simple reaction time task. *Psychophysiology*, 1969, **5**, 696-723.

Obrist, P. A., Webb, R. A., Sutterer, J. R., & Howard, J. L. The cardiac-somatic relationship: Some reformulations. *Psychophysiology*, 1970, **6**, 569-587. (a)

Obrist, P. A., Webb, R. A., Sutterer, J. R., & Howard, J. L. Cardiac deceleration and reaction time: An evaluation of two hypotheses. *Psychophysiology*, 1970, **6**, 695-706. (b)

Öhman, A., Björkstrand, P., & Ellström, P. Effect of explicit trial-by-trial information about shock probability in long interstimulus interval GSR conditioning. *Journal of Experimental Psychology*, 1973, **98**, 145-151.

Peeke, S. C., & Grings, W. W. Magnitude of UCR as a function of variability in the CS-UCS relationship. *Journal of Experimental Psychology*, 1968, **77**, 64-69.

Perkins, C. C., Jr. The stimulus conditions which follow learned responses. *Psychological Review*, 1955, **62**, 341-348.

Perkins, C. C., Jr. An analysis of the concept or reinforcement. *Psychological Review*, 1968, **75**, 155-172.

Pervin, L. A. The need to predict and control under conditions of threat. *Journal of Personality*, 1963, **31**, 570-587.

Price, K. P., & Geer, J. H. Predictable and unpredictable aversive events: Evidence for the safety-signal hypothesis. *Psychonomic Science*, 1972, **26**, 215-216.

Rachman, S. *The meanings of fear*. Middlesex: Penguin, 1974.

Rescorla, R. A. Pavlovian conditioning and its proper control procedures. *Psychological Review,* 1967, **74,** 71-79.

Rothbart, M., & Mellinger, M. Attention and responsivity to remote dangers: A laboratory simulation for assessing reactions to threatening events. *Journal of Personality and Social Psychology,* 1972, **24,** 132-142.

Sandman, C. A. Physiological responses during escape and nonescape from stress in field independent and field dependent subjects. *Biological Psychology,* 1975, **2,** 205-216.

Schachter, S. The interaction of cognitive and physiological determinants of emotional state. In L. Berkowitz (Ed.), *Advances in experimental social psychology* (Vol. 1). New York: Academic Press, 1964.

Schachter, S., & Singer, J. E. Cognitive, social, and physiological determinants of emotional state. *Psychological Review,* 1962, **69,** 379-300.

Seligman, M. E. P. *Helplessness: On depression, development, and death.* San Francisco, California: Freeman, 1975.

Seligman, M. E. P., Maier, S. F., & Solomon, R. L. Unpredictable and uncontrollable aversive events. In F. R. Brush (Ed.), *Aversive conditioning and learning.* New York: Academic Press, 1971.

Sime, A. M. Relationship of preoperative fear, type of coping, and information received about surgery to recovery from surgery. *Journal of Personality and Social Psychology,* 1976, **34,** 716-724.

Sokolov, Y. N. *Perception and the conditioned reflex.* New York: MacMillan, 1963.

Speisman, J., Lazarus, R., Mordkoff, A., & Davison, L. Experimental reduction of stress based on ego-defense theory. *Journal of Abnormal and Social Psychology,* 1964, **68,** 367-380.

Staub, E. *Reduction of a specific fear by information combined with exposure to the feared stimulus.* Proceedings of the 76th APA Annual Convention, 1968.

Staub, E., & Kellett, D. S. Increasing pain tolerance by information about aversive stimuli. *Journal of Personality and Social Psychology,* 1972, **21,** 198-203.

Szpiler, J. A., & Epstein, S. Availability of an avoidance response as related to autonomic arousal. *Journal of Abnormal Psychology,* 1976, **85,** 73-82.

Vernon, D. T. A. Information seeking in a natural stress situation. *Journal of Applied Psychology,* 1971, **55,** 359-363.

Vernon, D. T. A., & Bigelow, D. A. Effect of information about a potentially stressful situation on responses to stress impact. *Journal of Personality and Social Psychology,* 1974, **29,** 50-59.

Wachtel, P. L. Anxiety, attention, and coping with threat. *Journal of Abnormal Psychology,* 1968, **73,** 137-143.

Weiss, J. M. Somatic effects of predictable and unpredictable shock. *Psychosomatic Medicine,* 1970, **32,** 397-409.

Williams, J. G. L., Jones, J. R., Workhoven, M. N., & Williams, B. The psychological control of preoperative anxiety. *Psychophysiology,* 1975, **12,** 50-54.

Wolfer, J. A., & Davis, C. E. Assessment of surgical patients' preoperative welfare. *Nursing Research,* 1970, **19,** 402-414.

PERCEPTUAL AND JUDGMENTAL PROCESSES IN SOCIAL CONTEXTS[1]

Arnold Upmeyer

INSTITUT FÜR PSYCHOLOGIE
TECHNISCHE UNIVERSITÄT BERLIN
BERLIN, FEDERAL REPUBLIC OF GERMANY

I. Introduction to Theory

This contribution attempts to demonstrate systematically that social judgment should be considered a two-step process. The first step consists of the perception, storage, and internal representation of some stimulus or stimuli. The second step consists of a response which may be thought of as the external presentation of the internal representation.

The idea of breaking down the process into two separate parts is not new. In

[1]This contribution was supported by research grants from the Deutsche Forschungsgemeinschaft alloted to the Sonderforschungsbereich 24 ''Sozial- und wirtschaftspsychologische Entscheidungs forschung'' at the University of Mannheim, West Germany. I am grateful to Dr. H. S. Upshaw for his critical comments and to Laura Stevens for helping to improve my English.

257

the field of psychophysics, this idea forms a central part of the theory of signal detection (Swets, Tanner, & Birdsall, 1961) and of the input–output-transformation model of Curtis, Atneave, and Harrington (1968). In cognitive psychology, the notion is common to various models of information processing (Broadbent, 1958; Neisser, 1967; Norman, 1968; Erdelyi, 1974). Within the last 25 years, signal detection methodology has become routine in the study of perception, memory, problem-solving, discriminative learning, test construction, and so on.

In contrast, social psychologists have rarely employed signal detection methodology or any of the more sophisticated methods existing to isolate the effect of response modes in magnitude estimation. In our discipline and in the social sciences in general, we rely to a high degree on verbal reports about "perceived" variables, and usually we assess the effects of those variables with a single indicator, namely the mean of a response distribution on an absolute scale. From the point of view of a two-step theory of social judgment, this form of measurement confounds the internal representation and the response tendency when a person deals with a response mode. Of course, this becomes harmless if the state of the internal representation and the nature of the expressed response are congruent. However, we know intuitively and from experimental evidence that responses are often distorted and do not accurately reflect the state of the internal representation. Among the numerous well-known examples of such masking effects in social psychology are the Asch-type conformity response, the Rosenthal effect, acquiescence sets, negativity bias, social desirability bias, etc. This list of "special biases" can be expanded by consulting the literature on field research methodology which offers practical advice on how to avoid response sets in questionnaire construction.

What is needed in order to overcome confusion engendered by the accumulation of unsystematic biases is a theory of social judgment, and we feel that such a theory should be offered by social psychology. Figure 1 summarizes the processes and factors to be included in such a theory. This article is meant to constitute a major step toward the formation of such a theory.

A. DIFFERENTIATION

1. Differentiation Task and Stimulus Definition

A person is said to perform a differentiation task if there exist two sets of stimuli having different attributes and the individual must decide to which of the two sets a given stimulus belongs. In the psychophysical literature (see Luce, 1963) one usually finds a more detailed taxonomy of judgment tasks which resembles our definition, that is, detection, discrimination, and identification. In a detection task, the question is, "Has a particular stimulus been presented at all?" In the detection of an acoustical signal, the stimulus is usually a tone of

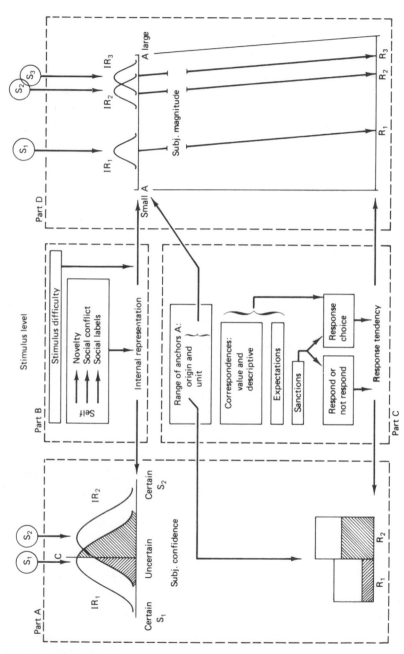

Fig. 1. Graphical summary of processes and factors. Part A, the differentiation process; part B, factors affecting internal representations; part C, factors affecting response tendencies; part D, the magnitude estimation process.

fixed frequency and fixed loudness which must be distinguished from background noise. In a discrimination task one asks, "Which of two stimuli has more
of a particular attribute?" This task was developed to determine the difference
limen of two stimuli on one particular stimulus dimension. The two stimuli to be
differentiated are physically well defined on the dimension to be judged. The
typical question in an identification task is, "Among all possibilities, which
stimulus has been presented?" In this case, the stimuli supposedly differ in more
than one attribute and, thus, the subjective distinction of the stimuli can be based
on many attributes simultaneously. Often the stimuli to be identified are more
than two, although two are sufficient to perform the task. Ethnic identification is
a well-known example from social psychological research.

A comparison of the definitions seems to show that each implies different
criteria, such as the number of attributes of perceived stimuli, the number of
stimuli to be judged, and the nature of background or context in the judgment
situation. The definitions are task-oriented and do not refer too much to the
nature of the underlying psychological processes. For a theoretical analysis, we
have to ask if each task will generate its own process or, alternatively, if the
common characteristics of task-induced processes prevail. We believe the latter
is more realistic in social judgment contexts, and we will discuss the reasons for
our position.

First, it is hard to imagine a discrimination task where we can be sure that a
subject uses only a single attribute on which the discrimination among stimuli is
based. Even in the psychophysical laboratory, there are usually so many context
variables correlated with the differences between two stimuli that even a well-
trained experimenter is unable to control for them. In the field of social psychology, we are not able to provide these controls, and often we do not want to
proceed like psychophysicists for other reasons.

Second, it is obvious that an observer in a detection task uses multiple
attributes to distinguish a signal from its background. In psychophysics, the
background is a complex stimulus aggregate, whereas the signal is comparatively
simple and well defined in terms of its physical parameters. Thus, the task of the
observer is to judge whether these attributes are existent or absent in a stimulus
situation. By way of contrast, the observer in a discrimination task does not
doubt that both stimuli can be distinguished from the background. However, this
conceptual difference between detection and discrimination refers to a categorization of stimulus situations, not to the psychological process of analyzing
stimuli. In both cases, the judgment of the distribution of attributes is the core of
the psychological process.

Finally, the same is true for identification tasks by definition. Thus, we
could have used the term identification instead of differentiation to summarize
the first kind of judgment processes. We hesitated to use it because the literature
on the psychology of judgment tends to employ this term for a task in which a

given stimulus has to be identified out of a whole set of possibilities, that is, more than two. The theory presented here assumes that a person is able to compare only two stimuli at the same time and that multiple-stimuli judgments are based on single comparisons. Our theoretical analysis will not consider how a person proceeds from single comparisons to the identification of a stimulus from a set of stimuli.

2. The Differentiation Process

Space does not allow the presentation of a detailed outline of signal detection theory which underlines the differentiation process. The interested reader is referred to the voluminous literature (e.g., Swets *et al.,* 1961; Green & Swets, 1966; Swets, 1973; Coombs, Dawes, & Tversky, 1970). Our presentation is confined to the essential features and to problems raised by adapting signal detection theory to social judgment. The differentiation process is depicted graphically in the upper section of Fig. 1A.

1. A person who begins a differentiation task must have an internalized concept of how two sets of stimuli may differ. Usually this notion is conveyed to the person by instructions, but it can also, though rarely, be self-developed. Internalized concepts are often derived from idealized cases such as skin color.

2. The two sets of stimuli are internally represented as Thurstonian discriminal processes. The ability to differentiate the two sets depends on the relative amount of overlap of the two subjective distributions. In the parametric case, differentiation ability is defined and measured as

$$d' = (M_{s+n} - M_n)/S$$

that is, by the difference between the means of the subjective distributions divided by their standard deviation if the two deviations are equal. Nonparametric analogs to d' are reported in the literature (e.g., Banks, 1970).

3. In setting up a differentiation task, the experimenter typically selects the attributes by which the stimulus sets may be exclusively defined independently of the subject. However, if the sets intersect on predetermined attributes, then the degree of intersection establishes the upper limit of differentiation performance.

4. The continuum underlying subjective distributions can be formally defined as a decision likelihood ratio, as in statistical decision theory (Wald, 1950). Psychologically, this continuum is interpreted as a bipolar confidence dimension (see Fig. 1). The individual's confidence is determined by the integration of a large number of attributes that contribute to the particular distribution of the two sets.

The analogy to statistical decision theory raises the problems of whether subjective elements forming the distribution are really independently sampled from stimulus populations and whether the elements will be invariant over time. These assumptions are most unrealistic in social psychology when meaningful material enters a signal detection analysis. Asch's work on impression formation has shown that nonindependence and ambiguity of meaning is more likely to be the rule than the exception. However, the amount of overlap of distributions formed by finite sets of observations can still be a fruitful measure of differentiation ability.

3. The Differentiation Response

The individual performing a differentiation task is usually provided with two response modes, R_1 and R_2, to indicate to which of the two sets, S_1 or S_2, a given stimulus belongs. The way in which a response mode is formulated often tends to circumscribe the sets to be differentiated and will then point specifically to certain subjective distributions. It can also happen that the person is reluctant to display an open response at all. Thus, the response process consists basically of two decisions: (a) to respond or not to respond, and (b) the choice between one of two response alternatives. A central feature of the present theory is the proposition that these two decisions are made largely independently of the differentiation itself. In other words, the forms of the subjective distributions and their relative amount of overlap do not affect the decision between response categories R_1 and R_2.

Empirical evidence for the proposition that the decision to respond or not to respond is largely independent of the acquisition of stimuli was provided by the work of Bandura and his associates (Bandura, 1965, 1971; Bandura, Ross, & Ross, 1963). Bandura was able to show that a set of stimuli can be stored at once depending on a person's level of attention; however, the decision to reproduce stimuli in terms of responses depends on the reinforcing properties of the situation in which they occur. In the present theory, no distinction in this regard is postulated between *verbal* or *behavioral* responses, for which we feel we can rely on results from cross-modality matching studies (Stevens, 1971).

Empirical evidence for the proposition that the choice between two responses is independent of the differentiation process has been reported by numerous signal detection researchers (e.g., Swets *et al.,* 1961). As shown in Fig. 1A, a variable decision criterion c is imposed on the subjective distributions when a person is asked to decide repeatedly between response alternatives R_1 and R_2. As a consequence, the person generates two frequency distributions of correct and wrong responses matching the areas under the subjective distribution left- and right-hand side of the imposed decision criterion.

If the criterion c is congruent with the ordinate at the point where the subjective distributions intersect, the response can be considered to be unbiased and stimulus-dependent, as assumed in Thurstonian psychophysics. If the criterion departs from the symmetry point, we can speak of a response bias and measure this tendency by $p(R_1)$.

The presence of the variable criterion is thought to have no effect on the distributions because they are stimulus-dependent. The only factor that changes is the relative proportion of incorrect to correct responses in each response category, but this proportion depends on the distributions.

Two exceptions to this rule should be discussed. First, consider the case of a finite set of elements which form discrete distributions—the realistic case in social psychological research problems. If a person is able to differentiate between the two distributions perfectly, he will answer R_1 when stimuli from S_1 are presented and R_2 when stimuli from S_2 are presented. In this case, responses are stimulus-dependent. Second, as shown by the Asch-type conformity experiments, we must take into account the fact that some individuals will only respond R_1 in the presence of S_2. Here, unanimous pressure from a group simply exerts more influence in determining the response than do the actual stimulus attributes. If we were able to remove all social influences from the judgment situation, we might then approach the Thurstonian ideal of a symmetrical, stimulus-dependent response criterion. However, in social psychology, the investigation of such response shifts may be as interesting as the study of differentiation. We may conclude from this discussion that the response criterion will be stimulus-dependent only under the condition that all other potential sources of influence are removed from the judgment context.

In order to better define the two stages in our theory, we introduce the following breakdown as a description of the typical course of events in information processing: (1) stimulus perception and representation in memory; (2) emergence of a differentiation task and formation of subjective distributions; (3) decision as to whether to respond; and (4) decision among response alternatives. *Differentiation ability* refers to processes (1) and (2); *response tendency* refers to (3) and (4).

4. Factors Affecting Differentiation Ability

An overview of the factors discussed below is presented in Fig. 1B.

a. Physical Stimulus Aspects.   As reflected in the early publications in signal detection, stimulus differentiation was believed to depend only on the physical features of the stimulus situation. In psychoacoustics, the term *signal strength* was coined and operationalized to be the loudness of a signal of fixed frequency to be detected in white noise. Detectability (a special case of our differentiation concept) was said to be influenced by the relative difference of physical events, that is, for the physical dimension loudness, the loudness of the signal relative to the loudness of white noise (Tanner & Swets, 1954; Swets, 1961; Swets et al., 1961). The remaining stimulus-independent sources of variance in a judgment task were referred to as *attitudes* (Swets et al., 1961) or *motivation* (Banks, 1970) and were supposed to enter the response bias measure. These views correspond to concepts within the traditional program of psychophysics with regard to the assessment of isomorphism between physical and subjective quantities. The new conception of detectability measure d' represents a major breakthrough when compared with the traditional psychophysical methods employed in threshold assessment, such as the method of average error, the method of minimal changes, and the constant methods. The shortcomings inherent in these methods became apparent in the controversy which emerged regarding research on the perception of taboo words.

The invariance of d' with respect to situational context is not an untestable theoretical assumption; it was, in fact, subjected to empirical research following Atkinson's (1963) proposal of the variable sensitivity theory of signal detection. Atkinson held that d' would be greatly affected by the motivational state of the subject in a detection task and thus challenged the invariance property of d'. Defending the virtues of invariance, Swets and Sewall (1963) performed an experiment in which they tested the variability of d' in the presence of different subject motivation. Although they claimed to have demonstrated that d' is largely unaffected by other than physical features of the stimulus, one can criticize their study as an example of the ability of psychophysicists to remove effectively social influences in a laboratory environment (for details, see Upmeyer, 1971, p. 285).

Expanding signal detection concepts to the more general process of differentiation in memory tasks where meaningful elements form subjective distributions, one comes to suspect that a much higher degree of variance exists with respect to individual differences and motivation as compared to the Swets and Sewall data. The extensive use of signal detection methodology in the study of memory (e.g., Banks, 1970) has gradually convinced researchers that differentiation ability is affected by factors other than stimulus properties. In our view, the term *stimulus difficulty* seems more appropriate than *signal strength*, thus indicating the dependence of d' on external stimulus-bound factors as well as on experientially derived internal factors.

Certainly one of the important external factors affecting memory is the number of elements in the sets to be differentiated, whereas a prominent internal factor is undoubtedly familiarity with the elements to be differentiated prior to exposure to motivational influences.

b. Selective Attention as a Response-Independent Determinant. In line with the traditional memory and perception research position, we believe that attention will affect differentiation ability. Unfortunately, attention itself is a rather vague concept. Psychologists agree that attention is selective; in our differentiation model, attention serves to bring forth a given class of stimuli against an undifferentiated background. This then results in better differentiation of the stimulus class to which attention is directed. Taylor and Fiske (1978) argued that attention determines what information is salient. Borrowing from Tversky and Kahneman (1973), they concluded that salient information is more available for subsequent processing because it is being encoded through more than one perceptual mode.

Within the present theory, attention is postulated to influence the individual's ability to differentiate but to have no influence on response tendency. That is, a set effect (Restorff, 1933) is expected to affect d' but not any of the response bias measures such as $p(R)$. In order to test this hypothesis, Upmeyer, Layer, and Schreiber (1972) conducted an experiment on the processing of information made up of two sets of verbal stimuli, each of which was labeled with the name of a country. Stimuli were taken from a translation of the Anderson list of adjectives (Anderson, 1968) provided by Busz, Cohen, Poser, Schümer, Schümer, and Sonnenfeld (1972) and rated by independent judges as to their appropriateness for stereotyped descriptions of these nations. Following the elimination of contradictory adjectives, the most appropriate 200 were selected from the total of 770 for use in a recognition experiment. During the learning period of the experiment, subjects were shown 100 adjectives which were randomly chosen from the total of 200 (these were called "old items"); during the recognition period, these adjectives were presented again but this time randomly interspersed among the remaining 100 adjectives ("new items"). The subjects were instructed to inform the experimenter for each item whether they had "seen it before" (R_1) or had "not yet seen it" (R_2). Selective attention was created by randomly dividing both the old and the new sets of 100 adjectives into subsets of 50 adjectives each and then combining these subsets with the labels Americans (AM), Russians (RU), Liechtensteiners (LI), Luxemburgers (LU), or with no label (NO). Liechtenstein and Luxemburg are known European countries, but there is little information about characteristics of their people.

Five groups of subjects were exposed to the two subsets of old items labeled as follows: (1) RU–LI, (2) RU–AM, (3) RU–NO, (4) LI–LU, and (5) LI–NO. To motivate the subjects to associate the labels with the adjectives, they were told that a student who had travelled in these countries had associated these particular adjectives with the respective peoples and thought that they were relatively characteristic. In the NO-label condition, subjects were told that the student had thought these adjectives to be characteristic of the peoples of many countries. In fact, the association was random and balanced to avoid familiarity effects due to adjectives. During the acquisition period, subjects were not told that their memory would be tested.

The pairs of labels were so constructed as to test the hypothesis that the imaginability of the label will increase memory differentiation ability but will not increase response bias. In contrast, familiarity with the label was hypothesized to influence response bias but not differentiation ability. Hypothesis 1 represents a simple extension of the von Restorff effect (or set effect). It was expected that the absence of a label would prevent subjects from forming images thus serving to facilitate retrieval during the recognition period. Subjective distributions were measured through the use of a confidence scale associated with each of the two responses, R_1 and R_2. The amount of distribution overlap, that is, differentiation performance, was measured by a nonparametric analogue to d'. The implications of the second hypothesis will be discussed more fully later, because it involves a factor thought to affect response tendency. It will suffice here to state our expectation that response R_2 ("not yet seen") will occur more frequently under conditions where the item is associated with an unfamiliar label. The results did, in fact, support this hypothesis. The meaningful labels generally generated higher differentiation ability between old and new items than did no label; the labels were statistically related as follows: LI > NO, RU > NO, RU ≈ LI, LI ≈ LU, and RU ≈ AM. However, the degree of familiarity of the label was the decisive variable on the response side, P("not yet seen"): LI ≈ NO, RU < NO, RU < LI, LI ≈ LU, and RU ≈ AM. Another comparison of the results (shown in Table I) demonstrates the experimental independence of differentiation ability from response tendency.

Upmeyer *et al.* (1972) further tested the independence of the differentiation variable by varying the instructions between incidental and intentional learning. This was achieved simply by informing the subjects in another LI–NO condition prior to the presentation of the label–adjective combinations that the experiment was actually a memory test. As expected from a shift of attention in the storage period (Anderson & Hubert, 1963), the previously obtained significant difference between LI and NO for the differentiation variable was no longer significant, but the response variable remained unchanged in both conditions.

In still another variation, the authors investigated the "input" aspect of the differentiation process. The LI–NO and LI–LU conditions were replicated, but all labels were omitted in the recognition period. (In the original experiment, old items *and* new items were labeled in both the acquisition and the recognition periods.) The results remained unchanged, thus indicating that the presence of labels during the retrieval period does not affect differentiation ability.

TABLE I

INDEPENDENCE OF DISCRIMINABILITY AND RESPONSE TENDENCY[a]

Response tendency	Discriminability	
	Variable	Constant
Variable	RU vs NO	RU vs LI
Constant	LI vs NO	LI vs LU
		RU vs AM

[a]From Upmeyer *et al.*, (1972).

Although this study seems to provide some convincing evidence regarding the difference between differentiation and response processes, this fundamental property needs to be further tested with respect to other social contexts.

  c. *Social Labels as Attention Triggers.*   In the preceding section, we focused on differentiation, that aspect of information processing for which selective attention is especially relevant. An experiment was reported in which social labels were employed to create selective attention among the subjects, thus illustrating the role of selective attention in the differentiation process. It is our strong belief that not only are social labels a convenient device for bringing out selective attention in experimental subjects, but that, in fact, they constitute one of the most important determinants of selective attention in social contexts. This belief is based partly on evidence found in the stereotype literature (i.e., Secord, Bevan, & Katz, 1956) and partly on research concerned with the classification of perceptual stimuli (Tajfel, 1969) and with the classification of groups (Tajfel, Billig, Bundy, & Flament, 1971).

It should be emphasized that labels are not simply single words, such as *Russian*. A label may often consist of a set of sentences which conveys information about the content of subsequent sentences. Labels may be transmitted through visual perception, such as a uniform which is interpreted to mean that the wearer of the uniform plays some social role, such as policeman. Skin color is another important and often investigated example of a label. Social labels serve effectively to aid the individual in screening incoming information from the social environment. At the extreme, an individual may choose to avoid information which is so labeled in order to convey the impression that such information is irrelevant to his present situation. From the point of view of the present theory, it is in such a situation that we should expect a breakdown in differentiation performance. However, a person not having exposed himself may still give responses as documented in several investigations (e.g., Kanungo & Das, 1960).

Readers who are familiar with selective-exposure research (e.g., Freedman & Sears, 1965; Sears, 1968) may tend to misunderstand the preceding discussion with regard to two premises, and these points should now be clarified.

First, we do not hold label-induced selection to be merely a consequence of the limited stimulus-encoding capacity of the organism faced with a large amount of information. This kind of phenomenon belongs to the realm of cognitive psychology (Broadbent, 1958; Neisser, 1970; Norman, 1968; Haber, 1966; Sperling, 1967; among others). Rather, we refer here to those situations in which the individual has ample time in which to analyze the information and store it in his long-term memory. A typical example of such a situation would be one in which a researcher screens the table of contents in a journal of his interest; the titles of the articles function as labels providing him with information that may or may not motivate him to read certain articles. It is postulated that the typical psychological antecedent to the processing of attitudinal or complex information will be the individual's more or less thorough comprehension of the label's meaning.

The second misunderstanding may have its origin in the selective exposure research (Freedman & Sears, 1965). Within selective exposure theory, confirmation seeking and avoidance of disconfirmation form the basis of information gathering. These two strategies will come into play, however, only when the information is correspondingly labeled as confirming or disconfirming. (In the relevant experiment, such labels are hidden within the instructions given to subjects prior to their making a stimulus choice.) More specifically, the labels are evaluated, that is, checked against the valence of one's own attitude, before they are taken as indicators of confirmation or disconfirmation. Now the misunderstanding may arise if the reader falsely assumes that the predictions of selective exposure theory in this regard are to be incorporated into our present theory simply from the fact that both theories suggest the importance of information labels. If the label indicates that the information may be *relevant* to the individual's situation, it will then be carefully analyzed irrespective of whether it is positive, negative, or even neutral in relation to the individual's own attitude. This view is in line with McGuire's critique of the selective exposure research (McGuire, 1969). Within the framework of the present model, the subjective analysis of relevant information is thought to result in improved differentiation.

We should now like to turn out attention to an additional internal process which we believe mediates between the perception of labels and the information they imply, on the one hand, and the resulting differentiation performance, on the other. Since the present model is confined to slowly incoming information, the notion that short-term buffers may influence the selectivity process (see Erdelyi, 1974) cannot be incorporated. In addition, the notion that persons avoid exposure to information has been rejected on theoretical grounds and has not been substantially proven to hold empirically. Among the internal mechanisms proposed within the cognitive psychology field are rehearsal (Norman, 1969; Bjork, 1970) and imagery (Paivio, 1971). We strongly favor the latter concept. It is proposed that relevant, labeled information will be internally evaluated and *elaborated,* that is, will generate additional thoughts and interpretations. The label, the information, and the elaboration will then be integrated and stored as a schema. The resulting complex of associations will, upon retrieval, serve to facilitate information differentiation (see Upmeyer *et al.,* 1972).

d. The Self as a Trigger of Attention.   As in other psychological theories, the concept of relevance (or importance or salience) raises the problem of vagueness. Ad hoc and ex post facto assumptions which are dependent on specific situations are primarily used as substitutes for a more general theoretical solution. Unfortunately, the present theory is also not able to provide a solution to this problem in that it cannot spell out an exhaustive index of salient social information categories.

However, we should like to introduce and discuss a distinction which can be used in partitioning information into more and less relevant classes. This is the concept of the self widely employed in social psychology (e.g., Wicklund, 1975). Incoming information is thought to be checked by the individual with respect to evaluative content about the self. In task-oriented groups, a competitive atmosphere will define information about the task as relevant. Another example may be the conformity conflict in the Asch paradigm. Moreover, information about the self may have been generated by the individual himself in the past, and it is predicted that, upon retrieval, this self-generated information will be well differentiated from other information. Unfortunately, an individual is normally more familiar with self-generated information than information generated by others, thus confounding the source of information with familiarity of the information.

The conception of the self presented here has its roots in Darwinian thinking. Dangers and challenges as well as the desire for security render self-relevant information more important and thus more salient than information concerning objects and events which are irrelevant to the self. A major drawback to this proposition derives from the well-established fact that an extreme challenge to the self may result in panic which, we suspect, will tend to markedly decrease differentiation performance. The current state of theory is unable to account for this phenomenon.

In concrete situations, it is still difficult to determine precisely to what extent the self is affected by information. The aim of establishing two exclusive classes of information—relevant and irrelevant—is certainly not achieved. Labels are again thought to function as structural mediators, indicating when incoming information is of personal relevance.

e. Novelty as a Trigger of Attention. The discussion in this section derives from the theory of exploratory behavior developed by Berlyne (1960) in which novel stimuli presented for a short time are treated as elicitors of orienting responses. We would like to suggest that the orienting response is an obvious and powerful determinant of differentiation.

For the case in which the individual has ample time for exposure to information, it is supposed that, where rare and unusual stimuli are to be processed, the central mediating process discussed in connection with labels will operate. Novel stimuli are supposed to be centrally elaborated, and, again, the extent of elaboration covaries with the preciseness of retrieval in the subsequent judgment situation. The present theory predicts that novel stimuli will be not only well differentiated from more common stimuli, but also highly differentiated among themselves.

A typical example of this kind of novel stimulus is provided by research on divergent thinking and creativity (Adams, 1968; Bouchard, Drauden, & Barsaloux, 1974). Such stimuli can be generated by asking subjects a question such as, "Usually, the purpose of a chair is for sitting. What else can you do with it?" Typical answers to this question will occur with varying frequency, and a probability distribution can be estimated by posing the question to a large number of subjects. A novel stimulus can then be defined objectively as an answer having a fixed low probability criterion. Another subjective measure of novelty would be to have the answers such questions rated for originality on absolute scales by independent judges (Bollinger, Hellingrath, & Upmeyer, 1977).

5. Factors Affecting Response Tendency

Within the original signal detection theory framework, the response bias parameter was conceived to vary according to (1) financial payoffs associated with certain responses and (2) the prior stimulus distribution, that is, the frequency of stimulus occurrence (Swets et al., 1961). Luce (1963) proposed that the ratio of two asymptotic learning parameters would operate as a third response determinant. In the present theory, these three classes of response determinants will be modified and conceived in a manner more in correspondence with the social psychological tradition. In line with this modification, we shall term the three types of response determinants, respectively (1) perceived sanctions, (2) expectations, and (3) perceived correspondence (see Fig. 1C).

a. *Perceived Sanctions as a Determinant of Response Tendency.* One method for varying the response bias distribution for a signal detection task is to define gains and losses in monetary terms and to make the respondent aware of this contingency. In the typical 2 × 2 S-R matrix (see Table II), gains are recorded for correct answers (in the diagonal) and losses for incorrect answers (in the off-diagonal). In the symmetrical case (Table II, left), gains and losses for both response categories ("Yes" and "No") will balance out, resulting in a symmetrical response distribution. This pattern will result, however, only in

TABLE II

EXAMPLES OF SYMMETRICAL AND ASYMMETRICAL
PAYOFF MATRICES

Stimulus	Symmetrical response		Asymmetrical response	
	Yes	No	Yes	No
S_1	+7	−3	+8	−2
S_2	−3	+7	−2	+4

those cases where the subject perceives, and therefore expects, equal stimulus frequency distributions. Let us consider for the moment what will occur in those cases where the subject expects equal frequency distributions but where, in fact, the distributions are asymmetrical (Table II, right). (In the "Yes" response category, the payoff is higher for a correct answer as compared to the "No" response category, whereas losses are equal in both categories.) If the subject feels sure that the signal has occurred, he will respond "Yes"; if he believes that noise rather than the signal has occurred, he will respond "No". If he is in doubt, he will prefer "Yes" because the rewards associated with this response are greater. In signal detection theory, the respondent is viewed as operating in such a way as to maximize the payoff, and, therefore, responses will be biased toward the alternative which will provide the greatest long-term reward.

The decision theory concept of utility analysis can be applied to social influence processes without major alteration. Prior to deciding on a definite response, the person who serves as the target of influence is thought to calculate roughly his expected gains and losses. Positive and negative sanctions are perceived and weighted in accordance with the individual's own value system. We prefer to use the term *sanction* rather than payoff to indicate the social origin and its nonmonetary content. For example, in the Sherif-type norm formation paradigm (Sherif, 1935), the person who holds an extreme individual position may expect to gain social approval by shifting toward the group norm. In making this decision, the person may calculate the losses he can expect to incur from the appearance of inconsistency, but this loss is probably assigned little weight relative to the expected gains, particularly if the extreme individual can assume that the group is not aware of his privately given responses. Another source of loss might be the individual's diminished self-esteem following the decision to alter the position, but, given the highly unstructured experimental stimulus situation, this loss may be compensated for by the belief that he has thereby improved his performance. A similar analysis can be applied to the Rosenthal effect or interviewer bias.

One technical problem involved in the straightforward transfer of the notion of payoff matrices to social influence situations is the specification of exact values for gains and losses which will encompass all relevant aspects of the process. However, in many cases the direction of social influence can be specified, and, thus, the most probable response preference can be predicted; this is particularly easy for those cases in which only two possible response categories exist.

In psychophysical experimentation, the stimulus configurations to be differentiated are constructed in such a way that payoffs are greater for correct answers than for incorrect answers. However, in the social psychological field, as well as in every day life, one is sometimes confronted with the possibility of receiving negative sanctions for correct responses. In the typical Asch paradigm,

TABLE III
THE ASCH-TYPE SITUATION AS A PAYOFF MATRIX

	Response	
Stimulus	Equal	Greater
S_1 (equal)	$+2$	-1
S_2 (greater)	$+6$	$+2$

social pressure will often cause the naive subject to judge a stimulus as being either smaller or larger than it actually is. This situation can be transcribed into payoff matrix language, as in Table III. Despite the fact that there certainly exist private rewards ($+2$) for giving what appears to be the objectively correct response, for example, self-esteem maintenance or expected blame when it is later revealed that one has responded incorrectly, group pressure in the unanimous situation is so strong that the payoff for yielding ($+6$) is greater than that for responding correctly, and, thus, the subject's response will in most cases contradict his own perception. We can state with some confidence that the subject's response in this case does, in fact, contradict his perception, since Asch employed objectively and perfectly discriminable stimuli.

Up to this point, we have discussed the role of sanctions only in connection with response decision type 2. On a common sense basis and from the evidence provided by matched-model dependent-behavior research, it is obvious that perceived payoffs (or reinforcement) will affect decision type 1 as well. In this case, varying weights will be assigned to the two alternatives, responding or not responding. The ratio of the two weights is hypothesized to vary directly with the probability of responding.

   b. Expectation as a Determinant of Response Tendency.   Swets *et al.* (1961) performed a detection experiment in which the relative frequency of occurrence of "signal + noise" (P) and "noise alone" ($1 - P$) was systematically varied to force subjects to adopt different response criteria. The methodological purpose of this variation was to obtain different empirical proportions of p(Yes, signal + noise) and p(Yes, noise alone) which would then generate empirical subjective distributions and which would be the basis for estimating the sensitivity parameter d'. For example, if the subject is exposed to 500 signal + noise trials and 500 noise alone trials in random order of succession and if the subject is further informed about this distribution, he will very likely respond with equal frequency: "Yes, the signal is present" and "No, the signal is not present." If, however, the subject is informed that P will now be equal to .750 and $1 - P$ equal to .250, then he will more likely increase correspondingly the number of "Yes" responses and decrease the number of "No" responses. Thus, the knowledge of the prior probability P (and its complement $1 - P$) will determine the subject's response distribution, and one would expect $P \approx p(\text{yes})$. The relation $P \approx p(\text{Yes})$ has been well established empirically for the case where subjects are informed about the stimulus distribution (Green & Swets, 1966).

For the case where subjects are given no information regarding stimulus distributions, assumptions or *expectations* develop. In memory experiments, subjects most often assume an equal distribution of the stimuli to be differentiated, and this assumption has been shown to generate symmetric and very stable response frequencies (e.g., Upmeyer & Schreiber, 1972; Upmeyer & Layer, 1972). A well-balanced experiment generally provides certain cues which are interpreted by subjects such that all conditions in the experiment are probably symmetrically or equally exposed.

The literal meaning of the term *response bias* applies to the judgment situation where knowledge about the objective stimulus distributions is not available. In such a case, the subject is forced to rely on past experience with similar situations or to develop reasoning strategies, which may result in the assumption of a false stimulus distribution. For example, in a group identification task involving the identification of ethnic minorities, the prejudiced person may overestimate the number of members of this minority ("the enemy is everywhere and numerous"). One way of explaining this bias is to invoke the implicit assumption that a "dangerous" minority must be numerous in order to be perceived as dangerous. More generally, our example may be derived from the representativeness heuristic of judgment proposed by Tversky and Kahneman (1973).

Note that a response tendency will be biased by the influence of expectations only in those situations where perfect differentiation is not possible. Where such differentiation is possible, the response distribution will always match the stimulus distribution. Thus, the influence exerted by expectations differs from that imposed by perceived sanctions in that expectations will produce bias only in the absence of objective differentiation ability, whereas perceived sanctions may influence the response even when perfect differentiation is possible.

c. Perceived Correspondence as a Determinant of Response Tendency. The principle of correspondence has been employed, under different semantic labels, as a common explanatory tool for a variety of social judgment phenomena. Asch (1956) pointed out that trait adjectives *change their meaning* depending on certain central traits. According to Wishner's (1960) analysis, traits are perceived to be intercorrelated to varying degrees, and responses which follow a particular set of stimulus traits will be determined by the subject's *a priori* perception of the degree of this covariation.

Through his *relevance* theory of accentuation, Tajfel (1957, 1959) attempted to reconcile the apparently contradictory results obtained in studies of coin estimation by arguing that the size of a physical object will only be accentuated if it covaries systematically with the object value. In other words, if the value of a coin does not covary with its diameter, value will not be a relevant parameter for size estimation, and, therefore, accentuation will not occur.

The principle of correspondence also underlies a number of causal schemata proposed by Kelley (1971) in his development of attribution theory. It would be a gross oversimplification to describe Kelley's various schemata as involving just one correspondence principle. However, for our purpose, it is sufficient to note that the probability that certain types of attribution will be made by the observer depends on the strength of covariation between the response mode variable and another variable associated with the response mode on the basis of a person's experience.

In the present analysis, the application of the correspondence principle is restricted to the response decision process. The concept would operate within a differentiation task as follows. If the person is unsure as to whether the presented stimulus is more representative of response category R_1 or R_2, he may consider a third variable category which differs from the stimulus variable but which is psychologically related to it. If the third variable V_1 is more correspondent with stimulus S_1 than with stimulus S_2, then the person will be more likely to respond R_1 than R_2. For example, within the series of German coins, a 5-pfennig coin (S_1) is actually somewhat smaller in size than a 2-pfennig coin (S_2). If a 2-pfennig coin were presented to a subject, the appropriate response would be "larger" (R_2). However, since the size difference is difficult to differentiate, the subject may be uncertain about his or her response. He or she may then consider a third variable, coin value, which should under most circumstances correlate highly with coin size. The state of this third variable would be V_1, that is, its value would suggest the larger size. As a consequence, the subject may then incorrectly choose the response "smaller" (R_1).

A further illustration of this phenomenon is to be found in an experiment conducted by Upmeyer et al. (1972). Within a recognition task, subjects were exposed to "old" and "new" trait adjectives. During the retrieval period, subjects were to describe each adjective as either "known" or "unknown," thus indicating whether the adjective had been presented previously. Thus, the known–unknown response mode was supposed to be used in a technical way. However, since the adjectives were experimentally associated with a third variable, that is, well-known (e.g., Russian) or unknown (e.g., Liechtensteiner) foreign groups, subjects' responses were, as predicted, affected by this third variable; stimuli associated with Liechtensteiner were more likely to be described as "unknown." Since a given response choice may be affected by several simultaneously operating "third variables," it is considered desirable for the development of our theory to attempt to specify those characteristics which will be important in determining the extent to which such variables will be influential in the judgment process. To this end, we should like to propose two concepts that were first introduced to the psychology of judgment by Peabody (1967). These are the *evaluative* dimension and the *descriptive* dimension of content. Within the present response theory, a distinction is made between *value correspondence* and *descriptive correspondence*.

Value correspondence is said to exist if the third variable reflects an evaluative attitude toward stimulus sets S_1 and S_2. For example, the elements of S_1 may generally be favorable, and those of S_2 may be generally unfavorable. Thus, if an observer is presented with a political statement and asked to attribute its source to one of two politicians, one of whom is generally viewed favorably and the other negatively, the observer's response may be influenced by the evaluative content of the statement—if it is negative, it may be attributed to the negatively evaluated source, if positive, to the positively evaluated source. Once again, this will occur when the observer is unable to make a definite differentiation. It is further assumed that value correspondence will be particularly important under conditions where (1) the person is in a highly emotional state and (2) the person is uninformed about the specific content of the stimulus sets.

If the observer feels well acquainted with the given stimulus situations but remains in doubt about a particular judgment, he may identify the class to which a stimulus element belongs by invoking certain descriptive characteristics of the element which correspond to general characteristics of the class. This correspondence may, of course, be simply illusory, but it is derived from the observer's past experience and perceived as real. In this way, those elements characterized as containing a trick may correspond to a specific politician, although in reality most politicians may play tricks on people. Descriptive correspondence will operate only if the subject under investigation knows some aspects of the character of that politician. This knowledge has to include more than "tricky is bad," that is, more than value correspondence. Moreover, it is thought that the politician under investigation is especially suspected of being tricky. It is evident that if value correspondence and descriptive correspondence operate, the probability of a judgment bias is particularly high (Upmeyer & Layer, 1974). Evidence for the effect of value correspondence alone on response tendency was provided by Upmeyer, Krolage, Etzel, Lilli, and Klump (1976) and Etzel, Lang, and Upmeyer (unpublished).

The concept of expectation can also be viewed as a special case of the correspondence principle in operation, the third variable in this case consisting of the frequency of response occurrence. The similarity between the concepts is heightened by the fact that both are based on the observer's past experience. However, before correspondence can come into play, the judging person must be able to interpret the *content* of the stimulus situation. (This feature is quite distinct from Luce's (1963) proposed asymptotic response learning process, which is also based on experience.) However, content is not implied in our concept of expectation, narrowly defined here as frequency of stimulus occurrence. The concept of correspondence is thought to play a role in many everyday situations where the prior stimulus distribution is often difficult to determine; however in the laboratory, especially where a well-balanced signal detection design is employed, expectation may constitute the primary response determinant.

6. *On the Independence of Differentiation Ability and Response Tendency*

Differentiation and response tendency will be independent to the extent that their respective determinants are independent. Having defined two exclusive sets of determinants for both processes, that is, for differentiation, physical aspects of the stimulus communicated through labels and selective attention deriving from personal characteristics of the observer, and for response tendency, perceived sanctions, expectations, and correspondence, the task of determining independence would seem to call for an empirical test making use of various orthogonal combinations of perceptual and judgmental variables. The application of such tests will be discussed in Section II. However, both differentiation ability and response tendency may be altered by a complex situation; therefore, it is necessary to develop our conceptualization further.

Let us consider, for example, a situation in which an individual must differentiate between stimuli which pertain to a strong personal attitude. The present analysis assumes that the person will (1) attempt to analyze the stimuli precisely and thus increase his or her differentiation performance and (2) issue responses which indicate the direction of his or her attitude.

In this example, the observed covariation between differentiation ability and response tendency is a result of the fact that two features of the theory coincide. Nevertheless, these features are psychologically different. The relevance of the attitude has a motivating property, and this may serve to define the set of stimuli to be differentiated, thus creating selective attention. Both increased motivation and cognitive selection will affect stimulus processing.

On the output side, the response decision may be affected by value correspondence; for example, a positively valenced response alternative will be chosen if the attitude object is generally also positive. In this case, the person's attitude produces the correspondence. However, if social sanctions operate in such a way as to force the response toward the opposite response alternative, then the influence of value correspondence may be overridden.

As shown in this example, response determinants are *directional* in the sense that they imply a cognitive guideline for response choices. An indication of the inherent difference between two processes is evident in the fact that while a person may often be cognizant of his or her predominant response tendency within a differentiation task, he or she may frequently be unaware of the quality of performance. The stimulus analysis process is apparently not accompanied by a conscious analysis of the differentiation process itself on the part of the subject, whereas the choice of the response takes place in the presence of constant checking of the various response possibilities for appropriateness. The response process must be viewed as a form of self-presentation, and we are convinced that the application of the consistency principle must be primarily restricted to response phenomena. Thus, a person may be perfectly capable of differentiating between various groups, but his or her consistent response will appear, externally, to be stereotyped.

Fortunately, several methodological approaches exist through which the independence of the two processes can be empirically assessed. (1) If the shape of the subjective distributions is known or can be confidently assumed, an operating characteristic curve can be fitted to empirical points generated by different pay offs and/or different prior distributions. The fit can be determined, for example, by the method of least squares, thus providing a criterion for the appropriateness of the model as a whole. (2) Differentiation ability and response tendency may be correlated, and a zero correlation would indicate the independence of the two processes. (3) The most powerful and theoretically fruitful approach would be to orthogonally vary the determinants of both the differentiation process and the response process. Independence would then be assumed if one of the processes was to vary while the other remained constant. Empirical evidence supporting the notion of independence between the two processes will be presented later.

B. MAGNITUDE ESTIMATION

Magnitude estimation processes are graphically summarized in Fig. 1D.

1. The Perceptual Process in Magnitude Estimation

In order to be able to estimate the magnitude of the difference between two stimuli, one must be able to differentiate between them. In most cases, and especially in those cases of interest to the social psychologist, the two stimuli are perfectly differentiable. As a consequence, we cannot obtain an empirical measure of the subjective distribution overlap generated by the stimuli, and, therefore, we cannot use the same measure to determine the preciseness of internal representation as would be possible in a differentiation task.

Although the interdependence of differentiation and magnitude estimation has been discussed in the field of psychophysics (Gravetter & Lockhead, 1973), an acceptable theoretical framework which might be extended to social judgment and to the present conceptual model has not yet been developed. The only indirect measure of the quality of internal magnitude estimation which comes to mind is that of internal consistency, or a test–retest correlation. In the absence of concrete data, we can only assume that the same determinants will operate in connection with magnitude estimation as were discussed above under differentiation.

In addition to the performance aspects of the internal representation of magnitude estimation, the dimensionality of the stimuli to be estimated must be considered as well. The individual can estimate magnitude only when the stimuli are internally represented on a continuum pertaining to one specific attribute only, whereas differentiations are made by taking several attributes into consideration. Most stimuli, of course, are describable in terms of several attributional dimensions; however, only one of these dimensions (although it may be complex) can form the basis of a magnitude estimation. A prominent example of a common dimension within social psychology is the attitude rating.

From early developments in psychophysics (Wertheimer, 1925) we know that magnitude dimensions are psychologically limited by anchors in a frame of reference. Different facets of this concept are incorporated in various social judgment theories (Helson, 1948; Volkmann, 1951; Sherif & Hovland, 1958; for an overview consult Eiser & Ströbe, 1972). Those of particular interest for our purposes are Parducci's range–frequency model (Parducci, 1965) and Upshaw's reference scale model and theory of variable perspectives (Upshaw, 1965, 1969a,b). As conceived in these models, the range principle signifies the existence of two anchors lying on the judgment dimension. They are conceptualized as psychological boundaries which specify the range of perceived stimuli. The stimuli lying outside this range are not taken into account by the individual and cannot be subjected to magnitude estimation. The range is determined by two parameters, width and absolute position with respect to the underlying dimension, respectively termed *unit* and *origin* by Upshaw (1969a). The range as a whole is highly dependent on the situation in which a judgment is made; as the situation changes, the range shifts quickly, and, thus, there is no enduring carry-over effect.

2. The Response Process in Magnitude Estimation

In the recent history of magnitude estimation research, one can discern a definite trend toward separation of the response process from the process of internal representation. This is a striking analog to the independent developments in the field of signal detection. We feel that the point may now have been reached where a merger of the two theories might be possible.

One fundamental notion which was advanced by S. S. Stevens (1971) is that quantities may be expressed in any conceivable response language; that is, it is possible to match magnitude across modalities. For example, Upshaw (1969a) has shown that moral judgment can be reliably expressed by volumes of sand piled on a table. The preferred response language in social psychological research has been the method of absolute scale limited by fixed end points. According to Upshaw's theory of variable perspectives, the process of matching internal representations with a given response language can be described as follows. When an individual is to estimate magnitudes, he or she first matches the anchors of the internally represented range to the end points of the response language to be used. The magnitudes of the stimuli lying within his or her subjective range are then linearly transformed to the response language dimension.

Within Parducci's range–frequency model, the range principle operates in precisely the same fashion (Parducci, 1965) except that his model is restricted to the categorical case. Upshaw, Parducci, and others have provided impressive empirical evidence to support the operation of this range principle. Ostrom and Upshaw (1968) have further pointed out the relevance of the theory of variable perspectives to attitude judgments.

At this point, we would like to compare the concept of the response process which we have been developing in connection with differentiation with that involved in magnitude estimation. One must consider whether the range principle is unique in its application to the process of magnitude estimation. As pointed out, the range in magnitude estimation tasks will be determined by two parameters (origin and unit), whereas in differentiation tasks one response parameter (the decision criterion) is sufficient. Since the response criteria can easily be summarize under the *origin* concept, it appears that magnitude estimation calls for one additional parameter, that is *unit*.

Let us now discuss in some detail the possible effects of the three response determinants—expectations, correspondences, sanctions—on the magnitude estimation process.

a. Expectation. Comparing the theory of signal detectability with Parducci's range–frequency model, we find a striking similarity concerning the application of the frequency principle. Parducci (1965) was able to show empirically that responses will shift toward the center of density of a distribution if the stimulus distribution on an absolute scale over a constant range is asymmetrical. Thus, a stimulus which objectively belongs to a category lying off center in a skewed distribution is not likely to be identified as belonging to this category; rather the probability is increased that the stimulus will be incorrectly placed in another category, one lying between the correct category and the center of the distribution. Parducci achieved this effect by informing subjects of the shape of distribution.

The effect can be transferred to a judgment of ethnic identification. Suppose someone meets a Caucasian person with a deep tan and has to judge whether this person belongs to the group of (1) white, (2) Caucasians, (3) mixed Caucasian and black, or (4) blacks. According to the frequency principle, the response to this task will depend on the individual's knowledge of how the four categories are distributed. If the person happens to be in Brazil, he or she will expect a greater percentage of blacks among the population and will tend to respond with the third category. If he or she is in Western Europe, the response might be the first category. Thus, the frequency principle appears to be simply an extension of the role of stimulus occurrence from two categories in signal detection to the k categorical case. It is only a minor step from Parducci's categorical model to the continuous case in magnitude estimation.

Parducci (1965) also demonstrated that the range principle and the frequency principle can be independently manipulated. If the two principles suggest different response tendencies to the judging individual, the final response will constitute a compromise between the two principles. According to Parducci, the compromise will represent the arithmetic mean of the two response tendencies, thus expressing the influence of both principles. Yet, the frequency principle has not attracted as much attention in the literature as the range principle; this lesser importance is reflected by the scarcity of experimental studies as well as by its absence in other theories of magnitude estimation. One reason for this may well be a psychological one—a distribution which lies on a judgment continuum seems to be more difficult to perceive, to memorize, and to use than the limits (anchors) of the continuum's range.

   b.   *Correspondences.*   Turning to correspondence as a response determinant, it becomes clear that the majority of examples demonstrating the effect are to be found in studies of magnitude estimation (see Eiser & Ströbe, 1972). Tajfel (1957, 1959), in his discussion of the concept of relevance, pointed out that only when the value of an object correlates with its size would one expect a relative accentuation effect, that is, a spreading of responses. In the coin estimation paradigm, for example, correspondence between the continuous variable (money value) forms the basis for a shift in response. Tajfel argued convincingly that this effect will not occur in a case where, for example, the size of a swastika is to be judged because the negative value associated with the swastika does not correspond to its size; a swastika is always negative, whether large or small (see Klein, Schlesinger, & Meister, 1951). In the present theory, Tajfel's accentuation concept is hypothesized to be restricted to the response process.

   c.   *Sanctions.*   Finally, the concept of perceived sanctions must be discussed as a possible response determinant in magnitude estimation. As in a differentiation task, the rewards associated with choosing a response suggested by others may be greater than those accompanying the decision to remain with one's own choice. A person being fully aware of the correctness of his response may nevertheless yield to preserve maximum reward without changing the range on the internally represented dimension. Lies are the best example.

II. Applications

A. SOCIAL INFLUENCE

At this point, it seems necessary to take a closer look at the results of the well-known Asch (1951) study of the effects of group pressure on judgment and reinterpret them in light of the conceptual model which has been developed in the preceding sections. Most reports on this series of experiments fail to distinguish between *distortion of judgment* and *distortion of perception*. Asch describes judgmental distortion as follows: "These subjects suffer from primary doubt and lack of confidence; on this basis they feel a strong tendency to join the majority" (p. 183). On the other hand, perceptual distortion, "under stress of group pressure," was described in the following terms: "These subjects report that they came to perceive the majority estimates as correct." We have argued that judgmental distortion operates on and is limited to the response process, whereas perceptual distortion as a result of social pressure occurs during the process of internal representation of stimuli; however, contrary to Asch, we feel that this perceptual process can hardly be described as distortion due to the fact that persons subjected to social pressure improve their perceptual performance (Upmeyer, 1968, 1971).

In order to attempt to explain social influence processes, one must consider three important concepts: the self, the other(s), and reality. The following enumerated points will be discussed individually in turn: When others are of a different opinion (1) with respect to some reality (2), the self feels threatened, resulting in a closer inspection and an improved internal representation of all aspects of that reality (3); if reality in this situation is ambiguous (4) and the social sanctions are perceived to be strong (5), the self will most likely yield to the others (6).

1. The differing opinion indicates that a social conflict exists, and, in order to be able to deal with that conflict, the individual must clearly understand the opinion. As pointed out by Moscovici and Faucheux (1972) and Nemeth and Wachtler (1973), this process is dependent on response styles, particularly on the consistency of the others' communications. It does not depend on the number of others—minority or majority—who advocate the opposite position. Furthermore, consistency does not consist simply of the repetition of the others' point of view; rather, it must be consistent with an underlying logic which the self attributes to the others. Possible patterns of consistency will depend on the task; for a discussion of the operation of consistency in this respect see Kelley (1971).

2. Reality can be viewed as any state falling between the two extremes of perfect clarity (as illustrated by the Asch situation, 1956) and total ambiguity (as exemplified by the Sherif situation, 1935). In line with the present differentiation theory, perfect clarity exists when the subjective distributions do not overlap, and

total ambiguity exists if the subjective distributions are congruent. The effect of stimulus ambiguity on the extent of yielding has been demonstrated by Luchins and Luchins (1955).

3. In the presence of a consistent and deviant communication from others, the self may feel threatened. The threat may stem from the insecurity the self expects to experience if it must abandon an attitude which it holds important. In a judgment task (our major task here), the threat emanates primarily from the expectation that errors will produce a negative evaluation. In an experiment, it is usually expected that the experimenter will make this evaluation. In such a situation, the person's choice is to yield or to stand by his or her point of view. In order to solve this problem satisfactorily, the individual will orient himself or herself to reality hoping, through careful inspection of the stimuli, to gather enough information to be able to substantiate one or the other of these alternatives. As a consequence, the internal representation of the stimulus situation will become sharper and the differentiation power of the human analyzer will be increased. In the language of the present conceptual model, differentiation will improve and magnitude differences will be more accurately estimated.

4. Despite this relative improvement in perception, the person may still be uncertain because of the difficulty of the stimulus situation. This stimulus difficulty is a supporting condition for yielding one's position. The extent to which the person will yield is directly proportional to the degree of ambiguity of the stimulus situation. At times, of course, it will be possible to improve one's analysis of the situation; in such cases, the actual state of the stimulus exerts little influence, but the individual's confidence is undermined.

5. In making the decision to yield, the person must calculate the subjective rewards and losses he or she can expect to be associated with each of the possible responses. If these stimuli are ambiguous, yielding will result in minimal loss of self-esteem. If the degree of ambiguity is constant, the payoffs may be affected by numerous influences like unanimous votes, sharpness (Moscovici & Faucheux, 1972, p. 178), consistency, status of the experimenter, and commitment to the person involved.

6. As demonstrated in numerous studies of conformity, yielding often represents a form of compromise. It should be noted on the basis of the concepts developed here that such compromises are more likely to occur in a magnitude estimation task than in a differentiation task because in the latter case the task defines the decision *a priori* as either right or wrong. However, in a repetitive differentiation task, the individual under pressure may compromise by yielding only part of the time. This generates a response frequency distribution which can be checked against the prior objective stimulus distribution, thus providing the opportunity to test our theoretical postulates within the signal detection paradigm.

In order to test the hypothesis that perception will improve as a result of yielding, Upmeyer (1968, 1971) conducted an experiment in which the Asch paradigm was modified. Perception was measured by the amount of overlap of subjective distributions observed in a differentiation task. Further, pressure was exerted on the subjects as to how to use a certain response scale. Two stimulus situations were to be differentiated. In situation A, two lights of unequal brightness were presented; in situation B, the two lights were equally bright. There were 240 trials, with each of the two situations occurring in 50% of the trials. Subjects were provided with a 4-point confidence scale ranging from 0 to 3, where 0 meant "very confidently B," 1 meant "confidently B," 2 meant "confidently A," and 3 meant "very confidently A."

According to Egan, Schulman, and Greenberg (1959), when subjects were asked to use such a scale in distinguishing between two situations, they will generally superimpose this external scale on the two subjective distributions which are generated by the two situations. Thus, the 240 responses from each subject can be exhaustively summarized within a 2×4 stimulus–response matrix, and this matrix will further reflect the empirical frequencies of the two subjective distributions. The manner in which the subject superimposes the category scale on his or her subjective distributions indicates his or her response style. Since the objective difference between the stimuli in situation A was very small, the cautious subject may prefer 0 and 1 responses (see Fig. 2). Other persons may see no reason not to respond 3 or 2—behaviors which might be

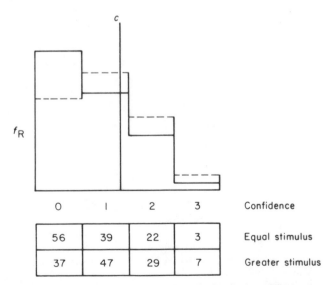

| 56 | 39 | 22 | 3 | Equal stimulus |
| 37 | 47 | 29 | 7 | Greater stimulus |

Fig. 2.   Example of a stimulus–response matrix (2 stimuli, 4 confidence responses) and its frequency distributions, reflecting a "cautious" criterion c. (———), Equal stimulus; (– –), greater stimulus.

termed uninhibited. Regardless of a person's response style, as long as he or she makes use of all categories, the distributions and the degree to which they overlap can be assessed from the 2 × 4 S-R matrix.

In this experiment, only those subjects who had demonstrated a "cautious" response style in a pretest (as reflected by the distributions in Fig. 2) were used.

For the experimental manipulation of social pressure, Upmeyer added a constant amount of response bias to each set of data for these subjects. As a result, the computed responses tended toward the uninhibited direction of 3 (see Fig. 3). This addition affected the mean of the unconditional response distribution, but not the amount of overlap of the conditional distributions.

Thus, the newly generated S-R matrix reflected both an identical differentiation performance and a different response tendency. The new table corresponding to the distribution (See Fig. 3) was the basis for what three confederates had to say in the following group session. More precisely, a random order of succession of trials for each confederate was established from the same 2 × 4 table for each individual. During the group session, one naive subject was placed with three confederates. The subject was required to respond first, followed by the confederates, who responded as described above. The confederates' responses were randomly determined so as not to be identical on each trial, but tending over trials toward the "greater" end of the scale. In contrast to the Asch paradigm, the subject could evaluate the pressure only after making his or her specific judg-

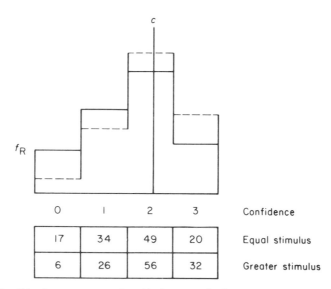

	0	1	2	3	Confidence
	17	34	49	20	Equal stimulus
	6	26	56	32	Greater stimulus

Fig. 3.   Stimulus–response matrix and its frequency distributions after adding a constant amount of response bias. Criterion c reflects a less "cautious" bias as compared to Fig. 2. (———), Equal stimulus; (- -), greater stimulus.

ment. Thus, yielding could be seen not as a consequence of each particular trial but rather as a general adjustment of the person's response style to correspond to the style of the majority. In addition, this arrangement provided the subject with the opportunity independently to produce correct responses. Further, the subject was allowed to believe that his or her responses may have influenced the others. A control condition was formed by having subjects respond by pressing a button. Thus, the subject was not aware of others' responses. Subjects were randomly assigned to either the experimental or the control group from among the pool of pretest subjects displaying response styles.

The results indicated that the experimental subjects yielded to the pressure to alter their response style by using the scale in a less cautious way. In general, their responses were located between their previous individual scale positions and that advocated by the confederates. The control group exhibited a slight tendency in the same direction, but this can probably be attributed to regression. So far, these results are exactly what one would expect from the conformity literature.

In addition, when compared with the pretest scores, the experimental subjects' differentiation performances improved significantly, whereas the performances of the control group significantly decreased. The increase among the experimental subjects was attributed to a raised attention level resulting from the conflict. The decrease in the control group was attributed to boredom resulting from the repetition of a task with which they were quite familiar. The variance among differentiation scores in the experimental group was significantly less than in the control group; thus, this is a strong indication of the motivational differences between the two situations. Finally, the correlation score between the two dependent variables—differentiation and response bias—did not depart significantly from zero. Thus, the independence of the two variables can be assumed.

Supporting evidence for the independence of differentiation ability and response tendency was also provided in a recent application of signal detection theory to social influence by Kriss, Kinchla, and Darley (1977). They proposed an interesting signal detection model allowing for trial-to-trial cues provided by another person before and after the subject gave his or her own judgments. They hypothesized that social influence will affect only response bias but not decrease sensitivity as might be inferred from the Asch study. Rather, sensitivity was supposed to and was found to vary only according to stimulus difficulty. Unfortunately, the authors did not discuss Upmeyer's hypothesis of increased sensitivity (Upmeyer, 1971), although they enclosed his article in their reference list. In fact, one is unable to draw from the Kriss *et al.* data conclusions about Upmeyer's motivation hypothesis because they did not incorporate a control group with no social influence into their experiment.

In order to evaluate their finding of influence-independent sensitivity, one has to take a closer look at their experimental manipulations. Their subjects were free to wait or not to wait until the (computer) confederate responded. The response latency of the simulated confederate ranged from .620 to .114 sec, and it was impossible to identify the trials in which the subject did or did not wait. Besides this, the time range was so short that an unknown latency of cognition could interfere with an exact measurement of the subject's waiting behavior. Nevertheless, the direction of the confederate's cues was properly manipulated, and the results suggest convincingly that these cues were effective in influencing response bias. However, the subject could always take the chance to compare his or her performance with the other. According to our theory, these comparisons are sufficient to keep the subject attentive, that is, to increase sensitivity rather than keeping it constant.

The latter hypothesis has been explored and confirmed by a series of earlier recognition memory experiments on social influence (Upmeyer & Schreiber, 1972; Upmeyer & Layer, 1972). In these studies, the response bias effect was held constant in group situations, but the differentiation process was systematically varied by having the subject believe that his or her response either agreed or disagreed with that of the group and that his or her overt performance was either superior to or inferior to that of the group. It was hypothesized that differentiation performance between old and new items in the recognition task would be increased when disagreement existed between the naive subject and the group, and when the subject's performance was seen as inferior to that of the others.

Upmeyer and Schreiber (1972) manipulated agreement and disagreement by giving the naive subject false feedback regarding the responses of two confederates after each trial in a series of recognition tasks. The feedback was delivered after the subject had responded. The subject was to respond with either "old" or "new" to indicate his or her judgment as to whether the item had appeared previously. Differentiation ability was measured by having the subject privately indicate confidence on each trial. The feedback information delivered by the two confederates was arranged in the following patterns: (1) both confederates agreed with the naive subject; (2) both disagreed; (3) confederate A agreed, confederate B disagreed, (4) confederate B agreed, confederate A disagreed. The four patterns were either equally (symmetrically) or unequally (asymmetrically) distributed over the whole series of identification trials. Within the asymmetrical distribution, patterns 1 (unanimous agreement) and 2 (unanimous disagreement) were varied such that one of the patterns was presented more frequently than the other, whereas patterns 3 and 4 were presented with an equal frequency. In addition, the extent to which the presentation of patterns 1 and 2 departed from equality was varied such that the difference was either weak or strong. A control condition was formed in which the two confederates were present but the subject did not receive feedback.

Following Festinger (1954), it was hypothesized that the level of attention directed toward the task will directly influence differentiation performance. More precisely, the level of attention was hypothesized to increase differentiation ability. Upmeyer and Schreiber were successful in confirming this hypothesis for weak disagreement but not for strong disagreement. The latter result may have been due to Festinger's (1954) qualification that in order for a certain degree of disagreement to be motivating, the subject should feel that a certain attainable performance standard above his or her present performance level existed and that this standard had not yet been reached. The theory of social comparison processes does not specify the exact extent of goal attainability. In the Upmeyer and Schreiber study a sufficient amount of attainability was apparently filled in the weak disagreement condition, but not in the strong disagreement condition. Upmeyer and Schreiber were also able to show that symmetrical feedback produces higher differentiation performance than no feedback.

Upmeyer and Layer (1972) used the same recognition task paradigm but did not provide trial-to-trial feedback. Rather, subjects who were working in a group without communication were given (fictitious) scoring results by the experimenter after blocks of trials as to the relative standing of an individual in the group. It was hypothesized and confirmed that a feeling of inferiority would increase achievement motivation and improve differentiation performance more than a feeling of superiority. Further, both conditions resulted in better performance than conditions in which the subject worked alone.

In both studies, response bias remained constant at about the .5 level. None of the manipulations exerted any effect on this result. In order to understand the surprising stability of response style, one should be aware of certain features of the recognition memory task. Usually, more than 100 items are presented in order to be able to achieve a stable estimate of the dependent variables; this is simply too many trials to be stored and immediately retrieved. Therefore, subsets of items (10 in the studies mentioned above) are formed to be presented in one block of consecutive trials during the acquision period. During the recognition period, these (10) items appear randomly interspersed within a subset of (10) new items. It is relatively easy for the subject to figure out that the number of "old" and "new" items presented in the recognition period is equal, thus forming a rather strong response expectation. This constitutes an implicit norm, leading the subject to structure his or her response style; therefore, the stability of the response bias measure at the .5 level is a strong confirmation of the present theory.

The finding which is most important, however, is the fact that the *response measure* was not affected by any of the variables which were hypothesized to, and actually did, alter the internal differentiation process. The classical means of manipulating motivation by disagreement and inferiority were chosen to add face validity to the attention-producing internal process; historically, the meaning of these variables is so well established that one can generalize as to the nature of the differentiation process.

The studies on disagreement and inferiority can be interpreted as follows. As soon as a conflict occurs between cognitions of the self and reported cognitions of others, the individual attempts to solve this conflict by mobilizing his or her internal analysis capabilities. The result is an improved analysis of the stimulus situation. However, the present social influence paradigm (including the expansion of the signal detection paradigm reported above) is limited toward a set of information presented by others. Additionally, we would suggest that the individual will actively seek information not to be found within the given set of stimuli. This secondary information might be provided by noninvolved others or past experience, or it could be concerned with the relative credibility of the opposing others. Regardless of which of the various factors operates in a given situation to direct attention to the stimulus, the result is not a distortion of reality. Rather, the individual becomes better informed.

The role of reality as an important third factor in this process has been generally neglected in the literature, both experimentally and theoretically. The experimental deficiencies are not surprising because the oversimplified response-gathering techniques widely used in social psychological research tend to mask the underlying process. Those techniques have merely documented the instrumental effect of social influence and have demonstrated a subject's dependency on others. In addition, the stability and strength of the conformity effect have undoubtedly led researchers to concentrate primarily on the investigation of variables which operate to modify the conformity effect itself. As for the theoretical deficiencies, it is more difficult to isolate specific sources of bias. The implicit assumption held by a great many experimenters, which characterizes the subject as a predominatly passive respondent, has certainly contributed to the general neglect of active information processing (see Berlyne, 1960). Furthermore, we find in the social influence literature a conception of reality as a constant. This is an important point, and we should like to discuss it in some depth and in relation to two lines of research, as represented by Deutsch and Gerard's study of social influence and Moscovici's and his co-workers' work on minority influence.

Deutsch and Gerard (1955) distinguished between two types of influence: normative and informational. Normative influence was said to represent the potential instrumental power of group members to exert pressure on the individual to comply with the group consensus. Informational social influence was said to apply in cases where the individual relies on the group to provide information about reality. In this case, the individual does not *conform* to others; rather, he or she voluntarily adopts their point of view. Deutsch and Gerard were unable to isolate experimentally a pure instance of informational influence and thus conceded that social reality would primarily result in an integration of the two types.

It is not our purpose to debate the relative value of such analytical distinctions. Rather, we should like to discuss the concept of reality implied in such a model. The stimulus reality dealt with in conformity studies is most often defined in objective physical terms, such as the size of bars, hues of colors, etc. In the typical conformity experiments, the subject is allowed direct experience with the stimulus object. However, in everyday situations, this is often not the case. The individual has no opportunity to directly experience a particular stimulus and is thus forced to rely on others' reports. Such a situation can clearly be defined as an instance of informational social influence. However, Deutsch and Gerard seem to generalize a step further by stating that the individual will accept the informational influence of others because past experience has taught that such reliance on others is generally beneficial. This implies that a person will be open to such influence, even when he or she has direct access to the stimulus. In such a case, normative influence may occur simultaneously, that is, it will coincide with informational influence, but is theoretically treated as an independent cognition.

If our interpretation of Deutsch and Gerard is correct, the implication is that a person will be open to informational social influence in so far as he or she believes in the utility of reliance of others. It is not difficult, however, to find examples of situations where reliance on the judgment of others will have negative consequences for the self. To the extent that the individual agrees with the others' viewpoint or is neutral with regard to the issue, no problem exists. Cases in which the others form the only existing source of information are also not particularly interesting. However, as soon as controversy exists between the individual and the groups of others, doubt will develop with regard to the utility of further reliance on the others, and, hence, informational influence will break down. In this situation, the person will seek an independent source of information. One powerful source is the stimulus basis of the judgment task, and this has been explored in the Upmeyer (1971) study.

Thus far, the discussion has considered the case in which a stimulus may be physically or logically defined (e.g., brightness of lights, solution of a mathematical problem). Let us turn now to stimulus situations which are defined by people, for example, a consensus of individuals about extent to which the pyramid of Uxmal is aesthetically pleasing. Again the trivial version of the situation occurs if one has not seen the pyramid and everybody who has seen it is enthusiastic about it. Here, one must rely "informationally" on others. However, the emergence of a suspicion that the pyramid is deteriorated and ugly (caused by direct inspection or by the reports of other persons) initiates a process of information analysis resulting in better differentiation of the information available and better differentiation of similar objects on one's evaluative dimension.

To summarize this issue, we think that the term *informational social influ-*

ence should be interpreted as a socially induced motivation to try to receive information independently of the persons in the present judgment situation. In order to assess this effect empirically, one should not employ the "yielding response," but rely on self-generated activity.

Moscovici and his co-workers introduced some important theoretical extensions to the literature and promoted a new look for the social influence process (Moscovici & Faucheux, 1972; Moscovici & Nève, 1973; Moscovici & Nemeth, 1974; Nemeth, Swedlund, & Kanki, 1974; Moscovici & Lage, 1976). A full account of the details of this research is beyond the scope of this article. Here, we will deal with Moscocivi's critique of the unilateral concept of social influence, according to which an influence is always exerted by the majority as a source of norms. Particularly, Moscovici criticized the conceptualization of minorities as mere recipients of those norms, with the majority always trying to influence the minority in order to ascertain its adherence to the norms. One can agree with Moscovici's critical position because such a model cannot explain the socially induced emergence of innovations.

Moscovici believes that innovations are introduced to society by active minorities. These minorities will be successful and influential only if they communicate by adopting a certain behavior style. The most important variable characterizing this style is consistency; for example, in the simplest case, as operationalized by Moscovici and Faucheux (1972) in a color perception experiment, consistency is achieved by repeating the same judgment on a stimulus situation over and over again. A consistent response style by a minority will be interpreted by members of the majority as an indication of confidence and will decrease their confidence in their own judgments. This creates the basis for accepting the innovative views of the minority.

The exact circumstances and the degree to which a majority yields to or polarizes the minority still remains unclear in Moscovici's work. However, he seems to suggest that the relative group size of the majority and the minority is a minor factor, whereas a consistent response style plays the major role. From this point of view, Asch's result can be interpreted as follows: Social influence does not originate in the power of a numerically superior majority to distribute rewards and sanctions; rather, it originates in a deviance from the existing stimulus norm communicated in a consistent manner. In the Asch case, consistency was produced by unanimity of the judgments.

Other forms of consistency were successfully investigated in experiments by Nemeth *et al.* (1974). According to these authors, there seems to exist a kind of consistency which can be termed *task adequate*. That is, for simple tasks, repetitions of the same judgment and unanimity may be sufficient to constitute a consistent response style. However, for complex tasks, such a style can well be interpreted as conveying stupidity, thus preventing the person from being influenced by the new norm. In order to be more successful in complex tasks, the influenceing agent should communicate a differentiated, stimulus-dependent response pattern, and he or she should use this pattern in a consistent way. Following this strategy, the agent will convey that he or she is dealing with the task adequately.

Although the ideas reported above seem to be very appealing, we are missing, from the point of view of our judgment theory, two concepts: (a) the enhanced orientation of the individual toward the stimulus reality as a consequence of a social influence attempt, and (b) the separation of the response tendency from the subjective analysis of the stimulus situation. To substantiate our concept, we have to inquire why it is possible that an individual believes a certain response pattern is adequate. In order to be able to judge "adequacy," a person must have performed a private, eventually incomplete analysis of the stimulus situation. The private stimulus analysis puts a person in a position to decide what is adequate and what is not adequate. Given a complex situation and a minority's purely repetitive response style, the person supposed to be influenced may conclude, for example, that the situation is too complex to be resolved so easily. In this example, the preexisting stimulus analysis implies the cognition of high complexity, but it may lack a particular solution; however, the solution suggested by the minority, however, may be disapproved because of its simplicity.

The theory advanced here conceptualizes consistency as more restricted than does Moscovici's; consistency merely provokes the attention of a person to be influenced. We agree with Moscovici that the size of group is unimportant for this process. When provoked by consistency, a person will first address himself toward the stimulus situation and will then improve his dissolving power of the stimulus elements. This improvement, under normal circumstances of data assessment, will be masked by the person's response pattern. That is, if a person is uncertain about the correct response, he or she may take over the suggested response from the agent exerting the influence; we believe a person does this to the extent of the agent's power to punish the person. If the power of the agent is very strong, the influenced person may yield even if convinced that the opposite is true.

In contrast to Moscovici's position, we argue that the existing stimulus situation is not an arbitrary norm that will be replaced by another norm as soon as a consistent opposing norm emerges. Although this situation may occur once in a while, de facto it seems to be a rare exception. In the language of signal detection theory, this occurs in a situation only if the stimulus alternatives generate a performance of random guessing. Even beyond physically defined stimuli, we believe there exist contents of meaning acquired by experience which are so firmly embedded by repetitive usage that they create a degree of confidence similar to (or greater than) that created by physical stimuli.

The results from the experimental studies of minorities do not appear to be quantitatively impressive. We believe this is largely due to the fact that the yielding response was used as the criterion of a minority's influential power. This objection is also valid when a classical constant method is applied to color perception judgments using the displacement or a normal ogive on a quasi-continuous judgment dimension as the criterion of a successful influence (Moscovici & Faucheux, 1972, p. 196). These data reflect the (low) power of minorities rather than a stimulus orientation produced by consistency. However, we would not decline to concede that minorities, in fact, sometimes have power, because power is not defined only by the number of group members.

B. SOCIAL ACCENTUATION

Since coming into existence, the concept of accentuation has undergone numerous alterations and reinterpretations. It plays an important role in the European literature, but it has almost disappeared in the American literature. Reviews of important studies contributing to the topic are provided by Eiser and Ströbe (1972) and Lilli (1975). Theoretically, Bruner and Postman (1951) established the concept and gave it prominent status in their hypothesized theory of social perception. In their classic coin estimation experiment, Bruner and Goodman (1947) defined the concept of accentuation as follows: "Perceptual objects which are habitually selected become more vivid, have greater clarity or greater brightness or greater apparent size" (p. 36). In other words, we are faced with the important problem of the extent to which the value (or importance) of an object will determine how it is perceived.

This problem was investigated primarily in the coin estimation paradigm. Bruner and Goodman (1947) asked children to estimate the diameter of coins and paper disks. They found that children tended to overestimate the size of coins as compared to disks. The primary results were later conceived as supporting the absolute version of accentuation theory, according to which a valued object is always perceived as larger on a physically defined stimulus dimension.

The first modification of this theory was proposed by Carter and Schooler (1949) when they found results indicating that a series of valued objects is more stretched out on a rating scale as compared to neutral objects—that is, large valued objects were relatively overestimated, whereas small valued objects were relatively underestimated. This effect was viewed as an accentuation of stimulus differences which was called the relative accentuation theory. Bruner agreed with this reinterpretation when the results were replicated, but Holzkamp and his co-workers (Holzkamp, 1965; Holzkamp & Perlwitz, 1966; Holzkamp, Keiler, & Perlwitz, 1968; Naatz & Hümmelink, 1971) continued to believe in the absolute variant of the theory and tried to present empirical evidence for it.

Unfortunately, experiments were published in the early 1950s showing no accentuation effect, although valued objects were employed. For example, Klein *et al.* (1951) could not demonstrate any effect. However, Tajfel (1957, 1959) was able to reconcile convincingly the apparent contradictions in the results by invoking a rule of relevance. This rule says that it is not sufficient for a value to exist in order to yield the accentuation effect, rather, value of an object must also covary with its size. By experience, this is true for coins because, on the average, coin systems are usually designed such that smaller coins have lower values and larger coins have higher values. However, for swastikas, value is irrelevant with respect to size because small swastikas are as negative as big ones. Later research showed that persons also accentuate if the value variable is replaced by a value-free variable which, nevertheless, indicated the direction of estimates on the accentuated variable (Tajfel & Wilkes, 1963). Hence, we would like to refer to those variables used as guidelines for estimation as *guiding variables*.

Tajfel's relevance theory of accentuation was empirically well supported by systematic variation of the statistical concordance of the variable to be estimated and its guiding variable (Lilli, 1970). Tajfel extended the application of his relevance theory of accentuation in two directions. First, he applied it to the process of stereotypes (Tajfel, 1969), that is, he demonstrated how differences between stimuli are apparently divided into two classes if a dichotomous guiding variable exists. Second, he transferred his ideas to studies of intergroup relations (Tajfel *et al.*, 1971). In these kinds of studies, he and others could demonstrate that payoffs toward others become accentuated depending on the ingroup–outgroup dichotomy. This paradigm presently is being widely explored by European researchers (Doise & Sinclair, 1973; Turner, 1975; Tajfel, 1976; Rabbie & Bekkers, 1978; and others). We believe that the different existing theories of accentuation can well be integrated into our two-step theory. A closer inspection of the existing models reveals that Bruner originally advocated a perceptual theory of accentuation. This view is supported by the quotation defining accentuation given above. Presumably, when watching the coins, a child's habitual motivations stimulate a selection process producing a better separation of the subjective distributions generated by each coin. However, this perceptual effect is superimposed by processes on the response level. It is on this level where Tajfel's accentuation model applies. Again, this can be substantiated by a quotation discussing the perceptual component of accentuation: "It is not particularly important to find out whether the stimuli are really 'seen' as larger or smaller. They are reproduced as such" (Tajfel, 1959, p. 197). For Tajfel, whether accentuation is a perceptual or a response process was a minor point, for he was concerned with demonstrating that he could reconcile the seemingly contradictory results of accentuation experiments by invoking a principle of relevance. Thus, the potential effect of motivation on perception was not a problem for him.

We believe that Tajfel's principle of relevance operates when internally represented stimuli are mapped out into a response language. In our theory, the decisive variable operating on this process has been termed *correspondence* because the choice of response alternatives is influenced by guiding variables when they covary with the response variable. In this sense, they are relevant by their correspondence property. For example, in coin estimation, it is the quantitative extent of coin value which affects the response. However, value per se could be conceptualized as relevant for the self-referring to the motivating properties of a stimulus such as money. Thus, we are proposing that value per se has no influence on the response process but will affect the quality of the subjective analysis of stimuli. This proposal is similar to Bruner's original concept of accentuation.

Given our basic definitions of perceptual and judgmental accentuation processes, we can discuss the range of application. There is not need to restrict the application to physically defined stimuli; we can also apply our theory to meaning, such as attitude. Furthermore, researchers should not confine the concept to the traditional paradigm of magnitude estimation but, rather, should expand it to differentiation tasks as well. When comparing magnitude estimation and differentiation, one should be aware of the difference in the factors affecting these two tasks. In differentiating two sets of stimuli, Tajfel's principle of relevance (i.e., the principle of correspondence) is sufficient to predict the response choice. However, it is necessary but not sufficient in magnitude estimation tasks (i.e., the domain of traditional accentuation research). More specifically, the principle of correspondence cannot explain why a *spread* of judgments has been found so often in experimental studies. In other words, why do we obtain results indicating an accentuation of differences (i.e., a relative underestimation of small coins as compared to disks)? We would like to suggest that the range principle can be made responsible for this effect. That is, subjects know by experience that coins form a smaller range of size of round objects than disks. As outlined in Section I,B,1, the range of the estimates on the response scale is inversely related to the range of anchors (Upshaw, 1969a). Thus, responses to coins are stretched out on a scale, as compared to responses to disks. In order to predict the extent of this relative accentuation effect, we have to take into account both parameters of range: origin and unit. This analysis may also solve the disagreement between advocates of the absolute (Holzkamp and co-workers) and the relative (Tajfel, Lilli) theory of accentuation. In fact, Holzkamp *et al.* (1968) pointed out the dependence of the relative concept on the judgment task, but they did not provide a general solution.

Empirical evidence for the theoretical analysis provided here was presented by Upmeyer and Cleary (1975), who tried to separate the internal representation of magnitudes from their external representation on an absolute response scale. They used the input–output transformation model of Curtis *et al.* (1968); some psychophysical applications of this model were published by Rule, Curtis, and Markley (1979), Rule and Curtis (1973), and Curtis, Paulos, and Rule (1973).

Upmeyer and Cleary asked subjects to estimate the sizes of two series of six

German coins and two equally sized series of disks in two different ways: (1) the size of the difference between all possible pairs of a series on a scale ranging form -5 (smaller) to $+5$ (larger) and (2) the absolute sizes of all six stimuli in a series on a scale from 1 (small) to 11 (large). The difference judgments were subjected to a multidimensional scaling analysis (Shephard, Romney, & Nerlove, 1972) and a one-dimensional solution was found. According to Curtis, Rule, and others, this solution was interpreted as the internal representation of the stimulus series, whereas the absolute judgments were interpreted as a combination of both the internal representation and the external mapping into a response language.

The two coin series and the equally sized disks, respectively, were different in that the value variable and the size variable corresponded to each other in either a monotonically ascending way or an alternatingly ascending way. This variation is illustrated when one compares the value of each coin with its diameter, respectively (diameters in parentheses): (1) *alternating*, .01 DM (2.15 cm), .02 DM (1.91 cm), .05 DM (1.85 cm) .10 DM (2.15 cm), .50 DM (1.99 cm), 1.00 DM (2.36 cm); (2) *monotonic*, .01 DM (1.66 cm), .02 DM (1.91 cm), .10 DM (2.15 cm), 1 DM (2.36 cm), 2 DM (2.68 cm), 5 DM (2.90 cm). It is important for understanding the experiment to notice the very small differences between the .02 DM coin and the .05 DM coin in the alternating series; this difference creates uncertainty in estimations. According to our theory, it was hypothesized that subjects will use the value of the coin as a guiding variable to judge the size. More specifically, in their absolute judgments, subjects will reverse the order of succession of the .02 DM coin and the .05 DM coin; however, the unidimensional solution of the difference judgments (as an indicator of internal representation) will not show this effect. The estimates of disks and all estimates in the monotonic series were also not supposed to show reversals. Second, it was hypothesized that, irrespective of the nature of the series, coins will yield a relative accentuation effect, that is, a more stretched mapping of responses than disks.

Nondistorted judgments on the internal as well as on the response level can be operationalized as a linear relationship between actual size and judged magnitude. Assuming a weak effect of value, this relationship is expected to be nonlinear but still monotonic. Given a strong effect, we expected nonmonotonicity, that is, a reversal of the true size relation.

The results indicated a strongly linear relationship in both disk conditions and in the monotonic-coin condition on both the internal level and the level of absolute responses. However, the absolute judgments showed a significant number of nonmonotonic reversals of the .02 DM coin and the .05 DM coin; the unidimensional scaling solution departed to some extent from linearity but did not show reversals. The relative accentuation hypothesis was strongly supported in both coin conditions. When these results were interpreted, one should keep in mind that internal representation was not operationalized as the amount of over-lap of the .02 DM coin and the .05 DM coin distributions; rather, the distance of their means was indirectly calculated. Consequently, the operationalization can be considered only as an inexact measure of differentiation. Besides this argu-ment, the difference scale which may not be free of response phenomena ex-pected from our theory. Despite these problems, the nonmonotonic relation between the internal scale and the absolute response scale supports the view that major distortions in judgments occur during the response process. Further re-search should take advantage of ideas promoted by Gravetter and Lockhead (1973).

In the field of differentiation, our two-stage accentuation theory was tested successfully by Upmeyer and Layer (1974). In this study, the subjects' attitudes toward politicians were taken as the value variable, and the stimulus dimension to be judged was established by positive and negative trait adjectives. A paired-associate method generated data which were analyzed by a nonparametric signal detection method. First, each subject was exposed to four sets of adjectives, pair-associated with four labels standing for two known politicians and two unknown groups of persons. Each of the sets was subdivided into two equal numbers of negative and positive traits. All the traits were selected in a pilot study in such a way that they characterized the German politician Strauss; at the same time, they were not characteristic of the politicians Brandt and Barzel. Strauss and Barzel were members of the same group in parliament, and they were generally negatively evaluated by the subjects, whereas Brandt was positively evaluated. One group of subjects received Brandt and Strauss as labels and another group obtained Brandt and Barzel. That is, the negative label within the two known labels was systematically varied with respect to appropriateness of description, whereas the positive label was kept constant.

After a paired presentation of labels and trait adjectives, the experimenter announced and performed a memory test. For this purpose, each adjective was presented again together with two labels, and the subject had to associate the correct label with the adjective.

Perceptual accentuation was documented by showing that the amount of overlap of subjective distributions was smaller among known politicians as com-pared to unknown groups of persons. The valence of the trait adjectives did not produce any difference. These results support our view that the importance of the attitude, not its valence, has a strong impact on the quality of internal representa-tion of information.

The response bias p(Brandt), that is, the relative frequency of associating triat adjectives to Brandt, was observed in one condition only. In this condition, both the principle of value correspondence and the principle of descriptive corre-spondence were fulfilled. That is, the adjectives characterized Strauss and they corresponded with the evaluated aspects of the subjects' attitudes toward Strauss.

(Strauss was negatively evaluated and negatively described.) In the remaining conditions, the stimulus distribution was matched by the response distribution in a fairly undistorted way. These results were attributed to the fact that value correspondence was absent in both conditions employing positive traits (Strauss–positive adjectives, Barzel–positive adjectives). Although value correspondence existed in the Barzel–negative adjectives condition (Barzel was disliked), it was not sufficient for a response distortion, apparently because the descriptive correspondence was lacking (all adjectives were characteristic for Strauss only).

Upmeyer and Layer (1974) reported another experiment using the same paradigm but without variation of the descriptive correspondence. The results showed that perceptual accentuation occurred again, but value correspondence alone was not sufficient to produce response accentuation. Summarizing this study, response accentuation can be expected only if both value and descriptive correspondence exist—at least when a known attitude object is to be judged. The Upmeyer and Layer study does not give evidence as to the exact amount a person must know in order to apply the principle of descriptive correspondence. However, from another memory study (Upmeyer *et al.*, 1976), we can roughly say that given a low level of knowledge and a high involvement of the self, value correspondence alone may be sufficient to shift responses into the direction of the value suggested by the attitude. In this experiment, active soccer players judged traits of their own and of a directly competing club, as well as traits of two clubs not incorporated in their own league. In one case, pure value correspondence was sufficient to bias responses according to the player's attitude. This study used groups (i.e., clubs) as labels for information; it can be assumed that these labels lack the conciseness needed to establish strong descriptive characterizations. Thus, value correspondence alone affected response tendencies of the players.

Although the results from the studies reported above appear to exhibit a common pattern, it seems to be recommendable to explore further the effects of value and descriptive correspondence.

C.   ATTITUDE AND MEMORY

This section is based on the same theoretical concept as the one on accentuation. However, in the literature, the research areas of "attitude and memory" and "accentuation" are kept totally apart. Since we are dealing here with the application part of the theory, we will maintain the arbitrary distinction.

The research on the relation between memory and attitude in social psychology is firmly embedded in the tradition of the Levine and Murphy (1943) study. At present, this research is not popular, apparently because the obtained results are contradictory and did not lead to an accepted theory. On·one hand, this is due to the ambiguous concept of attitude itself; on the other hand, the memory methodology (and theory) employed appears to be too primitive in view of recent developments in cognitive psychology. We expect a revival of this kind of research because of the progress achieved in memory theory. We will discuss some of the small range theories developed in social psychology and try to incorporate them into our own theory. A more detailed report on the relevant literature is provided by McGuire (1969) and Upmeyer and Layer (1973).

The theoretical substance of the study by Levine and Murphy (1943) can be summarized by the following hypothesis: Persons will remember information that corresponds to their own attitudes better than information that does not correspond to their attitudes. This hypothesis can be traced back to Freud (1904), who defined this process more generally as autism. Referring to Freudian thinking, we have to inquire as to whether or not autistic behavior is of a psychopathological nature and, hence, whether it applies to the majority of people. The maintenance of inner psychic balance has been widely assumed as the underlying motive for autistic behavior. However, theoretically, it seems to be more plausible that attitudes are changed when persons have to adjust to new environments. The latter position is known as *functionalistic* (see Jones & Aneshansel, 1956). One disadvantage of the functional view is its low predictability, that is, ex post facto one can always find a reason why persons adjusted their attitudes. Nevertheless, Jones and Aneshansel were successful in demonstrating (by announcing that antiarguments have to be reproduced later) that evaluation apprehension is able to reverse the Levine–Murphy effect. However, it can be argued that such a demonstration is atypical for information processing in everyday life.

Novelty was suggested as another factor in the attitude and memory literature and was found to increase memory performance (Greenwald & Sakumara, 1967). However, novelty was neither exactly defined nor satisfactorily explained. As we discussed (pp. 269–270), we believe that stimuli (in this case valenced information) must be defined as subjectively rare events to be perceived as novel. These events are a potential threat for the self because they may cause a revision of one's own attitude position. Consequently, novel information will be elaborated, resulting in an improved storage of information. This does *not* imply that the attitude will change in the direction suggested by the valence of the new information. However, we believe that novelty is responsible for findings that nonplausible arguments were retrieved easily (Jones & Kohler, 1958).

Garber (1955) proposed a theory to deal with attitude and memory which is closer to our theory than any other. It can be termed a sensitivity–repression theory. Garber suggested that ego involvment is a necessary prerequisite for selective storage of verbal material. However, the valence of the material does not influence the storing process. So far, Garber's position is the same as ours. However, the following kind of information will be centrally repressed after storing: (a) information considered to be wrong on the basis of one's own experience and (b) information incompatible with one's own attitude. Garber's repression mechanism was conceptualized as a central process. Contrary to his concept, we think it is a response process. If our assumption is correct, Garber's two-factor theory can be reinterpreted in terms of our two types of correspondence principles: (a) If information corresponds descriptively with one's cognitive experience (as a guiding variable), an appropriate response becomes more likely; this response is a complement of repressing wrong information; and (b) if information corresponds evaluatively with one's attitude, a response expressing the same valence becomes more likely; this response is a complement of repressing attitude-discrepant information. Garber did not provide precise details on which factor will dominate in a given situation. Without ignoring the basic difficulties to solve these problems, we have already made some suggestions (see pp. 273–276).

Garber's theory has been challenged on empirical grounds. For example, Jones and Kohler (1958) showed that nonplausible, attitude-discrepant information was particularly well retrieved. However, these findings could not be replicated by other authors (Waly & Cook, 1966; Brigham & Cook, 1969). Furthermore, novelty may have been a confounding variable, and the method employed to measure retrieval did not represent the recent standard in memory research. Particularly, these and other researchers in social psychology invariably confounded recognizability and response tendency.

The studies reported in Section II,B (Upmeyer & Layer, 1974; Upmeyer *et al.*, 1976) can be viewed as supporting our conceptualization of attitude and memory. We believe that the Levine–Murphy hypothesis is wrong in stating that information rejecting one's own attitude will be forgotten. On the contrary, all information relevant to a salient attitude will be stored more accurately, and this is particularly true if the information is novel. At the same time, the response may mask this central process because, when in doubt, a subject will respond according to his or her attitude. However, this kind of response tendency will only prevail if it is not counteracted by sanctions or descriptions contradictory to one's own experience. If sanctions and/or contradictory descriptions do not counteract the response suggested by the valence of the attitude, but rather support it, then we might observe a strong response-masking effect. In order to show that the Levine–Murphy hypothesis should be confined to the response system, it is advisable to control for sanctions and contradictory descriptions in an experiment.

This was done by Etzel *et al.* (unpublished). A set of 80 favorable and 80 unfavorable trait adjectives were selected from a list provided by Busz *et al.* (1972). Each subject was asked to describe three stimulus persons by checking the most suitable half of both the favorable and the unfavorable adjectives. The stimulus persons to be described were (1) a liked other, (2) a disliked other, and (3) the self. On completion of this task, the experimenter announced a recognition test. In this test, each trait was presented again together with the stimulus person printed beside it. For each item, the subject had to decide whether or not he or she checked this item to describe the given trait adjective. The response data of each subject can be analyzed in terms of signal detection analysis; the two sets to be discriminated were $\{S_1 \equiv$ previously checked$\}$ and $\{S_2 \equiv$ previously omitted$\}$ and the responses were $\{R_1 \equiv$ "Yes, I checked it"$\}$ and $\{R_2 \equiv$ "No, I did not check it"$\}$.

It was hypothesized and shown that differentiation performance was better for self-descriptive traits as compared to other descriptive traits, irrespective of the valence of the traits and the likability of others. This result clearly supports our theory that relevance (and not valence) determines the strength of internal representation. On the other hand, the response variable p(checked) was strongly affected by both the valence of the traits and the likability of others. When favorable items were analyzed, the "liked other" was assigned to having been more frequently checked than the "disliked other," whereas exactly the opposite was true for unfavorable items. The responses for the self-description were also biased toward favorableness, but not as much as in the other conditions (see Table IV). The response results can be interpreted well by our value correspondence principle; that is, if the stimulus person label and the underlying trait information covary in terms of value, responses are absolutely accentuated in the direction suggested by the valence of the label. Value correspondence alone was apparently sufficient to produce this effect, and we believe this is due to the descriptively poor content of the labels "liked other" and "disliked other."

Although our proposals for a solution of the problems faced in the field of attitude and memory certainly exceed the scope of earlier studies using one parameter for the assessment of memory, it seems to us that our own frame of reference is too narrow to deal with all problems emerging in this context. According to the terms widely used in the memory research area, our theory can be classified as a strength theory. We did not consider any assumption on the structure of human memory, like networks (Quillian, 1968) or scripts (Abelson,

TABLE IV

DISCRIMINATION PERFORMANCE AND RESPONSE BIAS OF VARIOUS
STIMULUS PERSONS

	Liked other	Disliked other	Self
Discrimination performance $P(c)$			
Favorable	70	71	78
Unfavorable	71	69	75
Response bias p (checked)			
Favorable	.67	.41	.60
Unfavorable	.36	.57	.42

1976). These structural properties seem to be indispensable for a thorough understanding of any memory theory, and we believe that attitude theory should include those new developments.

D. OTHER APPLICATIONS

Further possible applications of the present theory are enumerated below with some relevant literature provided. These applications do not seem to be central enough to justify more discussion because they are not very elaborated, they play a minor role in the literature of social psychology, or they are insufficiently documented by empirical evidence.

1. Ethnic Identification. Empirical applications of signal detection theory to the problem of identifying ethnic group members were provided by Malpass and Kravitz (1969), Dorfman, Keeve, and Saslow (1971), and Lang (1976). Upmeyer (1976) published a theoretical analysis based on the present theory. A more general review (without any signal detection applications) was authored by Brand, Ruiz, and Padilla (1974).

2. Subliminal Perception. This area of research was carefully reviewed by Erdelyi (1974), who discusses the application of signal detection methods (e.g., by Dorfman, 1967). An early, farsighted contribution to this problem was advanced by Dember (1960).

3. Interpersonal Attraction. Berman (1978) performed the first experiment in this field to separate perceptual from judgmental processes.

4. Stress. The effects of stress on sensitivity and response bias were explored by Chapman and Feather (1971), Clark and Greenberg (1971), and Neufeld (1975).

5. Sensitizers and Repressors. This well-known personality variable was subjected to a signal detection analysis by Van Egeren (1968).

6. Modeling. As outlined in Section I,A,3, Bandura's theory can be interpreted as a special case of our judgment model. One should try to apply our response parameters "expectation" and "correspondence" to choices between two different ways of behavior (e.g., between aggression and helping behavior). It is also possible to treat Bandura's accuracy measures of matched dependent behavior as a derivation of differentiation ability.

III. Final Discussion

This section is an attempt to dispense with two misconceptions which are, unfortunately, widespread among social psychologists concerning the role of psychophysics.

A. THE PERCEPTION-IS-NOT-MEASURABLE ARGUMENT

Researchers today share the view that perception is an intervening variable which, by definition, cannot be measured. On the measurement level, we always have to rely on individuals' responses, and the response process may contaminate reports on percepts.

However, this formal argument should not prevent us from finding *patterns* of responses which may turn out to be relatively stable and independent of a particular response mode. In other words, research may yield results showing that a particular pattern is invariant over a variety of ways in reporting what has been observed. At the same time, this pattern changes consistently when physical parameters of the stimuli are changed. One may or may not call such a pattern a measure of "perception"; irrespective of its scientific label, an actual progress is made in our understanding. In general, it is common practice in the sciences to infer the meaning of a measure from the meaning of the independent variables which were shown to affect the measure. Consequently, if we are able to establish one set of independent variables affecting d' and another set affecting $p(R_1)$, and if the psychological meaning of the independent variables varies between sets but is related within sets, then we feel certain that we have discovered a useful distinction.

Two related points should be emphasized here as well. (1) There is a tendency among psychophysicists to exclude unwanted confounds from any measure which is intended to refer solely to physical variables (e.g., see Swets & Sewall, 1963). These confounds are imprecisely called attitudes or motivational effects. For problems of a social psychological nature, however, they become as important as sensitivity measures and should be studied in their own right. This is the major reason that signal detection theory might ultimately prove to be more fruitful in social psychology than in psychophysics. In psychophysics, it is often possible to eliminate response bias effects through rigorous control of the laboratory environment, thus rendering the use of signal detection methodology unnecessary. (2) Social psychologists are certainly not primarily interested in constructing a "physical" measure of sensitivity. The properties of d' must be explored in detail in order to bring about a smooth transition to the use of signal detection methodology in the study of social perception.

B. THE DEPENDENCE-ON-A-PARADIGM ARGUMENT

Even those researchers who agree that the signal detection approach is not merely a method, but also encompasses a set of theoretical ideas, still tend to see it as having a very narrow range of application because it offers only a stringently defined set of relatively complex methods. More importantly, the complexity of the methodology may lead to the introduction of artifacts and, thus, the experimental judgment process may not stimulate judgments in everyday situations.

We think this is a fair argument, although it remains to be seen whether we will be able to completely free ourselves of the need for some investigation paradigm. A viable solution to this problem might be achieved by adding other research approaches to the central paradigm (in this case, to the signal detection paradigm) which share some important characteristics. Among these common characteristics, of course, should be included the basic separation of stimulus analysis and response tendency. In addition, the theoretically postulated mechanisms which determine the two basic processes should be the same for all considered paradigms; that is, on the operational level, there should be a high similarity between independent variables across paradigms. If these similar independent variables affect the two basic processes in the same direction, irrespective of the experimental paradigm employed, then we can feel more certain that the effect is a true one and not merely the product of artifacts engendered by the use of a particular paradigm.

It should be recognized that this is an empirical and not merely an analytical question. At present, we must rely solely on the analytical work and empirical evidence in the literature because no research has been carried out in which the independent variables were systematically varied over methodological paradigms. For such an integration, we have considered signal detection (Swets *et al.*, 1961), imitation learning (Bandura, 1965), variable perspective (Upshaw, 1965), and the input–output transformation model (Rule *et al.*, 1970). The first two of these paradigms involve differentiation judgment tasks and the latter two, magnitude estimation tasks.

As it stands now, the results encourage an integration, but more work has to be done before it is completed.

REFERENCES

Abelson, R. P. Script processing in attitude formation and decision making. In J. S. Carroll & J. W. Payne (Eds.), *Cognitive and Social Behavior*. Hillsdale, New Jersey: Erlbaum, 1976.

Adams, J. C. The relative effects of various testing atmospheres on spontaneous flexibility: A factor of divergent thinking. *Journal of Creative Behavior*, 1968, **2**, 187–194.

Anderson, N. H. Likeableness ratings of 555 personality trait words. *Journal of Personality and Social Psychology*, 1968, **9**, 272–280.

Anderson, H. H., & Hubert, S. Effects of concomitant verbal recall on order effect in personality impression formation. *Journal of Verbal Learning and Verbal Behavior*, 1963, **2**, 379–391.

Asch, S. E. Studies of independence and conformity: A minority of one against a unanimous majority. *Psychological Monographs*, 1956, No. 9.

Atkinson, R. C. A variable sensitivity theory of signal detection. *Psychological Review*, 1963, **70**, 91–106.

Bandura, A. Vicarious processes: A case of non-trial learning. In L. Berkowitz (Ed.), *Advances in experimental social psychology* (Vol. 2). New York: Academic Press, 1965.

Bandura, A. *Social learning theory*. Morristown, New Jersey: General Learning, 1971.

Bandura, A. Behavior theory and the models of man. *American Psychologist*, 1974, **29**, 859–869.

Bandura, A., Ross, D., & Ross, S. A. Vicarious reinforcement and imitative learning. *Journal of Abnormal and Social Psychology*, 1963, **67**, 601–607.

Banks, W. P. Signal detection theory and human memory. *Psychological Bulletin*, 1970, **74**, 81–99.

Berlyne, D. E. *Conflict, arousal, and curiosity*. New York: McGraw-Hill, 1960.

Berman, J. J. Factors affecting judgments of how much another likes us: A signal detection approach. *European Journal of Social Psychology*, 1978, **8**, 157–168.

Bjork, R. A. Positive forgetting: The non-interference of items intentionally forgotten. *Journal of Verbal Learning and Verbal Behavior*, 1970, **9**, 255–268.

Bollinger, G., Helingrath, C., & Upmeyer, A. Der Einfluß der Gruppenzugehörigkeit und des Antwortmodus auf die Verarbeitung origineller Informationen. *Zeitschrift für Experimentelle und Angewandte Psychologie*, 1977, **24**, 198–213.

Bouchard, T. J., Drauden, J., & Barsaloux, I. A comparison of individual, subgroup, and total group methods of problem solving. *Journal of Applied Psychology*, 1974, **59**, 226–227.

Brand, E. S., Ruiz, R. A., & Padilla, A. M. Ethnic indentification and preference: A review. *Psychological Bulletin*, 1974, **81**, 860–890.

Brigham, J. C., & Cook, S. W. The influence of attitude on the recall of controversial material: A failure to confirm. *Journal of Experimental Social Psychology*, 1969, **5**, 240–245.

Broadbent, D. E. *Perception and communication*. Oxford: Pergamon, 1958.

Bruner, J. S., & Goodman, C. C. Value and need as organizing factors in perception. *Journal of Social Psychology*, 1947, **27**, 203–208.

Bruner, J. S., & Postman, L. An approach to social perception. In W. Dennis & R. Lippitt (Eds.) *Current trends in social psychology*. Pittsburgh, Pennsylvania: Univ. of Pittsburgh Press, 1951.

Dusz, M., Cohen, R., Poser, U., Schümer, A., Schümer, R., & Sonnenfeld, A. Die soziale Bewertung von 880 Eigenschaftsbegriffen sowie die Analyse der Ähnlichkeitsbeziehungen zwischen einigen dieser Begriffe. *Zeitschrift für Experimentelle und Angewandte Psychologie*, 1972, **19**, 282–308.

Cantor, M., & Mischel, W. Traits and Prototypes: Effects on recognition memory. *Journal of Personality and Social Psychology*, 1977, **35**, 38–48.

Carter, L., & Schooler, E. Value, need, and other factors in perception. *Psychological Review*, 1949, **56**, 200–208.

Chapman, C. R., & Feather, B. W. Sensitivity to phobic imagery: A sensory decision theory analysis. *Behavior Research and Therapy*, 1971, **9**, 161–168.

Clark, W. C., & Greenberg, D. B. Effects of stress, knowledge of results, and proactive inhibition on verbal recognition memory (d') and response criterion (L_x). *Journal of Personality and Social Psychology*, 1971, **17**, 42–47.

Coombs, C. H., Dawes, R. M., & Tversky, A. *Mathematical psychology. An elementary introduction*. Englewood Cliffs, New Jersey: Prentice-Hall, 1970.

Curtis, D. W., Atneave, F., & Harrington, T. L. A test of two-stage model of magnitude judgment. *Perception and Psychophysics*, 1968, **3**, 25–31.

Curtis, D. W. Paulos, M. A., & Rule, S. T. Relation between disjunctive reaction time and stimulus difference. *Journal of Experimental Psychology*, 1973, **99**, 167–173.

Dember, W. N. *The psychology of perception*. New York: Holt, 1960.

Deutsch, M., & Gerard, H. B. A study of normative and informational social influence upon individual judgment. *Journal of Abnormal and Social Psychology*, 1955, **51**, 629–636.

Doise, W., & Sinclair, A. The categorisation process in intergroup relations. *European Journal of Social Psychology*, 1973, **3**, 145–157.

Dorfman, D. D. Recognition of taboo words as a function of a priori probability. *Journal of Personality and Social Psychology*, 1967, **7**, 1–10.

Dorfman, D. D., Keeve, S., & Saslow, C. Ethnic identification: A signal detection analysis. *Journal of Personality and Social Psychology*, 1971, **18**, 373–379.

Egan, J. P., Schulman, A. I., & Greenberg, G. Z. Operating characteristics determined by binary decisions and by ratings. *Journal of the Acoustical Society of America,* 1959, **31**, 768–773.

Eiser, J. R., & Ströbe, W. *Categorization and social judgment.* New York: Academic Press, 1972.

Erdelyi, M. H. A new look at the New Look: Perceptual defense and vigilance. *Psychological Review,* 1974, **81**, 1–25.

Etzel, G., Lang, S., & Upmeyer, A. *Cognitive schemata in social information processing: Effects on recognition and response-bias.* (Unpublished). University of Mannheim, Germany.

Fechner, T. *Elemente der psychophysik (Teil II).* Leipzig: 1860. (Reprinted by Bonset, Amsterdam, 1964.)

Festinger, L. A theory of social comparison processes. *Human Relations,* 1954, **7**, 117–140.

Freedman, J. L., & Sears, D. O. Selective exposure. In L. Berkowitz (Ed.), *Advances in experimental social psychology* (Vol. 2). New York: Academic Press, 1965.

Freud, S. Zur Psychopathologie des Alltagslebens, Über Vergessen, Versprechen, Vergreifen, Aberglaube und Irrtum. 1904. In S. Freud, *Gesammelte Werke,* Frankfurt: Fischer, 1964.

Garber, R. B. Influence of cognitive and affective factors in learning and retaining attitudional materials. *Journal of Abnormal and Social Psychology,* 1955, **51**, 387–397.

Gravetter, F., & Lockhead, G. R. Criterial range as a frame of reference for stimulus judgment. *Psychological Review,* 1973, **80**, 203–216.

Green, D. M., & Swets, J. A. *Signal detection and psychophysics.* New York: Wiley, 1966.

Greenwald, A. G., & Sakumura, J. S. Attitude and selective learning: Where are the phenomena of yesteryear. *Journal of Personality and Social Psychology,* 1967, **7**, 287–397.

Haber, R. N. The nature of the effect of set on perception. *Psychological Review,* 1966, **73**, 335–351.

Helson, H. Adaptation-level as a basis for a quantitative theory of frames of reference. *Psychological Review,* 1948, **55**, 297–313.

Holzkamp, K. Das Problem der "Akzentuierung" in der sozialen Wahrnehmung. *Zeitschrift für Experimentelle und Angewandte Psychologie,* 1965, **12**, 86–97.

Holzkamp, K., Keiler, P., & Perlwitz, E. Die Umkehrung der Akzentuierungsrichtung unter serialen Lernbedingungen: Theoretische und experimentelle Beiträge zum Problem der sozialen Wahrnehmung. *Psychologische Forschung,* 1968, **32**, 64–68.

Holzkamp, K., & Perlwitz, E. Absolute oder relative Größenakzentuierung? Eine experimentelle Studie zur sozialen Wahrnehmung. *Zeitschrift für Experimentelle und Angewandte Psychologie,* 1966, **13**, 390–405.

Jones, E. E., & Aneshansel, J. The learning and utilisation of contravaluant material. *Journal of Abnormal and Social Psychology,* 1956, **53**, 27–33.

Jones, E. E., & Kohler, R. The effects of plausibility on the learning of controversial statements. *Journal of Abnormal and Social Psychology,* 1958, **57**, 315–320.

Kahneman, D., & Tversky, A. On the psychology of prediction. *Psychological Review,* 1973, **80**, 237–251.

Kanungo, R., & Das, J. P. Differential learning and forgetting as a function of the social frame of reference. *Journal of Abnormal and Social Psychology,* 1960, **61**, 82–86.

Katz, J. J., & Fodor, J. A. The structure of a semantic theory. in L. A. Jakobovitz & M. S. Miron (Eds.), *Readings in the psychology of language.* Englewood Cliffs, New Jersey: Prentice-Hall, 1967.

Kelley, H. H. Causal schemata and the attribution process. In E. E. Jones, D. E. Kanouse, H. H. Kelley, R. E. Nisbett, S. Valins, and B. Weiner (Eds.), *Attribution: Perceiving the causes of behavior.* Morristown, New Jersey: General Learning, 1971.

Klein, G. S., Schlesinger, H., & Meister, D. The effect of personal values on perception: An experimental critique. *Psychological Review,* 1951, **58**, 96–112.

Kriss, M., Kinchla, R. A., & Darley, J. M. A mathematical model of social influences on perceptual judgments. *Journal of Experimental Social Psychology,* 1977, **13**, 403–420.

306 ARNOLD UPMEYER

Lang, S. Identifikationsleistung und Antwortpräferenzen von Personen mit unterschiedlichem beruflichen Status bei der Identifikation von Gastarbeitern. Diploma thesis, Mannheim, 1976. (Unpublished).

Levine, J. M., & Murphy, G. The learning and forgetting of controversial material. *Journal of Abnormal and Social Psychology,* 1943, **38,** 507-517.

Lilli, W. Das Zustandekommen von Stereotypen über einfache und komplexe Sachverhalte. Experimente zum klassifizierenden Urteil. *Zeitschrift für Sozialpsychologie,* 1970, **1,** 57-79.

Lilli, W. *Soziale akzentuierung.* Stuttgart: Kohlhammer, 1975.

Luce, R. D. Detection and recognition. In R. D. Luce, R. R. Bush, & E. Galanter (Eds.), *Handbook of mathematical psychology* (Vol. I). New York: Wiley, 1963.

Luchins, A. S., & Luchins, E. H. Previous experience with ambiguous and non-ambiguous perceptual stimuli under various social influences. *Journal of Social Psychology,* 1955, **42,** 249-270.

McGuire, W. J. The nature of attitudes and attitude change. In G. Lindzey & E. Aronson (Eds.), *The handbook of social psychology,* Reading, Massachusetts: Addison-Wesley, 1969.

Malpass, R. S., & Kravitz, J. Recognition for faces of own and other race. *Journal of Personality and Social Psychology,* 1969, **13,** 330-334.

Moscovici, S., & Faucheux, C. Social influence, conformity bias, and the style of active minorities. In L. Berkowitz (Ed.), *Advances in experimental social psychology.* (Vol. 6). New York: Academic Press, 1972.

Moscovici, S., & Lage, E. Studies in social influence III: Majority versus minority influence in a group. *European Journal of Social Psychology,* 1976, **6,** 149-174.

Moscovici, S., & Nemeth, C. Social influence II: Minority influence. In C. Nemeth (Ed.), *Social psychology: Classic and contemporary integrations.* Chicago, Illinois: Rand-McNally, 1974.

Moscovici, S., & Nève, P. Studies in social influence: II. Instrumental and symbolic influence. *European Journal of Social Psychology,* 1973, **4,** 461-471.

Naatz, T., & Hümmelink, W. Zur Realisation einer kognitiven Akzentuierungstheorie: Eine experimentelle Entscheidung zwischen dem serialen Ansatz (Tajfel) und dem modifizierten absoluten Ansatz (Holzkamp) bei serialer Stimuluskonstellation. *Zeitschrift für Sozialpsychologie,* 1971, **2,** 369-373.

Neisser, U. *Cognitive psychology.* New York: Appleton, 1967.

Nemeth, C., Swedlund, M., & Kanki, B. Patterning of the minority's responses and their influence on the majority. *European Journal of Social Psychology,* 1974, **1,** 53-64.

Nemeth, C., & Wachtler, J. Consistency and modification of judgment. *Journal of Experimental and Social Psychology,* 1973, **9,** 65-79.

Neufeld, R. W. J. Effect of cognitive appraisal on d' and response-bias on experimental stress. *Journal of Personality and Social Psychology,* 1975, **31,** 235-243.

Norman, D. A. Toward a theory of memory and attention. *Psychological Review,* 1968, **65,** 522-536.

Norman, D. A. *Memory and attention.* New York: Wiley, 1969.

Ostrom, T. M., & Upshaw, H. S. Psychological perspective and attitude change. In A. C. Greenwald, T. C. Brock, & T. M. Ostrom (Eds.), *Psychological foundations of attitudes.* New York: Academic Press, 1968.

Paivio, A. *Imagery and verbal processes.* New York: Holt, 1971.

Parducci, A. Category judgment: A range-frequency model. *Psychological Review,* 1965, **72,** 407-418.

Peabody, D. Trait inferences: Evaluative and descriptive aspects. *Journal of Personality and Social Psychology Monograph,* 1967, **7,** (whole No. 644).

Quillian M. R. Semantic memory. In M. Minksy (Ed.), *Semantic Information processing.* Cambridge, Massachusetts: M.I.T. Press, 1968.

Rabbie, J. M., & Bekkers, F. Threatened leadership and intergroup competition. *European Journal of Social Psychology,* 1978, **8,** 9-20.

Restorff, v., II., Über die Wirkung von Bereichsbildungen im Spurenfeld. *Psychologische Forschung*, 1933, **18**, 299–342.

Rule, S. J., Curtis, D. W., & Markley, R. P. Input and output transformations from magnitude estimation. *Journal of Experimental Psychology*, 1970, **86**, 343–349.

Rule, S. J., & Curtis, D. W. Conjoint scaling of subjective number and weight. *Journal of Experimental Psychology*, 1973, **97**, 305–309.

Sears, D. O. Selective exposure. In R. P. Abelson, E. Aronson, W. J. McGuire, T. M. Newcomb, M. J. Rosenberg, and P. H. Tannenbaum (Eds.), *Theories of cognitive consistency: A source book*. Chicago, Illinois: Rand McNally, 1968.

Secord, P. F., Bevan, W., & Katz, B. The Negro stereotype and perceptual accentuation. *Journal of Abnormal and Social Psychology*, 1956, **53**, 78–83.

Shepard, R. N., Romney, K. A., & Nerlove, S. B. *Multidimensional scaling* (Vol. 1). New York: Seminar Press, 1972.

Sherif, M. *A study of social factors in perception*. New York: Columbia Univ. Press, 1935.

Sherif, M., & Hovland, C. I. Assimilation and contrast effects of anchoring stimuli on judgment. *Journal of Experimental Psychology*, 1958, **55**, 150–155.

Sperling, G. Successive approximations to a model for short term memory. *Acta Psychologica*, 1967, **27**, 285–292.

Stevens, S. S. Issues in psychophysical measurement. *Psychological Review*, 1971, **78**, 426–450.

Swets, J. A. Detection theory and psychophysics: A review. *Psychometrika*, 1961, **26**, 49–63.

Swets, J. A. The relative operating characteristic in psychology. *Science*, 1973, **182**, 990–1000.

Swets, J. A., & Sewall, S. T. Invariance of signal detectability over stages of practice and level of motivation. *Journal of Experimental Psychology*, 1963, **6**, 120–126.

Swets, J. A., Tanner, W. P., & Birdsall, T. G. Decision processes in perception. *Psychological Review*, 1961, **68**, 301–340.

Tajfel, H. Value and the perceptual judgment of magnitude. *Psychological Review*, 1957, **64**, 192–204.

Tajfel, H. Quantative judgment in social perception. *British Journal of Psychology*, 1959, **50**, 16–29.

Tajfel, H. Cognitive aspects of prejudice. *Journal of Social Issues*, 1969, **25**, 79–97.

Tajfel, H. *Studies in intergroup behaviour*. (European Monographs in Social Psychology.) New York: Academic Press, 1976.

Tajfel, H., Billig, M. G., Bundy, R. P., & Flament, C. Social categorisation and intergroup behavior. *European Journal of Social Psychology*, 1971, **1**, 199–178.

Tajfel, H., & Wilkes, A. L. Classification and quantitative judgment. *British Journal of Psychology*, 1963, **54**, 101–114.

Tanner, W. P., & Swets, J. A. A decision theory of visual detection. *Psychological Review*, 1954, **61**, 401–409.

Taylor, S. E., & Fiske, S. T. Salience, attention, and attribution: Top of the head phenomena. In L. Berkowitz (Ed.), *Advances in experimental social psychology* (Vol. 11). New York: Academic Press, 1978.

Turner, J. C. Social comparison and social identy: Some prospects of intergroup behavior. *European Journal of Social Psychology*, 1975, **5**, 5–34.

Tversky, A., & Kahneman, D. Availability: A heuristic for judging frequency and probability. *Cognitive Psychology*, 1973, **5**, 207–232.

Upmeyer, A. *Diskriminationsleistung und Skalengebrauch unter sozialem Einfluß*. Unpublished Dissertation, University of Mannheim, 1968.

Upmeyer, A. Social perception and signal detectability theory: Group influence on discrimination and usage of scale. *Psychologische Forschung*, 1971, **34**, 285–294.

Upmeyer, A. Ethnische Identifikation. *Zeitschrift für Sozialpsychologie*, 1976, **7**, 143–153.

Upmeyer, A., & Cleary, P. D. Coin estimation as a two-stage process. *Berichte aus dem Sonderforschungsbereich 24, Universität Mannheim*, 1975.

Upmeyer, A., Krolage, J., Etzel, G., Lilli, W., & Klump, H. Accentuation of information in real competing groups. *European Journal of Social Psychology*, 1976, **6**, 95-97.

Upmeyer, A., & Layer, H. Effects of inferiority and superiority in groups on recognition memory and confidence. *Psychologische Forschung*, 1973, **35**, 277-290.

Upmeyer, A., & Layer, H. Attitüden und Gedächtnis bei sozialer Urteilsbildung. *Zeitschrift für Sozialpsychologie*, 1973, **4**, 181-194.

Upmeyer, A., & Layer, H. Accentuation and attitude in social judgment. *European Journal of Social Psychology*, 1974, **4**, 469-488.

Upmeyer, A., Layer, H., & Schreiber, W. K. Über die Verarbeitung stereotypisierter Eigenschaften fremder Völker. *Psychologische Beiträge*, 1972, **4**, 521-540.

Upmeyer, A., & Schreiber, W. K. Effects of agreement and disagreement in group on recognition memory performance and confidence. *European Journal of Social Psychology*, 1972, **2**, 109-128.

Upshaw, H. S. The effect of variable perspectives of judgments of opinion statements for Thurstone scales: Equal appearing intervals. *Journal of Personality and Social Psychology*, 1965, **2**, 60-69.

Upshaw, H. S. The personal reference scale: An approach to social judgment. In L. Berkowitz (Ed.), *Advances in experimental social psychology* (Vol. 4). New York: Academic Press, 1969. (a)

Upshaw, H. S. Stimulus range and the judgmental unit. *Journal of Experimental Psychology*, 1969, **5**, 1-11. (b)

Van Egeren, L. Repression and sensitization: Sensitivity and recognition criteria. *Journal of Experimental Research in Personality*, 1968, **3**, 1-8.

Volkmann, I. Scales of judgment and their implications for social psychology. In J. H. Rohrer and M. Sherif (Eds.), *Social psychology at the crossroads*. New York: Harper, 1951.

Wald, A. *Statistical decision functions*. New York: Wiley, 1950.

Waly, P., & Cook, S. W. Attitude as a determinant of learning and memory: A failure to confirm. *Journal of Personality and Social Psychology*, 1966, **4**, 280-288.

Wertheimer, M. Über das Denken der Naturvölker I. Zahlen und Zahlengebilde. *Zeitschrift für Psychologie*, 1925, 61. Reprinted in: M. Wertheimer *Drei Abhandlungen zur Gestalttheorie*. Darmstadt: Wissenschaftliche Buchgesellschaft, 1967.

Wicklund, R. A. Objective self-awareness. In L. Berkowitz (Ed.), *Advances in experimental social psychology* (Vol. 8). New York: Academic Press, 1975.

Wishner, J. Reanalysis of "impression of personality". *Psychological Review*, 1960, **7**, 96-112.

JURY TRIALS: PSYCHOLOGY AND LAW[1]

Charlan Jeanne Nemeth

DEPARTMENT OF PSYCHOLOGY
UNIVERSITY OF CALIFORNIA
BERKELEY, CALIFORNIA

[1]Preparation of this manuscript was partially supported by NIMH Grant No. 5 RO1 MH31401-03 receipt of which is gratefully acknowledged. I also wish to thank Wendy Alderson, Barbara Seibert, and Katherine White for their invaluable help in locating and organizing the materials contained herein.

ADVANCES IN EXPERIMENTAL SOCIAL
PSYCHOLOGY, VOL. 14

I. Introduction

In this article, we will be concentrating on trial by jury, an institution that has a long and cherished history but that is undergoing rapid changes; there are even calls for its abolition. This review of the difficult interface between psychology and law will cover the numerous empirical studies related to individual differences in conviction proneness and/or punitiveness, extra-evidentiary factors in individual decision making, and the dynamics of juror interaction that culminate in the verdict. We will also necessarily review evidence related to recent changes in the operation of juries, for example, in the size of jury and the requirements of unanimity, as well as various proposed reforms.

However, we would like to encourage researchers to go beyond these matters and apply their intellects and efforts to the broader issues, to conceptions of justice and to the processes by which these can best be achieved. Social psychological research is of considerable aid to an attorney whose purpose is to win his or her case. We have tools and knowledge pertinent to the selection of jurors, to the development of case strategy, and to the art of persuasion. We have also contributed to appellate issues such as the size and decision rules of juries. Yet, our research is often directed at a compilation of factors that "make a significant difference" or to the consequences of a decision once the court has already made its ruling. To aid the courts in their decisions of the future and, perhaps more ambitiously, to outline procedures that better ensure "due process" and "equal protection under the laws," we need to address the conceptual and value-laden issues involved in the notion of *justice* as well as study and devise procedures by which to ensure the attainment of this objective.

At present, our system of trial by jury is an adversarial process where evidence for both sides is presented to a (theoretically) impartial body of representatives of the community, usually 12 in number and typically required to deliberate to unanimity. Their decision is the final verdict.

Questions, of course, arise as to whether this is the best system to achieve justice and whether it best reflects the values intended by the framers of the Constitution in their provisions for due process, equal protection under the law, and trial by one's peers. For example, both critics and advocates have asked whether representation of the community is the best way to achieve justice. Are laymen sufficiently capable to render complicated judgments? Is representativeness the best way to achieve impartiality or lack of bias? Then there are questions on the specific forms representation should take. Is 12 the best number of jurors? Is justice curtailed if the size of the jury is reduced? Is unanimity necessary and for what reasons? Even if we decide representativeness is our desired goal, does our system select jurors so as to insure representativeness? By what means do we determine bias and by what mechanisms do we detect and remove it?

In attempting to investigate and hopefully to shed light on these issues, we should bear in mind that our present system is not the result of a carefully outlined set of theoretical and philosophical principles. Rather, it is the product of centuries of accumulated changes and adaptations which have given content and meaning to the term *trial by jury*. Thus, the jury trial must be understood in its historical context—how it began, what functions it has served, and the timing of its arrival and acceptance by the states. It must also be understood in the context of its relationship to the political and social structure. Many of the proponents of trial by jury see it as a "bulwark of liberty," a safeguard against political tyranny, or as a community lever against unpopular laws. They point to the controversial political trials of the 1960s as well as the frequent unwillingness of juries to convict violators of prohibition or drug laws. Even the debate over the role of the jury, that is, as fact finder versus interpreter of the law, can be viewed as a power struggle between judge and jury. Thus, as we attempt to understand the psychology and the law in the institution of trial by jury, we will start by exploring the origins of this deeply embedded tradition.

II. Antecedents and Historical Developments in Trial by Jury

The origin of trial by jury is difficult to trace, since it occurred in numerous forms over the centuries. While our particular conception of a jury trial bears most resemblance to that practiced during the reign of Henry II in England (1154–1189), there is evidence of widespread usage of jury trials in one form or another as early as 1200 B.C., during the Trojan period, when tribal democratic justice was observed. Both Greek and Roman law had versions of trial by jury. Socrates was condemned to death by a Greek jury of 501 members (of which apparently 30 could have swung the vote to acquittal). The Romans appealed to the *populus romanus* as a check on the magistrates. Ancient Germanic tribes practiced a form of democratic justice and are credited with the spread of the custom. This practice was developed further under the Carolingian kings in the latter part of the eighth century. The Danes used a form of group accusation of crime in the tenth century.

Though in existence and reasonably widespread for centuries, the important historical periods for the form of jury trials as we have come to know them were the Norman Invasion of Britain in 1066 and the reign of Henry II (see Cornish, 1968, pp. 9–18; Holdsworth, 1938; Howe, 1939, pp. 582–616; Pope, 1961, pp. 426–448; Thayer, 1892, pp. 295–319).

When the Normans invaded England, William the Conqueror introduced the notion of the Frankish inquest by sending inquisitors to investigate and record the property and claims of the populace, this becoming the famous Domesday Book. Henry II expanded the usage of local participation in adjudicating disputes and made it available for private disputes as well. In addition to charging a fee which added to his coffers, he submitted delicate disputes between the Crown and the Church to a jury and, in the process, won the approval of a populace who disliked trials by ordeal or battle and did not trust the fairness of the lords.

Although the practice became more widespread during Henry's reign, the importance of trial by jury as a right, as a guarantee of individual freedom and liberty, was marked by the signing of the Magna Carta on June 12, 1215, during the reign of King John. John, confronted by the barons at Runnymede, signed a document that made even the king subject to the law. Most important was clause 39, which stated that "No freeman shall be arrested and imprisoned, or dispossessed, or outlawed, or banished, or in any way molested; nor will we set forth against him, nor send against him, unless by the lawful judgment of his peers and by the law of the land."

Thus arose the importance of trial by jury as a basic democratic right, one that came to be described as a "bulwark of liberty," an institution which "ever will be looked upon as the glory of the English law" (Blackstone Commentaries, 1791, p. 379). It also came to be viewed as a protection of individual liberty against potential political tyranny. As late as 1956, Lord Devlin echoed the sentiments of Blackstone in the following quotation:

> The first object of any tyrant in Whitehall would be to make Parliament utterly subservient to his will; and the next to overthrow or diminish trial by jury, for no tyrant could afford to leave a subject's freedom in the hands of twelve of his countrymen. So that trial by jury is more than an instrument of justice and more than one wheel of the constitution: it is the lamp that shows that freedom lives. (as quoted in Cornish, 1968, p. 126)

Blackstone was hard pressed to document the independence of the jury against political tyranny prior to his statements. However, there is more corroboration for the independence of juries during the period of the French and American Revolutions (Cornish, 1968, p. 130).

III. The Jury in America

Though there was a century-long battle on the meaning of a jury trial in England, the trial by jury took on a special meaning as a safeguard against political oppression in the United States. It was used as a protection against unpopular laws and capricious English judges. It was part of our revolution. In the famous case of John Peters Zenger, an American jury refused to convict Zenger of libel and, in so doing, made it clear that the power of the British Crown could not be enforced without a conviction from an American jury.

Recognizing this show of independence, England wanted to get around the jury and attempted to enforce its hated Stamp Act of 1765 by placing the act under the jurisdiction of the admiralty courts. The outcry was great. The Americans saw the removal of a trial by jury as a mechanism for subjecting them to political repression. So deeply entrenched was this belief that all states used juries of various forms prior to the Declaration of Independence. The Articles of Confederation insisted on the right to trial by jury and the United States Constitution made it a fundamental right guaranteed to all citizens.

> The Trial of all Crimes, except in cases of Impeachment, shall be by Jury; and such Trial shall be held in the State where the said Crimes shall have been committed; but when not committed within any State, the Trial shall be at such place or places as the Congress may by law have directed. (U.S. Constitution, Article 3, Paragraph 2)

In addition, three amendments to the Constitution were added to specify more clearly the constitutional right to trial by jury. The Fifth Amendment requires indictment by a grand jury; the Sixth Amendment guarantees citizens the right to a speedy and public trial before an impartial jury in the jurisdiction where the crime was committed; and the Seventh Amendment allows for jury trials in civil matters where more than $20 is at stake. Thus, a country with deeply held suspicions of political tyranny and with fears of unchecked power developed a system of checks and balances and, with it, a belief in the protection afforded by community representation in the administration of justice (see generally Pope, 1961).

A. DETERMINERS OF FACT VERSUS INTERPRETERS OF THE LAW

Although the principle of trial by jury is deeply embedded in the roots of American history and has at times protected the populace against political repression or unpopular laws, there have been many attempts to curtail its usage or abolish it altogether. One form of curtailment can be best understood in the context of a struggle for power between judges and jurors, a struggle that has been waged for centuries.

Prior to 1670, judges had the power to control verdicts since, according to the practice of attaint, they could punish jurors for "error." This power was rendered obsolete by the famous Bushell case of 1670 involving William Penn, who attempted to conduct a Quaker meeting and was charged with unlawful assembly. When the jury returned a verdict of acquittal, "contrary to evidence," the judge (who was bent on conviction) confined the jury without food or water for three days. In a landmark decision, Chief Justice Vaughan ordered the jury freed and argued that the jury cannot be controlled by the judge. Thus ended the power to punish the jury. An important corollary to this decision was that the jury had the power to interpret the law as well as find for the facts since its general verdict could not be punished or controlled by the judge. Now came a new battle for power. Although the jury had the *power* to decide facts and interpret law, many argued that they had not the *right* to interpret the law. Thus, in the late seventeenth century when judges could no longer control verdicts by punishing jurors, they often sought to define the jury's role very narrowly, insisting that the jury should only determine the facts, not interpret the law. As one example, jurors in cases of sedition were asked only to determine whether an individual had published a given work, not whether the words were seditious. Whether or not the words were seditious was a question of law, not of fact, the judges argued. Juries resented this incursion into what they considered their role and eventually had the right to render a verdict on the entire question restored to them. This was effected by Fox's Libel Act of 1792 (Cornish, 1968, p. 131).

From the historical accounts, it seems clear that the jury was accorded the right as well as the power to interpret the law in the early days of this country. John Adams was quoted in 1771 as saying that it was not only the right of the juror but "his duty . . . to find the verdict according to his own best understanding, judgment, and conscience, though in direct opposition to the direction of the court" (as quoted in Van Dyke, 1970, p. 22). However, this right was soon contested and the issue was directly addressed in *United States* v. *Battiste* (1835) and *Sparf and Hansen* v. *United States* (1895). In *United States* v. *Battiste,* Mr. Justice Story argued that "it is the duty of the court to instruct the jury as to the law and it is the duty of the jury to follow the law as it is laid down by the court" (as quoted in Van Dyke, 1970, p. 18). It is this case that is credited "more effectively than any other decision to have deflected the current of American judicial opinion away from the recognition of the jury's right" (Howe, 1939, p. 590).

In *Sparf and Hansen* v. *United States,* two sailors were accused of throwing a third overboard from an American vessel near Tahiti and were charged with murder. Although the defendants asked that the jury be allowed to return a verdict of manslaughter, the judge refused to give such instructions, saying that the evidence did not warrant such a verdict. The Supreme Court upheld the judge's decision. In a majority opinion written by Mr. Justice Harlan, the Court held that the jury was obliged to follow the judge's instructions in matters of law even though, as the Court acknowledged, judges had instructed juries that they were judges both of law and of fact in criminal cases prior to 1835. The dissenting justices argued that it was preferable, for both historical and political reasons, to recognize that the jury had the right to disregard the court's instructions (Howe, 1939, pp. 588–590; Van Dyke, 1970, pp. 19–20).

The history of this struggle is lengthy and elaborate. It continues to this day and is poignantly illustrated in the contrast between instructions given to jurors in California and Maryland, where jurors are told, respectively

> Ladies and Gentlemen of the Jury: It becomes my duty as judge to instruct you concerning the law applicable to this case, and it is your duty as jurors to follow the law as I shall state it to you. (as quoted in Van Dyke, 1970, p. 17)

> Members of the jury, this is a criminal case and under the Constitution and the laws of
> the State of Maryland in a criminal case the jury are the judges of the law as well as of the
> facts in the case. So that whatever I tell you about the law, while it is intended to be helpful
> to you in reaching a just and proper verdict in the case, it is not binding upon you as
> members of the jury and you may accept the law as you apprehend it to be in the case. (as
> quoted in Van Dyke, 1970, p. 20)

Although the above instructions show that the issue is still very much alive, it appears that the judges are winning since only Maryland and Indiana instruct jurors that they are interpreters of the law as well as finders of fact. The rest of the states make it clear that the jurors have the duty to follow the law as the judge gives it to them.

Most of the concern about the diminishing power of the jury in this regard is raised in the context of political trials. It should be remembered that these are the same issues that marked the importance of the jury as a protection of individual liberty against political tyranny in the early days of this country. Thus, critics of the present judicial instructions (e.g., Van Dyke, 1970; Lefcourt, 1970) argue that the jury should be told that they have the right as well as the power to interpret the law, particularly in political trials involving crimes of conscience.

It is when judges presume to ask specific questions rather than allow the jury to simply return a general verdict (e.g., the Benjamin Spock case) or when there is evidence that the radical leaders of a movement for change are being selected for prosecution (e.g., the Black Panther 21 trial) that the jury must act on the totality of the evidence (Van Dyke, 1970, p. 24; Lefcourt, 1970, p. 63). It is here that we need the voice of the community, a lever against overzealous prosecutors and case-hardened judges. It is here that we need protection against possible political oppression, and it is in these types of cases that officials of the government lose their objectivity.

On the other side of the issue, critics of discretion on the part of juries point to the possibility of a "system in which the ultimate test of socially permissible conduct is, to a significant degree, the random reaction of a group of twelve people selected at random" (Fortas, 1970, p. 61). If a jury is prejudiced, discretion allows for unequal protection of the law. Some have argued that prejudice is manifested by findings that a black defendant is more likely to be convicted, to be convicted of a higher degree of crime, and, if convicted, to be more severely punished than whites (see Greenberg, 1959; Kalven & Zeisel, 1966; Kuhn, 1968 for related research), though other research does not corroborate these findings (Gleason & Harris, 1975; Nemeth & Sosis, 1973; Boone, 1973). However, it should also be mentioned that many authors concerned with racism have questioned whether manifestations of prejudice would be appreciably altered if a judge rather than a jury were rendering the verdict. (See discussions by McDougall, 1970; Rhine, 1969.)

B. COMPETENCE, REPRESENTATIVENESS, AND QUALIFICATIONS

Perhaps the most frequently voiced concern about the jury system has to do with competence of laymen to render just decisions in regard to complex problems. Writers from both sides of the Atlantic have voiced doubts about the quality and competence of juries. Some argue that verdicts should be left to judges and lawyers because of their presumed expertise in these matters. However, it is interesting that most of the criticism is not based on the supposed superiority of judges over laymen in rendering such decisions. Rather, the argument usually is that juries are not truly representative of their communities. Critics have especially emphasized the fact that professionals and the highly educated are underrepresented on juries. Given that clergymen, doctors, lawyers, dentists, chemists, etc. were exempt from jury service in England, Granville Williams expressed concern in 1955 as follows:

> The subtraction of relatively intelligent classes means that it is an understatement to describe a jury, with Herbert Spencer, as a group of twelve people of average ignorance. There is no guaranty that members of a particular jury may not be quite unusually ignorant, credulous, slow-witted, narrow-minded, biased, or temperamental. (quoted in Van Dyke, 1970, p. 21)

Thus, Williams fears nonrepresentation of the intelligent and educated on juries rather than the fact that it is laymen who serve. Interestingly, proponents of the jury system would agree with the critics on this issue of representation, although for less elitist reasons. They too argue forcefully for community representation. Juries "restricted to certain classes within the community are more likely to have some common prejudice" (Cornish, 1968, p. 141). Further, one needs representativeness in order to have the voice of a community conscience.

This issue of competence versus community representation has always been present in one form or another. Most of the arguments revolve around the definition of each of these terms and the links between them. One aspect of the dispute involves the premise that the most competent jurors are not random representatives of the community but, rather, the more educated, intelligent, and socially prominent. Thus, we have always had qualifications for jury service, many of which barred specific groups such as women and blacks. This is the first issue that we will explore. We will investigate the historical development and current status of qualifications for jury service and, with it, how the struggle for minimum qualifications has served to compromise representation of the community. A second issue that we will confront is the definition of competence. Granville Williams, and others as well, assumed that competence is linked to education and intelligence. He decried underrepresentation of the highly educated, not because of his belief in representation per se, but because of an assumption that these individuals would be better able to understand and comprehend complex issues and therefore render better and more just decisions.

Others have argued that competence is linked to representation rather than to education or intelligence. Competence to render justice is not an issue of scientific analysis, they contend, but of human insight, and this is not the sole province of the educated. One uses general knowledge and "familiarity with similar situations" to find the facts (McDougall, 1970, p. 532).

A third issue involves still another aspect of competence, that is, the jury's broader political and social role as protector against political oppression, as conscience of the community, and as a legitimating and symbolic institution for society. Thus, its competence must be viewed in terms of this broad mandate rather than a narrow definition related only to its fact-finding role.

1. Qualifications

Historically, the elitist answer to the question of how best to ensure just decision making has been to establish qualifications for jury service on the assumption that not all citizens are capable of the "onerous" duties. Athenian justice involved only male citizens and property holders and the Frankish kings summoned "important men" for their inquests. Pope (1961) argues that "every historical experiment which foreshadowed the modern jury required jurors to possess certain minimum qualifications . . . [and from] the beginning, jurors had to be freemen, had to own property and had to come from the vicinity of the dispute" (p. 437). Thus, the wealthy and socially prominent were favored for jury service.

In addition to selection procedures which barred particular groups, there is also a long history of the special jury, that is people chosen specifically for their qualifications to judge a particular issue at hand. Cooks and fishmongers may be called on to decide issues involving the selling of bad food. Merchants may be jurors in cases involving business practices. In England, both the special and the common petty juries existed until 1949. Special juries were used in civil cases where the issues were "of too great a nicety for the discussion of ordinary free-holders" (Blackstone Commentaries, III, p. 357). The assumption behind the special jury was that these individuals would most likely understand the issue and render a just verdict. The related assumption is that "like should be tried by like." However, as we will learn, the courts in both England and the United States have proven hesitant to favor this as a principle, particularly in the sensitive areas of sex and race.

Both England and the United States have a long history of discrimination in jury service. Originally, juries were composed of barons; women and indentured servants were specifically barred. When the institution of juries came to the United States, blacks were initially excluded as well, but as early as 1875 Congress made it a crime to exclude potential jurors on the basis of race. This act was upheld in a Supreme Court decision (Strauder v. West Virginia) in 1880 that specifically invoked the "equal protection under the law" clause of the Fourteenth Amendment. Kuhn (1968) reports that "express statutory exclusion of Negroes from jury duty disappeared soon after the close of the Reconstruction" (p. 251). As will be discussed in the section on race, however, this did not end racial discrimination, which has become more subtle and has raised more complex issues for legal opinions.

Women fared less well since the Supreme Court did not see fit to interpret the Fourteenth Amendment as prohibiting the exclusion of women. In this regard, it is interesting to note that, in a famous antidiscrimination case (*Hernandez* v. *Texas*), the Supreme Court in 1953 argued, "When the existence of a distinct class is demonstrated, and it is further shown that the laws, as written or as applied, single out that class for different treatment not based on some reasonable classification, the guarantees of the Constitution have been violated" (p. 478). The *Hernandez* case involved exclusion of Mexican-Americans, and the Court at that time was focusing on race and ethnicity. Although one might expect that the principle would apply to the sex as well as the other social categories, this was not the case. The Court specifically noted the categories of concern: "Exclusion of otherwise eligible persons from jury service solely because of their ancestry or national origin is discrimination prohibited by the Fourteenth Amendment" (p. 479). Even more pointed is Lindquist's (1967) comment with regard to the *Hernandez* decision: "Under this rule, the courts looked to the selection procedure only to prevent overt discrimination with respect to race, religion, color, national origin and economic status" (p. 33). Again, we note the omission of sex. Thus, for women, the right to serve on juries had to be established on a state-by-state basis, and as recently as the mid-1960s three states barred women from jury service (Alabama, Mississippi, and South Carolina) and three others required that they specifically ask to be called in order to be eligible (Florida, Louisiana, and New Hampshire).

Today, no state that we can find specifically bars women from jury service. However, Mississippi, in its 1972 statutes, has a special section on exclusion of women saying that "exclusion of women from jury service does not constitute an invalid discrimination" and that "the Fourteenth Amendment is not applicable on the issue as to whether or not women will be required to serve as jurors in a state court." They note that the power to prescribe qualifications rests with the state legislature and that they may include or exclude women. Legally, they are right, but such a practice underscores the problem with regard to discrimination based on sex. (See Kenyon & Murray, 1966; Nemeth, Endicott, & Wachtler, 1976, for further discussion.)

In the Federal courts, prohibitions against discrimination have been more clear and uniform. Congress passed the Jury Selection and Service Act in 1968, specifically stating that citizens shall not "be excluded from service as a grand or petit juror in the district courts of the United States on account of race, color, religion, sex, national origin, or economic status" (28 U.S.C.S. 1862).

Thus, any person is qualified for jury service in the Federal Courts except one who

(1) is not a citizen of the United States eighteen years old who has resided for a period of one year within the judicial district;
(2) is unable to read, write, and understand the English language with a degree of proficiency sufficient to fill our satisfactorily the juror qualification form
(3) is unable to speak the English language;
(4) is incapable, by reason of mental or physical infirmity, to render satisfactory jury service; or
(5) has a charge pending against him for the commission of, or has been convicted in a State or Federal court of record of, a crime punishable by imprisonment for more than one year and his civil rights have not been restored by pardon or amnesty. (Federal Code of Jury Qualifications, 28 U.S.C.S. 1864, 1865)

States, however, differ greatly in their qualifications for service. Most have an age qualification, usually 18 or 21; most require ordinary intelligence and the ability to read, write, and speak English; most disqualify convicted felons. However, some States require only these qualifications or slight variants thereof (e.g., California), whereas others include subjective provisions such as being "of well known good character and standing in the community" (Louisiana R.S. 13:3041), "of good character, of approved integrity, of sound judgment, and able to read and write the English language understandably" (New York juror qualifications, 1975, NY Judiciary Law, Art. 16, Para. 504), or "esteemed in the community for integrity, good character and sound judgment" [Ala Code § 12-16-60 1975 (Supp. 1979)]. Mississippi goes so far as to add that the person should not have "been convicted of an infamous crime, or the unlawful sale of intoxicating liquors within a period of five years and who is not a common gambler or habitual drunkard" [Miss. Code Ann. Sec. 13-5-1 (1972)]. The subjectivity of the wording and the lack of clear criteria by which to assess good character, ordinary intelligence, etc. obviously allow for discrimination. The problem is exacerbated when one considers that jury commissioners who compile original jury lists tend to be white males. Kuhn (1968) reports that every district judge (65), every jury commissioner (129), and every court clerk (28) in the federal district courts in the 11 Southern states in 1966 was white.

To make the situation even more subjective, many states still use the key-man system, a mechanism by which the jury commissioners contact prominent or *key* men to compile names for the jury lists. They may also contact organizations for this purpose. Many critics of this system (e.g., Lindquist, 1967; Rhine, 1969) have pointed to the fact that selection from organizations tends to favor white, professional, or business people who are better educated and who live in urban settings. The selection of key men uses arbitrary criteria as well; Lindquist (1967) reports criteria such as (1) previous jury service, (2) reputation in the community, (3) names in local newspaper articles, and (4) personal acquaintances as some of the ways in which key men are selected (pp. 37–39). These mechanisms tend to amplify uniformity and lead to overrepresentation of the white, male, middle-class population.

Such a procedure for jury selection was criticized in *Rabinowitz* v. *United States* (1966). In rejecting this mechanism for the Federal Courts, Title I of the Civil Rights Act established uniform juror selection procedures for district courts through the use of voter registration lists. Lindquist (1967), however, points out that this is applicable only to federal courts. While Title II provides that it is unlawful to distinguish on the basis of race, color, religion, sex, national origin, or economic status in any state, the phrasing prohibits discrimination but does not require a cross-section of the community. Nor does it establish random selection procedures for the states; state selection procedures are thus left alone and allowed to be nonrandom (note 74). Many advisory boards and court opinions have argued that these jury commissioners have a duty to find qualified jurors (*Cassell* v. *Texas,* 1950; U.S. Judicial Conference, 1966), but random and reviewable procedures are not mandated.

2. Competence

As noted earlier, the jury as an institution has long been charged with incompetence of one form or another. Many critics view it as ignorant and full of prejudice and passion (Frank, 1949). However, the little research that has been conducted does not offer so bleak a picture. Kalven and Zeisel's (1966) classic work concludes that jurors understand evidence and Simon's (1977) review of trials involving issues related to First Amendment civil liberties causes her to conclude: "During none of these periods is there any evidence, or indeed any suggestion, of the jury's lack of independence, or of the jury's failure to understand the issues or complexities of the problems involved, or of the jury's failure to do its duty" (Simon, 1977, p. 290). It should be remembered that these definitions of competence have more to do with comprehension and intellectual ability than human understanding or insight, although, even here, the jury looks quite competent. Another type of evidence offered on the issue of competence uses, interestingly, the criterion of what a judge's decision would have been. Many researchers have cited the work of Kalven and Zeisel (1966) in this regard. In that study, the jury verdicts were compared to the decisions that judges would have rendered in 3576 cases. While the juries were deliberating, the judges noted their own decisions. Subsequently, if there was a disparity between a judge's decision and the verdict rendered, the judge tried to give reasons for such a disparity. An analysis of these data shows agreement between judge and jury on 78% of the cases and, important for some critics' definition of competence, the disparity in judgments on the remaining cases can easily be understood. Kalven and Zeisel report that juries were generally more lenient than judges. Of the 22% of the cases on which there was disagreement, the jury was more lenient in 19% and less lenient in 3%. Kalven and Zeisel conclude that, of the disagreements in criminal cases, about 54% are due to "issues of evidence," 29% are due to "sentiments of the law," 11% to "sentiments on the defendant," and 6% to other factors. Of the disagreements due to "issues of evidence," most are largely due to the fact that the judge is privy to information that is considered "unduly biasing" to the jury, for example, the past criminal record of the defendant.

The varying "sentiments" reported by Kalven and Zeisel include tendencies to reduce the charge when damage is slight, leniency when the defendant had already been punished or when collaborators had received preferential treatment, leniency when the police had used improper methods, and so on, values that fall outside the official rules (Kalven & Zeisel, 1966). Thus, if one accepts the argument that competence is defined in terms of what the judge would have concluded, juries again appear quite competent. The disagreement appears to be in the application of values outside official rules, these being the community voice and conscience which our founding fathers valued.

The old political issues regarding the role of the jury are again apparent in discussions of the competence of juries. Erlanger (1970) argues that "the most sharply drawn issue in the debate over the jury's competence is the question of whether juries: (a) understand the judge's instructions; and (b) if they do, whether they follow them and therefore truly decide only issues of fact" (p. 348). The first part of this has to do with comprehension; the second is more political and subject to debate. With regard to comprehension, some critics point out that there are studies showing that as many as 40% of jurors do not under- stand judges' instructions (Hervey, 1947). While the issue of comprehensibility should be taken seriously, there is, of course, a question as to whether incom- prehensibility is the fault of jurors' lack of competence or judges' phrasing. Many researchers (e.g., Charrow & Charrow, 1979; Elwork, Sales, & Alfini, 1977) have documented outmoded phrasings and grammatical constructions in the law. These researchers and many concerned attorneys are attempting to substitute ordinary English for legalese.

Given adequate comprehension, the concern over whether jurors follow judges' instructions brings us back to the fact finder versus interpreter of the law issue and the general role of the jury as representative of the community and its conscience. One frequently cited example of the unwillingness or inability of juries to follow judges' instructions is in negligence cases. Jurors often substitute comparative negligence for compensatory negligence (Broeder, 1958, 1965a; Kalven, 1964). They usually consider who was more negligent (e.g., an indi- vidual vs. a company) rather than following a law that instructs them to award nothing to a plaintiff who "contributed proximally to the cause of his injuries." One may question whether or not jurors understand the distinction made in the law, but we must also consider the possibility that they choose to substitute what they consider to be a fairer or more equitable rule. (For further discussion of equity considerations by judges and jurors, see Austin & Utne, 1980; Austin, Walster, & Utne, 1978.)

Much of the foregoing discussion is related to many people's conception of competence, that is, analytic ability, knowledge, and comprehension. Critics of this approach (e.g., McDougall, 1970) point out that decision making in a criminal case is not a scientific process, dependent on technical knowledge, but is more often choosing between competing truths. Many times, it comes down to whom one believes, questions of credibility, likelihood of events, and inference of intentions. In such situations, many people (e.g., Kuhn, 1968; McDougall, 1970; Rhine, 1969) argue that personal experiences and background have more to do with the decision reached than scientific ability. It is here that one needs diversity of background and at least the presence of persons who have a background similar to that of the defendant.

The accuracy issue is difficult to document, as we will learn, since persons from different cultural backgrounds often make different decisions. Most of the arguments for the advantages of diversity for accuracy and competence are based on example. McDougall (1970) offers the illustration of a Park Avenue juror trying to understand a ghetto plaintiff's experience with shysters and shylocks. Other examples are easy to contemplate. If a person spotted at the scene of a crime runs away, is this an indication of fear of being wrongfully accused or is it an indication of guilt? One would expect race, class, and ghetto experience to be relevant to one's assumptions. Consistent with these arguments is the research of Triandis (1976) showing the importance of cultural background in interpreting events, including intentions. Thus, one could well argue that diversity of background and viewpoint is important for the fact-finding function of a jury and acts as a check on the prejudices of a particular group.

3. Representation

Although the preceding discussion argues for community representation on juries in order to render fact finding more competent or accurate, many of the issues involving representation of the community are political and social. They concern values that we wish to preserve. First, trial by jury is an important democratic principle; it provides for participation of the populace in the administration of justice. Perhaps no one understood its importance better than Jefferson: "Were I called upon to decide, whether the people had best be omitted in the legislative or judiciary department, I would say it is better to leave them out of the legislative. The execution of the laws is more important than the making them" (Jefferson, 1789, as quoted in Howe, 1939, p. 582).

In a democracy, each citizen should participate. Jury service, participation of the people in the administration of justice, thus requires representation of the citizenry. However, the fact is that our juries are not truly representative. We might be tempted to believe that the long history of discrimination is past. After all, the Supreme Court prohibited exclusion on the basis of race as early as 1880 in *Strauder* v. *West Virginia*. The Federal Jury Selections Act of 1968 required the use of voter registration lists and prohibited exclusion on the basis of race, color, sex, national origin, religion, or economic status. The struggle has been long and hard. Can we assume that representation has finally been achieved?

The available statistics do not support such optimism. Most studies still show underrepresentation of women on juries (Levine & Schweber-Koren, 1976; Simon, 1975; Mills, 1969; Alker & Barnard, 1978). Some indicate that blacks are underrepresented (Lindquist, 1967; Vanderzell, 1966), whereas others do not show significant differences (Mills, 1969; Alker & Barnard, 1978). Young people are consistently underrepresented (Simon, 1975; Mills, 1969; Alker & Barnard, 1978; Vanderzell, 1966). The less educated also tend to be underrepresented (Mills, 1969; Alker & Barnard, 1978). Thus, the picture painted by several studies is that the typical jury represents middle America and that there is underrepresentation of "blacks, women, lower and upper classes, young and old, core cities and exurbs" (Alker & Barnard, 1978, p. 221). The Prahl (1973) study confirms this picture, describing American juries as white, male, middle class, and suburban or rural. Lest we assume that this "middle" bias is an American phenomenon, Lord Devlin describes juries in England as "male, middle aged, middle minded and middle class" (Pope, 1961, footnote 10).

The reasons for this distribution are complex and the discrimination occurs at different phases in the selection process. Most states use either the key man system, previously described, or "objective" lists such as voter registration lists. The subjectivity of the key man system has been previously addressed and serves to exaggerate the presence of categories to which the jury commissioners belong. However, the objective lists have been seen as also contributing to the bias in race and age. Some states use taxpayer lists, with resulting overrepresentation of whites. Even voter registration lists (which are a great improvement over previous lists used) have a built-in bias. Lindquist (1967) points out that of the "1964 voting age population of 114 million, only about 80 million were registered to vote" (p. 47) and that available statistics suggest that this is discriminatory toward blacks, lower socioeconomic classes, and the less politically active. Young people tend to be underrepresented on these lists because many states update their master jury wheel every three or four years, meaning that persons newly eligible to vote may not appear. In addition, highly mobile students tend not to appear (Alker, Hosticka, & Mitchell, 1976, footnote 5).

The reasons for underrepresentation of women appear to be related more to the exemption or excuse processes than to the original master wheel. These processes produce an underrepresentation of the highly educated and professional classes as well. In our system of jury selection, certain groups of people are exempt from jury service (they are qualified but they are exempted). These exemptions are usually occupational in nature and cover members in active service of the armed forces, policemen or firemen, and public officials [18 U.S.C. #1863 (b) (6)]. The rationale is that it is in the public interest to exempt such individuals. England has the same kind of system, exempting lawyers, policemen, members of Parliament, peers, county councillors, doctors, firemen, priests, nuns, members of Mersey Docks and Harbours Board, and Elder Brethren of Trinity House from jury service (Cornish, 1968, p. 39). In addition, many groups of people can be easily excused. In England, these tend to be people with a one-person business who cannot be easily replaced, those who already have their holidays arranged, those who would lose a seasonal bonus, and those who must look after children or invalid relatives. In the United States, excuses are for those over age 70, ministers of religion, persons essential to the care of young children or aged persons, registered physicians, surgeons, dentists, pharmacists, and nurses, those who have served as jurors within the previous 2 years, university and other teachers, lawyers, sole proprietors of businesses, and anyone who has to come more than 80 miles or 2 hours of travel time to the court. There is also the discretion of the judge at the time the court is in session. There are myriad variations on the "no one can replace me" theme that, the judge willing, can be the basis for excuse [28 USC 1863 (b.) (5)].

It is clear that exemptions and excuses based on occupation tend to reduce the numbers of professional and highly educated persons. Excuse based on the care of children and the aged is credited with being the main reason for the great underrepresentation of women on jury panels (Alker & Barnard, 1978). While the preceding applies to federal courts, the states can be even more "chivalrous" in not requiring the services of women on juries. Copelon, Schneider, and Stearns (1975) report that four states (Alabama, Georgia, Missouri, and Tennessee) excuse women solely on the basis of their sex; our recent search shows that Georgia and Tennessee have repealed this automatic exemption. Many states give child care exemptions for women, and some even require that women specifically register for jury service.

The issue of exemptions and excuses is an important one. Apart from the question of whether or not certain occupations are so needed elsewhere as to be exempted or excused, many excuses are based on a simple preference by the person that he or she not serve. For one thing, some people claim that jury service poses an economic hardship on them since they are not paid at work while they serve and the $3-20 jury fee does not compensate them. Further, jury trials take a great deal of time, particularly since, according to some studies, only 21.5% of the entire service is spent in trial and deliberation and most of the time (61%) is spent in the waiting room (Simon, 1975; Pabst, 1973). Although 90% of jurors tend to be favorably impressed after service (Pabst, 1973), these are not inconsiderable hardships. Thus, there is an incentive to be excused from jury service, especially for particular categories of people.

Some would argue that a person should not serve who does not so wish.

Even Congress, in its defense of using voter lists for juries, said "Voter lists contain an important built-in screening element in that they eliminate those individuals who are either unqualified to vote or insufficiently interested in the world about them to do so" (as quoted in Alker & Barnard, 1978, p. 237). On the other hand, many have argued for a tightening of exemptions and excuses (Simon, 1975; Copelon, Schneider, & Stearns, 1975) on the basis that they contribute to the unrepresentativeness of the jury and, consequently, may harm the litigant, the community, and members of the excluded class. Nonrepresentation for any reason will probably affect the quality of jury decision making; it will certainly undermine representation of the community conscience, and it may serve to lessen public confidence in, and legitimacy of, the jury system. It should also be noted that the surveys reported in the beginning of this section probably underestimate the degree of discrimination. For one thing, most of those surveys were taken in northeastern states, and, although discrimination is not the sole province of any one section of this country, the strongest evidence of racial discrimination was found in the survey of eleven southern federal districts. The last states to allow women to serve on juries were also southern. The magnitude of this problem is perhaps better illustrated by specific cases and appellate decisions rather than surveys, since they demonstrate specific instances in which discrimination took on such a blatant form as to require reversal of the jury's decision as well as the setting of a legal precedent. We will concentrate mainly on cases involving race, since this is the category to which the courts have been most responsive.

C. COURT DECISIONS AND DISCRIMINATION

As mentioned previously, the Supreme Court as early as 1880 ruled that the states could not statutorily require that only whites could serve on juries. While one might hope that such a ruling would end discrimination by race, the discrimination only became more subtle. While state law no longer specifically excluded persons on the basis of race, actual practices of the jury commissioners were such that blacks did not serve. In 1935, the Supreme Court held in *Norris* v. *Alabama* that the practice of exclusion was forbidden by the Constitution (rather than just the explicit statute barring blacks from service). Yet, consider the evidence that was mustered to show discrimination in this case: "We think that the evidence that for a generation or longer no Negro had been called for service on any jury in Jackson County . . . established the discrimination which the Constitution forbids" [*Norris* v. *Alabama* (1935)]. In a case involving Mexican-Americans, the Court in *Hernandez* v. *Texas* found that Mexican or Latin American surnames comprised 14% of the population, 11% of males over the age of 21, and 6 or 7% of the tax rolls, but "for the last twenty-five years there is no record of any person with a Mexican or Latin American name having served on a jury commission, grand jury or petit jury in Jackson County'' (*Hernandez* v. *Texas,* 1954, pp. 480–481).

Needless to say, the forces of discrimination proved to be resilient. Token inclusion occurred, thus requiring further rulings. In *Smith* v. *Texas* (1940), a ruling of discrimination was based on the facts that blacks constituted 20% of the population and almost 10% of the poll tax payers but that only a fraction of 1% had served on juries during an 8-year period. One or two blacks were on the jury list each year and, with arrogant tokenism, the black juror was almost invariably numbered 16. In *Whitus* v. *Georgia* (1967), it was found that blacks comprised 27.1% of the taxpayers and 42% of the male population over 21, but only 3 of 33 prospective grand jurors were black, of whom 1 served on a 19-member grand jury, and only 7 of 90 were called for the petit jury, of which none was accepted (*Smith* v. *Texas,* 1940; *Whitus* v. *Georgia,* 1967).

Although the rulings were consistent when there was total exclusion, the Court stated to make distinctions when the exclusion was not total. The courts had generally established that there must be a prima facie case for discrimination, but they generally relied on their own intuitions as to when the disparity between the qualified population and the venire was sufficiently large. However, the courts have not sought proportional representation. In fact, they have specifically held that a defendant is not entitled to a proportional representation of groups, including his or her own, on the jury of 12 persons who try the case (*Hoyt* v. *Florida,* 1961; *Swain* v. *Alabama,* 1965; *Hernandez* v. *Texas,* 1954; *Akins* v. *Texas,* 1945). *Swain* v. *Alabama* made this particularly clear in their ruling that ''A defendant in a criminal case is not constitutionally entitled to a proportionate number of his race on the trial jury or the jury panel'' (*Swain* v. *Alabama,* 1965, p. 202).

What the Courts do want to prevent, and have fairly consistently ruled, is purposeful and sytematic exclusion of recognizable groups. This, they argue, would prevent an impartial jury selected from a fair cross-section of the community (*Smith* v. *Texas,* 1940; *Theil* v. *Southern Pacific Company,* 1946). The purposeful or intentional aspect arose in *Akins* v. *Texas* (1945), where the Court did not find evidence of purposeful or systematic exclusion on the basis of 1 out of 16 grand jurors being black. In *Swain* v. *Alabama* (1965), this is again articulated clearly: ''But purposeful discrimination may not be assumed or merely asserted'' (p. 205). In *Swain,* the Court argued that purposeful discrimination based on race was not ''satisfactorily proved by showing that an identifiable group in a community is underrepresented by as much as 10%'' (pp. 208–209). The evidence in that case was that 26% of the male population in the county were black, whereas only 10 to 15% of the members of grand and petit jury panels drawn since 1953 were black. No black had actually served on a petit jury since 1950, and none were on the jury in the defendant's trial (in 1964).

The issue of systematic exclusion basically means that the discriminatory practice must be shown to exist over a period of time. Thus, the *Norris* v. *Alabama* (1935) case used a generation; and the *Smith* v. *Texas* (1940) case used seven years. In *Akins* v. *Texas* (1945), "systematic exclusion" was not demonstrated since the evidence dealt with a single grand jury. The issue of a "cognizable" group is an interesting one which will be dealt with later. For present purposes, race has never been contested as a cognizable group.

Though some of these decisions, notably *Swain* v. *Alabama*, have been considered setbacks (e.g., McDougall, 1970), a series of recent decisions in the Fifth Circuit appear to be more progressive in this regard (Georgia Law Review, 1967). Sitting *en banc* in 1966 to review six state and federal cases pertaining to discrimination, this court ruled in *Davis* v. *Davis* (1966) that jury commissioners had the obligation to familiarize themselves with blacks who were qualified for service. Here, the discrepancy was 14.2%, and the court did not accept good intentions but, rather, insisted on active search by jury commissioners for qualified blacks. In *Brooks* v. *Beto* (1966), they upheld purposeful inclusion of blacks so long as it was a good faith effort to ensure proportional representation.

It has probably been noticed that these cases rest on the opportunity to serve and tend to concentrate on the jury pool list rather than the actual jury that hears a given case. In an extraordinary decision in a case in California (*People* v. *Wheeler*, 1978), the use of peremptory challenges to remove blacks on the actual jury was disallowed. Not only is this the strongest ruling against discrimination; it also deals with a specific sitting jury and, even more in contrast to previous decisions, the use of peremptory challenges. In this case two black defendants were convicted by an all-white jury of murdering a white grocery store owner in the course of a robbery. The conviction was overturned because the prosecutor used his peremptory challenges to remove blacks from the jury.

This ruling is in strong contradiction to *Swain* v. *Alabama*, which underscored the tradition that peremptory challenges may be made on any basis, including race. The rationale for this is in the long and cherished history of peremptory challenges. In its own wisdom, the Court has allowed for a challenge to a juror "without a reason stated, without inquiry and without being subject to the Court's control" *(Swain* v. *Alabama*, 1964, p. 220). The defendant should be able to remove a certain number of persons because of the belief that they will not be unbiased, even if he or she cannot articulate the reason for this belief. Although originally intended as a right and protection for the defendant, it has also become a right of the prosecution. The decision may be made on the basis of anatomy, dress, a smile, any of the "sudden impressions and unaccountable prejudices we are apt to conceive upon the bare looks and gestures of another" (4 Blackstone Commentaries, p. 353). The point of the peremptory challenge is that one should be able to remove a juror who is believed to be prejudiced against oneself or one who will not fully consider the evidence with impartiality, even if the reasons cannot be articulated and even if no one else would agree with the assessment.

Let us take an example to illustrate the phenomenon. A juror in a death penalty case was asked whether he had such conscientious objections against the death penalty that he could not vote for conviction under any circumstance, knowing that the death penalty could be a consequence (the death qualification process). Most jurors with no conscientious objections, or even those who favor the death penalty, respond with a simple no. This juror chose to add "that's the only way we can deal with *these* kinds of people," staring directly at the defendant. The clear and unmistakable impression that this man would not be impartial toward the defendant may have been difficult to articulate, and this is precisely the reason for the peremptory challenge. Needless to say, this juror was challenged peremptorily.

The problem is that peremptory challenges often are designed not to remove people with prejudice but, rather to get a "friendly" jury. Undoubtedly with this practice in mind, the California court in *Wheeler* pitted the right to peremptory challenge against a higher constitutional right, that is, representation of the community, in ruling that "the use of peremptory challenges to remove prospective jurors on the sole ground of group bias violates the right to trial by a jury drawn from a representative cross-section of the community" (p. 258). In distinguishing *group bias* from *specific bias,* the court is basically saying that one can challenge an individual but not a group. Needless to say, the distinction poses practical problems. As we will learn in the next section, most peremptories are based on assumptions of group attitudes, prejudices, etc. In one trial, you may search for a white female who is college educated. In another, you may want Catholics and Jews, preferably male. The problem that the *Wheeler* decision poses is that you cannot remove groups of people, at least not groups of blacks. As a practical matter, the court will ask for a reason (other than race) which is the basis of the challenge, thus allowing for a clever recasting of reasons.

Throughout this review of discrimination cases, it appears as though the courts have been quite responsive to issues of racial discrimination. Yet, as we have indicated previously, de facto discrimination still occurs. For other groups suffering from discrimination, for example, women and the young, even the law has not been very responsive. Though discrimination in any form violates representativeness and impartiality, the courts have set up a pecking order of minorities to be considered. In *Fay* v. *New York* (1947) for example, the Court ruled that if race was not the issue, the petitioner must demonstrate prejudice to his case.

From some of the cases reviewed, it appears as though the courts have close to a 10% tolerance level. If the discrepancies are very large between qualified populations and venires, the courts have ruled that discrimination has occurred.

However, the *Swain* decision allowed for a 10% discrepancy. With regard to other categories, the courts have been more tolerant of de facto discrimination. The case of *United States* v. *Di Tomasso* (1968) is revealing in this regard. In this case, the Court found "substantial representation" of blue collar workers when 18.6% of the jurors were from this group, though the qualified population was 29.3%. They also allowed for only 24% of jurors with less than a high school education when over 50% of the population comprised this group. As mentioned previously, less educated people are greatly underrepresented on juries. This Court also found "substantial representation" of 21- to 29-year-olds when 3.9% of the jurors drawn were from this category, even though they constituted almost 19% of the eligible population (see Jurymandering, 1973, p. 411). The Court went so far as to devise a pecking order in arguing that the achievement of substantial representation of sex, race, religion, and occupational groupings might make it necessary to sacrifice ideal representation in such categories as age and geography (*United States* v. *Di Tomasso, 1968*).

Although sex appeared as one of the more important categories in the *Di Tomasso* decision, the courts have, at times, been unresponsive to discrimination based on sex; as we have seen, surveys indicate that women are significantly underrepresented on juries. As Kuhn (1968) points out, "In the past, the Supreme Court has countenanced the exclusion of women from jury service" (footnote 25, p. 240; see also citations *Fay* v. *New York, 1947*; *Ballard* v. *United States, 1946*; *Glasser* v. *United States, 1942*). Thus, as we have noted previously, the fight for inclusion of women on juries was a state by state battle. Some states, however, have circumvented statutory exclusion by requiring specific registration by women. When this was challenged, the Court ruled that it was reasonable (*Hoyt* v. *Florida, 1961*). In this amazing ruling, the Court stated that "the relevant inquiry . . . is whether the exemption itself is based on some reasonable classification and whether the manner in which it is exercisable rests on some rational foundation" (p. 61). Previous courts found exclusion of Mexican-Americans (*Hernandez* v. *Texas*), blacks (*Norris* v. *Alabama*), and wage earners (*Thiel* v. *Southern Pacific*) unconstitutional, but the Court in *Hoyt* v. *Florida* found that requiring women to register is not unconstitutional because it is based on a reasonable classification:

> Despite the enlightened emancipation of women from the restrictions and protections of bygone years, and their entry into many parts of community life formerly considered to be reserved to men, woman is still regarded as the center of home and family life. We cannot say that it is constitutionally impermissible for a State, acting in pursuit of the general welfare, to conclude that a woman should be relieved from the civic duty of jury service unless she herself determines that such service is consistent with her own special responsibilities. (*Hoyt* v. *Florida*, pp. 51–62)

It is important to note, however, that more recent decisions have held that states may not systematically exclude women from juries (*Taylor* v. *Louisiana,* 1975; *Duren* v. *Missouri,* 1979), thus effectively overruling the *Hoyt* decision.

As unresponsive as the Court rulings may have been with regard to women, the underrepresented young (and aged) have an even more difficult time, since they are not viewed as cognizable (see Jurymandering, 1973, p. 408, footnote 84, for a list of case rulings on this issue). The definition given in *United States* v. *Guzman* (1972) is that the group must:

1) have a definite composition without arbitrarily chosen members;
2) be cohesive in terms of a basic similarity in attitudes, idea or experience; and
3) have a community of interest that cannot be adequately protected by the rest of the populace. (Jurymandering, 1973, p. 408)

These criteria prove to be difficult for age groupings and, we assume by analogy, for the less educated as well.

While the courts have proven unable to give clear guidelines and consistent rulings in discrimination cases, it should also be apparent that court rulings cannot fully eliminate discrimination. The rulings require proof of an unconstitutional situation in a particular case. Thus, a more effective mechanism to contain discrimination, and a more affirmative one, involves the selection process itself. The Jury Selections Act of 1968 was one such attempt to foster representation in its insistence on the use of voter registration lists. While even these lists are less than perfect, they are an improvement over the key man system or other subjective methods of juror selection. Suggested improvements over the voter lists have included recommendations that they be supplemented by city directories, social security, tax rolls, utility bill lists, etc. (Chief Justice Earl Warren Conference, 1977; Van Dyke, 1977). Other suggestions have pointed to problems at the clerical level—that, even with fully representative lists, there may not be random selection for specific juries if the clerical process is not random. In England, the Morris Committee found that some selection practices were random. Others selected people by street, by page, or alphabetically. One person confessed that he selected the watchdog mother of a lady he was courting (Cornish, 1968). In the United States, preliminary sorting, the "desk drawer" selection process, and the lack of follow-up on returned questionnaires have been reported as contributing to the lack of randomness in the procedures (Alker & Barnard, 1978).

IV. Does It Matter? Demographics and Jury Verdicts

In the foregoing treatment of discrimination in jury selection, it should be underscored that underrepresentation of a given group violates participation in a democratic institution. It may create problems for legitimacy of the process, for public confidence in the administration of justice, and in the stigmatization of the excluded class. Most court cases, however, have concentrated on fairness to the defendant due to the exclusion of a group of people to which he or she belongs. It is to this question that we now turn for empirical evidence. Are different identifiable groups likely to render different verdicts?

For those of you who like to read the ending before beginning the story, the answer is "Yes, but... " As you may well expect, our rearing, as females versus males, as black versus white, as rich versus poor, matter in jury selection. Whether we are in the early or later years of our lives also matters. However, there is no clear and simple relationship between such social categories and finding for the state versus the defendant or in finding for a plaintiff versus the defendant in a civil case. As with most areas of social psychology, the impact of these categories "depends." It depends on the evidence, characteristics of the defendant and the victim, rapport with the attorneys, etc. In addition, most attempts at jury selection depend on a combination of demographic characteristics. Women may differ from men, but women also differ greatly from one another. A young, urban, professional woman is different from an older woman who has spent her life raising nine children in a small town. Yet, even a single demographic quality can be of use in the selection process and provide a context which may be statistically helpful in ascertaining the sympathies and orientation of a juror.

One of the problems that we will find is that our evidence on the role of demographic characteristics in jury decisions is fragmentary. Part of the reason is that it is very difficult for researchers to obtain a sizeable sample of heterogeneous people to make judgments about the same case. Ideally, the investigator would want this sample to represent various age groupings, political orientations, national and ethnic groups, race, sex, and socioeconomic-status groups so that he or she could determine how these groups differ in the decisions they reach. Because of the enormity of such an undertaking, many researchers have opted for the most readily available population for such studies, the college undergraduate. Thus, while some sex and race differences have been studied, there is relatively less information on the effects of other categorizations. The college populations are relatively homogeneous with regard to age, socioeconomic status, and even political orientation. As a result, even the available evidence on the role of race and sex issues in jury decisions should be viewed with some caution since they may represent a relatively "emancipated" view and may well underrepresent the degree of discrimination against these groups.

A. SEX AND RACE OF JUROR OR DEFENDANT

The available evidence from empirical studies of how the sex of the "juror" influences decisions is mixed. Some studies have shown males more conviction prone and/or more punitive. For example, Kerr, Nerenz, and Herrick (1976) found males more likely to convict. Simon (1967) reported males more conviction prone in a case of housebreaking, and Steffensmeier (1977) found males more punitive in cases of homosexuality and resisting arrest. A survey of six-person juries in the Northwest Territories (Morrow, 1974) showed some tendencies for males to be more conviction prone in the number of cases. However, these data are difficult to interpret in the context of other findings because of the cultural disparity, the noncomparability of the cases being considered, and the fact that these individuals were not challenged nor did they "stand aside" (the Canadian version of our peremptory challenge).

Other studies have shown females to be more conviction prone and/or punitive. Mistretta (1977), using multidimensional scaling, found females more punitive across a number of crimes. Austin, Walster, and Utne (1976) found females to be more punitive in a purse-snatching case. Griffitt and Jackson (1973) reported females to be more punitive in a negligent automobile homicide case. Simmons (1975) stated that females gave longer sentences and greater periods of incarceration prior to parole. Scroggs (1976), using rape and robbery cases, and Simon (1967), using an incest case, found females more punitive.

Still other studies obtained no sex differences. Vidmar (1972) and Nemeth, Endicott, and Wachtler (1976) found no sex differences in murder cases, and Steffensmeier (1977) found no significant sex differences in cases involving shoplifting, public drunkenness, murder, embezzlement, child beating, and seduction of a minor.

The one area where there is a consistent sex difference is in cases of rape. As might be expected, females are consistently more conviction prone (Rumsey & Rumsey, 1977; Miller & Hewitt, 1978; Davis, Kerr, Atkin, Holt, & Meek, 1975; Bray, 1974; Ugwuegbu, 1973, 1976) and more punitive (Scroggs, 1976; Howitt, 1977; Bray, 1974; Ugwuegbu, 1973) than males. Although some studies (e.g., Jones & Aronson, 1973) reported no sex differences in a case of rape, sex differences are usually obtained, and the pattern of conviction proneness and punitiveness by females in this type of case is fairly well documented. Consistent with this is the finding that males are more likely to assume that the victim played a role in the rape than are females (Calhoun, Selby, Cann, & Keller, 1978).

With regard to race, most studies have involved white subjects as "jurors" and varied the race of the defendants. Many of these studies showed no statistically significant differences between conviction rates or sentencing of blacks versus whites (Gleason & Harris, 1975; Nemeth & Sosis, 1973; Boone, 1972), whereas a study by McGlynn, Megas, and Benson (1976) reported a marginal tendency for a greater likelihood of conviction if the defendant were a black male. This, of course, is in contrast to surveys (e.g., Wolfgang & Reidel, 1973) showing that blacks in the South are 18 times more likely to be executed for raping a white woman than any other racial combination of defendant and victim, as well as studies (e.g., Thornberry, 1973) which offer evidence that blacks are treated more harshly at the police level, the intake level, and the juvenile court level. In addition, there is the work by Broeder (1965b) and Greenberg (1959), who argued that blacks are more likely to be convicted, convicted of a higher crime, and, if convicted, given more severe sentences.

It is possible that experimental studies may underestimate the degree of bias against black versus white defendants, since their subjects usually consist of young white persons, often at fairly liberal institutions. Further, the cases are hypothetical. As indicated by the Wolfgang and Reidel survey mentioned above, the race factor may come into play when we consider characteristics of the victim and the type of crime involved. In their survey, the case was rape, usually interracial in nature. Recent evidence by Ugwuegbu (1974, 1976) indicates that prejudice does occur in these types of situations but that it goes both ways. In his studies, both races showed a bias for their own group. Whites were more severe if the victim was white, and blacks were more severe if the victim was black. Similarly, Miller and Hewitt (1978) reported that subjects were more likely to find the defendant guilty if the victim was similar in race to them.

B. AGE, POLITICS, AND EDUCATION OF JURORS

With regard to age and political orientation, the data are sparse but reasonably consistent. Several studies show younger jurors to be more acquittal prone (Scroggs, 1976; Stephen & Tully, 1977; Sealy & Cornish, 1973), though some studies (Reed, 1965; Simon, 1967, p. 112) show no significant differences as a function of age. The trend in the Simon study, however, is that persons under 35 years of age are more likely to vote not guilty (by reason of insanity, in this study). Politics tends to be important in terms of a liberal-conservative dimension. Nemeth and Sosis (1973) offer some limited evidence that jurors from a conservative junior college were more conviction prone than their liberal university counterparts. More direct evidence comes from Hermann's (1970) report on over 6000 jurors showing that registered Democrats tend to favor the plaintiff in a civil case both in judgment and in amount of award.

Ethnicity has mixed effects, though a north–south European dimension tends to appear in both folklore and empirical studies. Clarence Darrow (1936) indicated a preference, from the point of view of the defense, for "The Irishman and the Jew, (who) because of their national background, will put a greater burden on the prosecution and prove more sympathetic and lenient to a defendant, than an Englishman or a Scandinavian whose passion for the enforcement of the law and order is stronger" (as quoted in Simon, 1967, p. 104). Broeder (1958) found persons of German and British descent to be more likely to vote guilty and persons of Slavic or Italian descent to vote not guilty in his study with the University of Chicago jury project. Reed (1965) found Anglo-Saxon jurors of northern Louisiana to be more conviction prone than their French counterparts in the southern part of the state. Simon (1967, p. 111), however, found no significant differences between persons of southern or eastern European descent, those of central European descent, those of Scandinavian or British descent, and third-generation Americans.

Education and social class appear to be more important than ethnic background. Reed (1965), for example, finds that as education increases the likelihood of voting guilty increases. James (1959) reports that more highly educated persons emphasize procedures and instructions, whereas those with a grade school education are more likely to use personal life experiences and opinions from the trial in making their decision. Since education and social class are not unrelated, it is not surprising that there is also evidence (e.g., Rose & Prell, 1955) that higher status jurors (who define themselves as upper-upper class, lower-upper class, or upper-middle class) are more punitive than those of lower status (who define themselves as lower-middle class, upper-lower class, or lower-lower class). Simon (1967, p. 110) finds that persons with incomes over $450 per month are less likely to vote not guilty than those with incomes under $450.

Occupation, except for its correlation with social class, appears less helpful as a general predictor of jury decisions. Studies that rate the prestige of occupations (e.g., Adler, 1973; Reed, 1965) find that, the higher the prestige, the more one is likely to vote guilty. Specific occupations, however, offer a confusing pattern. Hermann (1970) reports on a study involving 6266 jurors questioned about civil cases. Butchers and skilled tradesmen were likely to find for the plaintiff on a liability case but would tend to give a below average award. Professionals were above average on both finding for the plaintiff and the award given. Blue collar workers were average on both finding for the plaintiff and the amount of the award. However, there were large differences within a category. Executives, for example, had to be divided into those who do editing and/or writing versus those who work for a corporation. The former tend to find for the plaintiff but to give him or her a low award, whereas the latter are less likely to find for the plaintiff but, if they do so, give an average award. Retired persons may be low on finding for the plaintiff, but the pattern changes when one considers retired real-estate persons versus retired sales clerks. The latter are higher on both liability and award. The complexity becomes even more apparent when one considers the occupation of the plaintiff. Here, however, the finding is fairly clear: People are kind to their own (Hermann, 1970, p. 152).

C. CHARACTERISTICS OF THE DEFENDANT

Probably the strongest effect for a defendant characteristic found in the experimental studies is the social and/or physical attractiveness of the defendant. Using descriptions that paint an individual as upstanding, middle class, having a good job,[2] and so forth, as opposed to less socially attractive descriptions, the evidence is quite clear that the socially attractive defendant is less likely to be convicted and, if convicted, is treated more leniently (Gleason & Harris, 1975; Kaplan & Kemmerick, 1974; Landy & Aronson, 1969; Nemeth & Sosis, 1973; Reynolds & Sanders, 1975; Sigall & Landy, 1972; Izzett & Leginski, 1974; Dowdle, Gillen, & Miller, 1974; Kalven & Zeisel, 1966). Although this documents the advantages of social status and social desirability in criminal cases, there is some evidence that higher status may have disadvantages when it comes to fines. Rose and Prell (1955) offer evidence that higher status persons may be fined more money for given criminal offenses, although this same study shows only minimal differences with respect to the sentencing of high-status persons in the same cases. One note of caution comes from Wilson and Donnerstein (1977), who offer evidence that the advantages of social attractiveness may be more important in hypothetical situations (which is the setting for most of these studies) than in reality. When real consequences are at stake, such advantages are not found, at least with regard to conviction. However, this study did show more severe punishment for the less socially attractive defendant in both real and hypothetical situations.

Attractiveness in the social sense is clearly an advantage. It also appears to be an advantage if one is physically attractive. A number of studies have simply varied the physical attractiveness of a "defendant" (ordinarily by photos) and found the more physically attractive person to be less likely to be convicted or, if convicted, to be treated more leniently (Efran, 1974; Levanthal & Krate, 1977). Physical appearance also makes a difference in civil cases. Stephan and Tully (1977) found that the physically attractive person wins more judgments and receives higher awards. However, there is also evidence that physical attractiveness can be a disadvantage, for example, in cases where it helps to effect a crime. Sigall and Ostrove (1975) found that physical attractiveness was an advantage for a female accused of a crime unrelated to attractiveness (in this case, burglary) but was a disadvantage when the crime was related to attractiveness (swindle).

Though jurors appear to like the physically and socially attractive regardless of how they themselves stand on these dimensions, much of the literature suggests that "like likes like," that is, that similarity leads to attraction leads to sympathy, an assumption that "they didn't do it," and leniency. We have seen that similarity on the basis of race and sex appears to follow this rule. Similarity of occupation was found to lead to higher awards. There is also evidence that workers favor labor and executives favor management if asked to imagine themselves as referees (Robinson, 1950). In addition, Adler (1973) found that the more similar the socioeconomic status of the defendant to that of the juror, the more likely is that defendant to be found not guilty.

[2]Note that these are the "qualifications" set by some states for eligibility for jury service.

This tendency to sympathize with those like oneself is even more apparent when we consider similarity of attitudes and beliefs. Griffitt and Jackson (1973) show that assumed similarity of attitudes leads to less likelihood of conviction and less severe punishments as well as recommendations of less time to be served prior to parole eligibility. Mitchell and Byrne (1973) find this tendency to be especially prominent when high "authoritarian personality" types are judging. Several researchers, notably Rokeach (1960), have argued that assumed similarity of belief is even more important than race.

Some research (e.g., Byrne, 1961) shows that highly prejudiced persons are likely to have negative evaluations of blacks while less prejudiced persons do not distinguish on the basis of race when responding to liking and work desirability scales. However, the Rokeach argument that similarity of belief is more important than race per se is supported by evidence showing that favorableness of evaluations is more tied to manipulations of assumed similarity of attitudes and beliefs than to race (Rokeach, Smith, & Evans, 1960). Even studies involving interaction between people show the possible supremacy of belief similarity over race for judgments (Hendrick, Stikes, Murray, & Puthoff, 1973).

Of course, comparing two such variables is a tricky research endeavor since it is hard to equalize the levels. Thus, other researchers have underscored the importance of race (e.g., Triandis, 1961) arguing that prejudice involves negative behaviors as well as the withholding of positive behaviors, and subsequent research (e.g., Stein, Hardyck, & Smith, 1965) shows that both race and assumed similarity are important for judgments. This bodes ill for the black defendant faced with an all-white jury since some studies (e.g., Byrne & Wong, 1962) show that whites tend to assume dissimilarity between themselves and blacks; highly prejudiced persons do this to an even greater degree. This would argue for the importance of having blacks and whites on juries simply in fairness to the litigant, not to mention the symbolic and community importance.

D.   ATTITUDES AND PERSONALITIES OF JURORS

While demographics appear to have limited generality to verdicts, the one area of psychological knowledge that offers quite good predictive capabilities is the personality "type" known as the authoritarian personality. Developed by Adorno, Frenkel-Brunswich, Levinson, and Sanford (1950), this personality is characterized by rigidity, a tendency to see things in terms of black or white, punitiveness, moralism, conservatism, intolerance of deviant behavior, and hostility toward low-status persons. It is measured by the famous F Scale (fascism scale) or more recently by a related measure designed specifically for legal attitudes, the Legal Attitudes Questionnaire (Boehm, 1968). Several studies using these measures have found that persons high on authoritarianism tend to be more conviction prone (Bray & Noble, 1978; Boehm, 1968), though some studies did not find the differences to be statistically significant (Sue, Smith, & Pedroza, 1975; Thayer, 1970). This tendency to convict is even more pronounced when high authoritarians are confronted by defendants who are dissimilar to themselves (Horstman, 1976; Mitchell & Byrne, 1972, 1973); this finding takes on additional importance when one considers the fact that high authoritarians are likely to assume dissimilarity with defendants who are lower status individuals. The one interesting anomaly is the situation where a defendant is an authority figure or has submitted to orders from an authority. Consistent with the personality "type," high authoritarians are less conviction prone and punitive when the defendant followed orders from an authority figure (Hamilton, 1976).

With regard to sentencing, the evidence is even more clear-cut. If persons high on authoritarianism convict, they tend to be more punitive (Centers, Shomer, & Rodrigues, 1970; Friend & Vinson, 1974; Bray & Noble, 1978; Mitchell & Byrne, 1973; Hamilton, 1976); Sue, Smith, and Pedroza (1975), however, find no significant differences in sentencing as a function of authoritarianism. Though some studies may show nonsignificance at the high levels of statistical confidence that are required for publication, the pattern of the evidence clearly supports the assertion that, by and large, high authoritarians are more prone to convict and, if they convict, to sentence more punitively.

E. JURY SELECTION: EFFICACY AND ETHICS

It is clear that some demographics characteristics may be related to jurors' decisions, but it is still difficult to compile a profile of an acquittal prone (or plaintiff prone) juror with only demographic information. After an extensive study of demographics, Simon (1967) concluded that it was "extremely difficult to predict the response or behavior of a given individual to a concrete situation on the basis of such gross characteristics as occupation, education, sex, or age" (p. 118). By and large, the preceding review shows sparse data and mixed results. Further, we have seen how often the influence of given demographic characteristics depends on the type of case, the characteristics of the defendant and the victim, issues of similarity, etc. Thus, most social scientists concerned with juror selection have used an empirically obtained profile rather than one that is theoretically based in deriving a profile for jury selection. These techniques involve sampling from the jurisdiction in which the trial is to be held. Demographic characteristics and attitudes are sampled and regression equations are used to determine which of them account for the most variance in a given criterion (i.e., a likely vote for conviction or acquittal). (See Berman & Sales, 1977; Christie, 1976; Kairys, Schulman, & Harring, 1975; Schulman, Shaver, Colman, Emrick, & Christie, 1963; for a discussion of procedures and specific cases.)

These empirically based profiles appear to have helped in a number of celebrated cases, for example, the Wounded Knee, Harrisburg, Camden, Angela

Davis, and Attica Prison trials (see Saks, 1976b). However, they appear to be of limited usefulness if one changes the jurisdiction. Women may be defense prone in Harrisburg, but men may be more defense prone in Gainesville (Schulman *et al.*, 1963). Further, Saks (1976b) points out that the profile can change not only with geography but even with the passage of time (p. 7). Certainly it changes with the case.

While not of direct theoretical use, the above techniques and empirically derived profiles have caused a surge of interest among lawyers and judges, not to mention social psychologists. The main reason is that these techniques have been used in widely publicized trials and, in general, have been on the winning side. The fact that these cases have been "won" has spurred controversy over both the efficacy of such social science help and its ethics. Let us deal with the efficacy issue first.

1.   Efficacy of Science

Although it would be difficult to ignore the impressive track record of social scientists using jury selection techniques in these publicized cases, it has been pointed out that the scientists were usually on the side of the defense and that the trials were mostly conspiracy trials. Some people believe that convictions are difficult to obtain in conspiracy trials. Therefore, some argue that the defense may have won without the help of social scientists. There are no control groups for these cases (Saks, 1976b, p. 13; Shapley, 1974; Zeisel, 1974).

Although there are no definitive answers about whether or not the scientific jury selection has won cases, most people who have aided lawyers in jury selection recognize the art as well as the science of this selection process. Even in developing the empirically based profiles, there is an art to selecting criteria questions and predictor variables. The design and phrasing of the questions takes judgment as well as training. However, the profiles are rarely used as the only basis on which to make the juror selections. Some (e.g., Saks, 1976b) argue that we should trust the "science" of the data that is collected rather than the "art" of our own clinical judgments. However, others would argue that one needs the combined wisdom, differential expertise, and cooperation of both attorney and psychologist (e.g., Christie, 1976). Further, the reality is that the profile is "statistical" in nature while the problem in court is to make a decision about a specific individual. As many (e.g., Saks, 1976a) have pointed out, the statistical approach means playing the odds. On the average one will win. The problem is that one wants to win the specific case. Furthermore, most statistical information is of too little predictive power to be of much help. One may find, for example, that in a given case females are likely to favor conviction 65% to 35% whereas males are likely to favor conviction 58% to 42%. If one wanted acquittal, one would pick males *on the average and if one knew nothing else*. The point, however, is to decide whether a specific male on the jury is one of the 58% or one of the 42%. Obviously, the job would be simpler if 98% of the males on a given case were likely to convict.

It is also the case that when one considers the specific 12 jurors, any given individual is a composite of social categorizations, attitudes, traits, and life history. One cannot have information on all the things he or she is and one probably wouldn't know how to weight them even if they were available. The empirically driven profile is of help since it orders variables by importance as predictors. It also gives composites. Again, however, one must make a decision on a specific individual. That person may fit the composite, but will he or she make the predicted judgment? To help in this decision, most favor expansive voir dire, a probing of the attitudes, values, and life experiences of the actual jurors to find those that "fit" the statistical profile. Most look for verbal statements and even nonverbal cues that "go together" with the demographics and attitudes that are assumed to underly a sympathy for the defendant (or the reverse). This is more the art than the science. Asking the questions in such a way as to receive authentic and revealing answers, recognizing that other jurors are influenced by the answers that are given, detecting the important information contained in both the verbal and nonverbal responses, and assessing the weight to give to each piece of information is, in part, an art. And the lawyer has his or her own experience and insights that must be considered as well.

2. Efficacy of the Lawyer's Insights

Although the judgments of an experienced trial attorney should be respected, it is difficult to document the insight and knowledge that such experience can bring. However, the articulated "rules" for jury selection promoted by some of the "greats" of the legal profession should provide some relief to social scientists obsessed by the inadequacy of their theories and findings. The advice offered by lawyers and judges in the books and manuals available to law students is different in two major respects from advice offered by social scientists. The lawyers' advice tends to be phrased definitively rather than probabilistically. It also derives from experience rather than from the systematic accumulation of data. It may also be more witty and entertaining.

Clarence Darrow (1936) recommended that a defense counsel should pick Catholics, Episcopalians, and Presbyterians over Baptists and Methodists, Irishmen and Jews rather than an Englishman or a Scandinavian. Donovan (1885) advised for the defense "better warm than cold faces; better builders than salesmen, better farmers than inventors. Avoid doctors, lawyers and pettifoggers" (p. 227). Bailey and Rothblatt (1974) tell us that persons between 28 and 55 are more alert and responsive to complex defenses and that married persons are more favorable to the defense than the unmarried. They further caution against women jurors when the defendant is a woman. While intriguing at some level, these generalizations have not been corroborated by available data, and the distinctions tend to be imprecise. For example, the age range of 28 to 55 is very wide, and most research finds distinctions within that range to be quite significant (e.g., 28 to 35, 35 to 45, 45 to 55). Unmarried persons can be widowed, divorced, or never married, distinctions that most scientists would make and that are psychologically meaningful. Women are not necessarily unfavorable to women defendants; some studies actually show the reverse (e.g., Rose & Prell, 1955; Nagel & Weitzman, 1972). Religion, nationality, and occupation are less consistent than lawyers have assumed.

Perhaps more revealing are the data from a survey of Chicago trial specialists chosen at random from the Martindale-Hubbell directory of lawyers. Kallen (1969) sent questionnaires to 88 trial specialists and received 50 responses. In an attempt to check the "truisms" that he learned as a law student, Kallen sought to learn whether or not there was agreement among trial specialists as to the relationship between juror background and verdict. The data showed that there were "no 'truisms' concerning the effect of background upon juror sympathies" (p. 146). Attorneys showed wide disagreement as to which demographic characteristics were good predictors and even disagreed as to the directions of the biases.

In a better designed study aimed at assessing the efficacy of lawyers' use of the peremptory challenge, Zeisel and Diamond (1978) studied cases before the Federal District Court of northern Illinois. For each case, the authors studied not only actual jurors but also their controlled counterparts; that is, they studied the jurors who were challenged peremptorily as well as the remaining venire. With the cooperation of the judges, all these individuals heard the entire case, were privy to exactly the same information, and were, to the extent possible, treated exactly as were the actual jurors. Comparing the "votes" of these individuals, Zeisel and Diamond were able to calculate a performance index for the prosecutor and the defense by taking into account the vote distribution of the entire venire. The authors report that the "collective performance of the attorneys is not impressive." The prosecutors made about as many good challenges as bad ones. The defense attorneys, though on the average a little more effective, were highly erratic. Some did very well; others did very poorly. To the extent that jury selection is not just a matter of technique and training, legal practitioners, like social scientists, will differ.

3. The Evidence

Though one could well argue that scientific jury selection techniques can help a lawyer in shifting the probabilities of winning a case, no one would argue that it is all-important or even the most important factor. The strength of the evidence appears to dominate the outcome. Most would argue that jury selection is important "all other things being equal." Zeisel (as cited in Shapley, 1974), for example, credits the evidence for the verdict in the vast majority of cases.

Saks (1976b) has data suggesting that "the amount of evidence was more than three times as powerful, and strength of evidence more than seven times as powerful" as attitudes. This latter finding should be taken with a grain of salt, since, as the authors themselves understand, the ranges of the variables under study are not comparable and one cannot take the conclusions about relative strength as definitive. However, the importance of the evidence is underscored by such findings. Further, the fact of agreement by judge and jury found in 78% of cases (Kalven & Zeisel, 1966) and the fact that jurors voted in line with the evidence 62% of the time regardless of personality differences (Boehm, 1968) supports the contention that it is the evidence that matters.

4. Ethics

It would be naive and irresponsible to equate the ethical issues in jury selection with its efficacy. In one sense, it may be true that charges of "stacking the jury" with a resulting diminution of justice may be less important if the jury selection techniques were found to be useless. Yet, the ethical issues involve more than efficacy, and most believe that social science knowledge can aid jury selection. The question then turns to the appropriateness and ethics of this aid.

Most people concerned with the shaping of a jury's composition tend to confuse the issue of cross-representation with the issue of peremptory challenge. As noted in the earlier sections, we presently do not have a cross-representation of the community with our existing qualifications for, and exemptions and excuses from, jury service. While one would be loathe to worsen the situation, the peremptory challenge originated from the idea that persons who are, or who are thought to be, biased against a defendant should be removed. It is further based on the insight that one cannot always clearly articulate the reason for presumed bias, which may be a look, a gesture. It is by its very nature a challenge "without a reason being stated" (*Swain* v. *Alabama,* 1964). Thus, one can challenge a given number of jurors for any reason, though the presumption is that the person is removed because of perceived bias.

The reality may well be that one attempts to create the most favorable jury. However, it is important to remember that the use of peremptories does not allow the selection of favorable jurors. It provides for the excusing of unfavorable jurors. This distinction is all too apparent to those who have done jury selection and have watched a favorite juror struck by the other side or have rethought a potential challenge when viewing the remaining venire. Given that the law provides the defendant (and the prosecution) with the right to strike unfavorable jurors, it makes sense that the effective use of this right requires information and judgment. To the extent that social scientists offer this information and judgment, they help the system to operate more effectively. Some (e.g., Mariani, 1975) argue that "the union of social scientists and attorneys serves to ensure the impartiality and fundamental fairness expected of our judicial machinery" (p.

81). One should recognize, however, that there is an implicit and very optimistic assumption in this reasoning. It is that both sides have access to this information and judgment.

Many critics of our system have been concerned that the prosecution has long had access to information not held by the defense, particularly government records and documents. Thus, some researchers (e.g., Christie, 1976) have tended to work for the defense. Others recognize the inequality of access to such information based on wealth of the defendant—some people can afford these services, others cannot. When it is provided at no cost, it is usually because of political sympathy—another nonequalizer. Thus, one should be concerned that the inequity that is evident throughout the criminal justice system, that is, that it helps to be beautiful and rich, becomes again evident in the use of social science aids in jury selection. It is also the case that this inequity has existed for some time in another form. As we saw earlier, some attorneys are better at jury selection than others. These are likely to be the attorneys that win. And the attorneys that win tend to be paid more, and, therefore, the wealthy tend to have greater access to them and to their knowledge. In this light, however, the issue becomes one of how to make the information available to the poor, not necessarily whether to ban it altogether.

F.   ATTITUDES TOWARD CAPITAL PUNISHMENT

1.   Exclusion of Those Opposed to Capital Punishment

An area where psychological research has been particularly needed and solicited by judges and lawyers alike is in cases involving the death penalty. For over a century, jurors with conscientious objections to the death penalty have been excluded from jury service in capital cases. The rationale for this was that when the death sentence is mandatory the only way a person could express scruples against capital punishment was to vote not guilty.

As early as 1820, in *United States* v. *Carnell,* all Quakers were challenged for cause because they did not believe in the death penalty, a practice that was upheld by the circuit court. In 1892, the Court ruled in *Logan* v. *United States* that the exclusion of veniremen who had conscientious scruples against the death penalty was constitutional. While this practice remained intact, most states started to allow juries to decide between penalties of death or life in prison rather than having a mandatory death penalty. Though this discretion changed the rationale for the exclusion practices, they remained until the mid-twentieth century. Although other cases have borne on the issue (see Cucinotta, 1968; Oberer, 1961; Gordon, 1969; Enborg, 1976, for reviews), the landmark decision came in 1968 with *Witherspoon* v. *Illinois.* Prior to *Witherspoon,* jurors with "general objections" to capital punishment were excluded. This could be as tentative as being "inclined that way," being that way in "most instances," requiring that the evidence be "very strong" to impose the death penalty, or even not knowing "whether he has such scruples" (Oberer, 1961, p. 547). Needless to say, many individuals were excused on this basis. Oberer (1961) reports a case involving murder in Erie, Pennsylvania in 1958 in which 142 prospective jurors were examined before 12 jurors and 2 alternates could be accepted. They exhausted the original panel of 100 and on three occasions sent out for more jurors. The reason was reported to be, in large part, that many persons had scruples against the death penalty.

After *Witherspoon*, only those jurors who would never impose the death penalty, that is, those irrevocably committed before trial to vote against the penalty of death, could be challenged for cause. The interesting legal point, however, is that this distinction was ruled necessary for the sentence phase, not the guilt determination phase, of the trial.

In the *Witherspoon* case, the defendant was convicted of first degree murder and sentenced to death by a unanimous jury. However, the venire members indicating conscientious scruples against the death penalty were challenged for cause and therefore removed. On appeal, the petitioner argued that the jury was neither representative nor impartial and therefore asked that his conviction and sentence be reversed. The Court ruled a reversal of the sentence, making it life in prison rather than death, on the argument that impartiality in the sentence required that the jury "express the conscience of the community on the ultimate question of life or death" (p. 1775). With this pronouncement, they noted that 42–47% of the people in a recent Gallup poll had expressed opposition to the death penalty; thus, a jury composed solely of persons with no scruples against the death penalty could not speak for the community. The Court also recognized the distinction between "general objections" to the death penalty and an inability to even consider that as an alternative. Some people can set aside their general scruples and consider the punishment that the state allows. Thus, the Court ruled that it is when a person would "automatically vote against the imposition of the capital punishment without regard to any evidence that might be developed at the trial of the case before them" (pp. 552–553) that is a basis for exclusion.

2. Death Penalty Attitudes and Readiness to Convict

The necessity of considering the available alternatives was underscored with respect to the sentencing of the defendant. However, the Court did not accept the argument that the removal of persons who had scruples against the death penalty would yield a conviction-prone jury. Thus, they did not reverse Witherspoon's conviction for they could not conclude that the "exclusion of jurors opposed to capital punishment results in an unrepresentative jury on the issue of guilt or substantially increases the risk of conviction" (p. 518).

In support of the petitioner's argument, three studies showing a relationship between death penalty attitudes and conviction proneness were submitted. However, they were all unpublished at the time (Wilson, 1964; Goldberg, undated; Zeisel, 1957), and the third study was a report on some preliminary analyses. The first study (Wilson, 1964) used 187 college subjects and found that those with scruples against the death penalty gave guilty verdicts significantly less often than those with no scruples. The second study (now published as Goldberg, 1969) studied 200 college students and reported that those with scruples against the death penalty found the defendants guilty in a greater percentage of cases than those without scruples, but such differences were not statistically significant. The third study reported some preliminary findings that were later published (Zeisel, 1968). This study involved actual jurors who had served in criminal cases. Zeisel asked each juror questions pertaining to capital punishment attitudes as well as the juror's first-ballot vote (and the first-ballot votes of the other jurors on that trial). In 9 out of 11 "first-ballot" jury votes, those without scruples against the death penalty voted guilty more often than those with scruples. Though not the strongest evidence in the world, the studies offered the argument (and at least were consistent with it) that jurors with no scruples against the death penalty would be more conviction prone. However, these studies were the only ones available to the Court at the time, and the Court saw fit to mention that even the amicus curiae brief filed by the NAACP on behalf of the defendant observed that "with respect to bias in favor of the prosecution on the issue of guilt, the record in this case is 'almost totally lacking in the sort of factual information that would assist the Court'" (footnote 11, p. 517). The Court found the evidence "too tentative and fragmentary" and was unable to determine "the precise meaning of the terms used in those studies, the accuracy of the techniques employed and the validity of the generalizations made" (p. 517). To reverse every conviction made by a "death qualified" jury as practiced for the past century was too great a decision given the evidence. Although the evidence was not considered conclusive, the Court agreed with the legal premise by stating that jurors could be excluded if their attitude toward the death penalty would prevent them from making an impartial decision as to the defendant's guilt.

Since the ruling in *Witherspoon,* more data have been collected and the pattern, while not perfect, supports the general contention in *Witherspoon* as to the relationship between death penalty attitudes and conviction proneness. (It should be pointed out that this link was made very clearly and persuasively by Oberer, 1961, prior to the *Witherspoon* case).

Some of the data both prior to and subsequent to this ruling are consistent with, but not a direct test of, the linkage between capital punishment attitudes and conviction proneness. Some (e.g., Crosson, 1968) link death penalty attitudes to conservatism. Jurow (1971) corroborates this and also relates death penalty attitudes to authoritarianism. Authoritarianism, as we saw in an earlier section, has been linked to conviction proneness and, especially, to punitiveness (Boehm, 1968; Bray and Noble, 1978, pp. 43–45). Capital punishment attitudes have been directly linked to punitiveness in numerous studies (Jurow, 1971; Goldberg, 1969; Hamilton, 1976). Those who favor the death penalty give longer sentences and are more likely to choose the death penalty relative to those who oppose the death penalty.

The most pertinent test, of course, is that between capital punishment attitudes and conviction proneness. Bronson (1970) made this specific connection but defined conviction proneness in terms of agreement with antidefendant legal attitudes. Those who favored the death penalty were more likely to agree with attitudes against defendants. While this may be correlated with conviction, it is not a precise test of the link we wish. White's (1973) report on the 1971 Harris Poll shows that "subjects who could vote for the death penalty were more likely to convict than those who would never vote for the death penalty" (p. 1186). However, these conviction data were based on voting guilty or not guilty from the evidence of a set of cards, each containing the facts of a criminal case. Although this is consistent with the proposed link, the problem is that not voting for the death penalty is not the legal definition of exclusion under the *Witherspoon* ruling. Furthermore, the "case" methodology is quite removed from its analogue. The Zeisel interviews, now published (Zeisel, 1968), report odds of 24 to 1 that jurors without scruples against the death penalty are more likely to vote guilty than persons with scruples. The data are powerful, and Zeisel makes a legally relevant distinction in assessing death penalty attitudes by asking the jurors if they had conscientious scruples against the death penalty which would preclude them from finding the defendant guilty if the crime were punishable by death. The problem, of course, is that conviction is defined as the first-ballot vote on noncapital cases; yet, the data are quite convincing since one could easily assume that conviction proneness in noncapital cases would transfer to capital ones.

Perhaps the best early study on this issue, which directly tests the link between capital punishment attitudes and conviction proneness (plus many other things), is that conducted by Jurow (1971). Recognizing that "general objections" to the death penalty was not a sufficient basis for exclusion, Jurow made the legal distinctions by including both a general attitudes toward capital punishment measure and one specific to the situation "if you were a juror." Five-point scales were used to assess the degree of "scruples" versus "no scruples." He also used tape-recorded cases and tested the hypotheses using two different cases (a liquor store robbery and rape). His findings basically support the contention that people with scruples against capital punishment are less prone to conviction. However, the findings are clear in this regard in the robbery case, whereas the data in the rape case show the predicted trend but did not reach the conventional level of significance (i.e., the chance factor must be less than 5 times out of 100). It is interesting to note that most subjects favored conviction in the rape case, whereas they favored acquittal in the robbery case. Though not explicitly stated by the authors, the pattern is that where the case evidence favors conviction, those who are for capital punishment are somewhat more likely to convict, but not significantly so. Where the evidence favors acquittal, those who are for capital punishment are significantly more likely to convict the defendant.

Ellsworth, Thompson, and Cowan (1980) conducted a study on this issue using a videotape of a single murder trial with subjects who were eligible for jury duty. Their findings show a significant difference between "death qualified" jurors (i.e., those who would consider imposing the death penalty) and those who would be excused under the *Witherspoon* ruling (i.e., those who would not consider it in any case).

The Supreme Court of California, *Hovey* v. *Superior Court* (1980), took quite seriously the whole sequence of studies pertinent to capital punishment attitudes and conviction proneness. However, California excludes not only those who would automatically vote for life imprisonment (i.e., not consider the death penalty in any case) but also those who would automatically vote for the death penalty. Thus, the studies did not make the appropriate comparisons for the *Hovey* case and the courts have yet to be convinced that the death qualification process, whether as defined by the *Witherspoon* ruling or by California law, leads to a greater probability of conviction and, thus, violates due process.

On balance, the evidence is quite strong for the link between death penalty attitudes and conviction proneness. Each study may have its flaws, and some of the results don't quite reach statistical significance, but the pattern of the results points very strongly to the contention that removal of persons with scruples against the death penalty is likely to lead to a conviction-prone jury. It certainly leads to a punitive one.

Another issue regarding exclusion of persons with scruples against capital punishment arises with regard to representation of cognizable groups, an issue we discussed earlier in this article. Though the *Witherspoon* decision concerned itself mainly with the conviction and sentence, the issue of representation of the community was also raised. In that context, it is important to note that most studies show fairly consistent demographic differences on the basis of attitudes toward the death penalty. In general, persons who favor capital punishment tend to be white rather than black, male rather than female, Republican or Independent rather than Democrat, wealthy rather than poor (Bronson, 1970; Zeisel, 1968; Harris polls cited in Vidmar & Ellsworth, 1974). These differences are strong and reliable.

Somewhat more complicated and less predictive are the demographic variables of age, occupation, religion, and education. The first two studies cited above report little differences in death penalty attitudes as a function of age, whereas the latter report, based on Harris polls, finds that older persons have a greater tendency to favor capital punishment. With regard to occupation, Bronson (1970) reports that professionals, executives, white collar workers, and skilled workers are more favorable to the death penalty than unskilled workers or housewives. The Harris polls reviewed by Vidmar and Ellsworth (1974) find that "white collar workers, manual laborers and farmers favor capital punishment [more] than do professonals and business persons" (p. 1253). With regard to religion, Bronson's (1970) ordering of death penalty attitudes from most to least favorable is Southern Baptists, Protestants in general, agnostics, Catholics, and Jews. However, Vidmar and Ellsworth (1974) report little difference between Catholics and Protestants, though the former are slightly more favorable to capital punishment. Both these studies show little relationship between education and death penalty attitudes, though Bronson (1970) reports a tendency for the highly educated and the poorly educated to oppose capital punishment.

Thus, one pattern becomes clear. We noted in earlier sections that the categories of persons underrepresented on juries are black, female, the highly and poorly educated, etc., exactly those groups of persons who would be further underrepresented in death penalty cases because of their scruples against capital punishment.

V.   Influence and Persuasion within the Jury

Up to now, we have concentrated on the jurors as individuals, people with a set of attitudes, values, and experiences that predispose them to view a case in one way or another. However, the jury is a group, usually 12 in number, who usually must deliberate to unanimity. (We will discuss the "usually" of these procedures in the next sections.) As a group, they inform each other, recreate the evidence, interpret it, and search to influence each other until consensus is reached.

As is undoubtedly apparent, not all individuals are equal in the art of persuasion. Even as a tactic in jury selection, lawyers and social science consultants try to keep the persuasive people who are in sympathy with their position and to remove the persuasive people who lean to the opposition. If one cannot persuade them to one's position, the strategy is to remove the independent and persuasive.

A.   THE FOREPERSON

In considering the categories of persons in terms of who is most likely to be persuasive, we must first consider who is most likely to be selected as foreperson. The available literature on this issue is very consistent. The findings are that the foreperson is most likely to be white, male, and of a higher status occupation. Strodtbeck, James, and Hawkins (1957), Gordon (1968), Davis *et al.* (1975), and Beckham and Aronson (1978) all find that males are significantly more likely to be elected as foreperson than females. By occupation, proprieters are most likely to be elected foreperson, followed by clerical workers, skilled laborers, and unskilled laborers (Strodtbeck *et al.*, 1957, James, 1959; Strodtbeck & Hook, 1961). Important in terms of influence, the foreperson is found to participate more than other jurors (Strodtbeck *et al.*, 1957; James, 1959; Simon, 1967), and participation is found to relate to maintenance of position and influence (Strodtbeck *et al.*, 1957).

Part of the reason that the white, male proprieter is most likely to be elected foreperson is because he tends to act in a highly confident manner. He usually takes the head seat at a rectangular table (Strodtbeck & Hook, 1961; Nemeth *et al.*, 1976), starts the conversation, and participates the most (Strodtbeck *et al.*, 1957). People usually elect as foreperson the person who takes the head seat at the table (Strodtbeck & Hook, 1961), and they usually elect the person who starts the conversation (Strodtbeck *et al.*, Gordon, 1968). The foreperson is in a position to control the discussion, suggest procedures, and give instructions (James, 1959). As an autocrat, he can suppress discussion and lead jurors to quick decisions; as a democrat, he can foster discussion and lengthen the deliberation process (Bevan, Albert, Loiseaux, Mayfield, & Wright, 1958). In any event, he has power and influence.

The fact that choosing the head seat, opening conversation, and participating more, that is, the behavioral manifestations of confidence, correspond to certain demographic characteristics (i.e., white, male, prestigious occupations) points to the possibility that it is the behavioral style rather than the category of person that determines influence and/or selection as foreperson. A study by Nemeth and Wachtler (1974) is informative in this regard. In that study, five "jurors" deliberated a personal injury case; unknown to the four who were subjects, the fifth person was a confederate of the experimenter. The confederate maintained a deviant position in favor of a decision for very low compensation, whereas the four subjects were in close agreement for a decision of much more compensation. Upon entry into the deliberation room, this deviant individual chose either the head seat at the table or one of the side seats. In two other conditions, he was assigned either the head seat or one of the side seats. Results showed that, although his arguments were exactly the same in each group, he exerted more influence when he chose the head seat than he did in any other condition. The other individuals significantly reduced their judgments of appropriate compensation. Further, they showed substantially lower judgments on different, but related, cases. This study shows the importance of the act of taking the head seat, the show of confidence that led to influence. Simple occupation of that seat was not found to affect influence; when the confederate was assigned the head seat, he was not influential.

Thus, the circle seems complete. Certain categories of persons are likely to perform the actions that foster their selection as foreperson. However, the emphasis on behavioral styles of confidence rather than the category of person suggests that the best predictor of foreperson and influence is the behavioral style of the person, that is, the indications of confidence, rather than the category of person. Although these tend to be correlated, it would behoove lawyers and social scientists alike to note the stylistic differences between jurors rather than just their demographic characteristics in making predictions regarding influence.

B. BEING IN THE MAJORITY OR THE MINORITY

It should also be noted that influence is not totally dependent on individual differences but is, in part, related to whether the person's position is in the majority or in the minority. Kalven and Zeisel's (1966) work shows that the majority position on the first ballot is highly likely to be the final verdict (in over 90% of cases). Part of the reason for this is the powerful conformity process. Decades of studies in social psychology point to the phenomenon where a person with a minority position will adopt the majority position even when the majority is incorrect (Asch, 1956; Allen, 1965). Thus, apart from the persuasive tactics of specific individuals, the fact of being in the majority is an advantage. It is particularly advantageous if the minority position is held by a single individual since the conformity process is drastically reduced if that individual has an ally (Allen, 1965).

Though it is statistically rarer, it is the case that the minority sometimes prevails. These may be our most interesting and controversial cases. Available evidence indicates that this process is more likely if the minority takes the position of "not guilty" rather than "guilty" (Nemeth, 1977). They are particularly more likely to prevail if they maintain their position, both resisting the conformity pressure and actively arguing their own position. This behavior, while creating dislike for them, tends to be effective in swaying majority opinion. (See Nemeth, 1979a, for a review of the influence of a minority.) Thus, it would appear that independence and confidence, while useful in general for influence, is particularly necessary when the person holds a minority position. Rather than yielding to a position with which they disagree, such individuals are more likely to resist and therefore "hang" the jury or possibly influence the majority to their position (see Nemeth, 1979b).

VI. Changes in the Form of the Jury

Court rulings have served to affect representation of the community on juries. Most notably, these have involved changes in the form of the jury—its size and its procedures for reaching a verdict. As noted earlier, the common law jury has been a body of 12 persons deliberating to unanimity ever since the reign of Henry II. Though some states have used smaller and nonunanimous juries, it is only in the last decade that the Supreme Court has ruled on both the size and the decision rule by which verdicts are reached. These decisions, many feel, are an erosion of the jury system. At least one author has suggested that the "1970's may well be remembered as the decade in which we almost lost the jury" (Sperlich, 1980, p. 263).

A. SIZE

In an historic and widely criticized ruling, the Supreme Court held in *Williams* v. *Florida* (1970) that state criminal juries of six were constitutional. Referring specifically to the sixth Amendment requiring an "impartial jury" in criminal cases, the Court concluded that the 12-person jury was an historical accident "unrelated to the great purposes which gave rise to the jury in the first place" (pp. 89–90). They further pointed to the distinction between the Sixth Amendment, covering criminal cases, and the Seventh Amendment, covering civil cases. The Seventh Amendment refers to jury trials according to the "rules of the common law." Common law juries were historically 12 in number. The Court did not dispute this. What it did dispute was the relevance of the common law jury to the "impartial jury" phrasing of the Sixth Amendment covering criminal trials. It thus left the question open with regard to civil trials.

The evidence that the Court mustered in support of this historically important and potentially damaging ruling is cause for particular concern. The issue raised by the Court was whether or not the 6-person jury was "functionally equivalent" to the 12-person jury. They were concerned with the values embedded in the jury system both as a protection against government oppression and in terms of community participation as well as its reliability as a fact finder. For support of functional equivalence on these issues, it used the following: (1) an undocumented statement by a judge quoting a book which stated that "it could easily be argued" that 6- and 12-person juries would deliberate equally well; (2) a judge's insight that 5-person juries over which he had presided were "satisfactory"; (3) the undocumented statement of a court clerk and the testimony of three lawyers that civil court verdicts were about the same for 6-person juries (with which they were experimenting) and 12-person juries; (4) reports by lawyers and a court clerk in a Massachusetts district court that the verdicts reached by differently sized juries were not different; (5) the fact that the Monmouth County Court of New Jersey was experimenting with 6-person juries; and (6) a judge's summary of the economic advantages that are likely to be derived from 6-person juries (see Zeisel, 1971, pp. 714–715; Sperlich, 1980, p. 270, for further details and commentary).

The reaction to this "evidence" was widespread and critical (Zeisel, 1971, 1972; Walbert, 1971; Stevens, 1971). It was seen as representing a concern for economics, that is, presumed time and money saved, over the preservation of a long and cherished democratic institution. The subjectivity and undocumented nature of the evidence especially caused concern, particularly in light of the sweeping changes that such a ruling could cause. In countering the arguments of the Court, Zeisel (1971) argued from a statistical point of view that 6-person juries would be less representative of the community and that minorities would be less likely to be represented. If represented, they would be less likely to have an ally, a situation that we know is likely to lead to conformity to the majority even if the majority is incorrect (Asch, 1956; Allen, 1965). Further, Zeisel argued that fewer hung juries would result with 6 person juries as consequence of yielding on the part of the minority.

Some of these points are consistent with the mathematical modeling approach to size of jury and decision making (e.g., Gelfand & Solomon, 1973, 1974, 1975, 1977; Nagel & Neef, 1975; Saks & Ostrom, 1975; see generally Penrod & Hastie, 1979, and Grofman, 1980, for thoughtful reviews and analyses of modeling approaches). These models, though they require interpretation because of some of their simplifying assumptions, tend to support the view that 12-person groups are more representative, more accurate, less likely to convict defendants when a case has "high apparent guilt," and will hang more often. The models tend not to assume large differences in the aggregate, much of this due to the fact that many cases are "clear," that is, most juries would make the same decision, as well as the fact that aggregate data tend to mask case by case differences (Kalven & Zeisel, 1966; Lempert, 1975).

In addition to the preceding arguments based on logic and modeling, there exists a sizeable literature on small groups pointing to differences in group performance and productivity as a function of group size. For example, a review of over 30 studies by Thomas and Fink (1963) concludes that larger groups are better, both qualitatively and quantitatively. These conclusions need to be tempered somewhat by the realization that the resources available to a group increase with size (though at a decreasing degree), but that coordination and motivation factors come into play, making the relationship between size and performance somewhat more complicated. Further, it is clear that the type of task affects this relationship, larger groups being superior when a correct answer is easily recognized as such (see generally Steiner, 1972, as well as Hoffman, 1965, for a review of these issues). Many studies show a superiority of larger groups when judgments are averaged, as might be the case with damage awards (see e.g., Lorge, Fox, Davitz, & Brenner, 1958), and the greater resources of large groups also appear to be relevant to recall of crucial facts (see generally Kelley & Thibaut, 1969). On the other hand, smaller groups tend to foster more equal participation and report more satisfaction (Hackman & Vidmar, 1970; Thomas & Fink, 1963). These, however, are not necessarily desirable in jury deliberations. Satisfaction may inhibit task performance (Hackman & Vidmar, 1970).

Although the evidence used by the *Williams* Court was subjective and undocumented and although there existed ample evidence illustrating the functional nonequivalence of 6- and 12-person groups, the message of the *Williams* v. *Florida* ruling was unmistakable. With the removal of the constitutional obstacles to reduction in jury size in state criminal trials, radical changes in civil litigation started. Gibbons (1972) reports that, starting on January 1, 1971 and continuing through June of 1972, more than 41 of 93 federal district courts reduced "the common law jury of twelve persons in all or specified categories of civil litigation" (p. 594). This was challenged in *Colgrove* v. *Battin* (1973), but the Court exacerbated the problem by upholding the reduction of jury size in civil juries.

In support of its ruling, the *Colgrove* Court not only repeated the errors of "evidence" in the *Williams* decision but found four new studies to support the contention that 6- and 12-person juries were functionally equivalent. Ignoring the criticism directed against the *Williams* Court as well as the available empirical data on the issue, the Court in *Colgrove* looked to four studies showing no statistically significant differences in verdicts as a function of 6- versus 12-member juries (the studies, however, proved to be methodologically flawed and are ably criticized by Zeisel & Diamond, 1974). These studies, which the Court found to be "convincing empirical evidence" (p. 159), were actual trial results from Washington (Bermant & Coppock, 1973), New Jersey (Institute of Judicial Administration, 1972), and Michigan (Michigan Study, 1973) as well as an experimental study (Kessler, 1973).

The first two studies collected data in systems that allowed litigants to choose between 6- or 12-person juries. Since the choice is a nonrandom event (lawyers have reasons for choosing a 6- or a 12-person jury), the groups cannot meaningfully be compared. In fact, the second study showed that the 12-person juries had bigger cases, that is, the settlements were, "on the average, three times as great as for the six-member jury cases" (Zeisel & Diamond, 1974, p. 284). The third study used a before and after design in which a 12-person system was changed to a 6-person system. The problem with this study is that, in addition to unknown corresponding events, there were two important "known" events—a mediation board was instituted and procedural rules involving insurance were established. The fourth study had the common problems of a nonrepresentative subject sample and an artificial situation. However, this study had additional problems in that only one case was used and this case overwhelmingly favored the defendant. The lack of statistically significant differences is not surprising given that practically all the subjects favored the same verdict. To make matters worse, the subjects were given instructions to deliberate until a 5/6 majority had been reached.

Since the *Colgrove* ruling, interested scientists have become even more alarmed at the increasing erosion of the jury system, particularly when the evidence does not support such a sweeping change. In fact, the change flies in the face of both historical precedent and good empirical data. Many have assumed that the courts favor a reduction in size because of presumed economic saving, an intolerable consideration when pitted against the constitutional protections. However, the available evidence shows that even such savings are minimal, if they exist at all. Pabst (1973), for example, finds virtually no differences in voir dire times, trial times, and number of challenges. While the Chief Justice estimated that $4 million could be saved by reducing federal civil juries to six persons (New York *Times,* 1971, as reported in Zeisel, 1971, p. 711), Zeisel (1971) points out that this represents "little more than a thousandth part of one per cent of the total federal budget." In even more concrete terms, Sperlich (1980) translates this into "two cents of savings per person per year" and compares it to the "annual outlays of $631 million for golf equipment" (pp. 276–277). The savings, if any, will be quite small when compared to the other wastes in the judicial system, particularly when the importance of democratic participation in the administration of justice is considered.

Not all the criticisms have come from scientists and concerned citizens, however. The conferees of the Chief Justice Earl Warren Conference on Advocacy in the United States (1977) openly disagreed with the views of the Supreme Court. They backed 12-person juries and called for a resistance to the trend for 6-person juries. As part of the advantages of 12-person juries, the conferees noted that there would be better representation of the community, that there would be more resources and more likelihood of correcting errors in larger groups, and that deliberation would be more vigorous and more encouraging of dissent.

Of great service to this issue and to subsequent rulings was an article by Lempert (1975), who provided summaries of available literature as well as methodological critiques of the evidence pertinent to the issues raised by the *Williams* and *Colgrove* rulings. Given the balance of its presentation and the review it provided, this article came to be heavily cited (along with the articles by Zeisel, 1971, 1974, and Saks, 1977) in a ruling that was to follow.

In 1978, the Court stopped the erosion of the jury by calling to a halt the reduction in size. In *Ballew* v. *Georgia,* a case involving the distribution of obscene materials, the Court ruled that Georgia's jury of five persons was unconstitutional. The Court did not, however, correct its ruling in *Williams* v. *Florida.* In fact, it reaffirmed its position that 6- and 12-person juries were functionally equivalent and that 6-person juries were therefore constitutional. However, the *Ballew* ruling said that 5-person juries were not constitutional because "the purpose and functioning of the jury in a criminal trial is seriously impaired, and to a constitutional degree, by a reduction in size to below six members" (p. 1030). The Court recognized the importance of the available data for demonstrating functional nonequivalence based on group size. Yet, it used much of the data (which actually compared 6- and 12-person juries) to find an impairment of functioning in juries consisting of 5 members while still affirming the functional equivalence of juries of 6 and 12 members. Though this is still of concern to many who feel that the allowance of even 6-person juries is an erosion of an important institution, the Court at least has called a halt to the diminution of the jury.

In an impressive use of available scientific data, Mr. Justice Blackmun pointed out that reduction in jury size can impair quality of performance and productivity. It lessens the likelihood of remembering each of the important pieces of evidence; it is less likely to overcome the biases of its members; the likelihood of convicting an innocent person increases (Type I error); the variability of the decisions is greater; the minority is less likely to be represented and, if represented, less likely to adhere to its position; fewer hung juries will occur; and the opportunity for meaningful and adequate representation of the community decreases (see pp. 1035–1037). For these conclusions, the Court relied on an extensive list of published studies (see footnote 10, p. 1034), many of which were included in the Thomas and Fink (1963), Lempert (1975), Saks (1977), and Zeisel (1971, 1974) articles. Not all the complexities of the relationship between group size and performance were noted, or perhaps understood, but the message of functional nonequivalence was understood and utilized. For many of us, the *Ballew* ruling was indeed welcome because it halted a process that may have caused serious underrepresentation of minority viewpoints and a reduction in the conflict of diverse viewpoints that are part of the robust process necessary to reach a verdict.

Since *Ballew,* even better evidence has accumulated. In one of the most realistic and controlled studies on the issue of 6- versus 12-member juries, Padawer-Singer, Singer, and Singer (1977) studied 828 jurors from the central jury room. The experiment was conducted in the authentic setting of a courtroom, and the trial was a 3-hr videotaped reenactment of a real trial. A judge gave the jury instructions and the jury was allowed to deliberate as long as needed. The results from this extensive and well-designed study show that, although verdicts in the aggregate are not statistically different for 6- and 12-person juries, 6-person juries are much more likely to have consensus at the start of deliberation (23.9%), which did not occur in the cases of 12-member juries. The 6-person juries were more "unstable," being highly variable, and 12-person juries "hung" more often. This, together with the experimental evidence of Valenti and Downing (1975) showing that 6-person juries are more likely to convict when apparent guilt is high, tends to underscore the functional nonequivalence of 6- and 12-person juries.

B.   MAJORITY VERSUS UNANIMITY OF VERDICTS

Ordinarily, the robust conflict needed to reach a verdict means the robust conflict needed to reach consensus. Historically, the common law jury has been defined not only as 12 people, but also as 12 who would reach a unanimous decision. That definition has changed this past decade. In another sweeping change in the early 1970s, the Court ruled in *Apodaca, Cooper and Madden* v. *Oregon* (1972) and in *Johnson* v. *Louisiana* (1972) that the allowance by some states of less than unanimous verdicts in criminal trials was not unconstitutional. In Oregon, verdicts can be reached by a vote of 10 to 2, except for capital cases. Louisiana has a three-tier system in which capital cases require 12 persons deliberating to unanimity, cases where punishment is necessarily imprisonment at hard labor can be decided by a 9 to 3 vote, and cases where punishment might be imprisonment at hard labor require 5 persons reaching a unanimous verdict.

In the Oregon case, Apodaca was convicted by a vote of 11 to 1, Cooper by 10 to 2, and Madden by 11 to 1. They argued that their constitutional rights to an impartial jury under the Sixth Amendment and equal protection under the law under the Fourteenth Amendment were violated. The Court disagreed. In the Louisiana case, Johnson made a similar plea. He also pointed out that requiring 5 persons to be unanimous was a stricter requirement than a 9 to 3 majority and that he should at least have been accorded the same protections as he would have received if charged with a less serious crime. The Court disagreed with this premise and argued that "If appellant's position is that it is easier to convince nine of 12 jurors than to convince all of five, he is simply challenging the judgment of the Louisiana Legislature" (*Johnson* v. *Louisiana,* p. 4527). The Court split 5 to 4 in these decisions. The majority opinion concluded that the constitutional rights of the defendants were not violated in either Oregon or Louisiana. In so ruling, the Court considered evidence from Kalven and Zeisel (1966) that 5.6% of juries required to deliberate to unanimity "hang," whereas, in those states requiring less than unanimity, hung juries result in only 3.1% of the trials, a difference the Court did not find particularly significant. Since almost no empirical data were available to the judges on this issue, they relied on their intuitions about conviction–acquittal rates as well as other legally pertinent issues. The Court did consider the issue of preservation of minority viewpoints. Would the minority whose votes were not needed for conviction be ignored? Would the nature of the deliberation be adversely affected? Would community confidence in the administration of justice suffer? While considering these issues, the justices had different intuitions, with the majority believing that little of consequence would be affected by the allowance of nonunanimity. The underlying premise for much of the logic seems to have been that the majority would win in any event, and, thus, majority rule will not change verdicts substantially; they will simply eliminate the occasions when one juror is stubbornly, and without reason, holding out. Given this (as we will learn, incorrect) set of premises, the Court argued that

We have no grounds for believing that majority jurors, aware of their responsibility and power over the liberty of the defendant, would simply refuse to listen to arguments presented to them in favor of acquittal, terminate discussion, and render a verdict. On the contrary it is far more likely that a juror presenting reasoned argument in favor of acquittal could either have his arguments answered or would carry enough other jurors with him to prevent conviction. A majority will cease discussion and outvote a minority only after reasoned discussion has ceased to have persuasive effect or to serve any other purpose— when a minority, that is, continues to insist upon acquittal without having persuasive reasons in support of its position. (p. 1624)

Such an optimistic view that the majority will only outvote a minority when it ceases to have persuasive reasons of its own provides a certain irony, since the majority justices, numbering five, outvoted a minority who offered persuasive reasons for an opposing position. Mr. Justice Douglas, writing a dissenting opinion, argued as follows:

Non-unanimous juries need not debate and deliberate as fully as most unanimous juries. As soon as the requisite majority is attained, further consideration is not required either by Oregon or by Louisiana even though the dissident jurors might, if given the chance, be able to convince the majority . . . the collective effort to piece together the puzzle of historical truth . . . is cut short as soon as the requisite majority is reached in Oregon and Louisiana. . . . It is said that there is no evidence that majority jurors will refuse to listen to dissenters whose votes are unneeded for conviction. Yet human experience teaches that polite and academic conversation is no substitute for the earnest and robust argument necessary to reach unanimity. (pp. 1647, 1648)

The available evidence tends to support the dissenting opinion. Unfortunately, most of these studies were conducted after the decisions were rendered. First, in regard to the issue of verdict and hung juries, studies on verdict distribution as a function of decision rule show mixed findings. Davis *et al.* (1975) find no statistically significant differences between experimental groups required to deliberate to a 2/3 majority or unanimity in a rape case. Nemeth (1977) finds no significant differences over a number of cases. However, she does find greater conviction rates in the majority rule situation if the minority favors a not guilty verdict. Under these circumstances, that is, when the majority favors conviction and the minority favors acquittal, the minority is more resistant and ultimately is more likely to prevail if the jury must deliberate to unanimity. Kerr, Atkin, Stasser, Meek, Holt, and Davis (1976) find majority rule more likely to lead to conviction than unanimity in a study using a rape case. Thus, the pattern, though not strong, tends to support the assumption that allowance of nonunanimity may increase conviction rates.

More clear-cut is the evidence on the frequency of hung juries as a function of unanimity versus majority rule. Numerous mathematical models (e.g., Gelfand & Solomon, 1973; Davis, 1973; Saks & Ostrom, 1975) support the contention that groups required to deliberate to unanimity hang more often. This greater likelihood of reaching a verdict in majority rule groups is accomplished by higher errors of both Type I (convicting an innocent person) and Type II (acquitting a guilty person). Empirical evidence supports this as well, with most of the studies conducted showing greater percentage of hung juries under unanimity conditions (Davis *et al.*, 1975; Kerr *et al.*, 1976; Nemeth, 1976; Padawer-Singer *et al.*, 1977). Juries required to deliberate to unanimity also tend to deliberate for a longer time (Davis *et al.*, 1975; Kerr *et al.*, 1976; Nemeth, 1976).

The Court raised still other issues which are pertinent to due process. One major theoretical difference between the Court and the dissenting justices has to do with whether minorities whose votes are not needed for conviction will be ignored. The Kalven and Zeisel (1966) data show that unanimity requirements lead to verdicts that are nonunanimous (i.e., to hung juries) in only 5.6% of cases. In contrast, those states allowing for nonunanimity show 25% of the verdicts as not having been reached by consensus (see Saks & Hastie, 1978, p. 85). In an experimental laboratory study involving a murder case and in a study involving a series of cases presented in an actual courtroom, Nemeth (1977) found that groups required to deliberate to a 2/3 majority did not stop as soon as the requisite votes were achieved, but they did stop short of full consensus. Relative to the unanimity groups, the juries required to deliberate to a 2/3 majority stopped significantly short of consensus. As a result, jurors reported more dissatisfaction and felt that justice was less well served when the decision rule was a 2/3 majority rather than unanimity. It appears that it is the minority in these majority rule groups that reports the most dissatisfaction; this finding is corroborated by Kerr *et al.* (1976).

The Justices also disagreed on whether the nature of the deliberation would be altered by nonunanimity. Would polite and academic conversation (particularly after the requisite votes were achieved) replace robust conflict? In Nemeth's (1977) study, a technique was used to test this. Using a procedure known as *valence* (Hoffman & Maier, 1964, 1967), a running count was kept of all comments, including for each one whether it was pro-prosecution or pro-defense. When the number of comments for one position (regardless of who uttered the comment) exceeded the number of comments for the other position, Nemeth (1977) found that she could predict all but one of the verdicts (i.e., she could accurately predict the outcome of 97% of the deliberations). Since this measure so accurately predicts the outcome, it was used as a measure of "functional deliberation time." The assumption was that if the outcome of a deliberation could be predicted very quickly this was not a deliberation of robust conflict. Groups required to deliberate to unanimity required more functional deliberation time than majority rule juries. Unanimity groups were harder to predict. In addition, unanimity groups made more comments in "conflict" categories (e.g., giving information and giving opinions) than did majority rule groups. The individuals also reported that they felt significantly more conflict in the unanimity groups than in the majority rule groups.

Still another issue raised by the justices in the Apodaca decision was community confidence. Mr. Justice White commented as follows:

> Community confidence in the administration of criminal justice cannot but be corroded under a system in which a defendant who is conspicuously identified with a particular group can be acquitted or convicted by a jury split along group lines. The requirements of unanimity and impartial selection thus complement each other in ensuring the fair performance of the vital functions of a criminal court jury. (p. 1627)

Though there are very limited data, the Nemeth (1977) study finds that persons required to deliberate to unanimity tend to report that justice has been better served than those persons deliberating to a 2/3 majority.

The issue of community confidence is an important one that deserves more scientific attention. We do not know whether, on a statistical basis, individuals in Oregon and Louisiana, for example, feel that justice is less "fair" since unanimity is not required in many of their trials. Yet, history shows us that a single case can be of paramount importance. Imagine a situation where a black man accused of a criminal charge against a white victim is faced with a jury of 9 whites and 3 blacks in Louisiana. If the vote followed racial lines, the perception of justice by the black community could be seriously jeopardized. At the time of this writing, 3 days of rioting in Miami were stimulated by the acquittal of 4 white policeman charged with shooting a black insurance man. The jury was all white.

Though there is not a great deal of evidence on the unanimity issue, the data that do exist tend to support the concerns of the dissenting justices in *Apodaca* and *Johnson*. The allowance of nonunanimity raises serious questions for preservation of minority views. Even if a minority does not convince the majority of their position, unanimity at least fosters the robust conflict and the full consideration of all views that leads to consensus. The consequence is more satisfaction and a perception that justice has been served. In a number of possibly important instances, minorities who cannot be outvoted can effect hung juries, a right that many would want to preserve. Thus, those concerned with the rulings in the early 1970s that reduced both the size of juries and the degree of consensus required to convict are relieved by the recent ruling in *Burch* v. *Louisiana* (1978). As the *Ballew* judgment limited the reduction in size of juries to 6, the *Burch* decision stopped the reduction in unanimity by ruling that conviction by a nonunanimous 6-person jury for a nonpetty offense was unconstitutional under the Sixth and Fourteenth Amendments. In support of this ruling, the Court relied on the reasoning in *Ballew* but offered no additional empirical evidence.

While the erosion of the jury thus seems to have been halted, many are still concerned about the losses in community representation, in preservation of minority views, in "robust conflict" in deliberations, and in the perception that justice has been served that the allowance of less than 12-person and less than unanimous juries may have been created.

VII.   The Future

The preceding sections cover areas where social science is particularly able to aid lawyers and judges in the difficult decisions they have to face. On the one hand, a recognition of the historical values and the history of court decisions involving this treasured institution of trial by jury can serve to help us frame questions that are legally and even politically relevant. Further, it is hoped that the importance of the issues that have surrounded this institution (e.g., death qualification, reduction in size and consensus, representation of all sectors of the community) will serve to interest researchers in combining their talents and efforts into making this the instrument of justice that was originally intended. In addition to creating the relevant empirical base, social scientists need to present their studies in ways that are helpful to those making the decisions. Though pertinent evidence existed prior to the *Williams* v. *Florida* decision, the justices were seemingly unaware of it. With the Lempert (1975) review, this evidence came to the attention of the *Ballew* Court.

The problem, of course, is twofold. As scientists, we must make our research available in a coherent form that is critically analyzed and legally relevant. On the other hand, judges have to want to know the data and ideas pertinent to their decisions. Their passivity in this regard has been problematic since they tend to rely on lawyers' briefs to bring forth the pertinent evidence. Sperlich (1980) has some recommendations in this regard. Judges can let lawyers know they expect "complete and responsible treatments of social fact issues, which must include all relevant scientific evidence" (p. 286); they can take it upon themselves to search the scientific literature (as Mr. Justice Blackmun did in the *Williams* case); or they can delegate the task to a body of scientific experts.

The onus, of course, is on the scientists to provide well-designed and comprehensive studies that are pertinent to legal issues prior to rulings. One of the problems is that much legally relevant research has been conducted after decisions have been rendered. It is when we realize that an error has been made that we start to address an issue. Scientists cannot be expected to anticipate every decision where well-designed research will be needed. Yet, we can address questions that will always be relevant, such as the improvement of the jury trial. If we want representation, robust conflict, and preservation of minority views, we can ask questions about the best selection procedures and best mechanisms for encouraging participation and even dissent. We can ask questions pertinent to raising the quality and the creativity of decision-making groups.

Perhaps most important is the contribution we can make in regard to the citizens' views of, and participation in, this democratic institution. At one level, people's perception of whether justice has been served can affect their regard for the institution, their feelings of pride in their citizenry, even their willingness to obey the laws. The rioting in Miami over an acquittal that had strong racial implications serves to remind us that the clauses of due process and equal protection under the laws must have meaning and be believed by the populace. At perhaps a more mundane level, we also need to consider the little issues, the encounters that most people have with the courts. Most of us will, happily, not be personally involved in a death penalty trial. Most of us will, at one time or another, be involved in traffic citations, divorces, child custody cases, eviction proceedings against "professional tenants," or the like. Though not of constitutional importance, the delays in such proceedings, the emotional trauma, and the perceptions that justice is not served will be the important determinants of confidence in our system of justice. The interface between psychology and law is an area filled with issues of intellectual and human importance, one that deserves "the best and the brightest" research we can bring to bear.

REFERENCES

Adler, F. Socioeconomic factors influencing jury verdicts. *NYU Review of Law and Social Change*, 1973, Winter, 73, **III**, 1.

Adorno, T. W., Frenkel-Brunswich, E., Levinson, D. J., & Sanford, R. N. *The authoritarian personality*. New York: Harper, 1950.

Akins v. *Texas*. 325 U.S. 398, 403, 1945.

Alker, H. R., Jr., & Barnard, J. J. Procedural and social biases in the jury selection process. *The Justice System Journal*, 1978, **3**, 220.

Alker, H. R., Jr., Hostica, C., & Mitchell, M. Jury selection as a biased social process. *Law and Society Review*, 1976, **11**, 9–41.

Allen, V. L. Situational factors in conformity. In L. Berkowitz (Ed.), *Advances in experimental social psychology*. New York: Academic Press, 1965. Pp. 133–175.

Apodaca, Cooper and Madden v. *Oregon*. 92 U.S. 1928, 1972.

Asch, S. E. Studies of independence and submission to group pressure: I. A minority of one against a unanimous majority. *Psychological Monographs*, 1956, **70** (Whole No. 417).

Austin, W., & Utne, M. K. Discretion and justice in judicial decision making. In B. D. Sales (Ed.), *Psychology in the legal process*. New York: Prentice-Hall, 1980 (in press).

Austin, W., Walster, E., & Utne, M. K. Equity and the law: The effect of a harmdoer's 'suffering in the act' on liking and assigned punishment. In L. Berkowitz & E. Walster (Eds.), *Advances in experimental social psychology* (Vol. 9). New York: Academic Press, 1976. Pp. 163–190.

Bailey, F. L., & Rothblatt, H. B. *Fundamentals of criminal advocacy*. Rochester, New York: Lawyers Co-operative, 1974.

Ballard v. *United States*. 329 US 187, 1946.

Ballew v. *Georgia*. 435 US 223 (1978).

Beckham, B., & Aronson, H. Selection of jury foremen as a measure of the social status of women. *Psychological Reports*, 1978, **43**, 475–478.

Berman, J., & Sales, B. D. A critical evaluation of the systematic approach to jury selection. *Criminal Justice and Behavior*, 1977, **4** 219–240.

Bermant, G., & Coppock, R. Outcomes of six- and twelve-member jury trials: An analysis of 128 civil cases in the State of Washington. *Washington Law Review*, 1973, **48**, 593–596.

Bevan, W., Albert, R. S., Loiseaux, R. R., Mayfield, P. N., & Wright, G. Jury behavior as a function of the prestige of the foreman and the nature of his leadership. *Journal of Public Law*, 1958, **7**, 419–449.

Blackstone, W. *Commentaries on the laws of England.* Oxford: Clarendon, 1791.

Boehm, V. R. Mr. prejudice, miss sympathy, and the authoritarian personality: An application of psychological measuring techniques to the problem of jury bias. *Wisconsin Law Review,* 1968, No. 3, 734-747.

Boone, J. S. The effects of race, arrogance, and evidence on simulated jury decisions. (University of Washington, 1972). *Dissertation Abstracts,* 1973, 7018-A.

Bray, R. M. *Decision rules, attitude similarity, and jury decision making.* Unpublished doctoral dissertation, University of Illinois, 1974.

Bray, R. M., & Noble, A. M. Authoritarianism and decisions of mock juries; evidence of jury bias and group polarization. *Journal of Personality and Social Psychology,* 1978, **36,** 1424-1430.

Broeder, D. W. The University of Chicago jury project. *Nebraska Law Review,* 1958, **38,** 744-761.

Broeder, D. W. Voir dire examinations: An empirical study. *Southern California Law Review,* 1965, **38,** 503-528. (a)

Broeder, D. W. The negro in court. *Duke Law Journal,* 1965, Winter, 19-31. (b)

Bronson, E. J. On the conviction proneness and representativeness of the death-qualified jury: An empirical study of Colorado veniremen. *University of Colorado Law Review,* 1970, **42,** 1-32.

Brooks v. *Beto.* 366 F2d 1, 1966.

Burch v. *Louisiana.* 47 L.W. 4393, 1979.

Byrne, D. Interpersonal attraction and attitude similarity. *Journal of Abnormal and Social Psychology,* 1961, **62,** 713-715.

Byrne, D., & Wong, T. J. Racial prejudice, interpersonal attraction, and assumed dissimilarity of attitudes. *Journal of Abnormal and Social Psychology,* 1962, **65,** 246-253.

Calhoun, L. G., Selby, J. W., Cann, A., & Keller, G. T. The effects of victim physical attractiveness and sex of respondent on social reactions to victims of rape. *British Journal of Social and Clinical Psychology,* 1978, **17,** 191-192.

Cassell v. *Texas,* 399 U.S. 282, 1950.

Centers, R., Shomer, R., & Rodrigues, F. A field experiment in interpersonal persuasion using authoritative influence. *Journal of Personality,* 1970, **38,** 392-403.

Charrow, R. P., & Charrow, V. R. Making legal language understandable: A psycholinguistic study of jury instructions. *Columbia Law Review,* 1979, **79,** 1306-1373.

Chief Justice Earl Warren Conference on Advocacy in the United States: *The American Jury System,* 1977.

Christie, R. Probability v. Precedence: The social psychology of jury selection. In G. Bermant, C. Nemeth, & N. Vidmar (Eds.), *Psychology and the law.* Lexington, Massachusetts: Heath, 1976. Pp. 265-281.

Colgrove v. *Battin.* 413 U.S. 149, 1973.

Copelon, R., Schneider, E. M., & Stearns, N. Constitutional perspectives on sex discrimination in jury selection. *Women's Rights Law Reporter,* 1975, **2,** 3-12.

Cornish, W. R. *The jury.* London: Penguin Press, 1968.

Crosson, R. F. An investigation into certain personality variables among capital trial jurors. *Proceedings 76th Annual Convention, APA,* 1968, 371-372.

Cucinotta, S. J. Witherspoon—Will the due process clause further regulate the imposition of the death penalty? *Duquesne Law Review,* 1968, **7,** 414-445.

Darrow, C. Attorney for the defense. *Esquire,* 1936, 36-213.

Davis, J. H. Group decision and social interaction: A theory of social decision schemes. *Psychological Review,* 1973, **80,** 97-125.

Davis, J. H., Kerr, N. L., Atkin, R. S., Holt, R., & Meek, D. The decision processes of 6- and 12-person mock juries assigned unanimous and two-thirds majority rules. *Journal of Personality and Social Psychology,* 1975, **32,** 1-14.

Davis v. *Davis.* 361 F2d 770, 1966.

Donovan, J. W. *Modern jury trials and advocates* (3rd ed.). New York: Banks & Brothers, 1885.

Dowdle, M., Gillen, H., & Miller, A. Integration and attribution theories as predictors of sentencing by a simulated jury. *Personality and Social Psychology Bulletin*, 1974, **1**, 270–272.

Duren v. *Missouri*. 439 US 357, 1979.

Efran, M. G. The effect of physical appearance on the judgment of guilt, interpersonal attraction, and severity of recommended punishment in a simulated jury task. *Journal of Research and Personality*, 1974, **8**, 45–54.

Ellsworth, P. C., Thompson, W., & Cowan, C. *Juror attitudes and conviction proneness: The relationship between attitudes towards the death penalty and predisposition to convict*. Unpublished manuscript, 1980.

Elwork, A. Sales, B. D., & Alfini, J. J. Juridic decisions: In ignorance of the law or in light of it? *Law and Human Behavior*, 1977, **1**, 163–189.

Enborg, K. D. Case note. *Journal of Urban Law*, 1976, **53**, 557.

Erlanger, H. S. Jury research in America: Its past and future. *Law and Society Review*, 1970, **4**, 345–370.

Fay v. *New York*. 322 U.S. 261, 1947.

Federal Code of Jury Qualifications, 28 U.S.C.S. 1864, 1865.

Fortas, A. Follow-up/The jury. *Center Magazine*, 1970, **3**, 60–61.

Frank, J. *Courts on trial*. Princeton, New Jersey: Princeton University Press, 1949.

Friend, R. M., & Vinson, M. "Leaning over backwards: Jurors' responses to defendants' attractiveness. *Journal of Communication*, 1974 (Summer), 124–129.

Gelfand, A. E., & Solomon, H. "A study of Poisson's models for jury verdicts in criminal and civil trials. *Journal of the American Statistical Association*, 1973, **68**, 271–278.

Gelfand, A. E., and Solomon, H. A. Modeling jury verdicts in the American legal system. *Journal of the American Statistical Association*, 1974, **69**, 32–37.

Gelfand, A. E., & Solomon, H. A. Analysing the decision making process of the American jury. *Journal of the American Statistical Association*, 1975, **70**, 305.

Gelfand, A. E., & Solomon, H. A. An argument in favor of 12-member juries. In S. S. Nagel (Ed.), *Modeling the criminal justice system*. Beverly Hills, California: Sage, 1977.

Georgia Law Review. The fifth circuit: New history for an old problem—jury selection. *Georgia Law Review*, 1967, **1**, 674–690.

Gibbons, D. J. "The new minijuries: Panacea or Pandora's box? *American Bar Association Journal*, 1972, **658**, 594–599.

Glasser v. *United States*. 315 U.S. 60, 1942.

Gleason, J. M., & Harris, V. A. Race, socio-economic status, and perceived similarity as determinants of judgments by simulated jurors. *Social Behavior and Personality*, 1975, **3**, 175–180.

Goldberg, F. *Attitude toward capital punishment and behavior as a juror in simulated capital cases*. Unpublished manuscript, Morehouse College, undated.

Goldberg, F. Toward expansion of *Witherspoon*: Capital scruples, jury bias, and the use of psychological data to raise presumptions in the law. 5 *Harvard Civ. Rights—Civil Liberties Law Review*, 1969, 53.

Gordon, R. I. *A study in forensic psychology: Petit jury verdicts as a function of the number of jury members*. Unpublished doctoral dissertation, University of Oklahoma, 1968.

Greenberg, J. *Race relations and American law*. New York: Columbia University Press, 1959.

Griffitt, W., & Jackson, T. Simulated jury decisions: The influence of jury–defendant attitude similarity–dissimilarity. *Social Behavior and Personality*, 1973, **1**, 1–7.

Grofman, B. Mathematical models of juror and jury decision making: The state of the art. In B. D. Sales (Ed.), *Perspectives in law and psychology: Vol. II. The trial process*. New York: Plenum, 1980.

Hackman, G., & Vidmar, N. Effects of size and task type on group performance and member reactions, *Sociometry*, 1970, **33**, 37.

Hamilton, V. L. Individual differences in ascriptions of responsibility, guilt and appropriate judgment. In G. Bermant, C. Nemeth, & N. Vidmar (Eds.), *Psychology and the law.* Lexington, Massachusetts: Heath, 1976. Pp. 239–264.

Hendrick, C., Stikes, C. S., Murray, E. J., & Puthoff, C. Race vs belief as determinants of attraction in a group interaction context. *Memory and Cognition,* 1973, **1**, 41–46.

Hermann, P. J. Occupations of jurors as an influence on their verdict. *The Forum,* 1970, **5**, 150–155.

Hernandez v. Texas. 347 U.S. 475, 1954.

Hervey, J. C. Jurors look at our judges. *Oklahoma Bar Association Journal,* 1947, **75**, 1508–1513.

Hoffman, L. R. Group problem solving. In L. Berkowitz (Ed.), *Advances in experimental social psychology* (Vol. 2). New York: Academic Press, 1965.

Hoffman, L. R., & Maier, N. R. F. Valence in the adoption of solutions by problem-solving groups: Concept, method, and results. *Journal of Abnormal and Social Psychology,* 1964, **69**, 264–268.

Hoffman, L. R., & Maier, N. R. F. Valence in the adoption of solutions by problem-solving groups: II. Quality and acceptance as goals of leaders and members. *Journal of Personality and Social Psychology,* 1967, **6**, 175–182.

Holdsworth, Sir Wm. *A history of English Law, XI.* Boston: Little, Brown, 1938.

Horstman, D. A. S. *Testing a jury selection scale and theory in court.* Unpublished doctoral dissertation, The University of Oklahoma, 1976.

Hovey v. Superior Court of Alameda County. 28 Cal. 3d 1, 1980.

Howe, M. D. Juries as judges of criminal law. *Harvard Law Review,* 1939, **52**, 582–616.

Howitt, D. Situational and victims' characteristics in simulated penal judgments. *Psychological Reports,* 1977, **40**, 55–58.

Hoyt v. Florida. 368 U.S. 57, 1961.

Institute of Judicial Administration. A comparison of six- and twelve member juries in New Jersey Superior & County Courts, 1972.

Izzett, R., & Leginski, W. Group discussion and the influence of defendant characteristics in a simulated jury setting. *Journal of Social Psychology,* 1974, **93**, 271–279.

James, R. M. Status and competence of jurors. *American Journal of Sociology,* 1959, **64**, 563–570.

Johnson v. Louisiana. 92 U.S. 1935, 1972.

Jones, C., & Aronson, E. Attribution of fault to a rape victim as a function of respectability of the victim. *Journal of Personality and Social Psychology,* 1973, **26**, 415–419.

Jurow, G. L. New data on the effect of a 'death-qualified' jury on the guilt determination process. *Harvard Law Review,* 1971, **84**, 567–611.

Jury-Mandering: federal jury selection and the generation gap. *Iowa Law Review,* 1973, **59**, 401–419.

Jury Selection and Service Act, 1968 (28 U.S.C. 1862).

Kairys, D., Schulman, J., & Harring, S. (Eds.) *The jury system: New methods for reducing prejudice: A manual for lawyers, legal workers and social scientists.* National Jury Project and National Lawyers Guild, 1975.

Kallen, L. Peremptory challenges based upon juror background—A rational use? *Trial Lawyer's Guide,* 1969, **13**, 143–165.

Kalven, H., Jr. The Dignity of the Civil Jury. *Virginia Law Review,* 1964, **50**, 1055.

Kalven, H., Jr., & Zeisel, H. *The American jury.* Boston: Little, Brown, 1966.

Kaplan, M. R., & Kemmerick, G. D. Juror judgment as information integration: Combining evidential and non-evidential information. *Journal of Personal and Social Psychology,* 1974, **30**, 493–499.

Kelley, H. H., & Thibaut, J. W. Group problem solving. In G. Lindzey & E. Aronson (Eds.) *Handbook of social psychology* (Vol. 4, 2d ed.). Reading, Massachusetts: Addison-Wesley, 1969.

Kenyon, D., & Murray, P. *The case for equality in state jury service.* Unpublished memorandum in support of ACLU proposal to Amend. S. 2923, 1966.

Kerr, N. L., Atkin, R. S., Stasser, G., Meek, D., Holt, R. W., & Davis, J. H. Guilt beyond a reasonable doubt; effect of concept definition and assigned decision rule on the judgements of mock jurors. *Journal of Personality and Social Psychology,* 1976, **34,** 282–295.

Kerr, N., Nerenz, D., & Herrick, D. *Role playing and the study of jury behavior.* Unpublished manuscript, Univ. of California at San Diego, 1976.

Kessler, J. B. An empirical study of 6- and 12-member jury decision making processes. *University of Michigan Journal of Law Reform,* 1973, **6,** 712–734.

Kuhn, R. S. Jury discrimination: The next phase. *Southern California Law Review,* 1968, **4,** 235–328.

Landy, D., & Aronson, E. The influence of the character of the criminal and his victim on the decisions of simulated jurors. *Journal of Experimental Social Psychology,* 1969, **5,** 141–152.

Lefcourt, G. B. Follow-up/the jury. Center Magazine, 1970, **3,** 62–64.

Lempert, R. O. Uncovering non-discernible differences: Empirical research and the jury size cases. *Michigan Law Review,* 1975, **73,** 644–707.

Levanthal, G., & Krate, R. Physical attractiveness and severity of sentencing. *Psychological Reports,* 1977, **40,** 315–318.

Levine, A. G., & Schweber-Koren, C. Jury selection in Erie County: Changing a sexist system. *Law and Society Review,* 1976, **11,** 43–55.

Lindquist, C. An analysis of juror selection procedure in the United States District Courts. *Temple Law Quarterly,* 1967, **41,** 32.

Logan v. *United States.* 144 US 263, 1892.

Lorge, I., Fox, D., Davitz, J., & Brenner, M. A survey of studies contrasting the quality of group performance and individual performance. *Psychological Bulletin,* 1958, **55,** 337–372.

McDougall, H. The case for black juries. *Yale Law Journal,* 1970, **79,** 531–550.

McGlynn, R. P., Megas, J. G., & Benson, D. H. Sex and race as factors affecting the attribution of insanity in a murder trial. *Journal of psychology,* 1976, **93,** 93–99.

Mariani, G. Peremptory challenge—Divining rod for a sympathetic jury. *Catholic Lawyer,* 1975, **21,** 56–81.

Michigan Study. Six member and twelve member juries: An empirical study of trial results. *University of Michigan Journal of Law Reform,* 1973, **6,** 671–695.

Miller, M., & Hewitt, J. Conviction of a defendant as a function of juror–victim racial similarity. *Journal of Social Psychology,* 1978, **105,** 159–160.

Mills, E. S. A statistical profile of jurors in a United States District Court. *Law and the Social Order,* 1969, 329–339.

Mississippi, 1972, Sec. 13-5-1.

Mistretta, M. J. Criminal law and the collective conscience: Multi-dimensional scaling of perceptions of crime. *Dissertation Abstracts International,* 1977, **38,** 6–A, 3743.

Mitchell, H. E., & Byrne, D. *Minimizing the influence of irrelevant factors in the courtroom: The defendant's character, judge's instructions, and authoritarianism.* Paper presented to Midwestern Psychological Assn., Cleveland, Ohio, May 1972.

Mitchell, H. E., & Byrne, D. The defendant's dilemma: Effects of jurors' attitudes and authoritarianism on judicial decisions. *Journal of Personality and Social Psychology,* 1973, **25,** 123–129.

Morrow, W. G. Women on juries. *Alberta Law Review,* 1974, **XII,** 321.

Nagel, S., & Neef, M. Deductive modeling to determine an optimum jury size and fraction required to convict. *Washington University Law Quarterly,* 1975, **4,** 933–978.

Nagel, S., & Weitzman, L. Sex and the unbiased jury. *Judicature,* 1972, **56,** 108–11.

Nemeth, C. Interactions between jurors as a function of majority vs. unanimity decision rules. *Journal of Applied Social Psychology,* 1977, **7,** 38–56.

Nemeth, C. The role of an active minority in inter-group conflict. In W. G. Austin & S. Worchel (Eds.), *The psychology of intergroup relations.* Belmont, California: Brooks-Cole, 1979. Pp. 225–236. (a)

Nemeth, C. Group dynamics and legal decision making. In L. E. Abt & I. R. Stuart (Eds.), *The social psychology of discretionary law*. New York: Van Nostrand-Reinhold, 1979. (b)

Nemeth, C., Endicott, J., & Wachtler, J. From the '50s to the '70s: Women in jury deliberations. *Sociometry*, 1976, **39**, 293-304.

Nemeth, C., & Sosis, R. Simulated jury study: Characteristics of the defendant and the jurors. *The Journal of Social Psychology*, 1973, **90**, 221-229.

Nemeth, C., & Wachtler, J. Creating the perceptions of consistency and confidence: A necessary condition for minority influence. *Sociometry*, 1974, **37**, 529-540.

New York Juror Qualifications, 1975, NY Judiciary Law, Art 16, Para. 504.

Norris v. *Alabama*. 294 US 598, 1935.

Oberer, W. E. Does disqualification of jurors for scruples against capital punishment constitute denial of fair trial on issue of guilt? *Texas Law Review*, 1961, **39**, 545-567.

Pabst, W. R., Jr. What do six member juries really save? *Judicature*, 1973, **57**, 6-11.

Padawer-Singer, A. M., Singer, A. N., & Singer, R. L. S. An experimental study of twelve- vs. six-member juries under unanimous vs. nonunanimous decisions. In B. D. Sales (Ed.), *Psychology in the legal process*. Jamaica, N.Y.: Spectrum Publications, 1977.

Penrod, S., & Hastie, R. Models of jury decision making; a critical review. *Psychological Bulletin*, 1979, **86**, 462-492.

People v. *Wheeler*, 22 Cal. 3d 258-295, 1978.

Pope, J. The jury. *Texas Law Review*, 1961, **39**, 426-448.

Prahl, W. G. The civil petitioner's report to representative grand juries and a statistical method of showing discrimination in jury selection cases generally. *UCLA Law Review*, 1973, **20**, 581-654.

Rabinowitz v. *United States*. 366 F2d 34 (5th Cir. 1966).

Reed, J. P. Jury deliberations, voting and verdict trends. *Southwestern Social Science Quarterly*, 1965, **45**, 361-370.

Reynolds, D. E., & Sanders, M. S. Effect of defendant attractiveness, age, and injury on severity of sentence given by simulated jurors. *The Journal of Social Psychology*, 1975, **96**, 149-150.

Rhine, J. The jury: A reflection of the prejudices of the community. *The Hastings Law Journal*, 1969, **20**, 1417-1445.

Robinson, W. Bias, probability, and trial by jury. *American Sociological Review*, 1950, **15**, 73-78.

Rokeach, M. *The open and closed mind*. New York: Basic Books, 1960.

Rokeach, M., Smith, P. W., & Evans, R. I. Two kinds of prejudice or one? In M. Rokeach (Ed.), *The open and closed mind*. New York: Basic Books, 1960. Pp. 132-168.

Rose, A., & Prell, A. Does the punishment fit the crime? A study in social valuation. *American Journal of Sociology*, 1955, **61**, 247-251.

Rumsey, M. G., & Rumsey, J. M. A case of rape: Sentencing judgments of males and females. *Psychological Reports*, 1977, **41**, 459-465.

Saks, M. J. Social scientists can't rig juries. *Psychology Today*, 1976, January, 48-50. (a)

Saks, M. J. The limits of scientific jury selection: Ethical and empirical. *Jurimetrics Journal*, 1976, **17**, 3-22. (b)

Saks, M. J. *Jury verdicts*. Lexington, Massachusetts: Heath, 1977.

Saks, M. J., & Hastie, R. *Social psychology in court*. New York: Van Nostrand-Reinhold, 1978.

Saks, M. J., & Ostrom, T. M. Jury size and consensus requirements: The laws of probability *vs* the laws of the land. *Journal of Contemporary Law*, 1975, **1**, 163-173.

Schulman, J., Shaver, P., Colman, R., Emrick, B., & Christie, R. Recipe for a jury. *Psychology Today*, 1963, **6**, 37-84.

Scroggs, J. R. Penalties for rape as a function of victim provocativeness, damage, and resistance. *Journal of Applied Social Psychology*, 1976, **6**, 360-368.

Sealy, A. P., & Cornish, W. R. Juries and their verdicts. *Criminal Law Review*, 1973, April, 208-223.

Shapley, D. Jury selection: Social scientists gamble in an already loaded game. *Science*, 1974, **18**, 1033–1071.

Sigall, H., & Landy, D. Effects of the defendant's character and suffering on juridic judgment: A replication and clarification. *Journal of Social Psychology*, 1972, **88**, 149–150.

Sigall, H., & Ostrove, N. Beautiful but dangerous: Effects of offender attractiveness and nature of the crime on juridic judgment. *Journal of Personality and Social Psychology*, 1975, **31**, 410–414.

Simmons, V. M. Decisions of simulated jurors: influence of sex, locus of control, judicial instructions, and biasing information about the defendant. (Emory University, 1975). *Dissertation Abstracts*, 1975, 2484-B.

Simon, C. K. The juror in New York City: Attitudes and experiences. *American Bar Association Journal*, 1975, **61**, 207–211.

Simon, R. J. *The jury in the defense of insanity*. Boston: Little, Brown, 1967.

Simon, R. J. "The American jury: Instrument of justice or of prejudice and conformity. *Sociological Inquiry*, 1977, **47**, 254–293.

Smith v. *Texas*. 311 U.S. 128, 1940.

Sparf and Hansen v. *United States*. U.S. Reports, 1895, Vol. 156.

Sperlich, P. W. . . . And then there were six: The decline of the American jury. *Judicature*, 1980, **63**, 262–279.

Steffensmeier, D. J. The effects of judge's and defendant's sex on the sentencing of offenders. *Psychology*, 1977, **14**, 3–9.

Stein, D. D., Hardyck, J. A., & Smith, M. B. Race and belief: An open and shut case. *Journal of Personality and Social Psychology*, 1965, **1**, 481–489.

Steiner, I. D. *Group processes and productivity*. New York: Academic Press, 1972.

Stephen, C., & Tully, J. C. The influence of physical attractiveness of a plaintiff on the decisions of simulated jurors. *Journal of Social Psychology*, 1977, **101**, 149–150.

Stevens, W., L. Defendant's right to a jury trial: Is six enough? *Kentucky Law Journal*, 1971, **59**, 996–1002.

Strauder v. *West Virgina*. 100 US 303, 1880.

Strodtbeck, F. L., & Hook, L. H. The social dimensions of a twelve man jury table. *Sociometry*, 1961, **24**, 396–415.

Strodtbeck, F. L., James, R. M., & Hawkins, C. Social status in jury deliberations. *American Sociological Review*, 1957, **22**, 713–719.

Strodtbeck, F. L., & Mann, R. D. Sex role differentiation in jury deliberations. *Sociometry*, 1956, **19**, 3–11.

Sue, S., Smith, R. E., & Pedroza, G. Authoritarianism, pretrial publicity, and awareness of bias in simulated jurors. *Psychological Reports*, 1975, **37**, 1299–1302.

Swain v. *Alabama*. 380 U.S. 202 208, 1965.

Taylor v. *Louisiana*. 419 US 522, 1975.

Thayer, J. B. The jury and its development. *Harvard Law Review*, 1892, **V**, 295–319.

Thayer, R. E. Attitude and personality differences between potential jurors who could return a death verdict and those who could not. *Proceedings, 78th Annual Convention APA*, 1970.

Theil v. *Southern Pacific Company*. 328 U.S. 217, 1946.

Thomas, E. J., & Fink, C. F. Effects of group size. *Psychological Bulletin*, 1963, **60**, 37.

Thornberry, T. P. Criminology, race, socioeconomic status and sentencing in the juvenile justice system. *Journal of Criminal Law and Criminology*, 1973, **64**, 90–98.

Triandis, H. C. A note on Rokeach's theory of prejudice. *Journal of Abnormal and Social Psychology*, 1961, **62**, 184–186.

Triandis, H. C. *Interpersonal behavior*. Monterey, California: Brooks-Cole, 1976.

Ugwuegbu, D. C. E. *Is justice color-blind?: The racial factor in jury attribution of criminal responsibility*. Unpublished doctoral dissertation, Kent State University, 1973.

Ugwuegbu, D. C. E. Black jurors' personality trait attribution to a rape case defendant. *Social Behavior and Personality,* 1976, **4,** 193-201.

United States Judicial Conference, 1966.

United States v. *Battiste.* 24 F. Cas. 1042, (C.C.D. Mass. 1835).

United States v. *Carnell.* 25 F. Cas. 650 (No. 14, 868) (C.C.R.I. 1820).

United States v. *Di Tomasso.* 394 U.S. 934, 1968.

United States v. *Guzman.* 337 F. Supp. 140 (S.D.N.Y. 1972).

Vanderzell, J. H. The jury as a community cross-section. *Western Political Quarterly,* 1966, **19,** 136-149.

Valenti, A. C., & Downing, L. L. Differential effects of jury size on verdicts following deliberation as a function of the apparent guilt of a defendant. *Journal of Personality and Social Psychology,* 1975, **32,** 655-663.

Van Dyke, J. M. The jury as a political institution. *Center Magazine,* March 1970, 17-26.

Van Dyke, J. M. Selecting a jury in political trials. *Case Western Reserve Law Review,* 1977, **27,** 609.

Vidmar, N. Effects of decision alternatives on the verdicts and social perceptions of simulated jurors. *Journal of Personality and Social Psychology,* 1972, **22,** 211-218.

Vidmar, N., & Ellsworth, P. Public opinion and the death penalty. *Stanford Law Review,* 1974, **26,** 1245-1270.

Walbert, D. F. The effect of jury size on the probability of conviction. *Case Western Reserve Law Review,* 1971, **22,** 529.

White, W. S. The constitutional invalidity of convictions imposed by death-qualified juries. *Cornell Law Review,* 1973, **58,** 1176-1220.

Whitus v. *Georgia.* 385 US 545, 1967.

Williams v. *Florida.* 399 US 78, 1970.

Wilson, C. *Belief in capital punishment and jury performance.* Unpublished manuscript, University of Texas, 1964.

Wilson, D. W., & Donnerstein, E. Guilty or not guilty? A look at the 'simulated' jury paradigm. *Journal of Applied Social Psychology,* 1977, **7,** 175-190.

Witherspoon v. *Illinois.* 391 US 510, 1968.

Wolfgang, M., & Reidel, M. Race and the death penalty. *Annals of the Academy of Political and Social Science,* 1973, **407,** 119-133.

Zeisel, H. *Some insights into the operation of criminal juries.* Unpublished manuscript, University of Chicago, 1957.

Zeisel, H. Some data on juror attitudes toward capital punishment. University of Chicago Center for Studies in Criminal Justice, 1968.

Zeisel, H. . . . And then there were none: The diminution of the federal jury. *University of Chicago Law Review,* 1971, **38,** 713-715.

Zeisel, H. The waning of the American jury. *American Bar Association Journal,* 1972, **58,** 367.

Zeisel, H. Twelve is just. *Trial,* 1974, Nov-Dec, 13-15.

Zeisel, H., & Diamond, S. S. Convincing empirical evidence on the six member jury. *University of Chicago Law Review,* 1974, **41,** 281-295.

Zeisel, H., & Diamond, S. S. The effect of peremptory challenges on jury and verdict: An experiment in a federal district court. *Stanford Law Review,* 1978, **30,** 491-530.

INDEX

CONTENTS OF OTHER VOLUMES